D0252590

To Raise an Army

★

THE DRAFT COMES TO MODERN AMERICA

John Whiteclay Chambers II

THE FREE PRESS
A Division of Macmillan, Inc.
NEW YORK

Collier Macmillan Publishers
LONDON

Copyright © 1987 by John Whiteclay Chambers II

All rights reserved. No part of this book may be reproduced
or transmitted in any form or by any means, electronic or
mechanical, including photocopying, recording, or by any
information storage and retrieval system, without permission
in writing from the Publisher.

The Free Press
A Division of Macmillan, Inc.
866 Third Avenue, New York, N.Y. 10022

Collier Macmillan Canada, Inc.

Printed in the United States of America

printing number
2   3   4   5   6   7   8   9   10

Library of Congress Cataloging-in-Publication Data

Chambers, John Whiteclay.
    To raise an army.

    Bibliography: p.
    Includes index.
    1. Military service, Compulsory—United States—History.
2. United States—Armed Forces—Recruiting, enlistment, etc.—
History.   3. World War, 1914–1918—United States.   I. Title.
UB343.C483   1987   355.2′2363′0973   87–15150
ISBN 0–02–905820–1

For
Annette K. Baxter
William E. Leuchtenburg
Allan Silver

CONCORDIA UNIVERSITY LIBRARY
PORTLAND OR 97211

Contents

(Illustrations are after page 148 and page 244)

Preface

Like a persistent specter, the military draft keeps reappearing as a public issue in the twilight of the 20th century. In fact, a combination of factors—demographic, strategic, economic, and political—appears to make a return to some form of draft possible within the near future. Yet it had seemed an institutional casualty of the Vietnam War, killed by the antiwar movement and interred by President Richard M. Nixon in 1973. Within seven years, however, President Jimmy Carter had resumed compulsory draft registration, a measure renewed in 1982 by President Ronald Reagan, whose administration began prosecuting registration resisters. Once again television screens showed young people in the streets and in courtrooms protesting against the draft. Without a war, without even induction, the draft had flared again as a national issue.

Even in the late 1980s, after such intense opposition had faded from the headlines, problems with the All-Volunteer Armed Force led to renewed speculation about the need for some kind of military draft. A decline in the number of 18-year-olds, and growing economic opportunities due to the end of the recession of the early 1980s, led to decreasing enlistment and spurred a debate over the quality and appropriateness of a military force obtained solely through voluntary means.

With the Reagan administration pursuing a tough foreign policy against the Soviet Union and against anti-American governments in the Third World, the status of the All-Volunteer Armed Force raised additional questions. Would such an army be capable of fighting successfully the kind of wars that might result? Could voluntary enlistment by itself obtain soldiers who were able to master the skills demanded by new and complex weapons systems? In a vitally important issue, was the NATO defense of Western Europe overly reliant upon the use of nuclear weapons to deter a potential Soviet invasion or threat of invasion? A number of influential civilian and military figures have suggested that the western Allies could reduce their reliance on nuclear arms, and the risk of nuclear war, by significantly expanding their ground forces, an action which could require resumption of the draft in the United States.[1]

More than a decade after it began in 1973, the All-Volunteer Armed Force—including the largest volunteer army ever maintained in America in peacetime—remained still a largely untested experiment. Although it retained considerable support, this military format sustained significant criticism from both civilian and military communities. The public debate over the volunteer army, focusing primarily on combat readiness to meet strategic goals, was also concerned with other aspects of the issue. As *The Washington Post* observed, "the volunteer force has been criticized heavily in Congress, with a growing number of lawmakers contending that it costs too much, puts too much of the defense burden on minorities and the poor, and is providing 9 a.m.-to-5 p.m. soldiers who see the military as just another job, not an obligation."[2] The use of terms like "obligation," "cost," and "burden" implied that the debate went beyond such issues as whether voluntarism provided enough qualified recruits, or arguments over military effectiveness, or the U.S. role in the world. It concerned differences over the nature of society, citizenship, and government in America.

The national draft and the question of whether the United States should have an entirely volunteer army or a mixed force of draftees and volunteers remain important policy questions. With the era of the Vietnam war growing ever more distant, domestic support has increased for building up America's military strength. But while the Reagan administration focused on the development and production of expensive weapons systems, the costs of the defense build-up had caused much concern. By the winter of 1986–87, a number of Democrats had come to believe that circumstances favored an emphasis on military manpower, including a possible resumption of some form of compulsory service.[3] The draft might then be part of a program for improving the military by cutting spending and reducing the deficit, particularly since it has long been shown that it is less expensive to raise an army by conscription than by the economic incentives needed to sustain an all-volunteer armed force. Further, although in recent years Americans have continued to be divided over the draft, compulsory registration has been implemented successfully. The widespread support for a stronger defense establishment, particularly among voters in the South and the West, might indeed make it politically tempting for the Democratic party, seen since the late 1960s as predominantly antimilitary, to advocate some form of compulsory service in the final decade of the 20th century.

Whatever the future of the draft, some basic questions remain: How did the national draft come to a country that traditionally emphasizes the liberty of individuals, and is suspicious of centralized governmental power, of standing armies, and of national conscription? How did the draft come to dominate American thinking about military formats? And why is the issue still with us today? The answers stem in large part from the first successful American experience with national conscription. It was in World War I that the modern draft first came to America.

JOHN WHITECLAY CHAMBERS II
New Brunswick, N.J.
March 13, 1987

Acknowledgments

DURING THE MANY YEARS of research and writing this book, I
have received the help of such a large number of people that it
is impossible to list them all here. I wish to thank these colleagues,
archivists, librarians, and students, and the many members of my
family.

In the final stages of production, I received valuable assistance
from two graduate students at Rutgers University, Kimn Carlton-
Smith and G. Kurt Piehler, and from a diligent copy editor, Victor
Rangel-Ribeiro, and dedicated production supervisor, Celia Knight.
I am particularly indebted to my editor, Joyce Seltzer, for her encouragement and for her insistence and direction in making this a
shorter and better book. In addition, I want to express my gratitude
to two historians who have read the entire manuscript and offered
excellent criticism: J. Garry Clifford of the University of Connecticut and Arthur S. Link of Princeton University. Any errors of fact or
judgment are, of course, the author's responsibility.

This book is dedicated to three persons whose guidance and sup-
port have had a profound influence on my life and work. William E.
Leuchtenburg, now William Rand Kenan Professor of History at the
University of North Carolina, Chapel Hill, served as a model for me
even before I studied under his direction at Columbia University;
Allan Silver, Professor of Sociology at Columbia University, also
became an insightful adviser and friend; the late Annette K. Baxter,
Adolph S. and Effie Ochs Professor of History at Barnard College,
Columbia University, was more than chair of the department during
most of the decade that I taught there, she was a constant and
enthusiastic champion of my work. Like countless other former
students, many of them now scholar-teachers themselves, I owe a
great debt to these three fine people.

J.W.C.

xi

Introduction

O N A DAMP AND MISTY MORNING in April 1918, a giant troopship, dappled in wartime camouflage, churned out of New York harbor on a historic voyage across the Atlantic. Jammed to the topmost railings were draftees on their way to the trenches of the Western Front. Not only did these khaki-clad soldiers differ strikingly from the civilian passengers normally carried aboard this converted luxury liner, but more importantly the mass conscript army to which they belonged signaled a major departure in American military policy. Unlike the traditional U.S. Volunteers, these wartime citizen-soldiers had been obtained primarily through a national draft. They were also part of the first American army ever sent to the battlefields of Europe.

This wartime mass army, eventually numbering more than 3,500,000 troops, dramatized the emergence of the United States as a major world power. Domestically, it represented an unprecedented assertion of the authority of the national government. In all, 72 percent of the "doughboys" were draftees, conscripted through the new Selective Service System. The national draft had come to America as a result of a new level of international intervention and the creation of a modern State. Symbolically, the troopship which began the convoy of this mass conscript army to Europe bore the name U.S.S. *Leviathan*.[1]

Looking askance at the conscription systems of Europe and Asia, Americans historically had viewed such military formats as fostering tyranny and aggression and as being at odds with individual liberty and republican virtue. How then did the United States arrive at a mass conscript army in World War I? Was conscription in the New World different from conscription in the Old? What was the result of the adoption of the draft? By the end of the war, the Selective Service System had proven quite successful in raising soldiers and was widely accepted in the United States, at least as a

1

wartime instrument. What did this experience portend? How would it affect popular and elite attitudes towards the proper wartime military format in subsequent years? To what extent did the experience with a drafted force, then and later, continue to influence attitudes about means of raising America's armies?

How should a nation raise its armies? Although this question has been central to the existence of nations, states, and empires over the centuries, it has no simple answer. And it is even more difficult when applied to the United States with its uniquely mixed heritage of military and foreign policy, for it raises other pressing questions concerning the nature of the army and society and the strategic goals of the State. Since military formats vary in size, composition, service, and leadership, costs and advantages differ from one system of military service to another. How, for example, does a professional force of volunteer career soldiers compare with an army composed largely of short-term draftees? What is the relationship of a nation's military format to the structure and dominant ideas of its society, and to its international position and goals?

The issues of how to raise an army and what kind of army to raise have always proven particularly troublesome to Americans. For while Americans have often been bellicose and frequently violent, they have traditionally been suspicious of professional standing armies. Historically, in wartime they relied upon citizens to leave their civilian employment and come forward temporarily to fight the declared enemies of the colony, state, or nation. For ideological as well as material reasons, Americans kept only a small constabulary force of regulars under arms. Only in the Cold War era since World War II has the United States maintained comparatively large standing forces.

The nation's divided military tradition—its episodic but intense willingness to wage war and its unwillingness to impose military obligations upon the citizenry except when absolutely required—has left the United States ill prepared for the global leadership it has sustained since World War II. But the engines of U.S. foreign policy have been economic and ideological more than military. So in planning for the new postwar order, American policy-makers initially saw international organizations like the United Nations, the International Monetary Fund, and the World Bank, as the primary vehicles for U.S. global leadership. With the onset of the Cold War, air power and the atomic bomb seemed to offer a military trump card for America's expanded geopolitics, but the diplomatic and military effect of that nuclear monopoly was reduced when the Soviet Union developed its own nuclear arsenal. Furthermore, atomic weapons proved largely irrelevant to anti-colonial and other guerrilla-style

insurgencies in the Third World. As has been repeatedly demonstrated in smaller wars around the globe since the end of World War
II, the existence of nuclear weapons has not eliminated the importance of effective armies.

During two world wars, the mobilization of a mass conscript
army through the Selective Service System proved an effective and
consensual military format. But in the more than forty years since
the end of World War II, the United States has sought in vain to find
a comparable model, a militarily effective and politically acceptable
military format for maintaining both a peacetime garrison force and
deterrent as well as an army capable of effective combat in Europe
or the Third World. Instead, the country has experimented with a
variety of formats. These have included a brief postwar return to
the old small standing army; a number of unsuccessful appeals for a
system of universal military training and service or national service;
a sustained reliance on a mixed force of draftees and volunteers (but
with widely fluctuating selective draft calls); and, since 1973, reliance on a large, all-volunteer force. This last format, a controversial one as yet untested in war, remains an experiment.[2] The United
States still searches for a durable military system for its new and
unprecedented role as a continuing world power.

Raising an army and determining its nature are more than matters of military efficiency. Naturally, professional soldiers prefer a
format based only upon military criteria, as physicians might prefer
to think only in strictly medical terms. But reality is usually more
complex. Ideally, military commanders would like to know in advance the goals and potential enemies of the army. Then they could
recommend the kind of forces needed for success. Although the
current debate has focused largely on precisely these military questions of missions, adversaries, and the quantity and quality of American forces, military formats are seldom determined by questions
solely of military concern. In America, as in most other countries,
because the nature of the military format can have such an important impact upon the citizenry, its determination is generally based
on politico-economic as much as military grounds.

Theoretically, a variety of possible formats exist. Soldiers can be
volunteers, obtained through various incentives. They are usually
enlisted from the home population, but some countries have supplemented these with foreign mercenaries. The government can compel
military training and service among its residents, a conscription
which can be selective or "universal"—that is, comprehensive
among particular age groups of able-bodied men, and (in some countries) women. Training and service can be relatively brief, as with
militia or short-term draftees. Or service can be for the duration, as

in the world wars. In contrast with temporary citizen-soldiers, the core of the regular army is usually composed of long-term professionals, career soldiers who re-enlist until retirement. The nature of the officer corps is vital to the army's military efficiency and political loyalty. In countries like the United States, with an effective tradition of civilian control of the military, there are periodic efforts to ensure that the social origins and attitudes of the officer corps are broadly in line with predominant civilian views about society and government. In regard to all of these various criteria, the most important distinctions among military formats have in practice been largely those between local militia and national forces, and between long-term regulars and temporary troops.[3]

In considering which of these formats, or what combination of them, to apply in particular circumstances, policy-makers have been limited by existing traditions as well as contemporary constraints. In addition to institutional and strategic considerations, political and economic costs are important considerations to civilian decision-makers. How will various socio-economic, ethnic, and racial groups be involved? When the greater financial costs of a larger or volunteer army must be met through higher taxes, increased borrowing, or cuts in social or economic programs, what will be the impact on society, and what reaction can be expected? How would the temporary transfer of large numbers of workers into the army affect the economy? Politically, what degree of public opposition or disorder might be caused by a particular format?

Americans have been rather limited in their acceptance of national conscription. How could it be otherwise? For most of its history, the United States was relatively secure, without aggressive and militarily powerful nations on its borders, and without a far-flung empire to defend. For a variety of reasons—demographic, economic, political, and ideological—Americans developed a society with a significant degree of individual freedom and local autonomy. In the formative years of the Republic, the majority of the population, including the predominant, agrarian elites, had a fear of strong central government and of a national standing army, regarding them both as being unduly expensive and potentially threatening to local autonomy, to individual liberty—initially, at least, among adult white males—and to the ideal of republican government.

It is difficult to see how such an individualistic, fragmented, and governmentally suspicious society could mobilize its military resources on a national scale. The United States long remained divided among regions—Northeast, South, and West—with conflicting interests and attitudes. Under American federalism, political and mili-

tary authority was divided between the national and state governments and, within those, between the legislature and the executive.
The idealization of individualism and opportunity and the desire to
protect local and regional interests helped keep the nation rudimentary and the central government wary of asserting authority directly upon citizens. Unlike such fundamental charters in Europe,
the basic documents of the United States, from the Declaration of
Independence to the Bill of Rights, asserted only the rights of the
citizenry, and not its obligations.[4]

When even the framers of the national government were politically unwilling to assert direct military obligations, how could such
a nation defend itself and its interests? The dominant ideology of the
early republic, which emphasized freedom from governmental interference, also supported the belief that, because of their inherent
superiority and sense of public virtue, republican citizens would
eagerly enlist when needed and would triumph over the professional "hirelings" of their adversaries. But what would happen if
too few citizens volunteered, or if part-time citizen-soldiers proved
inferior to full-time professionals, or if the long-term protection of
national interests required a continuing force? Could a standing
army prove acceptable? Was conscription compatible with liberty?
More pragmatically, in a political system with widespread suffrage,
in which most of the potential citizen-soldiers were also citizen-
voters, could popularly elected legislators be induced to vote to
draft their constituents?

Military institutions reflect the societies that create them. While
few would disagree with such a general assertion, the more controversial and important questions involve precisely how much military institutions reflect civilian society.[5] Why and to what extent are
they modified by changes in the larger society? Why is one military
format chosen over another? Most intriguingly, why are some formats created and maintained despite the opposition of the military?

In seeking to explain what has been responsible for the major
changes in the nature of armies, particularly in the last few centuries, theorists have developed varying and often conflicting interpretations. Many emphasize changes in the nature of warfare. Some
of these point to the importance of *technology*, either new weapons
such as firearms, machine guns, or guided missiles, or explosives
like gunpowder, TNT, or nuclear fission and fusion, or nonmilitary
inventions such as railroads.[6] Others stress *military theory and
doctrine*, crucial concepts of military strategy and organization con-
ceived by military thinkers like Clausewitz and Liddell-Hart, or by
commanders like Frederick the Great, Napoleon, Grant, or Moltke.[7]
Even the "new" military history, which has studied the institutional

development of the armed forces rather than the campaign narratives that were the focus of the old "drum and bugle" school, at least in the American case has emphasized debates within the professional officer corps over what should be the proper type of army.[8]

What dominant influences shape military institutions? Those who stress large social forces rather than purely military factors disagree over the identity of the primary causal forces. Some highlight the importance of ideas while others point to the material bases of social change. An emphasis on *political ideology* concentrates on differences in military systems resulting from dominant beliefs, whether in monarchy or republicanism, localism or nationalism, totalitarianism or democracy.[9] Others stress the importance of *structural aspects* of a society and their impact upon the military. To Marx and Engels, the *class structure* based upon the nature of the economy was determinative.[10] More recently, historian William H. McNeill has noted especially the influence of *demography*, particularly increases in population, upon the nature of war and the military.[11] Some have linked evolving military organizations to developments in the social and economic structures of society as well as to resulting attitudinal changes, a *socio-cultural* approach sometimes linked to a "cosmopolitan-localistic" dichotomy or the so-called "organizational" or "bureaucratic" synthesis.[12]

Major changes in long-term military formats have been causally related to long-term alterations in domestic and international circumstances. The present author has identified several such long-term patterns, sometimes lasting a century or more, within which, despite some differences among specific formats for particular wars, there remained a general similarity and continuity.[13] There have been six long-term "general military format models" over the course of American history from 1607 to 1987, encompassing a number of specific military formats.

Beginning with the *Settlement Model* of the local community-in-arms in the early 1600s, the pattern shifted after the 1650s to the less burdensome *Colony Model* of minimal local defense and ad hoc expeditionary forces. The American Revolution produced a short-lived system, the *Confederation Model*, composed of temporary wartime multi-state forces. But the format which served the new republic for more than a century began to emerge in the 1790s. The *New Nation Model* of a combined local-national military survived until 1917. It was in World War I that the United States achieved a truly national wartime mass army for world use in the *Nation-State Model:* wartime national mass mobilization. That model was used in both world wars. Currently, in seeking a durable *World Power Model*, the United States since 1973 has experimented with a large, volunteer, professional standing army. All of these general format models have been related to long-term changes in the nature of American society and its international context.

Over the past four centuries, the nature of America's armies has been the product not simply of military theory and technology but, more importantly, of forces in the civilian society and the international system. Externally, the most important factors have been regional or global changes in the structure of geopolitical and economic interests and in relative military power. Domestically, the most significant determinants have been both socio-economic forces and the political culture. The former includes the nature of the economy and social structure as well as the demographic mix. The political culture includes political processes, prevailing ideology and popular and elite beliefs (particularly in regard to concepts of citizenship and its military obligations), and the distribution of political power, including, most importantly, the relative power of the State.[14]

In American history, the nature of military formats has in the final analysis been shaped not by the military, but primarily by civilians in the public arena. There the outcome is the result of competition among various groups and elements (including the State itself), attempting to establish or maintain political power and to determine prevailing cultural forms and meanings. At issue has been not simply the military defense of regional or national interests as perceived by particular groups, but also changing definitions of the military obligations of citizens, and alterations in the role of the State. In such an analysis, the influence, or the lack of it, of various groups is crucial. For in determining the manner and extent of military mobilization that is actually possible, it is essential to consider not only the legal authority and institutional capability of the State, but also popular legitimacy and public consent.[15]

The most important changes in long-term general military format models have been related to changes in the power of the State, its expansion or diminution, the relationship of the citizenry to the State, and the international relationships among nation-States. The process of *State-building*, at least among Western nations, has been one in which various groups have expanded the control of the central government over a body of land and people, generally for a combination of domestic and foreign purposes. The centralizing States which began to emerge in Europe in the 16th century were, at the same time, also responding to each other and creating a modern State system in that area of the world.[16]

Crucial to this development, from the beginning, was the ability of

the central authorities—the monarchy and the growing bureaucracy—to obtain military forces. To compete effectively with
each other as well as to consolidate power internally, these governments sought to monopolize the means of organized violence. Consequently, the decentralized feudal levies of peasant-soldiers, raised
by the nobility, were gradually replaced by military forces linked
more closely to the central government. Initially, this took the form
of temporarily conscripted, largely unpaid, local militia under
county officers appointed by the Crown. Subsequently, with increased financial powers, the monarchy hired professional soldiers.
By the end of the 17th century, the major States of Europe had
obtained the legal authority and institutional ability to raise professional forces which were highly disciplined, militarily efficient, and
politically loyal. Although smaller than the feudal peasant levies,
these standing armies were considerably more expensive to maintain. Consequently, they not only fought limited wars against the
regulars of other States, but they were often used to put down anti-
tax riots and other direct challenges to their own State's extractive
powers, which had been increased largely to finance the armed
forces. Indeed, by the 18th century, a government without the
powers of both "the purse and the sword" did not qualify as a
"modern State."[17]

These early States were not "nations" in the modern connotation
of the term, for they lacked nationalism, that powerful sense of
group or national consciousness among masses of people which
swept through Europe in the 19th century. In the process of *nation-
building*, modernizers characterized an entire population from different subregions, ethnic, religious, and socio-economic groups as a
national citizenry for purposes of political and economic integration. This was often accompanied by such an intensive commitment
to national ideals and purposes that it dramatically expanded the
power of the national government into that of the *nation-State*.[18]
Modern nation-States found that they were able to mobilize large
numbers of citizens into military forces through popular enthusiasm and, when necessary, through widespread conscription. The
mass conscript army was first developed on the national level by
Revolutionary and Napoleonic France at the end of the 18th century.
Later, in the second half of the 19th century, monarchical Prussia
and republican France extended it through a system of widespread
and ultimately "universal" military training and service (UMT&S).
The nation-State had created the mass conscript army and the
means for "total war."[19]

The wave of national consciousness and democratic spirit had, in
the wake of the French Revolution, altered the nature of armies,

warfarc, and thc State. As Michael Howard, the eminent British military historian, explained:

> The dichotomy between princes and peoples, between the state apparatus and the community, was violently resolved in a series of grcat rcvolutions, foreshadowed by the American Declaration of Independence, that swept Europe between 1789 and 1918, when in one country after another the representatives of 'the people' or 'the Nation' (the terms were initially interchangeable), assumed control of the States.
>
> But so far from inaugurating the expected reign of peace, this 'nationalization' of the State meant simply the nationalization of war; and the new *international* conflicts were fought with an intensity inconceivable under *l'ancien regime*.[20]

The political and military evolution of European States differed from the evolution in the United States because of the strength of localism in America and the comparative weakness of the central government. In the Old World, the rise of the modern centralized State came well *before* the arrival of nationalism and the subsequent transformation of States into nation-States. In America, however, the sequence was almost completely reversed. Among the thirteen former colonies, their first central government was created only in the 1770s during the revolution and it had only minimal powers. From the beginning of settlement, each colony had maintained its own military forcc—the militia and its offshoots. In the Revolution, these thirteen militia were augmented by a temporary Continental Army composed of longer-term units which were also supplied by the states. A stronger national government was established under the Constitution of 1787, but although it and a small national standing army expanded over the next century, they grew slowly and remained rudimentary compared to those of European States.

In America, the differing interests of local and regional elites, together with strong popular fears of governmental corruption and tyranny, contributed to the decentralization of a dual system of federalism. The political-legal system was based on cooperation between the national government and thc scmi-sovercign states. For a bare minimum of national coordination and direction, the country relied upon three factors: a largely self-regulating market, the judiciary, and a national political party system. American citizenship, first defined during the Revolutionary period, combined local social and political loyalties with a rather vague and circumscribed legal link to the nation. Given such conditions, how could such a decentralized country raise and maintain national armies that would be both militarily effective and politically acceptable? How could it become a true nation-State?

Unlike the European experience, in America a sense of nationalism preceded and grew more rapidly than the central State. The feeling of common purpose and destiny, based on ideals of independence and republicanism, strongly emphasized individual rights and local autonomy. These were part of the opposition to the idea of strong central government which was integral to the initial definition of Americanism. Largely divorced from the national government, nationalism flourished mainly through common experiences, symbols, and beliefs rather than, as in Europe, in connection with strong national institutions such as the State, the established Church, and the standing Army. The United States sustained only a limited government and a small standing army. Emphasis upon American national greatness coexisted in the early 19th century with a widespread apathy bordering on disdain towards the national government and the U.S. Army, both of which were widely viewed as largely irrelevant to the progress of American society. The former colonies still had only a tenuous sense of unity and nationhood.

Nationalism increased in the 19th century, but it took the crucible of civil war and the forging of a national industrial marketplace for many Americans to identify themselves as a nation, rather than as simply a series of disparate communities and regions. During the Civil War and Reconstruction, national citizenship was redefined and declared supreme in certain legal areas. The Spanish-American War of 1898 intensified the sense of nationalism. But despite the burgeoning, spread-eagle Americanism of the closing decades of the 19th century, the United States lacked a powerful, continually active central government—a modern State. Such a State was precluded by the continued distrust of governmental corruption and of interference in class and regional interests; by an emphasis on largely unrestricted individualism in the economic sphere; and by the continuation of a governmental philosophy of laissez-faire. Even as it finally became a nation, the country retained important individualistic and localistic traditions.[21] The industrial giant, in which individuals created the most powerful corporations in the world, lacked a national government with either the institutional means or the popular legitimacy to project an army into the international arena to an extent commensurate with its status as an economic world power.

Only in the 20th century did a modern, activist, interventionist State emerge on a regular basis in America. When it began in the progressive era, it followed the intense nationalism of the turn of the century. It arrived as the nation-State, created by a desire for efficient coordination and legitimated by popular consciousness and a sense of political participation by and benefit to the citizenry. The development of an institutionally strong and popularly legitimated State, together with intensive nationalism, helped make possible the successful establishment and operation of the American mass conscript army in World War I. Unlike continental Europe, the creation of the mass army in America was accomplished with a deference to the continued importance of localism and an emphasis upon the temporary, selective nature of the draft. With its decentralized system of local boards, the Selective Service System contributed greatly to public acceptance of a wartime national draft. This politico-military formula, integrating nationalism and localism, provided the mechanism for raising America's mass armies in war and cold war for most of the 20th century.[22]

A broad historical examination of the evolution of the means of raising America's armies and their nature, particularly in regard to the relationship of the citizen to the State, is especially useful today. It helps understand what led to the important decision to use drafted citizen-armies in the 20th century and it can correct the misuse of history in recent debates over the proper military format for America. Current partisans have frequently identified their choice of format with the American military "tradition." While understandable as rhetorical efforts, such claims often distort the historical reality.

In the current policy debate, those who seek a return to the mixed force of draftees and volunteers that existed before 1973 often have portrayed that as the traditional format, ignoring the fact that the peacetime use of national conscription, at least during the non-war years between 1948 and 1973, represented a major departure from American traditions. At the same time, defenders of the All-Volunteer Armed Force have usually portrayed the current exclusive reliance upon voluntarism as entirely within the American tradition, despite the fact that never before in its history has the United States maintained such a large peacetime volunteer military force. Nor, regardless of the arguments of libertarians, is the draft always "un-American."[23]

The present debate cannot be adequately understood without an accurate knowledge of the origin and legacy of the modern American military format first adopted in World War I. That model, and the politico-military formula which enabled it to succeed, coincided with changes in American society and the international order. Today, any contemporary American system of military service—the mixed force of draftees and volunteers that characterized most of the Cold War era, the present all-volunteer army, or whatever format that will surely and eventually replace it—must derive partly from the dramatic developments of the First World War. No format in the foreseeable future can be fully comprehended without an awareness of these pivotal changes of the early 20th century, or of the historic evolution of the means of raising America's armies* and their relationship to society and the international order, all of which is the larger subject of this book.

---

* The nomenclature of America's armies has varied. In this study, "American army" refers to the wartime and Cold War armies of the United States which contained citizen-soldiers (whether in units of the U.S. Volunteers, Additional Army, National Army, or Army of the United States) and professionals; "militia" and "National Guard" indicate the citizen-soldiers of the states; and "U.S. Army" denotes the nation's standing army of regulars.

1

"Soldiers When They Chose to Be," 1607–1861

WITH THE SUCCESSFUL CONCLUSION of the Revolutionary War, Congress saw no further need for a national army. Consequently, on June 2, 1784, it discharged the entire Continental Army, keeping only 83 veterans to guard the accumulated military supplies at West Point and Fort Pitt.[1] The belief that the United States did not need and would not accept a sizable standing army accurately reflected predominant American attitudes and traditions. It would remain a powerful influence for generations. But it would also continue to pose a dilemma: How could the United States raise its armies in a manner that was both militarily effective and politically acceptable?

When the English colonists arrived in America in the early 1600s, they brought weapons and ideas about military organization and warfare as well as a few hired captains, like John Smith and Miles Standish, to defend them. But the early settlers soon became dissatisfied when these swashbuckling disciplinarians tried to turn them into soldiers. Most colonies quickly turned to a more "civilianized" and less demanding military system. Political leaders rejuvenated the decaying local militia organization from Tudor England and transformed it into an acceptable and effective civilian-led force for temporary local military action against the Indians.

Ironically, while the Americans revived the militia concept of using the civilian community as an occasional fighting force, Europeans abandoned such short-term, amateur, defensively oriented forces, whether militia or feudal levies. In a "military revolution" beginning between the mid-16th and mid-17th centuries, European monarchs obtained the authority and institutional ability to raise and sustain large new, offensively oriented, professional standing

13

armies. These forces were maintained and controlled directly by increasingly centralized States which employed them in a wide variety of tasks, both foreign and domestic. The power of the purse and the sword—the ability to raise internal revenue in order to sustain a large professional army—was seen as an essential characteristic of the modern State.[2]

England's North American colonies lacked strong central governments and, in a land where men and money were in short supply, they were unable to afford standing forces of long-term, paid professional soldiers. They chose a different military format. Although specifics varied according to colony and era, a general pattern emerged: the *Settlement Model: the local community-in-arms*. With the exception of pacifist Quaker Pennsylvania, all the colonial legislatures declared able-bodied freemen (males who had a property stake in society) between the ages of about 17 and 60 to be members of the local militia. Initially, the lawmakers excluded second-class citizens, apprentices, indentured servants, and black slaves, except in emergencies. They also frequently exempted certain occupations, such as iron-makers, master mariners, and others whose skills were deemed essential to the community's welfare; some colonies with Quaker settlements, like Pennsylvania, Rhode Island, and North Carolina, also exempted conscientious objectors.

Politically and economically the system fit the early needs of the colonies because the militia reflected the predominant social order (with officers drawn from local elites) and because the burden although widespread was minimal. Militiamen had to arm themselves, train a few days a year, and respond to calls for defense of the colony or local retaliatory attacks. Service seldom lasted more than three months, usually in the summer between planting and harvesting season, and since most militiamen were farmers, it generally did not adversely affect them or the economy. Although less of a deterrent than regulars stationed on the frontier would have been, the militia proved to be an instrument of great destruction in numerous conflicts between Indians and colonists. The obligation for periodic, unpaid, compulsory training and short-term service was widely accepted as necessary to defend highly vulnerable outposts in the wilderness. As one historian explained, "all were soldiers because all lived on the battlefield."[3]

As the frontier and the battlefield shifted westward, however, and the colonial population swelled, the need to mobilize most adult males became increasingly infrequent. By the end of the 17th century, the militia in most colonies, although maintained through compulsory training days, had in practice ceased to be the community's principal military instrument. Only occasionally between

1675 and 1775 did a colony deem it necessary to mobilize a substantial percentage of the citizenry. Governing elites in most colonies concluded that it was neither militarily necessary nor politically nor economically wise to disrupt the economy and the electorate through such intervention unless absolutely necessary. For garrison duty and regular patrolling on the Indian frontier and for most extended expeditions against French or Spanish colonists and their Indian allies, the colonists turned increasingly to specially organized, ad hoc, military units, composed primarily of paid volunteers. Technically, these units—to be discussed in detail later—were neither militia nor a standing army, for they were created anew each year if needed. Rather, these were temporary, hybrid organizations, between short-term defensive militia and long-term, offensively oriented regulars. This general format can be described as the *Colony Model: minimal local defense and ad hoc, contracted active-service forces.*[1]

Even as it atrophied as a fighting system, however, the militia remained important as a politico-military concept. Militarily, it provided a manpower reserve, in which officers developed leadership skills and from which they obtained many active-service recruits. In the West, it remained an instrument of frontier defense and warfare against the Indians. In the North, it was used against riots and other civil disturbances in the growing seacoast cities. In the South, where blacks were generally excluded from the militia, it served as a vehicle to deter or suppress slave insurrections and as a basis for routine nighttime patrols to keep slaves from leaving the plantations. Most effective in New England, the militia there was used against Indians and to protect an extensive seacoast and a long border with Canada. Its relative importance among the Yankees derived perhaps from their considerable ethnic and cultural homogeneity and sense of common purpose as well as from the fact that New England had a more town-centered and urban population than most other colonies.

Massachusetts drew upon its militia for ad hoc, contracted, active-service expeditionary forces in four wars which pitted Yankee and British forces against the French and their Indian allies between 1689 and 1763.[5] In the mid-1750s, during the early stages of the French and Indian War, the Bay Colony successfully fielded large annual, six-month expeditions which amounted to nearly one-third of the young men aged 16 to 29. It was not through impressment that such a mobilization was achieved (only 2 percent were draftees and 10 percent substitutes); rather, 88 percent enlisted voluntarily, inspired by economic, religious, and patriotic reasons, and sometimes by the sheer desire for adventure.[6]

These young men were successfully recruited as temporary citizen-soldiers. The key to this large-scale mobilization was not the
government's authority and ability to conscript, which it used spar-
ingly if at all, but rather its ability to mobilize the community,
through religious and secular appeals, and to raise funds to hire and
supply the temporary force. Community enthusiasm and support
was generated largely through the Puritan leadership's portrayal of
the conflict against the Catholic French and the heathen Indians as a
retaliatory, religious crusade, one which also offered substantial
opportunities for material gain. There were limits to the average
New Englander's sense of military obligation. According to their
diaries and account books as well as contemporary observers, these
Yankees did not serve out of any sense of inherent obligation or
obedience to their officers or to governmental authorities in Boston
or London. Rather, to the astonishment and disgust of British regulars, these provincial American troops emphasized the importance
of contractual relationships in their military service as in their
everyday civilian life.

The contractual ideal was, in fact, central in New England. It
proved essential in a money-scarce economy in which people turned
to carefully-tallied records of goods and services owed to each other.
The contract idea held a central place in the Puritan religion which
stressed the covenant with God by individuals and the church. Massachusetts' citizen-soldiers held to the letter of their enlistment
contracts, which they saw as obligating them only to serve for a
specified period for contracted terms of pay and sustenance under
the local officers who had recruited them. Attempts to alter these
terms by the army or the government were seen as nullifying the
soldier's contractual responsibilities, leaving him free to leave and
return home. Many officers, American as well as British, recognized
the extremity and inefficiency of such a military system, but colonial officers and officials had to accept it because the sense of
individualism, voluntarism, and contractualism was inherent in
New England society.[7]

Free blacks posed a politico-military issue in virtually every
colony. Should they be included in the polity? In the militia? Increased fear of insurrection, due to the growing numbers of Afro-
American slaves and the belief that rebellion was often instigated by
free blacks, led to their exclusion from the militia, first in Virginia
as early as 1639 and later throughout the South and even in many
areas of the North. Nevertheless, in a labor-scarce society, periodic
pressure for military manpower as well as the unwillingness of
many middle-class whites to serve for more than a few months and
the reluctance of elected legislators to force voters into the army

against their will, led to some modification of these restraints. Periodically, some colonies actively recruited free blacks as soldiers. In the 18th century, many northern blacks fought in integrated units in the wars against the French and Indians. In the South, however, particularly after a number of slave conspiracies and insurrections, the lawmakers became increasingly unwilling to arm and train any Afro-Americans. Although many blacks were eager to fight for their independence and advancement, the degree to which they were included in the militia or contracted expeditionary forces depended largely upon the prevailing racial attitudes in white society and the severity of the military situation.[8]

The periodic problem of how to raise troops for extended service of up to a year was often resolved by enticing voluntary enlistments from adventurous militiamen and impecunious members of the underclass. Most legislators saw the inclusion of unfranchised, second-class citizens as the solution to their dilemma. The political problem, however, was how to get the propertyless to accept a conscription which excluded the middle class. One solution, popular in New England, was "substitution," in which conscripted middle or upper class militiamen paid substitutes to serve in their place. Another, more common in the South, was for the legislators to exempt property-owning voters from conscription and to aim the draft specifically at the unemployed and transient poor, an extension of the concept of compelling vagrants to perform civilian labor in lieu of payment of fine, this time compelling rootless and impoverished men to serve in the military.

But conscripted transients often made reluctant soldiers, so extended-duty troops were generally hired rather than conscripted. What emerged in Britain's 18th-century American colonies, at least outside New England, were two quite different types of military institution: a short-term militia of established citizens, and a temporary, ad hoc, active-service expeditionary force drawn mainly from poor farmers, servants, apprentices, transients, "vagrants," impecunious recent immigrants, laborers and others among the landless white poor, as well as some white-Indian halfbloods, mulattoes, free blacks, and occasionally some black slaves. Despite the differences in the rank and file, officers in both the militia and the expeditionary forces came primarily from the middle and upper classes.[9]

The class-bound nature of most of the active-service expeditionary forces was evident in the manner in which Virginia mobilized during the French and Indian War.[10] Unlike the middle-class force fielded by Massachusetts in 1756, Virginia sought, that same year, to exclude the upper-class gentry and middle-class farmer-voters of the militia, through socially selective conscription. The Old Dominion tried to raise an extended-term expeditionary force composed of those the planter-legislators referred to as the "lesser sort," "common herd," and "ignorant vulgar." However, the colony proved unable to conscript such a force. Rural conscripts forcibly resisted or fled into the mountains. In contrast to its willingness to help control black slaves, the middle-class militia refused to impose the gentry's will upon drafted poor whites, probably because the growth of black slavery had heightened the value that all whites placed upon freedom for themselves. Effective resistance to "involuntary military servitude" became so widespread that the colony failed to raise even a regiment. Virginians, one frontiersman explained, were "soldiers [only] when they chose to be."[11]

Not until a new British Ministry decided in 1758 to pay for American troops could the Old Dominion obtain an adequate expeditionary force. With London paying the bill, the House of Burgesses jettisoned the unsuccessful draft and enthusiastically launched a recruiting campaign based on a handsome enlistment bounty which produced two full regiments of volunteers within six months. The lower classes of Virginia served neither out of direct coercion nor from any sense of deference to their "betters," or sense of obligation to colony or Crown. Rather, in a colony characterized by a relatively scarce supply of white labor, and in which the common people were making increasingly successful challenges to gentry control of political and ecclesiastical institutions, these people insisted on the liberty to pursue their own interests in military institutions as well.[12]

By the time the French were driven out of Canada and the Ohio Valley in 1763, a number of American colonies had employed provincial forces distinct from the militia and which, like the Virginia regiments, included men who had enlisted for one- or two-year terms. For the first time, London had also introduced significant numbers of British regulars into the colonies. Despite initial setbacks, their ultimate military success, particularly in the assault on Quebec, led a few American military men to accept the combat superiority of professional soldiers. However, the British forces also caused considerable problems. Provincial troops resented the arrogance of British officers and their attempts to impose discipline and control over them in violation of the colonists' enlistment contracts. With the tightening of imperial rule after the war, many colonists viewed the garrisoning of British regulars here without the consent of local legislatures as part of a larger threat to American liberties.

Hostility to British regular forces reinforced the popular belief in the ideal of the militia and the citizen-soldier. The anomaly between the myth of the community-in-arms and the reality of generally lower-class, active-service expeditionary forces had failed to become a major political issue in the colonial period because of the relative infrequency of war and combat. In fact, the economic inducements of pay and wartime plunder provided opportunities for many. The ideal, if not the reality, of the citizen-soldier continued, and it was soon elevated into a major element of the practical and ideological dispute with Britain during the two decades of crises which preceded the Revolution. Americans drew upon the ideology of radical English Whigs who had argued that the "Glorious Revolution" of 1688 had been betrayed by a conspiracy in which a powerful State was created by the Hanoverian monarchs and by the London financial and commercial magnates who dominated their "Court" party. The new and large professional army was seen as a vehicle for political corruption, manipulation, and tyranny by this State. In contrast, the Whigs argued that the relationship between the civil and military responsibility of property-owning citizens was essential to guaranteeing free institutions and limiting the corruption of the political system and the establishment of arbitrary, centralized power. The citizen-militia, composed of the property-owning yeomen and freeholders who were the backbone of the country, was portrayed as both the guardian of individual liberty as well as public virtue.[13]

American colonists, however, eschewed standing armies for more than purely ideological reasons. Labor and financial resources were scarce and war was episodic. Government was small, taxes few, and an enforcement body relatively non-existent. In the struggle for local control, colonial assemblies forced royal governors to rely upon short-term militia or other temporary troops rather than on standing forces which would be paid by and loyal to a governor who represented not the colonists as much as the political and economic interests in London. The growing confrontation with England that began in 1763 helped convince many Americans that the Crown sought to curtail local liberties and was employing British redcoats as an instrument of domestic control. In their emphasis upon individual liberty, republicanism, and civic virtue, the colonists idealized the citizen-soldier of the militia; hostility towards standing armies became an integral part of the American ideology. When the revolution began in 1775, the colonists faced an apparent dilemma: How could they reconcile this belief and yet raise and maintain military forces sufficient to defeat the British Army and force London to recognize the independence of its former colonies?

The American Revolution was seen as a people's war: a fight for individual liberty, local autonomy, and the restoration of public virtue. Citizens would serve in arms, it was believed, because of patriotism, not pay. Unlike the more restricted wars in Europe fought between professional standing armies, the revolution meant extensive mobilization and involvement of society. As in the earlier conflicts against "savage" Indians and "cruel," "papist," Spanish and French forces, the colonists converted a war over clashing interests into an ideological "crusade" to drive the enemy from the continent. Since the Americans did not have a standing army, such "emotionalization" was needed to persuade the population to accept considerable temporary personal, military, and financial burdens, to mobilize a people in arms.[14]

In numbers alone, the militia provided the bulk of American forces. The use of short-term (from a few weeks to six months), largely unpaid, primarily volunteer citizen-soldiers for local defense was geared to the agricultural seasons. Protecting their own lives and property, the militia often served effectively, if sporadically, against invading enemy forces, particularly when firing from behind defensive positions, as they demonstrated at Bunker Hill. They also harassed the enemy's lines of communication and supply, and controlled dissident loyalists, playing a vital part in denying the British control over extensive rural areas.[15]

Despite the existence of similar weaponry and doctrine, the military formats of various states differed considerably, reflecting sociopolitical and economic circumstances and traditions as well as strategic contexts. Massachusetts employed the most efficient military system—a select, well-equipped, volunteer, ready reserve (the "Minute Men" ready for duty at a "minute's" notice), prepared in advance for active duty of up to six months. Virginia chose the least efficient system—a short-term general militia—in which relatively untrained, semi-equipped, bodies of men would be haphazardly organized and called forth briefly and sporadically when needed. The government of the Old Dominion remained politically or institutionally unable to implement effective conscription. Governor Thomas Jefferson complained to John Adams in 1775 that Virginians were simply too jealous of their liberty to accept conscription.[16] Instead, he relied upon some enlistment bounties and a semi-draft in which the government readily accepted substitutes and tolerated a great deal of evasion and desertion. Only when the British Army invaded the state in 1780–81, did Williamsburg turn reluctantly to a *levée en masse*, which was rejected by planters as well as by the common people.[17] In Massachusetts, as Adams explained to Jefferson, the draft was not considered onerous. When not enough citizen-soldiers volunteered, local militia officers drafted the more affluent citizens who, in turn, hired men to serve as substitutes. This selective draft functioned mainly as a kind of tax for raising individual enlistment bounties. Although military obligations were stronger in New England, its citizen-soldiers also enjoyed more rights and privileges, including determining their contract and electing their officers.[18]

As a revolutionary conflict, the War for Independence showed the difficulty faced even by a professional army in defeating a de-centralized agrarian population, mobilized behind a powerful com-bination of ideology and self-interest. Yet it also demonstrated the limitation of militia in securing a national political goal, indepen-dence. To carry on the war, the colonies created a weak coordinating authority, a confederation of sovereign states. Under the Con-tinental and then Confederation Congress, they created a new military format: the *Confederation Model: temporary wartime multi-state forces.* Initiated in June 1775 to augment New England militiamen besieging Boston, the Continental Army was composed of paid, long-term (two- to three-year) enlistees. This force lasted until the end of the war in 1783, and continued as a concept for a decade after that. Since the weak central government had neither the power to tax nor to conscript, it relied upon the states to supply and maintain units of the Continental Army in addition to their own short-term militia.[19] Even this multi-state standing army had been established only after considerable controversy because it ran coun-ter to the republican idea of virtuous citizen-soldiers. It also implied an expansion of the central government, of taxation, and public debt. It threatened the states' desire to ensure that their military resources would always have the defense of local interests as their first priority.

At first, Congress had enrolled Continental soldiers for six- or twelve-month enlistments, but by 1777 many of the initial recruits had been killed or captured, or had left the army. With the war showing no sign of ending, the legislature in desperation appealed for three-year enlistments. The creation of a wartime standing army of disciplined regulars was portrayed by George Washington and other traditionalists as a military necessity. Only a few professional officers, like the political and military radical General Charles Lee, believed the revolution called for a different kind of national "cit-izens army," somewhere between regulars and militiamen.[20]

The longer-term regulars of the state-raised units of the Conti-nental Army differed considerably from the short-term citizen-sol-diers of the militia. Unlike the celebrated "embattled farmers" of the militia, the rank and file of the Continental Army—if the units from Maryland, Massachusetts, and New Jersey were typical—eventually became composed overwhelmingly of the young and the poor whites and blacks—the sons of marginal farmers, laborers, drifters, indentured servants—and recent immigrants without roots in America.[21] They also included thousands of women who served officially and for pay, primarily as nurses in the medical corps and with the artillery as carriers of water (the so-called "Molly Pitchers") to keep excess powder swabbed out of cannons. A few women disguised themselves and enlisted in combat units, but as this was a role defined by law as male, they were discharged if discovered.[22] Among the men in the ranks, service in the Continental Army differed from that in the militia, not simply in the length of enlistment and socio-economic status, but in the attempts of Washington and Von Steuben to turn the Continentals into regulars. To do so, they ended the New England practice of election and fraternization of officers and enlisted men and imposed strict standards of discipline and obedience.

As the war dragged on, state and national governments increased their patriotic appeals and boosted enlistment bounties in paper currency bonuses or western land grants. But when too few signed up for three-year terms, the states expanded eligibility to the poor and non-citizens, such as British and Hessian prisoners of war, and then purchased the freedom of indentured servants and pardoned convicted felons if they would enlist. The recruitment problem, plus the British policy of offering freedom to slaves who joined their army, led white Americans gradually to encourage black enlistment. In New England, free blacks had served from the beginning, some in Afro-American combat companies under black officers. Although a number of mid-Atlantic states accepted black enlistment in 1777, the South refused until after the British invaded the region in 1778. Then every southern state except Georgia and South Carolina enlisted some free blacks and slaves in labor units. The military role of Afro-Americans in supporting the war together with evolving concepts of republican citizenship contributed to the ending of slavery in several northern states and the liberalization of manumission laws in the upper South.[23]

Difficulties in sustaining the ranks of the Continental Army led many states to augment recruiting efforts with drafts or, more frequently, with draft-induced substitutions. Maryland first drafted vagrants. Most states exempted married men and certain occupations; all allowed the middle and upper classes to avoid personal service by hiring substitutes. The widespread use of state drafts to maintain the Continental Army in the late 1770s appears, in practice, to have been New England–style "quasi-drafts," in which local militia officers "drafted" affluent militiamen who then hired substitutes to serve for them in the Continental Army.[24]

Although the revolution spurred national consciousness, it also reinforced the localism and regionalism of a "segmented society." Most of the 200,000 Americans who served under arms had not all served at the same time, but in smaller numbers and for brief periods; most had served in the local militia. The maximum strength reached by the Continental Army was 16,800 in 1778, but it generally averaged considerably less.[25] Despite a new sense of national identity among some groups such as the Continental Army officer corps, few former colonists had much conception of a collective community beyond their town or region. No matter how much the Revolution would later be celebrated as the formative national experience, parochialism remained predominant at the time.[26]

Following their successful rebellion, Americans debated the nature of postwar military institutions as part of a larger controversy over republicanism and centralized power, a debate shaped by ideology and the self-interest of particular groups, states, and regions.[27] Calling themselves Federalists, nationalistic State-builders sought a more powerful central government, including a national bank, bureaucracy, and army. Allied with financial and mercantile interests concerned with the new problems and interests of a growing commercial society, they organized a political coalition of cash crop planters in the tidewater South and business and professional elites in the urban, commercial North. In opposition the localistic, states-rights Anti-Federalists were joined by discontented republican nationalists. This anti-Statist coalition, the Jeffersonian Democratic-Republicans, drew its political support from small farmers of the rural South and West and artisans, workers, and entrepreneurs in the cities of the Mid-Atlantic region.[28]

Determining a national military format in such an evolving political context proved particularly problemmatic. Federalists sought an effective standing army to intimidate or overcome hostile Indians, deter European encroachments, and make the United States a "respectable" part of the emergent international State system. Many of these nationalists also feared internal disorder and possible sectional fragmentation into regional republics each pursuing its own interests. Consequently, they argued that a strong national military establishment was needed to help consolidate as well as maintain the Union. They dismissed fears of a standing army, by asserting that in a properly governed republic such a force was not a threat to liberty.[29]

There remained, nevertheless, much support for local, ad hoc citizen-soldiers. Many Americans continued to believe that the revolution had demonstrated the superiority of local, volunteer citizen-soldiers over career regulars, a belief epitomized in the celebration of the "embattled farmers" and the "Minute Men."[30] At the end of the war, opponents of standing armies, like Elbridge Gerry, a wealthy member of the Confederation Congress from Marblehead, Massachusetts, called for complete elimination of the Continental Army. In place of a standing army, Gerry and others argued for reliance upon militia units or ad hoc contracted troops, as in the colonial period.

The resulting compromise was weighted against a standing army, and the Confederation Congress did discharge the Continental Army, except for a few dozen storehouse guards. However, to awe the Indians in the Ohio Valley, Congress also summoned 720 volunteers from the militia of the Mid-Atlantic states to serve for one year (subsequently extended to three years) in a nationally coordinated, regional, ad hoc contracted active-service force. This temporary, multi-state frontier constabulary provided an initial alternative to a peacetime national standing army.[31]

For more than a decade, State-builders like Washington and Alexander Hamilton sought to overcome the opposition to an effective regular army. A traditional soldier himself, like the European professionals he admired, Washington rejected the militia concept that every male citizen was also a soldier. Like other specialized trades, soldiering required a long apprenticeship to be effective. Although he preferred disciplined, long-term regulars, Washington recognized that popular opinion required at least some deference to the citizen-soldier. In 1783 and 1792, therefore, he proposed a mixed national force which would include a small standing army of 2,600 to 4,000 regulars, augmented by a selected national militia (a "Continental Militia") of young men, enlisted or drafted, subjected to regular army training and discipline, and led by nationally appointed officers. In line with recent developments in Europe, Washington suggested a national military academy to ensure a continuing supply of trained professional officers.[32]

Some of Washington's aides offered alternatives which took more account of the prevailing localism, regionalism, and republicanism. In an attempt to win popular support for the general's suggestion, Secretary of War Henry Knox argued that the military training would produce better citizens. In the annual "camps of discipline," he said, undisciplined, self-centered youths could be moulded into virtuous republican citizens as well as effective national militiamen, but this was still a proposal too extreme for acceptance.[33] In a bid to win states-rights advocates, Knox suggested that the states be allowed to appoint field officers and supervise the organization and training of the select national militia (although the central government would appoint general officers, keep the weapons locked in federal arsenals, and have authority to conscript militiamen in war-time). With greater deference to regionalism, Washington's drill-master, Baron Von Steuben, suggested regional military academies and select militia "Legions" in New England, the Mid-Atlantic, and the South, coordinated only by a nationally appointed general. Former Quartermaster General Timothy Pickering of Massachusetts suggested a different regionalization, dividing the frontier and the coastline into sections and having each group of states supply 800 continental constabulary troops for its region's defense. The state militia would remain the main defense forces, their officers linked to society despite military training because that training would be at local civilian colleges rather than national military academies considered "nurseries of aristocracy."[34]

Such fears delayed a national military academy for years, but during the 1780s, Congress did create a small but permanent regular army. The temporary, nationally coordinated, 700-man multi-state militia force which had been sent to the Ohio Valley frontier in 1784 was soon converted to a permanent national unit, the 1st U.S. Regiment, the initial unit of the U.S. Army. From the beginning, the regulars' primary responsibility was constabulary duty on the Indian frontier.

The militia continued to be viewed as the Republic's main bulwark of internal order and national defense, but Congress, reflecting conflicting interests, could not agree on an acceptable manner of turning the citizen-soldiers of the states into a national force. Representatives from New England, with the greatest wealth and best equipped militia, feared nationalization would mean its resources would be exploited to protect poorer regions along the Indian frontier. The South, West, and Mid-Atlantic states, each worried that nationalization might sacrifice their particular needs (whether use against Indians, protection of the seacoast, or control of slaves or urban rioters) to whichever region dominated the national government. Furthermore, since the local militia was still viewed as the major bastion against the tyranny of centralized power, many feared the corrupting effect of linking the careers and loyalties of state militia officers to a national military establishment.[35]

In the face of such widespread opposition to standing armies and national control of the militia, it is surprising how much the nationalizing Federalists were able to achieve in the U.S. Constitution and the single decade during which they controlled the national government. The majority at Philadelphia and in most state ratifying conventions accepted the argument of moderate Whigs that a standing army did not threaten liberty in a republican government characterized by limited and separated powers, and that modern warfare required the preparation of some units before hostilities. Thus the framers gave Congress the power "to raise and support Armies," and to declare war, and they designated the president as commander-in-chief with responsibility for overall direction of the army. Some critics tried to establish a specific constitutional limitation on the size of the peacetime army, but failed. To assuage anti-militarist fears and ensure congressional control, the Federalists—following the English example—limited all military appropriations to no longer than two years.

Although the Constitution clearly authorized a national army, it was necessarily much less specific on the means by which the central government could raise such a force. Did the national government have the power to draft as well as hire soldiers? As practical politicians as well as theorists, the framers had sought to avoid being drawn into a debate over the ultimate powers of the new government. Although almost nothing was said about conscription in the closed-door sessions in Philadelphia, Edmund Randolph of Virginia warned his colleagues that "draughts stretch the strings of government too violently to be adopted."[36]

Aware that state governments had the authority to compel short-term militia training and service, the nationalists also understood that an attempt to give the new central government such authority would have been unprecedented and might well have led to popular rejection of the Constitution. (Even the British Army did not draft, and American colonists had resisted attempts by the Royal Navy to impress them.[37]) In awarding Congress the power "to raise and support Armies" the farmers did not specifically grant the new government the power to conscript. However, they did not expressly prohibit it. They left the issue to future generations. There seems little doubt, however, that most of the nationalists believed at that time that the U.S. Government, like other modern States, would hire its army. Unlike the Articles of Confederation, the Constitution provided the power to tax. Hamilton declared that revenue would be the "essential engine" of national defense.[38]

Unlike most other nations, the United States, in keeping with American federalism, retained a dual military system, with both the nation and the states having their own forces. In the early Republic, the nationalists failed to establish a fully predominant position for the central government, either with exclusive control of the military obligations of the citizenry or clear superiority over the state militia. As with the taxing power, the founders accepted concurrent authority by both the national and state governments. To ensure the independence of the militia, the states were guaranteed authority over the appointment of officers and supervision of training. The central government could provide uniform standards of organization and training, but it was empowered to call out and control the militia only in carefully prescribed circumstances: to enforce national law, suppress insurrection, and repel invasion.[39] Implicitly then, the state militia were retained as counterweights to the regular army and to arbitrary action by the central government.

Yet thirteen separate militia of varying quality did not produce a militarily effective reserve. One alternative, as Washington had recommended, was a selected, well-trained, national (or regional) militia corps. Anti-centralizers blocked such alternatives because they feared—not without reason—that such plans could be a wedge for eventually eliminating state control of the officers and men who made up the core of the militia, by subsuming them under an enlarged national military establishment of regulars and reservists.[40]

Nationalization of the militia and the creation of a militarily effective and politically acceptable national reserve force was impeded by the fragmentation of power in federalism and the nature of citizenship in America. A highly individualistic, predominantly locally oriented people, Americans had little sense of responsibility to the nation or the new central government. Nor did they view citizenship in strictly political and legal terms. Rather, the concept was also nurtured within local social and cultural institutions as well as a sense of spaciousness and opportunity favorable to voluntarism and pluralism. This context encouraged an emphasis upon individual security and the freedom to try to improve one's situation, to engage, in Jefferson's felicitous phrase, in "the pursuit of happiness." On a legal and political level, the concept of American citizenship which began to emerge during the revolution linked the civic loyalties of citizens to their states; only in a larger, less tangible sense, were these linked to the new nation. By 1789, Madison had concluded that in order for the new U.S. government to gain increasing public acceptance, it would have to recognize the limits on its actions by local loyalties and the fear of central government.[41] American federalism reflected a dual and quite ambiguous citizenship.

Similarly, the legal concept of citizenship also failed to clarify military obligations to the nation. In the process of formulating early definitions of citizenship, American jurists and political thinkers tried to define principles of membership that adequately encompassed ideals of individual liberty and community responsibility. They portrayed political allegiance as resting upon individual volition and consent. Although volitional citizenship helped to legitimate withdrawal from the British Empire and justified a new government, it contained difficulties and dangers of its own. Emphasis upon individual consent clashed with community acceptance, particularly where long-standing prejudices excluded women, blacks, resident Indians and others considered alien or inferior, from full membership in the sovereign community. Such emphasis also failed to clarify the ambiguity between state and national citizenship. In fact, the emphasis upon the individual's consensual rights contributed to inadequate attention to obligations. Although male citizens could be obligated for short-term state militia service, it was not clear whether they had any military obligation to the nation.[42]

To the extent that they dealt with citizenship, the fundamental charters of the American national government—the Declaration of Independence, Articles of Confederation, U.S. Constitution, and the Bill of Rights—emphasized rights and privileges, not obligations, as they sought to build popular support for a new national government. Unlike the basic documents of Revolutionary France, none of these put forth the obligations of individual citizens.[43] The republican ideal had portrayed a selfless, independent citizenry as the cornerstone of public virtue, social harmony, and community defense. But the nexus had been between citizens and republican states, not between citizens and a distant central government with a potential for corruption and domination. By the late 18th century, expanding commercialization encouraged Americans to shift their celebration from selfless yeomen to aggressive, individualistic entrepreneurs. The drive for private wealth came to be hailed as a public virtue. In such an evolving context, Americans increasingly favored a national government which would leave them free to engage in their private economic pursuits.[44]

In regard to military service, this emphasis upon individual liberty and limited central government meant that except in a clear emergency the vast majority of citizens did not expect to have their careers interrupted to serve in the army. Since threats to the national security were generally limited and sporadic, Americans developed a two-army tradition. The standing army—the U.S. Army—remained minuscule compared to the expanding population and wealth of the country and compared to the armies of other nations, its main function being to provide a constabulary force on the Indian frontier and an experienced wartime leadership cadre. In wartime, the country relied upon temporary armies, raised only when needed. Only in part were these the militia. Congress honored the militia in principle, but generally ignored it in practice. In 1792, the Uniform Militia Act declared that "every free able-bodied white[45] male citizen of the respective states between 18 and 45 should be enrolled in the militia by local militia captains. . . ." But far from being the foundation of a national military obligation, this first national militia law was a hollow measure. Because of a continued deadlock among states and regions, Congress proved unable to agree on implementation or on uniform national standards.[46] Instead, for the bulk of its wartime forces, the United States relied upon ad hoc armies of citizen-soldiers.

The primary mechanism for raising these temporary citizen-armies, from the Indian wars of the early 1790s to the Spanish-American War of 1898, was the "U.S. Volunteers."[47] These ad hoc units were locally raised and officered, but funded by the U.S. government and directed by federally appointed generals. The process was simple: upon congressional authorization, the governors would nominate local notables who would receive commissions as temporary officers from the president. They, in turn, would recruit men in their areas into temporary units of federal volunteers, signing up the men who would elect the junior officers and follow them into battle. The system drew upon the essentially local basis of American society to serve national purposes; it enabled the central government to raise a large temporary army in a country where political power was fragmented by federalism. Because they were temporary, these armies were paid for only when needed, and there were no Constitutional limitations on the use of the U.S. Volunteers. Militia in federal service could not be held for more than nine months and not be sent outside the country. In contrast, the Volunteers enlisted for one- to three-year tours and, during the 19th century, fought both within the United States and as expeditionary forces in Canada, Mexico, Cuba, and the Philippines.[48]

Beginning in the early 1790s, a successful and acceptable format had begun to emerge. This fourth American military format-model, the *New Nation Model: the local-national military*, included three major components: a small permanent regular army, some organized militia units as ready reserves which could be mobilized for local defensive operations, and most importantly, previously unorganized units of locally raised, federally directed U.S. Volunteers which enabled a relatively weak central government to create sizable temporary wartime forces to carry out national policy.

The legitimacy and early limits of this format were quickly discovered when the Federalists exceeded them. In the 1790s, Federalist-dominated Congresses used crises with Indian nations and Revolutionary France to enlarge the national military establishment. Combined with Hamilton's aggressive national fiscal policies, this contributed to the formation of an opposition "Country" party, led by Jefferson and Madison, which concluded that the Hamiltonians were using manipulative "Court-style" national politics favoring northern commercial and financial interests to the detriment of agrarians and the republican experiment. The "Country" party was particularly concerned about the growth of the national debt as a source of patronage and power, and the army as a dangerous source of expense and repression. Under the Federalists, the cost of the regular army had risen from $600,000 in 1789–91 (14 percent of the federal budget) to $2,600,000 in 1794 (37 percent of the budget).[49] Equally as alarming to Jeffersonians was that the regular army, expanded to 5,000 men to defeat the Indians of the Ohio Valley, was not cut back after it destroyed their power in 1794. That same year, encouraged by Hamilton, the Washington administration in a highly unpopular move summoned 13,000 militiamen into federal service to suppress the so-called "Whiskey Rebellion," a protest by western Pennsylvania farmer-distillers against the federal excise tax on bottled whiskey, a tax designed to pay for a regular army which had just been tripled in size.[50]

Fears of Federalist expansion of the military reached their peak during the undeclared naval war with France, 1798–99. The Hamiltonian nationalists used the crisis to obtain congressional authorization for another tripling of the regular army to 12,000 men and the creation of 30,000 temporary federal volunteers. Since there was little real threat of invasion by France, the authorization for 42,000 troops was probably designed to make the United States appear a major power (and possibly to seize New Orleans, the key to the entire Mississippi Valley). Although few enlisted men were recruited, the administration appointed hundreds of new officers, an attempt to create a large Federalist national officer corps (Jeffersonians were systematically excluded) which would be an instrument of national cohesion and conservative stability.[51]

In part, the expanded, Federalist-led military force was designed, as Jeffersonians feared, to be a loyal instrument capable of intimidating or quashing public criticism and organized political dissent. Yet Federalists went beyond the limits of contemporary acceptance when they branded Jeffersonian criticism of their policies as seditious libel and treason and employed the federal judicial and military power to suppress it. When another tax-resistance movement— Fries' "Rebellion" of 1798–99—arose in eastern Pennsylvania, President John Adams sent regulars and federal volunteers to ensure compliance. This proved a costly mistake, for these Federalist soldiers violated civil liberties so wantonly (at least one Jeffersonian editor was publicly horsewhipped) that moderate Federalists joined Democratic-Republicans in condemning them.[52]

In their State-building, Federalists had exceeded the bounds of the republican consensus and, after their loss of the presidency in 1800, their political base was confined to New England and a few Mid-Atlantic states. Consequently, for most of the years between 1801 and 1861 the national government was controlled by a southern-dominated "Country" party (the Jeffersonian Democratic-Republicans followed by the Jacksonian Democrats) in alliance with elements in the Mid-Atlantic states and the expanding West. By taking control of the government away from those groups most interested in State-building, the localistic, agrarian-oriented, "Country" party helped ensure that, for the first century of its existence, the United States would not develop a strong central government at all comparable to those of other strong modern States in the international system.[53] Such a minimal State was possible in large part because, except for 1812–14 and 1861–65, the United States remained largely immune from major wars, and because it had developed a military format which enabled it to raise substantial wartime forces when necessary.

The agrarian dominated "Country" party believed that in international affairs America could maintain its prosperity and security largely through commercial diplomacy—by skillfully marketing its agricultural surpluses among different nations so as to assure favorable postures towards the United States. Jeffersonians and Jacksonians sought a much more limited, less expensive national military establishment than their predecessors. Once in office, although he cancelled the Federalist authorization for the 42,000-man force, Jefferson maintained the regular army at around 4,000 men, but concentrated on creating a loyal republican officer corps.[54] Skillfully, he forced out only the most partisan and incompetent Federalist officers, while increasing the pay of those who remained. More importantly, in 1802 he established the U.S. Military Academy at West Point, a tuition-free public institution which he hoped would open the officer corps to young men of ability from all levels of society, not merely upper-class, privately educated Federalists, and which, with the proper faculty, would inculcate sound republican principles in addition to military tactics and engineering.[55]

"While our [military] functionaries are wise, and honest, and vigilant, we have nothing to fear," the sage of Monticello explained to a friend.[56] A republicanized officer corps was one reason why Jefferson was not necessarily concerned about "raising standing armies." As the Napoleonic wars increased tensions between the United States and Britain and France, Jefferson employed economic sanctions and doubled the regular army to more than 9,000 men.[57] The Republican Congress rejected Jefferson's proposal for a specially trained national militia of 190,000 young men, but authorized him to call upon the states to supply 100,000 short-term militiamen if necessary. Simultaneously in 1808, Congressmen from the less affluent South and West voted to use $200,000 annually in national revenues (derived largely from the affluent and largely Federalist Northeast) to help buy weapons for the militia, the first federal grant to the states.[58]

When the United States finally went to war with Britain in 1812, the Democratic-Republican administration of James Madison demonstrated the difficulty of mobilizing a governmentally weak and regionally divided country for major war. Federalist New England bitterly opposed the conflict brought on by the "War Hawk" Republicans of the South and the West and refused to support the conflict with its money or militia.[59] The administration planned to invade Canada and hold it hostage to British recognition of American maritime rights. Because of New England's vigorous dissent, Madison initially sought to by-pass the militia and rely primarily upon offensively oriented, nationally loyal, regular or other national forces. The 5,500-man standing army was authorized to expand to 10,000. Yet, this "Old Army" would remain on the western Indian frontier. The invasion was to be carried out by a temporary new force, the "Additional Army," or "New Army." It was to be composed of 25,000 troops raised in temporary regular army units by local officers directly appointed by the president. In addition, Congress authorized the president to call for 50,000 locally raised federal Volunteers (and 100,000 militiamen if necessary). Both Republicans and Federalists expressed concern that control over 85,000 national troops would give the president enormous patronage and influence and the power to drain off the best state troops and thus destroy the militia.[60]

Such fears proved unfounded, however, for the national government proved unable to raise more than a third of the 85,000 troops. Failure resulted from the War Department's sheer inability to mobilize, supply, and coordinate such a large force, as well as from the active opposition of New England, and the defeat of a premature expedition into Canada. Federalist governors refused the president's call for their quota of militia units, arguing that since the United States had not been invaded, the chief executive's directive was invalid. This bold assertion of state supremacy in determining the constitutionality of presidential requests for the militia was upheld by the Federalist judges of Massachusetts' highest court and was not legally overturned by the Supreme Court of the United States for more than a decade.[61]

Despite inadequate mobilization and the failure to conquer Canada, the United States was not threatened militarily until the defeat of Napoleon freed the British to turn against America. In 1814, with 25,000 veteran regulars, Britain launched a number of expeditions against the United States. In the face of ineffective central government and continued military assaults, political authority began to fragment back to the states. Even Democratic-Republican governors began to abandon hope of effective national action. To protect their coastlines against the possibility of direct British attack, they turned to raising ad hoc state armies beyond the formal militia—an act of dubious constitutionality but obvious desperation. "The people must look for protection to the *State Govts.*," a young Federalist member of Congress, Daniel Webster, wrote home to New England. "This Govt cannot aid them—or will not—or both."[62]

Despite governors' pleas for local defense, the Madison administration continued to support its offensive strategy for the conquest of Canada. For such an invasion, Madison and his secretary of war, James Monroe, decided to ask for national rather than local troops, "regulars" not militiamen. "It is nonsense to talk of regulars," Jefferson rebuked Monroe. "They are not to be had among a people so easy and happy at home as ours. We might as well rely on calling down an army of angels from heaven."[63] Ignoring the former president's advice and his suggestion to classify the militia by age groups and call out the younger men for offensive operations while leaving the older men to local defense, Madison and Monroe asked for authority to raise an additional force of 70,000 temporary "regulars" who would bring the national army of 34,000 up to 104,000 troops.[64]

Despite its suspicion of centralized power, the "Country" party in control of the government in 1814 was led by the exigencies of war and its desire to preserve the nation to put forward the boldest assertion of national power yet attempted in America—a recommendation for direct national conscription, if voluntary enlistment failed. The task of justifying such a radical proposal fell to the secretary of war who, despite his concern about his political future, forcefully supported the proposal for the president to bypass reluctant state governors and personally to direct county militia officers to obtain soldiers from the free male population. Such a national force, Monroe argued, could be used more efficiently than disparate local militia. He also assured Congress that the government sought primarily the "unmarried and youthful, who can best defend the country and best be spared from the economy."[65] Emphatically, Monroe stressed that the administration asked only a temporary, not a permanent, alteration in American military institutions. National conscription was an emergency measure, justified by military necessity and the inherent right of government to defend the community. "[T]he Commonwealth has a right to the service of all of its citizens," Monroe declared, "the citizens composing the Commonwealth have a right collectively and individually to the service of each other, to repel any danger which may be menaced."[66]

Not surprisingly, such an assertion of national coercive power was received with little enthusiasm, particularly since even many of Madison's supporters disagreed with his continued strategy of Canadian invasion. Recognizing the administration's vulnerability, Federalists focused on the unpopular proposal for conscription, rather than the less onerous alternatives Monroe had offered. They assailed the draft as unconstitutional and a tyrannical instrument of Napoleonic despotism. Already a powerful orator, Daniel Webster denounced conscription as "a horrible lottery" based upon the throw of "the dice of blood."[67]

Given the unpopularity of the idea of national conscription and its clash with localism, individualism, and the republican consensus, only a handful of Democratic-Republicans in Congress supported Monroe's proposal. They defended it as a temporary military necessity and declared it was constitutional under a broad interpretation of the power to "raise and support Armies." However, the majority in Congress, including the Republican leadership, ignored the conscription proposal and adopted less odious measures. As the party in power, Republicans realized they had to adopt some constructive program, so they first sought to enhance recruitment in the temporary wartime Additional Army by doubling the enlistment bounty and expanding the eligibles to include non-citizens and blacks. When this proved insufficient as an alternative to national conscription, they tackled the previously irreconcilable problem of creating an effective national militia. Only after an obfuscating series of complex bills and intricate parliamentary maneuvers were the reluctant lawmakers able to reach a compromise which would authorize the president to call for state militia units totaling 80,000 officers and men. These militiamen would be put in federal service under nationally appointed generals for an unprecedented 18-month period. State drafts would be used if necessary. The vote to create this national militia was determined more by regional interest than party affiliation. The versions of the two houses differed slightly and when the legislators learned in late December 1814 that peace was near, they tabled the entire matter with obvious relief.[68]

The war experience of 1812–14 was subject to different interpretations. Many nationalists and professional soldiers believed it showed the need for a larger regular army and an improved War Department. Yet 86 percent of the people who had borne arms had done so in local units not directly under the control of the national government.[69] For most Americans the war, particularly victories such as Andrew Jackson's at New Orleans, reinforced the popular faith in citizen-soldiers when properly led by their local officers.

Despite the growing population, burgeoning economy, and westward expansion in the four decades after the War of 1812, the United States continued to maintain a small regular army and to rely primarily upon temporary citizen armies in wartime. The peacetime standing army did expand incrementally—from 3,000 in 1801, to 6,000 after the War of 1812, to 11,000 after the Mexican War of 1846–48—but it shrank in proportion to the soaring civilian population. In the 1790s there was one regular soldier for approximately every 1,000 civilians; for the first half of the 19th century, it dropped to one for every 2,000 civilians.[70]

After the Napoleonic wars ended at Waterloo in 1815, the balance of power in Europe precluded any major military threat to U.S. interests for nearly a century. In the meantime, Americans relied for coastal defense upon their navy and an extensive system of fortifications, the latter relatively unmanned in peacetime, but backed up in case of war by the ad hoc U.S. Volunteers.[71] The minimal army was also grounded in the agrarian "Country" party desire to restrict the financial cost of the national government, and not incidentally to minimize customs duties which would fall disproportionately upon the imports of the agrarian South which dominated the Democratic party. By the 1850s, many southerners also feared that an expanded national army might eventually be used to help crush slavery in the South.

In the 1820s and 1830s, however, a few southern nationalists like Secretaries of War John C. Calhoun and Joel R. Poinsett argued for an effective national alternative to a large standing army and to amateur, local forces. They advocated what Calhoun called an "expansible [regular] army" in which a compartively over-officered small peacetime regular army would act as a skeleton force which could be fleshed out in the ranks in wartime without seriously diluting its professional leadership. But the public and Congress, particularly in the Jacksonian era, expressed considerable skepticism about professions, including soldiering (the most radical sought to eliminate West Point as the source of a "military aristocracy"), and continued to support the primary emphasis upon the citizen-soldier serving temporarily when needed in the militia or in the U.S. Volunteers. Furthermore, there was increasing northern concern that southerners might use a strong army for the expansion of slavery into the West.[72]

Although the U.S. Army was small, it was comparatively expensive, since soldiers' pay, like the civilian wage scale, was higher in

America than in most other countries because of the relative scarcity of labor. Still, it was low compared to civilian wages, and
recruiting was therefore easiest among the unemployed and impoverished. The ranks of the peacetime army were filled largely
with recent immigrants, mostly Irish and German. Afro-Americans, who had supplied many regulars in earlier times, were excluded beginning in 1820 by order of Secretary Calhoun of South
Carolina, a policy not altered until the Civil War, when the South
lost its predominant influence in the federal government.[73]

In regard to periodic proposals for national militia reform, particularly the selection of some young men for a few weeks of annual
training followed by assignment to a uniform national reserve, all at
federal expense, Congress remained too divided by state and regional differences to adopt such suggestions.[74] Even the threat of
war was not sufficient to establish an organized federal reserve. In
1837, faced with a crisis with Mexico over an independent Texas,
Poinsett asked Congress for authority to raise a select federal militia of 100,000 men, through voluntary enlistment or conscription.
Rejecting his proposal, the northern-dominated House Committee
on the Militia explained in its report: "The people entertain an
aversion to any kind of conscription for military purposes unless an
exigency requires it."[75]

When President James K. Polk provoked war with Mexico in
1846 to gain its western lands and Pacific harbors, the southern
Democratic chief executive, facing vociferous opposition from
northern Whigs, relied entirely upon volunteers to fight the war.
This wartime force included a regular army, temporarily enlarged to
42,000, about 12,000 militiamen from the gulf states who patrolled
the border, and most importantly, 61,000 U.S. Volunteers, most of
them from the South and the West.[76] Despite occasional difficulties
(such as when seven regiments of Volunteers refused to continue
the invasion of Mexico at the end of their one-year enlistment
contracts), the combination of long-term regulars and temporary
U.S. Volunteers enabled the administration to achieve its original
war aims.[77]

The one major change in military format in the first half of the
19th century was the elimination of compulsory militia training and
the transformation of the militia in the northern states. The militia
had changed greatly since the Revolution. With the expansion of
citizenship, and of membership in the militia, to include large numbers of poor and working-class men, and with the end of major
threats to national security, increasing numbers of the urban middle
and upper classes shunned attendance at the semi-annual militia-

training days, by paying a fine instead. Declining interest and consequent financial neglect led to the spectacle, lampooned by the urban
press, of "rabble" or "scarecrow militia," engaged in a parody of
military drill, many without weapons or uniforms. The militia-train-
ing days, critics argued, had degenerated into loafing and inso-
briety. Increasingly, in the urban and industrializing North, universal compulsory militia training was viewed as an archaic remnant of
the pre-industrial past, an institution which had become socially
disruptive, economically wasteful, and militarily inefficient. Having
clearly lost popular and elite support, and with the state governments too weak to insist upon its continuance, the old institution
was easily toppled by a coalition of artisans, owners of small businesses, and middle-class economic and humanitarian reformers.
They persuaded Jacksonian-era legislators to abolish, as inequitable, fines and imprisonment for non-payment of the fines, as well as
the entire system of debtors' prisons. Between 1831 and 1851, most
northern legislatures also repealed the ancient laws requiring compulsory militia training. "The notions and habits of the people of the
United States," Alexis de Tocqueville wrote after a visit in 1831, "are
so opposed to compulsory recruiting, that I do not think it can ever
be sanctioned by the laws." A Massachusetts legislator explained
the end of compulsory militia training quite simply: "the country
outgrew its institutions."[78]

Yet neither was entirely correct. While the northern states abolished compulsory militia training, it continued in the South. In that
agrarian area, a few days spent annually in militia training was
not a significant loss to the economy. More importantly, with millions of Afro-Americans in the region, most southern whites viewed
the local militia and slave patrol as essential instruments of race
control. Adroitly, southern leaders emphasized that the militia encouraged martial skills and virtues, highly prized among rural residents, and also forged a bond among white males. In the deep South,
some states made membership in the militia a prerequisite for suffrage for white males of military age.[79]

Although the northern states ended compulsory militia training,
the lawmakers had not abandoned the concept of the general militia
nor relinquished the states' authority to compel militia service. Yet
the general militia, legally composed of all able-bodied white male
citizens, aged 18 to 45, had clearly become less important. Ironically, in the "age of the common man," while the vote was being
extended to all white males, the new state constitutions restricted or
eliminated suffrage for blacks. Despite the argument that free
blacks had earned the right to vote by combat service in the Revolution and the War of 1812, Afro-Americans now found themselves

excluded from both the polity and the militia in most of the North as
well as the South.[80]

In part, the northern states had been able to abandon the regular
assembly or compulsory training of the old common militia because
of declining need and because of the emergence of special new
volunteer militia companies. Composed of like-minded men from
the same town or ethnic group who enjoyed the pomp and comarad-
ery of a military brotherhood, these units were, like the volunteer
fire-fighting companies, part of the proliferation of associational
groups in urbanizing, Jacksonian America. Created by social forces
rather than by the government, these independently organized, volunteer militia companies were part private association and part
public body, and they nicely served the purposes of the states as
part-time military instruments for maintaining public order and
local defense at minimal public expense. Concerned about riots in
an increasingly unruly and heterogeneous urban society, northern
business and professional groups helped to have them obtain official recognition from the state governments. As the "organized militia," or more commonly the "National Guard" (a term they adopted
in part to distinguish themselves from the disreputable general or
common militia), they became eligible for funding as well as deployment as the "soldiers of the states."[81]

By allowing private individuals, rather than the previously appointed county lieutenants, to raise the only trained militia units,
the state governments had lost significant control over the composition of their military forces. Initially unimportant, this became
of considerable concern when the growth of nativist and anti-Catholic sentiment, stemming from the immigration of millions of impoverished Irish Catholics in the 1840s and 1850s, raised public
fears about the loyalty and reliability of such ethnic National Guard
units in a society increasingly divided along ethnic, religious, and
class lines. In the 1850s, nativists seeking to create a "pure American" militia, demanded the exclusion of immigrants from the National Guard. In response, the governors of Massachusetts and Connecticut confiscated the weapons of all so-called "foreign militia"
and ordered the dissolution of militia companies composed primarily of Irish Catholics.[82]

Like the South, many in the North had come to view the community as dangerously divided between groups of different ethnicity
or race and they sought to keep military power exclusively in the
hands of the dominant socio-economic groups. While "purging"
many ethnic units (many of which reorganized as hunting clubs,
retained their martial skills, and in 1861 marched off to join the
Union Army), a number of the urban northern states continued to

build up well-armed and well-disciplined volunteer organized militia. When the Civil War broke out, the Massachusetts National Guard numbered 5,000 well-trained troops, a force nearly one-third the size of the United States Army.

The 19th century American military format was not primarily the result of military theory or technology. It stood opposed to predominant professional military theory on both sides of the Atlantic. Until the 1860s, except briefly for the mass conscript citizen-armies of revolutionary and Napoleonic France, most European States relied mainly upon standing armies of long term professionals, since citizen-soldiers were viewed by the monarchs, aristocrats, and professional soldiers as militarily inefficient and politically unreliable.[83] The United States employed a different format, one in which there were really two armies the peacetime regulars and the wartime citizen-soldiers. The two-army concept reflected the social and political realities of 19th century America, a country without powerful threatening neighbors and with a system of federalism which reflected and reinforced divided and relatively weak national political, judicial, and military institutions. The embryonic nationalism encouraged by the final victories of the War of 1812, by a westward expansion justified through "manifest destiny," and by dynamic economic growth, failed to alter the predominant American emphasis upon individualism, localism, and a largely self-regulating marketplace economy. To the degree that there was national coordination, it came primarily through political parties, the judiciary, and the marketplace. In the evolution of American federalism by the mid-19th century, the central government had not yet established clear predominance over the states.[84]

However, the nature of American federalism, of the military obligation of citizens to the nation, and of the central government's ability to mobilize and command the full military resources of the nation, would be forged anew in the flaming crucible of civil war. The titanic struggle of 1861–65 would force Americans to go beyond their traditional emphasis upon individual liberty and local autonomy to emphasize the very existence of the national community. In that effort, Americans would confront national conscription as a means of raising their wartime armies.

CHAPTER

2

The Civil War Draft and After, 1861–1914

T HE STATUE of the proud and handsome Civil War soldier erected in the mid-19th century in the squares of thousands of American towns was more than a monument to the men of 1861–65 in blue or gray. It was also a testimonial to an ideal: the local citizen-soldiers who fought righteously as Volunteers. As those who designed and dedicated these statues knew, they were certainly not memorials to those who had been drafted. The Civil War had produced the first national conscription acts, but unpatriotic "conscripts" and unsavory substitutes seemed ignominious parts of the great American struggle. Indeed, the wartime experience with national conscription, the first in American history, had been widely denounced as tyrannical, oppressive and un-American, as class legislation designed to draft the destitute and make it "a rich man's war, but a poor man's fight." Such resentment helped retain the wartime format of local-national U.S. volunteers for the next half century, through the Spanish-American War and the Philippine Insurrection. What is surprising, given the intense opposition, is the degree to which conscription ("under the best management, a delicate measure to carry out" Boston financier John Murray Forbes had cautioned in 1863) played an important part in enhancing the authority and determination of the central government and in maintaining a mass wartime army, through its impetus to the volunteer system.[1]

When the Civil War began, few realized that it would last for four years. Yet determination by the South to achieve independence and by the North to maintain the Union led each side, after the first bloody and indecisive battles, to call for massive wartime armies. Like freshets flooding into the sea, the local units of Volunteers

41

surged at the beginning into a mighty torrent of troops. By the end of 1861, the North had 660,000 soldiers in the field, the largest military force since Napoleon's revolutionary *Grande Armée*.[2]

The North started with the traditional format: regulars, militiamen, and Volunteers. Although temporarily expanded somewhat beyond its prewar size of 16,000 soldiers, the regular army remained comparatively small and its units were kept intact by the West Pointers in an attempt to provide a solid core of disciplined troops. In the initial attempt to suppress the southern rebellion, Lincoln called for 75,000 militia and some one- and two-year Volunteers. When their three-month terms expired, many of these militiamen then joined the more than 600,000 other northerners who responded to the president's July 1861 call for three-year U.S. Volunteers. During the course of the conflict, the U.S. Volunteers composed more than 92 percent of the 2,100,000 men (and several hundred women) who served in the Union Army.[3]

The raising of units of U.S. Volunteers was repeated hundreds of times throughout the land, drawing upon the still dominant local loyalties. After Congress had authorized a specific number of troops, the War Department apportioned these among the states according to population and prior enlistments, and governors determined quotas for cities and counties. The state executive would then authorize prominent local men to recruit, train, and lead units of the Volunteers, which upon approval by a regular army officer would be mustered into federal service under their own officers. Initially, company officers (lieutenants and captains), like non-commissioned officers, were elected by the men. This was finally prohibited in 1863 by the U.S. War Department as adverse to discipline and good leadership, but it remained predominant practice in the South. In the North, the governors commissioned all officers of the Volunteers, except for general officers; these, and all regular army officers received their commissions from the president (in the South, Jefferson Davis commissioned all Confederate officers). Although both North and South filled all the top commands with professionally trained officers, nearly half of the generals on each side were amateurs, including a few "political generals" appointed in the first year to attract less enthusiastic constituencies to the war effort. Despite the opposition of the professionals, they were, like elected junior officers, an important aspect of raising citizen armies in a divided and highly politicized democratic society, which relied primarily upon voluntary enlistment.[4]

For example, from the towns and farms southwest of Philadelphia came the 97th Pennsylvania Regiment of the U.S. Volunteers, composed, as was rural Chester County, primarily of white, Protestant,

Republican farmers and villagers. Among the local notables who recruited it in 1861 were a former state senator, an ex-member of Congress, and a descendant of one of the signers of the U.S. Constitution. Additionally, in the county seat of West Chester, Irish Catholics raised Mulligan's Company, a unit of working-class countrymen. While technically amateurs, many of those who became officers in the Chester Country regiment had seen service as Volunteers in the Mexican War or had been with the local National Guard units which had responded to Lincoln's call and fought at the battle of Bull Run. The first regimental commander, Col. Henry Ruhl Guss was a 36-year-old heir to a substantial property-owning German-American family who had helped organize a volunteer militia company in West Chester in 1846 and in 1859 became its captain and company commander. When the Civil War broke out, he had rejected a colonelcy and command of a regiment of militiamen from another part of the state in order to lead his local company as a captain. When the unit returned from Bull Run, Guss was authorized by the governor to raise a regiment of U.S. Volunteers from Chester County and virtually the entire militia company enlisted under his command in the 97th Pennsylvania Volunteers. All of those original militiamen of the spring of 1861 who remained in the service through 1865 eventually became officers.[5]

Units of the U.S. Volunteers, like the 97th Pennsylvania Infantry, retained close ties with their local community throughout their federal service. The townspeople helped provide them with uniforms, gave them food and other supplies while they drilled nearby, and cheered them when they marched off to war. Neighbors followed their exploits, through local newspapers which proliferated to cover what many saw as the most historic American event since the Revolution. The community helped care for the veterans who came home wounded or disabled and consoled the relatives of those who died in the service. The degree to which the Union Army was representative of the northern population remains debated. Nevertheless, the importance of the ties of its units to local communities is indisputable. That connection, as a Wisconsin volunteer described it, was "the care, not of a socialized impersonal state, but of a big, generous hearted community of neighbors."[6]

Initially, the rush of volunteers and the task of mobilization overwhelmed the central governments, both North and South. The two war departments proved unable even to supply enough weapons or uniforms. In Washington, the secretary of war, a Republican party boss from Pennsylvania, actually halted the acceptance of Volunteers and closed down the recruiting stations, a mistake not rectified until he was replaced in 1862 by Edwin M. Stanton, the former attorney general and an aggressive and indomitable administrator. Opponents of the war also hampered mobilization on each side: Peace Democrats in the North, supporters of the Union in the South. Nevertheless, through appeals to patriotism and by temporarily expanding centralized power, the Lincoln and Davis administrations overcame those who sought a compromise peace and negotiation instead of the use of military force. With the support of a majority in each section, the two "national" governments defined the war aims as complete territorial, socio-economic, and cultural integrity, indeed of national existence. With this rejection of compromise, with no substitute for total victory acceptable, this became the precursor of modern total war.

Mass armies, armed with mass-produced rifled muskets, made the Civil War tremendously costly in human life. Major battles often involved nearly 200,000 men. Predominant Napoleonic tactics usually meant leading soldiers in direct assaults across open fields. But now defenders no longer stood in rows, but took whatever protective cover they could find. Furthermore, rifling increased the effective range of the old smoothbore musket from 200 to 600 yards, thus tripling the "killing zone" across which advancing infantry had to march under fire. The consequence was unprecedented casualties, which averaged 10 to 20 percent, or 20,000 to 40,000 Union and Confederate soldiers killed or wounded in each major battle of the war. More than 600,000 troops died of wounds or disease over the next four years.

High casualty rates even in the early battles helped discourage enlistments in the second year of the war, but there were additional reasons for the slackening of volunteering. Among these were reports of poor food and inadequate supplies, irregular pay (some Union soldiers received nothing from federal paymasters for more than a year), and unsanitary camp conditions which contributed to widespread illness and death from disease. (Such conditions would have been considered by colonial New England citizen-soldiers enough to negate their enlistment contracts, but by mid-19th century the regulars who ran the army treated such premature leave as desertion.) Union soldiers also expressed discontent over menial, make-work tasks, boredom with long periods of inactivity, and the hardships caused by Lincoln's decision not to exchange prisoners of war (designed to exacerbate the South's comparative manpower shortage, it meant that northern P.O.W.s suffered much greater deprivations, since food was scarce in southern prison camps). Many potential volunteers were also encouraged to remain at home by soaring prices and high wages in the civilian sector. While thousands continued to volunteer, few came from among the northern Peace Democrats who opposed Lincoln's Emancipation Proclamation and other radical emergency war policies, as well as the administration's unwillingness to negotiate a compromise settlement. Other potential volunteers were deterred by the North's inability to achieve clear progress towards victory until 1863–64. Throughout the war, the administration faced a dilemma between increasing the effectiveness of the military manpower recruitment system and generating such political opposition that it might breakup the governing coalition and bring a halt to the prosecution of the war.

From the beginning, the Confederacy outpaced the North in emphasizing a higher degree of military effectiveness over political acceptability in its military format. The absence of a regular army in the South was offset by the fact that nearly one-quarter of 750 officers in the U.S. Army, almost all the southerners in the officer corps, resigned their commissions in order to lead Confederate units. Additionally, a month before the attack upon Fort Sumter and the beginning of the North's mobilization, the Confederate Provisional Congress authorized Jefferson Davis to call out the militia for six months and to accept 100,000 twelve-month Confederate States Volunteers. After Sumter, the southern lawmakers approved the call for an additional 400,000 Volunteers, some for "any length of time" that the president of the Confederacy prescribed (initially, he set it at three years) and others for the war's duration.

While both North and South faced military manpower problems during the summer campaigning season of 1862, it was the Confederate government which first turned to a national draft. The Conscription Act of April 16, 1862 was designed less to raise additional manpower than to retain the one-year Confederate Volunteers, many of whom planned to return home when their enlistments expired later that spring. By the second year of the war, the "Boys of '61" had become veteran soldiers and formed the valuable core of both the Union and Confederate armies. The national conscription acts of both sections of the country, although operating in significantly different ways, were designed in large part to retain these experienced citizen-soldiers until the end of the war.[7]

The Confederate government, however, was willing to do what the U.S. government could not even consider: violate fixed-term enlistment contracts and compel volunteer citizen-soldiers to remain in the army for the duration. The Conscription Act declared all able-bodied white males between 18 and 35 (including those in the army whose enlistments were due to expire) to be liable for national conscription for three year's service. This enabled the veterans to be kept in the field. Three years later when this term was due to expire in the spring of 1864, the Confederate Congress passed a new law requiring all soldiers to remain in the army until the end of the war.

In addition to retaining the gray-clad veterans, the southern draft of 1862 was soon extended to augment additional volunteers with conscripts. As with traditional militia drafts, national conscription authorized draftees to hire substitutes. By the end of 1863, however, the price of substitutes had soared to $6,000 in Confederate currency (or $600 in gold) and was thus clearly available solely to the rich, causing discontent among the poor and the middle class. Once again the Confederate government acted more forcefully than the North. It prohibited substitution and in its place, created a long list of specific occupational exemptions, first granted by statute, then subsequently by executive discretion through a military-run Conscription Bureau. Yet these exemptions were also seen as class-bound, for they excluded many middle-class professionals and skilled artisans, as well as overseers needed to control the slaves on the larger plantations belonging to the planter aristocracy which dominated the South.[8] In 1864, Richmond extended the draft to virtually all white males 17 to 50 and in desperation in the final months of the war, conscription was extended to black slaves, who would be freed if they fought for the Confederacy.

Given its ideological emphasis upon states-rights, it was ironic that the South developed a more centralized, coercive government than the North. Indeed, in the quest for military efficiency, the Confederacy mobilized its manpower to a degree never before matched in American history and seldom equaled in any nation. It put nearly half the adult white males into the army. Although only 21 percent of the one million Confederate soldiers were obtained through the draft, the Conscription Acts had been used to keep in the service for the duration the 79 percent who had first entered as volunteers.[9]

How was this extraordinary effort possible? Partly, it was due to the fact that the Confederacy was outnumbered in total population by more than two to one. Yet, in the early years of the war, this inferior position was partially offset by more imaginative and successful southern campaign strategies, particularly those of Robert E. Lee, and the widespread belief in the superior fighting qualities of southern outdoorsmen over northern city-dwellers.[10] But there was also the matter of incentive. In part, the South chose to rely upon conscription to a greater degree than the North because of its smaller population, in part also because of the comparative scarcity of financial resources in the region. The South simply could not offer volunteers the sizable enlistment bounties that were available in the North.

Jefferson Davis, besides being personally rather authoritarian, was a West Point graduate and former secretary of war, familiar with European military systems, and so responsive to suggestions for a centralized system. By early 1862, proposals for national conscription were advanced by Davis' leading military advisers, Generals Lee and Joseph E. Johnston, as well as by several newspaper editors, who argued that the military efficiency of a centralized system outweighed potential political costs stemming from the undermining of state-rights autonomy and the potential erosion of popular support. A number of people dissented from this view, among them several editors, the governors of Georgia and North Carolina, and even Vice-President Alexander Stephens, a former Whig from Georgia, but they proved unable to stop its adoption. Pushing aside such opposition, Davis ignored the Confederate Constitution's proclamation of the sovereignty of the states, and won a majority in the southern Congress for a national draft as a military necessity.[11]

"[W]e must follow her example," admonished Union General William Tecumseh Sherman as he urged the U.S. government to conscript as the South had done.[12] But northern public opinion, Congress, and the Lincoln administration were divided on the necessity and wisdom of such a policy. "Let it be our boast that while the rebels fill their waning ranks by compulsory service, we defend the nation by the heroic volunteer," declared the Democratic governor of New Jersey."[13] To encourage volunteers, Republican opinion-moulders had called upon nationalism and evangelical Protestant ism through such emotional anthems as "The Battle Hymn of the Republic" and "We Are Coming, Father Abraham, 300,000 More." Augmenting such appeals, enlistment bounties offered by the local, state, and federal governments, reached $500, the equivalent of a blue-collar worker's annual earnings, by the end of 1862. Nevertheless, the enthusiastic mass enlistment of 1861 failed to reoccur the following year, except when Confederate armies threatened to invade the North. Consequently some Republican leaders began to advocate national conscription. "I have all along feared a draft might be found indispensable," Secretary of State William H. Seward, former New York governor, observed in July 1862. "But we must first prove that it is so, by trying the old way."[14]

The old way, of course, was voluntarism augmented by state drafts if necessary. The Lincoln administration maintained the local-national military format, but encouraged state governments to use their authority to draft. With the terms of the one-year volunteers expiring in the summer of 1862, the U.S. government sought to encourage their re-enlistment and the addition of more new troops, calling for 300,000 three-year U.S. Volunteers and also 300,000 nine-

month militiamen. While offering enlistment bonuses as inducements, the U.S. government simultaneously threatened to use a new
"federal militia draft" to compel service, if too few volunteered.
Building upon the assertion in the 1792 Uniform Militia Act that all
able-bodied male citizens were members of the militia, the Federal
Militia Act of July 17, 1862 rather obliquely empowered the president (if a governor refused or declined to act) to draft citizens into
the state militia if that state failed to fill its quota through voluntarism. A halfway measure of dubious constitutionality, the Federal
Militia Act sought to prod state efforts rather than replace them.
Under this law, the army conducted door-to-door registration in a
number of areas where antiwar sentiment had led to unfilled
quotas, and in doing so often encountered considerable evasion and
resistance. Despite this registration, the U.S. government never
instituted the threatened federal militia draft. For through a combination of patriotic and financially induced volunteering, the
threat of federal conscription, and some local drafts actually conducted by the states of Ohio, Indiana, and Wisconsin, the Union
Army obtained more than it had sought in 1862: some 520,000 enlistments and re-enlistments.[15]

Although these efforts bolstered the Union Army to 900,000 by the
beginning of 1863, the enlistments of the militiamen and of two-year
volunteers from 1861 would soon expire and the summer campaign
undoubtedly would require substantial numbers of replacements
for casualties. Traditionally, therefore, inadequate volunteering and
unfulfilled manpower needs have been cited as the explanation for
the enactment of the first national conscription law adopted by the
United States, the Enrollment Act of March 3, 1863.[16]

Within the context of raising the Union Army, it appears, however,
that contrary to traditional explanations, the first national draft law
was shaped more by political and economic influences than purely
military attitudes.

Militarily, it was not strictly an inadequate number of citizen-
soldiers that led to the adoption of national conscription in 1863.
Plausible alternative solutions for obtaining additional soldiers had
been put forward: higher enlistment bounties (with deferment of
payment until discharge in order to reduce the problem of "bounty-
jumpers" who deserted after enlistment); dramatic pay increases
(from $13 to $30 a month) to attract and keep soldiers;[17] expansion
of the pool of potential recruits to include minors, sympathetic
Indians, prisoners of war, foreign nationals from Canada or Europe,
and southern blacks. To help fill their enlistment quotas, some
northern industrial states like Massachusetts actively recruited
units of southern blacks in areas behind Union Army lines. Even-

tually, Congress authorized the federal government to recruit freedmen directly into special national units of U.S. Colored Troops. In all, there were approximately 200,000 black soldiers in blue, representing 10 percent of the Union Army. In addition, during the war years, some 800,000 foreign white immigrants arrived in the North; many of the young males among them joined the service. The foreign-born composed nearly 25 percent of the Union Army.[18]

Union generals like Sherman, U.S. Grant, and Henry W. Halleck who urged bold national action (unlike states-rights Democratic colleagues like Gen. George B. McClellan) endorsed conscription to obtain recruits in a predictable and regular manner. Conscription, they argued, would enable them to plan and sustain their campaigns and use the North's numerical superiority to the fullest to crush southern resistance. They disdained the "spasmodic soldiering" which produced recruits in periodic waves of frenzied emotionalism.[19]

Conscription was also advocated by a number of conservative civilians. Although northern elites were divided by 1863 many had concluded that the volunteer system which operated on a combination of popular emotionalism and costly financial inducements was, as one businessman put it, "the poorest thing possible."[20] In their view, the excessive costs of the volunteer bonus system (which in a small way was redistributing income) threatened to undermine the economy through increased inflation and mounting public debt. Furthermore, emotional recruiting campaigns exacerbated ethnocultural and political divisions in the already unstable northern social order. Conscription would be cheaper and less disruptive of society and the economy.

Politically, the volunteer system had produced increasingly unacceptable results, particularly as the war continued and the casualties mounted. Enlistment figures showed that the states of the rural Middle West had supplied considerably more soldiers per capita than many of the more populous eastern states which had failed to meet their quotas. With industry booming, many eastern workers failed to join the army. Neither did the apathetic and the pro-southern, states-rights "Peace Democrats" who included many former southerners in the unseceded border states and the lower Middle West, as well as many impoverished immigrants (Irish-Americans were the most numerous) in the urban North who feared an influx of competitive black labor as a result of emancipation. Important political pressure for national conscription to force dissenters to serve came from the Midwestern wing of the Republican party as well as from the citizen-soldiers and their officers in the field. The veterans in the Union Army resented home front "shirkers" who opposed the war and who refused either to volun-

teer or purchase war bonds. Increasingly, the Lincoln administration came to see some kind of national conscription as necessary to
sustain the morale and effectiveness of the Union Army and the
Republican party.[21]

Symbolically, the conscription act was important as powerful
evidence of the national government's determination and ability to
prevent disunion. Indeed, this was probably the single most important reason for its adoption. For, particularly after two years of
indecisive warfare, there was a widespread belief among many
nationalists that only a forceful demonstration of the power and
determination of the U.S. government could control the centrifugal
forces of American society and enable the Republic to survive.[22]

Strong central leadership was supported by nationalistic, Republican politicians who represented new industrialist entrepreneurs
and also many common people, through the mass-based party. Republicans had constructed a northern coalition of eastern business
people, middle-class pietistic Protestants, skilled workers, and western entrepreneurial farmers. Prominent in the new "republican"
ideology that (along with specific government benefits) helped cement this coalition was the view that the State could play an active
role in establishing a moral and prosperous society and in giving
everyone an opportunity to become a successful capitalist.[23] Although it was put forward primarily as a matter of military necessity, the national draft thus also fit within this dynamic concept of a
more strongly interventionist government which was part of Republican ideology. The benefits of citizenship offered by the new
national government could, of course, also be accompanied by increased obligations, including (during wartime) the nation's first
income tax and national conscription, both primarily Republican
measures.[24]

The exercise of such national power, however, was questioned by
Peace Democrats and, what is more surprising, also by a number of
Republicans and Unionist Democrats who retained too much Jeffersonian suspicion of a strong central government to support national
conscription.[25] Even within the Republican party, antidraft sentiment was strong among influential contributors in the New England
business wing. Industrialists feared that conscription would rob
them of skilled workers and managers, and impede production. If
they could not block it, they sought to ensure that their workforce
would be protected in the operation of any conscription system.[26]
Furthermore, conservative Republican patricians were afraid of
unforeseen results of the unprecedented power and policies demanded by extreme nationalists. Charles Francis Adams, Jr., warned
his father that the radicals would "bankrupt the nation, jeopardize

all liberty by immense standing armies, debauch the morality of the nation by war, and undermine all our republican foundations to effect the immediate destruction of the one institution of slavery."[27]

Given such conflicting sentiments, even within the Unionist governing coalition, Lincoln moved cautiously. Already accused by critics of creating a "military dictatorship" by imprisoning a number of dissenters, the president decided to remain intellectually aloof from the conscription issue and have such a controversial proposal originate in the national legislature. Authorship accordingly fell to Senator Henry Wilson, chairman of the Military Affairs Committee, a Radical Republican from Massachusetts. Few politicians could be better prepared for such a delicate political task. A self-made man, who rose from an indentured servant to become a cobbler, then a wealthy shoe manufacturer, and finally a United States Senator, Wilson was one of the founders of the Republican party and was seen as a political champion of both the common man and the industrialists in the Bay State. During the winter of 1862–63, Wilson, in consultation with the secretary of war, several Union generals, and Francis Lieber, a German-born professor at Columbia College who was familiar with European systems of conscription, carefully crafted a national conscription act. It was designed, as might be imagined—particularly since Wilson was facing re-election in 1864—to accommodate the various and often conflicting military, political, and economic interests.[28]

By necessity, the first national conscription act adopted by the U.S. government was largely a symbolic measure. Although it bristled with bold assertions of national authority and harsh penalties for non-compliance, the statute offered a variety of legal means to escape personal service. As Wilson told his colleagues, such a law had to appear both determined and equitable. Yet it could not work an undue hardship upon industry or the middle class who were the backbone of the Republican party and, as Wilson and others argued, the most productive elements of society.[29]

Consequently, the Enrollment Act of March 3, 1863 began by implicitly redefining the traditional military obligations of citizenship in America. Avoiding any mention of the militia, the statute provided instead for enrolling and calling out "the national forces." This was an entirely new term and concept.[30] The national forces were declared to include all able-bodied male citizens, as well as immigrants who had legally declared their intention to become American citizens (declarent aliens) between the ages of 20 and 45. All of these were liable for military duty "in the service of the United States" if called upon by the president.

Statutory exemptions from the draft were few: some federal and state officials as well as narrowly defined dependency hardship cases and those deemed physically, mentally, or morally unfit for service. Unlike the Confederate and most state militia statutes, this federal draft act did not provide exemptions for specific occupations, probably because they had proven so controversial and class based. Instead, to avoid political responsibility for such decisions and to provide a semblance of equity, the northern lawmakers left the choice of service up to the individuals and the operation of the marketplace. In keeping with Anglo-American militia tradition and the policy being incorporated into the new national conscription systems of Europe and the Confederacy, Henry Wilson chose to allow draftees to purchase substitutes. But to make the system at least appear equitable, Wilson added an innovation, a "commutation fee" of $300 which draftees could pay to avoid service. It would keep down the price of substitutes, the senator argued, and, like a tax, would raise a federal bounty fund to induce more men to volunteer. Commutation and substitutions were included so that national conscription would be acceptable to industrialists and the middle class (many of whom, like Grover Cleveland, then a young district attorney, hired substitutes), and to the Republican and War Democrat majority coalition in Congress.[31]

As a symbol of Unionist determination, the law created a powerful federal conscription agency. Influenced by the centralized, military-run systems in the Confederacy and Continental Europe, Henry Wilson and his advisers provided for the establishment of a federal military bureaucracy of unprecedented size and power in the United States. In a land where the only federal presence had been an occasional postman or customs clerk, the act authorized the army to assign provost marshals to be in charge of the draft in every congressional district. These officers (who as military police were also charged with apprehending deserters and arresting suspected Confederate informants and spies) were authorized to conduct door-to-door registration, hold lotteries to select potential draftees, and examine and induct eligible conscripts. Claims for exemption would be decided in each district by an "enrollment board," composed of a provost marshal, a physician, and a third person, all appointed by the president. Contrary to the traditions of American jurisprudence, the decisions of these boards were to be considered final; they could not be appealed.[32] Resisting the draft or encouraging resistance to it were declared to be federal crimes, punishable by two years in prison. In a divided and demoralized North, with Democratic opponents in many state and local government offices and in the courts, the Republican Congress established conscription machinery designed to intimidate the opposition through dramatic assertion of the emergency powers of the national government.

Recognizing how unprecedented and controversial this was, yet resolved to adopt some kind of conscription act, the Republican majority in Congress curtailed legislative debate and enacted it as quickly and as quietly as possible. The vote came in the lame-duck session in late February 1863. In the Senate, Republicans pushed it through in one day, enacting the bill by a voice vote.[33] (The avoidance of a roll-call, which would have recorded each senator's position, was particularly helpful to supportive Unionist Democrats.) In the House, where Peace Democrats had increased their minority position in the 1862 election, the Republican leadership proved less dictatorial and debate was allowed. Peace Democrats denounced national conscription as unconstitutional and unfair class legislation, the commutation clause being cited as particularly inequitable. The House then adopted the draft 115 to 49, with all Republicans and a number of War Democrats voting in support of the bill.[34]

Despite their fears of the political consequences of such a radical step, the Republican majority in both Houses had responded to considerable political and military pressures and enacted national conscription. Understandably, these elected legislators had done so "with fear and trembling," as Republican Senator John Sherman of Ohio had written to his brother in the field.[35] This cautious concern had led them to enact a largely symbolic measure, which in Senator Wilson's evocative phrase would "bear as lightly as possible upon our people—upon our productive industry—and [yet] shall fill up our armies."[36]

Nevertheless, initiation of draft lotteries in many areas of the North in the summer of 1863 set off the worst rioting in the nation's history. Armed resistance broke out in New York City, Albany, Boston, and Rochester and in many other towns and rural counties from the eastern seaboard to the Middle West. Scores of people were killed, including 38 of the federal enrolling officers. In the bloodiest riot, thousands of poor and working-class men and women, mainly recent Irish immigrants, overcame the police and raged through the streets of lower Manhattan for four days. They burned down the draft headquarters, sacked the homes of draft officials, the mayor, and a number of wealthy and prominent Republicans. The rioters also turned their wrath against the blacks, lynching several black men from streetlamps. It took six regiments of troops, marching back directly from the aftermath of Gettysburg, to restore order. Although traditional estimates ranged from 500 to 1,200 dead, some recent accounts put the figure closer to 120. Still the New York City antidraft riot of July 13–16, 1863 was the worst riot in American history.[37]

Although opposition to conscription in the North was widespread, the national government clearly strengthened its authority through its determination to conduct the draft lotteries and its ability, in conjunction with local authorities, to crush violent resistance. Lincoln and Secretary of War Stanton were prepared to use the Union Army when necessary to enforce the draft.[38] In general, however, they relied upon state and local authorities to suppress open, armed resistance and to restore law and order. In Boston, when a mob of more than a thousand persons from the Irish ghetto tried to seize the National Guard Armory, Col. Stephen Cabot ordered his artillerymen to fire canister and grapeshot directly into the crowd. Two dozen people fell dead or mortally wounded and the riot ended the first night. Even the leading Peace Democratic newspaper there applauded: "Lead and steel must end this frantic attempt at revolution and assert the supremacy of the law."[39] From the field, General Sherman also cheered the suppression of antidraft rioters as demonstrating the inherent power of the national government. "Our Government, though [a] democracy, should in times of trouble and danger, be able to wield the power ['the most despotic power,' he added later] of a great nation."[40]

In winning the support of the middle and upper classes through the appeal for law and order, it served the purpose of the national government to discredit antidraft rioters and resisters as poor, "ignorant," Irish immigrants aroused by southern agents or unscrupulous snake-like, "copperhead" Peace Democratic "demagogues." Although the urban rioters were mainly poor or working-class immigrants, primarily Irish Catholics, their motives were neither necessarily ignorant nor simply the result of manipulation by others, but can be seen as consistent with one view of their own class and ethnocultural interest. In 1863, Irish Catholic immigrants provided the majority of the unskilled urban and industrial workforce in the North. Many of them feared potential labor competition from black freedmen and also possible suppression of Roman Catholic culture and religion by a powerful government controlled by crusading, nativist, Protestant Republicans. With these fears in mind, many Irish immigrants opposed the draft and resisted conscription in a war they opposed, conducted by a political party they distrusted.[41] Still, more than 140,000 Irish-born Americans served in the Union Army, the majority as volunteers.

As dramatic as the antidraft riots were in the cities, draft resistance and evasion was much more widespread.[42] The provost marshal general reported after the war that 160,000 men failed to show up for examination when called by their draft boards. Systematic analysis of samples among these "illegal draft evaders by choice and deserters by law" shows that they included not only urban immigrants but also large numbers of rural, poor or lower middle-class, native-born, primarily Protestant Americans. Both groups were traditionally part of the Democratic party, whose Jeffersonian-Jacksonian states-rights concept of limited central government was being challenged by dramatic economic and emergency war policies being adopted by the new Republican party that was responsive to abolitionists, business interests, and middle-class agrarians and urbanites. Both of these lower-class Democratic groups felt threatened by the idea of competition from millions of freed black slaves who might subsequently migrate into the North and West. While much of the attitude of many of these individual resisters, and the Peace Democratic faction as a whole, is morally objectionable, particularly the blatant racism and the acceptance of slavery in the South, it should be noted that the majority of Republicans were also racist (as well as anti-Catholic), even though they supported an end to slavery on moral and economic grounds.[43] Draft resistance and evasion among such economic and cultural groups can perhaps be better understood not simply as personal avoidance of military service but also as a challenge by less affluent, more parochial segments of society to the activist national policies that Republicans were employing to establish their particular interests and vision of America.

In America, great political issues ultimately also involve constitutional issues as well, for legitimation cannot be obtained outside of the Constitution without seriously weakening its unifying power. During the Civil War, however, the constitutionality of national conscription remained unresolved, because the issue proved too divisive for a judicial ruling to be accepted as definitive, particularly since it did not come before the Supreme Court of the United States.

The conscription act never reached the highest court in the land largely because the Lincoln administration knew that the chief justice, Roger Brooke Taney, was hostile to it and prepared to hold it unconstitutional. The 86-year-old Marylander and former adviser to Andrew Jackson was a staunch defender of slavery and states' rights. Like many Democratic judges, he was a bitter opponent of the actions of the Republican administration. In regard to the draft act, an uncirculated memorandum shows that Taney took an extreme states' rights position, understandable only in the context of civil war. He was ready to argue a radical concept of American federalism, involving mutually exclusive rather than concurrent governmental powers between the state and national governments, and a dual citizenship in which "the citizen owes allegiance to the general government to the extent of the power conferred on it, and no further." He did not believe that the congressional power to "raise and support Armies" authorized national conscription.[44] However, when the draft was challenged in the state courts, most Democratic judges who ruled against it did so on less radical grounds. Taking a traditional view of the need and authority of the states to maintain their militia so that they could protect their own interests and sovereignty, these judges held that national conscription violated this essential control of the states over their forces by threatening to draft into a national army the very class of men who constituted the state militia. This challenge to the militia was the basis for the initial judgment of the Supreme Court of Pennsylvania, the highest court to rule on the national draft law during the Civil War. In its first ruling in the case of Kneedler v. Lane, the Pennsylvania court split along party lines and held, by a vote of three Democrats to two Republican judges, that the conscription act was not constitutional.[45]

As the controversy over conscription mounted, Lincoln considered taking a bold step: a direct appeal to the people urging them to ignore opponents' arguments and obey the law. In late summer, he scrawled out a public statement, defending the necessity and constitutionality of the draft in simple, yet forceful, Lincolnesque language:

> The case simply is, the Constitution provides that the Congress shall have power to raise and support armies. This is the whole of it. . . . The Power is given fully, completely, unconditionally. It is not a power to raise armies if State authorities consent; nor if the men to compose the armies are entirely willing; but it is a power to raise and support armies given to Congress by the Constitution without an if.[46]

Perhaps realizing that by endorsing the principle of virtually unlimited national power unless specifically prohibited by the Constitution he would unnecessarily open himself up to additional charges of "dictatorship," Lincoln shelved the document and decided simply to protect the operation of conscription. In a brief proclamation, he suspended the use of the writ of habeas corpus, thereby preventing civil courts, hostile to the administration, from obtaining the release of draft resisters, antiwar editors, or other advocates of active resistance who were being held by the government in military prisons.[47]

The Union victories at Gettysburg and Vicksburg and the subsequent Republican gains in state and local elections in the fall of 1863 enhanced both the legal and political position of the administration. In Pennsylvania, the election reversed the composition of the state's Supreme Court, giving it three Republicans and two Democrats.[48] The new majority then reversed the first *Kneedler* decision and by a 3–2 vote *upheld* the constitutionality of the national draft law. In support of their decision, the Republican jurists accepted a broad construction of the congressional power to raise armies. They also stressed the inherent right of national defense, asserting that the founders had intended to institute a new nation within the family of nations and to give it "every attribute of sovereignty" including the right and ability to defend itself.[49]

Since the 1863 draft law had been written as a compromise, with opportunities for both substitution and commutation, it actually produced very few conscripts. The first federal call for Volunteers which included the threat of a draft, made in July 1863 for several hundred thousand troops, did in fact obtain several hundred thousand Volunteers. In contrast, of the 300,000 men summoned by draft authorities, 40,000 failed to report for examination, 165,000 were examined and then exempted because of physical or other disability or dependency, 52,000 escaped service by paying the commutation fee (contributing $15 million to the federal bounty fund), 26,000 provided substitutes, and only 10,000 were held to personal service.[50] Thus in 1864, the government was again confronted with various pressures for and against a more effective draft, this time in a national election year.

The problems were many. Militarily, the three-year enlistment contracts of the 1861 volunteers were due to expire. If these veterans went home the North would lose the best and most experienced half of the Union Army's combat troops. Consequently, the U.S. government relied upon patriotic appeals and other inducements to get these men to re-enlist (such as a 30-day furlough, a $300 federal bounty in addition to state and local bonuses, and distinctive chevrons on their uniform to identify them as "veteran volunteers"). But the veterans also complained bitterly about the antiwar "shirkers" and "traitors" back home and wanted the government to draft these men and make them share the military burden.[51] Pressure for more soldiers also came from a change in military leadership and strategy. Although the public looked to the new commander, Ulysses S. Grant, for a quick end to the war, Grant remained skeptical of the possibility of a single decisive battlefield victory and was convinced instead that the Union would win largely through application of its superior numbers. That would mean a larger army which together with continual engagement would lead to

larger casualties and the need for more replacements. Inequity of
service was still an important political issue. Congress came under
renewed pressure from Midwestern representatives who protested
that their region continued to provide a disproportionate share of
soldiers. New pressure also came from within the War Department
where, as a result of his experience in directing the draft since 1863,
the provost marshal general, Brig. Gen. James B. Fry, an authoritarian and enigmatic West Pointer, joined Secretary of War
Stanton in recommending a tightening up of the draft law.[52] All of
these emphasized the need to eliminate the $300 commutation
clause.

The commutation "escape" clause became a major political issue
in the early phase of the 1864 election. This was because the pressures to eliminate it were countered by support for it from the New
England industrial wing of the Republican party and from both the
Peace and Unionist wings of the Democratic party. Representatives
of the industrialists, like Senator Wilson, argued that commutation
was needed for business to maintain essential production. Republican James G. Blaine of Maine, then beginning an illustrious career
in the House, supported commutation because it favored "the great
'middle interest' of society—the class on which the business and
prosperity of the country depend."[53] Surprisingly, these Republicans were joined in 1864 by the Peace Democrats who reversed their
opposition of 1863 and now supported the commutation clause.
They argued that, without the $300 commutation fee, antiwar work-
ing-class draftees would have no protection against inflationary
increases which would put the price of substitutes far beyond their
reach.[54]

The dilemma of the Republican administration and party leaders
was how to meet the demands for a stricter draft, more troops, and
a demonstration of national determination, without losing financial
and popular support from New England and without providing the
Democrats with the kind of highly charged emotional issue which
could tip the election. Caught between such conflicting pressures,
the majority in Congress sought at first to evade the issue and seek
other alternatives: in February 1864, it expanded the pool of eligible
soldiers by finding new sources of troops, particularly southern
blacks and foreign-born immigrants.

In attempting to sustain the northern armies and the governing
coalition, Unionists began to refine further the concept of national
citizenship and its obligations. Rather than focus on the *obligation*
of citizens to serve the nation militarily, most Republicans had
stressed the *authority* of the national government to conscript when
necessary to preserve the Union. In part this was because the

federal government sought a selective rather than a universal draft, but it also resulted from the traditional American emphasis on individual liberty. Widespread resistance to conscription in the summer of 1863 first led some Republicans to assert that national military service, when demanded, was a major obligation of citizenship. Some nationalists argued that such a duty was inherent; others drew upon liberal political theory to link the obligation with the rights and benefits of citizenship in a democracy characterized by universal male suffrage. New York's adjutant general defended national conscription by declaring that: "Where the whole population participates in the rights, privileges, and immunities of a free people, they must share equally also in its burdens."[55]

State-builders with the most conservative political and economic views went further and argued that American citizens who refused to fulfill their military obligations should be stripped of their political rights, and foreign-born citizens should be deported. "If any man, North or South, withholds his share of taxes, or his physical assistance to this, the crisis of our history," General Sherman declared, "he should be deprived of all voice in the future elections of this country, and might be banished, or reduced to the condition of mere denizen [a resident without the legal or political rights of citizenship] of the land."[56] A number of Republicans supported such a forfeiture of the "rights of citizenship" and many editors in 1864 repeated approvingly the epigram of Senator Garret Davis, a Unionist Democrat from Kentucky, that every man should "fight, pay, or emigrate."[57] The wartime popularity of the idea demonstrates the intensity of divisions and contemporary nationalism during the Civil War. When combined with the intense anti-immigrant nativism of the preceding decade, this chauvinistic nationalism led Congress to adopt legislation incorporating it. An 1864 amendment to the draft law provided that declarent aliens (but not naturalized or native-born American citizens) could be deprived of their political rights and even deported if they refused to be conscripted.[58]

Tens of thousands of resident aliens now became subject to conscription. The amendment expanded liability beyond declarent aliens (because they could renounce their declaration) to include any foreign-born male who had "at any time assumed the rights of a citizen by voting."[59] Thus draft officials had only to prove that the alien had voted (as many did in urban politics) in order to make him subject to conscription. However, by making the exercise of a right such as suffrage, which was conferred by state law, the basis for an obligation owed to the national government, the 1864 legislation offered a dramatic example of how the balance of power in American federalism was shifting in favor of the national government.

The expansion of the military manpower pool was also linked to the emergent concept of reciprocal rights and duties of national citizenship when northern authorities turned to American blacks to help fill up the armies. Although they had been excluded from service in the Union Army in the first year of the war, due to white opposition and Lincoln's belief that their use as combat troops would drive border slave states into the Confederacy, black volunteers were recruited into segregated combat units after the Emancipation Proclamation went into effect in 1863. Thus it was not surprising that in 1864 Congress included able-bodied, free black males among those liable to conscription, (these included the slaves in the Confederate states whom Lincoln had declared to be legally free, but not the slaves of the non-seceded border states which Lincoln had, for political and strategic reasons, excluded from his proclamation).[60] Few blacks were drafted, but nearly 200,000 enlisted. Their extraordinary valor and high casualty rates (the Confederate army refused to treat former slaves as prisoners of war and summarily executed black soldiers) began to alter some northern images of Afro-Americans, particularly as Republicans emphasized the contrast between the treacherous activities of white "copperhead" Peace Democrats at home and the heroism of black soldiers on the battlefield, fighting for their freedom and the Union.[61]

As black abolitionist Frederick Douglass predicted, military service offered black men a chance to establish a strong claim to the rights of first-class citizenship. Thus, Lincoln abandoned his earlier support for foreign colonization of the freedmen and instead endorsed their right to live in the country for which they fought. In his last public address, he asserted that suffrage should be conferred on "the very intelligent [black men] and those who serve our cause as soldiers." During Reconstruction, Republican-controlled Congresses formally recognized the claim of black men to the rights of citizenship for which many of them had fought. In a series of laws and constitutional amendments, Congress established and defined a concept of national citizenship that was, in certain aspects, superior to state citizenship and which included black Americans among the national citizens who, as stated in the Fourteenth Amendment, were entitled to "the privileges and immunities of citizens of the United States . . . [and] the equal protection of the laws."[62]

Expansion of the manpower pool through the inclusion of aliens and black freedmen did not, however, satisfy those military and political interests pressing in 1864 for a stronger national draft law. Too many opponents of the war continued legally to avoid personal service. Indeed, General Fry reported that only 10 percent of the men being examined in the spring draft call were being held for personal service (10 percent furnished substitutes, 35 percent paid the commutation fee, and 45 percent were exempted for physical or other reasons). Since the Peace Democrats now argued that the $300 commutation fee aided their poor and working-class antiwar constituents, the Republicans, particularly after the heavy Union casualties suffered in Grant's spring offensive in Virginia, voted in late June to repeal the commutation clause. Unlike the Confederacy, they were unwilling, however, even to consider ending substitution, an old militia practice that still existed in European conscript armies, and which enabled the middle and upper classes to avoid service if they desired. Substitution, the *New York Times* declared bluntly, offered "the only means of sparing the class of the community whose labors are of most value to the nation, and who, once lost, cannot readily be replaced; namely those who work with their brains—who do the planning and directing of the national industry."[63]

For all the strident rhetoric about national determination and compulsion which accompanied the end of commutation, the northern draft still remained in practice a rather weak instrument for conscripting an army. At the same time that it eliminated commutation, Congress tried to minimize the need actually to conscript by boosting bounties to increase voluntary enlistment and by authorizing northern states to help fill their quotas by recruiting southern black freedmen so they would not have to draft industrial workers and other residents.[64] And in practice the draft was not particularly coercive; it still failed to result in mass conscription. Not only did increased governmental financial inducements attract volunteers, but even among low-paid, unskilled workers, significant numbers of draftees were able to purchase substitutes and avoid personal service, because many sympathetic state and local governments gave them direct financial relief. Since draftees, along with most of their male relatives, could vote, elected officials increased the public debt in order to provide grants to help local draftees to buy substitutes, despite the soaring prices.[65]

Thus, even after the adoption of a national draft law, the northern experience largely perpetuated the military format of wartime armies based primarily upon locally raised and officered units of U.S. Volunteers. National conscription in the Civil War provided very few men directly and served mainly to encourage voluntary enlistment. The primary reliance was upon voluntarism, individual decisions, patriotism and the market system. Enlistment bounties were an attempt to shape the distribution of manpower by influencing rather than abandoning the marketplace ideal. The state and local draft relief funds, in effect, augmented the bounty system and the market mechanism rather than replacing them. The four federal drafts between 1863 and 1865 directly produced only about 46,000 conscripts (about 2 percent of the Union Army) and 118,000 substitutes (about 6 percent). Influenced by patriotism, increased enlistment bounties (which in some districts reached $1,000 in federal, state, and local bounties by 1864), or the desire to escape the stigma of being a "conscript"—most conscripts were viewed as unpatriotic and unreliable in the field—nearly 92 percent of the 2,100,000 citizen-soldiers in the Union army were volunteers.[66] But while the local-national format remained, the war had shown that the two central governments, each in a different manner, had gained the authority and the ability to mobilize and maintain massive citizen armies in the field.

The Civil War demonstrated once again the importance of more than military influences upon military format even in wartime. Both sides employed similar weapons and, for the most part, were schooled in the same military theories. Since both were American, they had much in common in thought and tradition. Yet the two regions were also significantly different and their military formats reflected those socio-economic and political as well as strategic differences.

Most striking is the degree of military efficiency achieved by the South in raising its armies. Despite considerable division, the Confederate government adopted national conscription early and tightened it eventually to exclude even substitution. It compelled veterans to remain in the army. Through a combined system of voluntary enlistment and compelled service, the South obtained nearly a million soldiers, one-sixth of the white population of the region, and was able to keep a much larger percentage of veterans in the field until the closing months of the war.

In contrast, the North's mobilization effort was much less militarily efficient, even though it eventually proved sufficient to defeat the Confederacy. The U.S. government relied only minimally upon compulsory service and then its military function was largely indirect. It helped prod some reluctant volunteers to enlist and even more it served to raise enormous sums of money for enlistment bounties or the hiring of substitutes. It was not coercion which raised the Union armies or kept them in the field, but rather a greater willingness and ability to use financial inducements and to expand the pool of eligibles by including blacks and aliens. A combination of patriotism, financial incentives, and the draft raised more than 2 million soldiers for the Union Army, one-tenth of the population of the North.

The contrast between the two formats—in army size compared to population, willingness to draft effectively and compel veterans to continue to serve, and the manner of appointment of all officers—derives not simply from the population imbalance of the two regions or the consequent strategic difficulty of the South.[67] Clearly the decision not to use blacks in combat stemmed directly from the social and economic nature of southern society. Similarly, the comparatively limited use of enlistment bounties was a reflection of the region's scarce financial resources. Presidential appointment of all Confederate officers (except in the militia) was largely a consequence of Jefferson Davis' professional military background, as was the decision to send individual replacements into veteran units instead of allowing governors to appoint new officers and create entirely new replacement units as was the practice in the North. In part the greater readiness of the South to use conscription may have been influenced by the continuation in that region of compulsory training and service in the militia in the antebellum period, a practice which had been discontinued in the North but had continued to reinforce the sense of military obligation among white male citizens of the South.

Most important, however, was the absence of a two-party system in the Confederacy: lacking the vigorously competitive national political parties of the North, the new Confederate government was less accountable to the voters and so was readier to adopt and implement, even early in the war, such unpopular coercive measures as national conscription. The fact that the Confederate president was limited to a single, non-renewable, six-year term reinforced Jefferson Davis' self-assured, unbending personality and made him even less amenable to political pressure and compromise. Since he did not face re-election, he had little motive to build up a political organization of his own, which would have linked the loyalty and self-interest of legislators, editors, and others to the executive. Without such an organization, Davis was forced, as the war continued and the Union Army occupied larger areas of the South, to draw increasing percentages of congressional support for such coercive measures from legislators who were freed from antidraft constituent pressures because their districts in the western theater of the war were either directly threatened or already occupied by northern armies.

Paradoxically, the centralization and absence of an effective two-party system which initially produced effective military mobilization in the Confederacy also eventually contributed to the disintegration of the southern war effort. From the beginning, Davis' centralizing, coercive measures had generated considerable opposition from states' rights advocates and business and small farmer critics of the planter-dominated central government. In the absence of national political parties in Richmond, the opposition became increasingly difficult to manage and incorporate, precisely because it was individual and nonpartisan. The absence of a political party made it difficult for Davis to mobilize his increasingly slim majority in the Confederate Congress. His centralizing and coercive policies contributed significantly to the rapid decline of the popular legitimacy of the Confederate government, particularly after the military reverses of 1863. His attempts to tighten the draft and ultimately to arm slave-soldiers were not simply a result of Confederate loses but also of the widespread draft resistance and mass desertion within the South in 1864–65. As Senator William L. Yancey of Alabama, one of the original "fire-eating" secessionists and most ardent of states-righters, declared shortly before his death in 1863, if the southern government had to become a despotism, it would be better to have a Lincoln, "not a Confederate dictator."[68]

Unlike the South, the North had a vigorous two-party system, with elected politicians linked to the mass electorate through a party apparatus and a partisan press. Because of opposition within the Democratic party to abolitionism, conscription, and many other Republican policies, Lincoln moved much more cautiously and slowly than Davis. The politicization of the draft as an issue limited the government's ability to establish a truly effective national draft. Yet the existence of national parties also helped skillful politicians like Lincoln to mobilize a popular majority behind the war through a Unionist coalition of Republicans and War Democrats. By the end of 1863, Republicans had won nearly all the northern state governorships, thus linking Washington and the state capitals through ties of party loyalty and mutual interests. The votes of Union soldiers helped re-elect Lincoln over the Democratic candidate (a former general, George McClellan), and gave the Republican party major state and national victories. That and the approaching end of the war helped reduce conscription as an issue.

The northern draft has often been applauded for the "spur it gave to volunteering."[69] Although this is accurate, it is also misleading. For the primary spur it gave was not in prodding men to volunteer in order to escape being a "conscript," as generally portrayed, but rather in persuading elected officials to raise much higher bounties to entice men to enlist and thus avert the need for governmental coercion. (The enormous public debt caused by the Civil War bounty system, in which state, local, and national governments paid out probably half a billion dollars in enlistment bounties, was condemned then and was one of the reasons that enlistment bounties were subsequently prohibited in the two world wars.) From the standpoint of military efficiency—of raising troops regularly and predictably—its success was limited at best. The North continued to rely primarily upon voluntarism throughout the war. Yet from a political standpoint, the first national draft represented a considerable achievement, balancing the interests and desires of various constituencies in the Unionist coalition and helping to maintain both that coalition and the army. It was a symbol of Unionist determination and the authority of the U.S. government, and in being that symbol lay its greatest importance.[70]

The victory of the Union and its avenging army ("God's terrible swift sword," Julia Ward Howe called it in "The Battle Hymn of the Republic") contributed to the growth of nationalism and national power. Although the draft and federal income tax were quickly ended, the war and reconstruction firmly established the concept of national citizenship and the supremacy of the national government over the states in certain important areas of citizenship.[71] In some cases, military service had contributed directly to this concept; the war record of black soldiers bolstered the Republican argument that the federal government must protect certain rights of citizens, such as the right to vote.[72] Not surprisingly, measures like the Fourteenth Amendment, that defined the *rights* of national citizenship, said nothing about the *obligations* of citizens. Like the Federalists before them, Republican nationalists sought to build a constituency by demonstrating the ability of a strong central government to protect property and other rights, and to enhance economic growth, rather than its ability to impose obligations upon its citizens.

In the last third of the 19th century, the industrializing nations of the world experienced many new developments in military technology and theory as well as dramatic changes in military formats, but few of these had any immediate impact upon the United States. Most Americans viewed the Civil War and the U.S. need for mass armies as an aberration. They were content to return to the prewar format of a small standing army on the Indian frontier (at 27,000 larger than its prewar strength of 17,000, but still a minimal force among nations), with National Guard volunteer militia units as the ready reserve and instrument for domestic order. For more than a decade, of course, these could have been augmented in an emergency by the youthful veterans in their own organizations like the Grand Army of the Republic and Sons of the Confederacy.[73] But there was no great emergency or military threat and Americans returned to their primary focus upon economic development within the United States, a task in which the standing military establishment seemed almost superfluous.

The U.S. Army suffered not simply from neglect in the era of industrialization, but from outright public hostility. Its use in the occupation of the South had alienated many southerners, already traditionally suspicious of a large standing army because of their Jeffersonian agrarianism. In an era of laissez-faire, and conservative opposition to expanded government as potentially responsive to "demagogues" and harmful to economic growth, many northern business leaders sought to limit expenditures on the army (the largest item in the federal budget) as a drag on the economy (except for the local economies of those western states who benefited from the scores of little posts in which the soldiers were stationed). Furthermore, the dramatic expansion of international commerce and the dominant belief in progress led many civilian leaders to believe that the growing commercial bonds between nations would reduce the incidence of major wars and that sizable standing armies were a costly, wasteful, and potentially dangerous anachronism from the feudal, aristocratic, premodern times. Especially after the conclusion of the Indian Wars on the Great Plains in the 1870s, the army had little to do except round up renegades from the reservations, maintain a professional leadership cadre, and occasionally help maintain order during labor strikes. While officers were accepted socially, promotion was painfully slow (many served as lieutenants for twenty years) and the enlisted regulars were considered social outcasts. No wonder this period was considered "the dark age" of the U.S. Army.[74]

Domestic security needs in the industrializing nation were met not by regulars but by revitalized state units, the National Guard. Southerners had employed the militia during reconstruction. In the North and West, local economic and political elites built up predominantly middle-class volunteer militia units, complete with castle-like armories in the cities, to maintain order in a society increasingly strained by massive new immigration and outbreaks of bloody violence between industrial labor and management. By 1891, the National Guard totaled 104,000 part-time citizen-soldiers, who cost the states $2 million, in contrast that year to the 27,000-man regular army which cost the federal government $49 million. This certainly made the militia more attractive to taxpayers. But its predominant mission of strike duty alienated the growing organized labor movement and threatened to erode the National Guard Association's political support in Congress, as well as to undermine its claim to be the institution of the citizen-soldier and the nation's second line of defense.[75]

The Spanish-American War of 1898 and American military conquests in Cuba, Puerto Rico, and the Philippines, and the subsequent construction of the Panama Canal, marked the beginning of a turning point for the army. As the United States plunged overseas and established an empire of colonies and protectorates in the Caribbean and the Pacific, it became evident that the nation must have the ability to project its military power outside the continental limits of the United States, at least into these regions now directly connected to the interests of the nation. Despite the hopes of regular officers for an orderly expansion of the army in the Spanish-American War, President McKinley and Congress bowed to public desires and authorized instead a flood of locally raised U.S. Volunteers. Thus, although the U.S. Army was expanded to 60,000, there were more than 200,000 Volunteers, including the First U.S. Volunteer Cavalry Regiment, Theodore Roosevelt's famous "Rough Riders." And while the regulars made up the bulk of the brief expeditions to Cuba and Puerto Rico, U.S. Volunteers played a large part in the much longer and heavier fighting involved in the conquest of the Philippines. To the American public, the war once again demonstrated the success of the traditional format with its emphasis upon temporary, locally raised wartime U.S. Volunteers, even for such overseas expeditions. The press saw the main problem as the inefficiency of the War Department which was once again overwhelmed by the sudden mobilization of large numbers of Volunteers.[76]

When the war was over and the Volunteers returned home, the army resumed its role as a constabulary force, but this time the frontier garrisons were not simply in the West but more importantly in strategic overseas territories like the Philippines, Hawaii, and the new Panama Canal Zone. Although Americans remained divided over the acquisition of populous colonies like the Philippines, McKinley and his successor, Roosevelt, obtained expansion of the regular army to around 80,000 for overseas colonial garrison duty. This, while representing a small force and a small empire compared to those of major European powers, was still a departure from America's continental traditions. In exerting temporary military pressures in the Caribbean and Central America, the U.S. government under Roosevelt and his successors relied much more upon the easily deployable Marine Corps and the U.S. Navy.

The Navy had been the country's main defense against invasion by world powers as well as its main instrument for quickly projecting American power overseas. It was therefore the major focus of the modernization of American defenses in the late 19th and early 20th centuries. In large part the change stemmed from important technological developments, especially the development of all steel, steam-propelled warships with rifled cannon firing high explosive shells at ranges up to 20 miles. Influenced by the modernization of

European fleets as well as a variety of domestic economic and
political factors, an influential group of business and imperial-
minded civilian "navalists" began in the depression of the 1880s to
obtain congressional authorization for the construction of a modern
"new navy." In the 1890s, this "big navy" coalition of politicians,
business people, expansionist editors, and naval officers drew upon
a variety of arguments—including that of Admiral Alfred Thayer
Mahan, linking seapower with national greatness—to overcome
ideological and financial opposition from isolationist agrarians,
pacifists, and many concerned taxpayers who argued instead for a
less expensive, defense-oriented coastal protection system of mines,
torpedo boats, submarines, and modernized fortifications. The
Spanish-American War did lead to the construction of modern long-
range coastal artillery emplacements in the harbors of the United
States and its new overseas territories. But more importantly, the
war helped the "big navy" advocates achieve a modern, offense-
oriented high seas fleet of cruisers and battleships. With Theodore
Roosevelt in the White House, the United States joined the international battleship-building race, by 1914 ranking behind Britain and
Germany, but ahead of the other major naval powers: Japan, France,
Italy, and Russia.[77]

But the United States did not join the dramatic changes in military
formats in Europe and Asia. Between 1870 and 1914, virtually every
European nation except Britain abandoned primary reliance upon
long-term professional armies of regulars and adopted variations of
the successful Prussian emphasis upon mass conscript armies of
easily mobilized reserves already prepared through a national system of nearly universal military training and service (UMT&S).
What made this system unique was its emphasis on widespread,
intermediate-term training (generally two years), rather than the
long-term service (five- to seven-year enlistments) that had characterized professional armies and helped give them their military
discipline and political reliability. Hundreds of thousands, even
millions of citizen-soldier reservists provided the mass for these
conscript armies, while a highly professionalized officer corps and
regular army supplied the core and means of leadership and control, and a central general staff did the planning and coordination.
For both economic and military reasons, the German General Staff
developed the strategic doctrine of short, total war in which such a
massive number of citizen-reservists would be mobilized, transported, and led to a quick and decisive victory. The quickness was
important not simply for military surprise but also to avoid domestic economic, social, and political strains which might accompany a
long and indecisive conflict of mass mobilization in which the army

was no longer isolated from the civilian society but an integral part
of it. In the Franco-Prussian War of 1870–71, the system worked
with startling effectiveness, defeating the French Army, previously
considered the best in Europe.[78]

During the last quarter of the 19th century, most European nations began to mobilize their populations, increasingly shaped as a
national citizenry, in these mass conscript-reservist armies designed for large-scale war with adjoining states or alliances of
states. Their military, supported by various civilian elites, developed doctrines of extensive warfare in which specialized general
staffs and a professional officer corps directed the activities of mass
conscript-reservist armies. Continental nations naturally adapted
UMT&S to their own politico-cultural, economic, and strategic circumstances. For example, given the spread of socialism among its
industrial working classes, Germany drew its conscripts disproportionately from the agrarian population. France exempted clerics
and much of the middle class, until its declining birth rate and
increased tensions with Germany forced it to more extreme measures. In a number of poorer countries, like Italy, budgetary considerations led politico-economic elites to seek a middle way between a
mass and a professional army. Overruling the military, they reduced
the period of training, or created two categories of trainees—those
given only one year's training, which the military considered worth-
less, and a smaller number given from three to five years of training.
Many in the elite still considered it dangerous to provide military
training to the masses. Given the fragility of Vienna's control over
its heterogeneous subject peoples, the Austro-Hungarian Empire
feared the centrifugal result of building truly effective regional
reserve units among its nationality groups. Conversely, extreme
nationalists like General Colmar von der Golz in Germany argued
that nationalism inculcated through UMT&S could provide an effective antidote to the divisiveness of ethnic, regional, class, and religious loyalties and antagonisms. France also used the national
army to turn provincials into Frenchmen.[79]

The increased international rivalry of the second half of the 19th
century, combined with the greater social and political acceptability
and economic feasibility of mass armies through the use of reservists, helped most ruling elites to shed their suspicion of conscription and led to wide-spread adoption of the mass conscript-reservist
army. Although colonial warfare in the same period was conducted
by separate, long-term professional forces, sometimes augmented
by native auxiliary troops, planning for war on the European continent was increasingly seen as preparation for mass mobilization and

short, total war. Like the American Civil War, it was based upon the widespread mobilization of citizen armies, but unlike that conflict, it was based totally upon conscripted standing and reservist forces rather than on previously untrained and unorganized, temporary volunteers. In the late 19th century, among major nations, only Britain and the United States avoided the new mass conscript-reservist armies and retained their traditional military formats. Except for a few soldiers, like Brig. Gen. Emory Upton, Americans largely ignored the developments on the continent or joined in denouncing them as Prussian "militarism."[80]

The growing international role of the United States, as well as public discontent with the War Department's inefficiency in the Spanish-American War, led in the early 1900s to some adjustments in the country's military format. Through Secretary or War Elihu Root, a leading corporation lawyer, Uptonians in the officer corps and efficiency-minded civilian elites were able to obtain congressional authorization for a general staff, although a very limited one, and expansion of postgraduate educational facilities for officers. Root was too astute to ask for a conscripted reserve, but he did request a solely national (voluntary) reserve of 100,000 veterans. The militia officers' lobbying group, the National Guard Association, killed such a competing ready reserve. Instead they obtained the Militia Act of 1903 which designated the National Guard as the nation's ready reserve, to be called up before the U.S. Volunteers.[81]

The Militia Act of 1903 proved a first, major step in the 20th century achievement of clear federal supremacy over the militia. The new law recognized two types of militia: the common or unorganized militia which included the great mass of males of military age (18–45) who had state and federal military obligations only in emergencies, and more importantly, the Organized Militia (the National Guard) which was designated the nation's pretrained ready reserve and put under dual federal-state control. Under the 1903 act, Guardsmen agreed to increased regular army supervision in return for federal recognition that their primary role was in national defense (thus relegating unpopular strike duty to a secondary function) and consequently they were entitled to greatly increased federal financial assistance.[82]

The traditional animosity of regulars towards militiamen increased as a result of the Guard's success in blocking a solely national reserve. The regulars suggested that the Constitution did not allow the president to send the militia outside the United States; thus the soldiers of the states could not be a part of the projection of American power overseas. The issue was a sticky one. In the War of 1812, New England militiamen had refused to cross the border into

Canada and in another famous incident, in the Spanish-American War, members of the famous, elite 7th New York Regiment refused to enlist because of a disagreement with the War Department over procedures. In 1908, the National Guard Association influenced Congress to remove the traditional nine-month limitation on militia called into federal service and to declare that the "federalized" National Guard could be used outside as well as within the United States. It was in response to this that under the advice of Enoch H. Crowder, the army's judge advocate general, Attorney General George W. Wickersham issued an opinion in 1912 that the Constitution prohibited federal use of the militia outside of the United States, an opinion hotly disputed by the National Guard.[83]

Faced with revolution across the border in Mexico, Congress adopted the Volunteer Act of 1914, the first prewar legislation in the nation's history for the U.S. Volunteers. While not organizing them in advance of hostilities, Congress spelled out the procedure for their enlistment and sought to avoid a number of Civil War practices which had proven militarily and economically inefficient. In this attempt to modernize the Volunteer system, the 1914 act provided, for example, for individual replacements into veteran units and granted the War Department authority to refuse to accept soldiers whose skills were deemed vital to industrial war production.[84]

Thus as late as 1914 the military format of the United States, despite increased professionalization of the officer corps and the creation of an embryonic general staff, remained in theory and in statute, quite similar to what it had been throughout the 19th century. The local-national military format still consisted of a small regular, constabulary army, pretrained state militia units, and, if necessary, locally raised and officered ad hoc units of the U.S. Volunteers. The format was suited for a relatively secure, decentralized society with strong attachments to individual liberty, private pursuits, and localism, in which governmental authority was divided through American federalism. Although nationalism had increased dramatically in the 1860s and 1890s, the U.S. government had not begun to qualify as a powerful, active modern State until well into the second decade of the 20th century. By then, although agrarian, localistic, individualistic, laissez-faire characteristics continued, modern America was rapidly emerging as an urban, industrial, ethnically heterogeneous nation with a more active and interventionist government at home and abroad. Part of that growth of governmental power had been the creation of the "new navy" but it was not at all clear how, when, and in what manner the rest of the American military format would be similarly "modernized."

CHAPTER

3

The Conscription Crusade, 1914–1917

AMERICA'S PAINFUL CIVIL WAR EXPERIENCE with limited national conscription made it all the more surprising that in World War I, the federal government chose from the beginning to rely upon a national draft to raise the wartime army. The conscripted doughboys who filled the *Leviathan* when it steamed out of New York Harbor in the spring of 1918 were the first of millions of draftees to serve overseas. In the Civil War, fewer than 8 percent of the Union Army were draftees. In World War I, 72 percent of the 3.5 million citizen-soldiers were conscripted. Instead of relying upon individual choice and the operation of the market system as earlier, in 1917 the United States established a comprehensive draft and the Selective Service System. In 1918 this agency prohibited voluntary enlistment as inefficient and disruptive. Little wonder that contemporaries described the change in American military policy as "revolutionary."[1]

Some supporters portrayed the World War I draft as inevitable—a consequence of the modernization of American institutions. In the midst of congressional debate over the draft act in April 1917, Henry Watterson, renowned editor of the *Louisville* (Ky.) *Courier-Journal*, declared:

> The volunteer system, like the stagecoach, served its purpose in primitive times, but like that stagecoach, it proved unequal to the expanding needs of modern time. . . . [The people] know that the volunteer system has been a failure wherever tried, and seeking efficiency they prefer the selective draft system, just as seeking speed they would prefer a locomotive to an oxcart.[2]

73

It was an alluring metaphor. Watterson equated the draft with modernization, linking organizational change to technological development and describing both as indicators of progress. Yet such a description ignored the continued importance of the local volunteer tradition, even at the price of complete national military efficiency. As the editor of a rival Louisville paper, the *Evening Post*, responded: "The volunteer system [is] the very life of American democracy. The conscript system means the subjugation of America to military oligarchy such as that which has cursed Germany."[3] Since the draft was adopted and successfully implemented without subjugating America to any such military oligarchy, many have accepted the position of contemporaries like Watterson who portrayed it as an inevitable and desirable development for the effective use of force in defense of American ideals and interests against aggressive major powers like Germany, a necessary aspect of a great nation's "modernization" in the early 20th century.[4]

But who were the agents of this "modernization"? What were their motives? What were the results of the adoption of the draft? To the extent that historians have identified those responsible for the 1917 draft, they have differed over whether primary responsibility belongs to President Woodrow Wilson, ex-President Theodore Roosevelt, Maj. Gen. Leonard Wood (the "prophet of preparedness"), Maj. Gen. Hugh L. Scott, army chief of staff from 1914 to 1917, or Maj. Gen. Enoch H. Crowder, the judge advocate general who wrote the draft law and became wartime head of the Selective Service System.[5] Also controversial is the role of the "preparedness" movement of 1915–17.[6]

The core goal of this elite-dominated, multi-faceted social movement for greater military "preparedness" was a national mass conscript reserve army raised and prepared through universal military training and service (UMT&S). Like the continental European nations, the United States would have a pretrained mass army of citizen reservists, trained and commanded by regulars and coordinated by a general staff. Unlike the major European forces, however, training would be for six months rather than two years and thus there would be no mass standing army in peacetime. Although it lasted from 1915 to 1920, the campaign for UMT&S reached such intensity between 1916 and 1917 that it became a virtual conscription crusade.

The movement's leading spokespeople—ex-president Roosevelt and General Wood, army chief of staff from 1910 to 1914—and such leading preparedness organizations as the National Security League and the Military Training Camps Association (named "Plattsburgers" after the site of their original training camp) advocated complete reorganization of the traditional military format. As champions of nationalism and a stronger central government, they rejected both the militia and the U.S. Volunteers as anachronistic remnants of a parochialism obstructive to national efficiency and progress, which, they believed, required a single, unitary, national military force.

Although the regular army represented such a force, it was not sufficient for these modernizers. With only 100,000 soldiers, it was too small to be effective against a first-class power. Even when supplemented by the 112,000 "ready reserves" of the National Guard, the ground forces of the United States were only slightly larger than those of Mexico or Belgium, and insignificant compared to the prewar forces of Germany or France. Before the outbreak of war in 1914, these two world powers had mass conscript standing armies of 800,000 which could be raised to 2 million within a few weeks by calling up units of young first-line reservists, and subsequently more than quadrupled by summoning millions of older men organized in second line reserves.[7]

American conscriptionists believed that reliance upon the regular army was not simply militarily inadequate but economically inefficient. Partly because it had to compete with civilian wage rates which were higher than in most other nations, the U.S. Army was the most expensive force, per soldier, in the world. Although American regulars were paid only $15 a month in 1914, the annual cost of maintaining each soldier was $1,700. This helps explain why, despite an annual expenditure of $200 million, which amounted to more than one-quarter of the federal budget, the United States had the smallest standing army among the great powers.[8] The preparedness movement proposed a more cost-efficient instrument than the regular army as a means of increasing the size of the ground forces without a prohibitive increase in cost.

They proposed a severely modified version of the European mass-conscript-reservist army, in which the emphasis would be on short-term training and national reserve organizations rather than on maintaining a large standing army. Each year 600,000 able-bodied, 18-year-old American males would spend six months in military training camps. The best of these would be selected for additional training as reserve officers. All would be assigned to geographically organized reserve units. During their civilian careers, the citizen-reservists would also progress, as they grew older, from first-line to second-line and, ultimately, into inactive reserves. Under the conscriptionists proposals, reservists could not be drafted into military service except in case of war or other national emergency.

The idea was to employ a small regular army for training and

leadership and continued constabulary and garrison duty but to replace the old locally oriented and led National Guard and U.S. Volunteers with these new nationally oriented pretrained reserves. Universal military training and service (UMT&S) would be defined as a
military obligation of citizenship. Consequently, the trainees would
not be paid during training or their extended period in the reserves.
Nor would there be enlistment bonuses in wartime, since the government would simply call up the millions of reservists. Citizen-
soldiers, conscriptionists believed, should not expect compensation
merely for fulfilling their duty to the nation. The result would be a
large reserve force without a proportionate increase in the cost of
the military establishment.

Scholars continue to disagree about the nature of the preparedness movement and its relationship to international and domestic
developments. Differences also remain over the necessity and success of the draft of 1917.[9] As the present study shows, the preparedness movement, like the new military doctrines and technology,
were important in the evolution of this new military format, but the
adoption of the Nation-State Model: wartime mass mobilization was,
more significantly, the result of larger changes in the structure of
power relationships and attitudes within American society and the
world.[10]

If military institutions reflect the larger society, they should be
affected by significant changes in that society. Certainly, the progressive era was a time of pivotal changes. By the turn of the
century, mass production was creating new centers for labor and
immense new sources of wealth. Dramatically expanding trade created an increasingly interdependent national and even international
economy. Industrialization provided an opportunity in which new
elites came to power in industry, transportation, and finance, and in
the law firms, trade associations, and other institutions which assisted the giant new corporations. Seeing the new industrialism as
the major source of personal and national wealth, these new corporate and professional elites sought to ensure a politico-economic
environment conducive to the evolving system of big business and
domestic and international interests.

Industrialization, of course, created major social problems. Millions of largely poor, agrarian workers immigrated from southern
and eastern Europe, and the influx of so many Roman Catholics and
Orthodox Jews triggered a renewed wave of nativism in America.
Rapid industrialization also led to widespread poverty, crime, and
disease in urban slums. While urbanization and industrialization
greatly increased the wealth of the rich and expanded opportunities
for many in the middle class, it also exacerbated the gap between the

rich and the poor, and increased ethnic and regional tensions. Increasing social unrest and regional protest was aggravated by the depression of the 1890s and the consolidation of big business at the turn of the century.

As a result of these developments, many Americans began to modify their belief in unrestrained individualism, laissez-faire, and the self-regulating marketplace. They turned in varying degrees to collective action and often to the government for assistance in ameliorating social problems and enhancing their own economic position. This growing acceptance of active interventionism applied not simply to domestic circumstances but to international affairs as well. In the progressive era, the United States began to emerge as a world power, economically at least, projecting its influence into different areas of the world. In part this resulted from the growth of American industry and world trade, in part from an interventionism in which American presidents and foreign policy elites sought to go beyond simply reacting to external events, seeking instead to shape international affairs, particularly in the Caribbean and Central America, but also in East Asia, and Europe.

American interventionism was itself a reaction to major changes in the international system in the late 19th and early 20th centuries. A strong, unified yet politically unstable Germany challenged both the status quo and the balance of power. Imperialist European powers carved Africa into colonies and with expansionist Japan began to intervene in East Asia. Such imperialism threatened traditional U.S. interests in China and many Americans feared that the well-armed, aggressive imperialist powers, like Germany and Japan, might turn next to Latin America. To join the imperialist race or to defend American interests against it, internationally minded Americans sought to move beyond traditional political and military isolationism and pursue an active, interventionist foreign policy. Accordingly, American business people, diplomats, and presidents like Roosevelt, Taft, and Wilson began to play major roles in international diplomacy.

It was one segment of this new, internationally oriented, cosmopolitan expansionist elite which was responsible for the preparedness movement and its key military component, the conscription crusade. Departing from the American liberal tradition with its emphasis on commerce, rational behavior, and law as the tools of international relations, and the oceans and coastal defense as protection against external threats to national security, preparedness leaders saw an increasing need for extensive military and naval forces which could be projected overseas. An expanded military force was important, not merely for the emergency of the world war,

but on a long-term continuing basis for the United States to defend
its expanding interests and act as a major world power.

Theodore Roosevelt and Leonard Wood provided the twin symbols of preparedness in the mind of the public. Undeniably Roosevelt had an extraordinary talent for capturing attention through his
exuberant personality and his ability to fuse America's ideals and
self-interest. The bellicose old Rough Rider had long believed in
expanding the nation's armed forces in support of his foreign policy.
As president, he had built up the navy, but in regard to the army he
had been much more cautious, simply obtaining a general staff and
a doubling of the regular army. Roosevelt had not been one of
founders of the movement for UMT&S; rather, as in his earlier
campaign for conservation of natural resources, he was more the
popularizer than the initiator of the movement, helping to provide
the idea with a national forum.[11]

Similarly although Leonard Wood was probably the single most
important figure in the movement for a mass conscript army in
America, he probably received more credit than he deserved. Often
portrayed as a military evangelist, Wood has been pictured as the
"prophet" of preparedness, wrestling with and seeking to convert to
UMT&S both rigid Uptonian professionals in the army and liberal
internationalists in civilian society. His admirers considered him a
martyr engaged in a long and largely thankless struggle to ensure a
powerful America. To his liberal detractors, he appeared to be a
politically ambitious and dangerous military commander who, with
conservative support, might become the "man on horseback" who
could threaten American democracy. A graduate of Harvard Medical School, Wood had entered the army as a surgeon rather than a
line officer and to most professional military officers he remained
an outsider, a mere "doctor." His career advanced through his personal friendship with influential politicians, particularly with Presidents McKinley and Roosevelt, leading to his becoming army chief
of staff from 1910 to 1914. It was from the army's top post that he
began to seek to transform America's military establishment.[12]

Like the Uptonians, Wood had taken the idea of the pretrained
conscript-reservist army from the mass armies of Europe. As a
military observer in 1902, he had marvelled at the massive German
Army in its annual maneuvers. He listened to General Colmar von
der Goltz, who disputed traditional views and argued that the mass
conscript army could be made loyal through intense nationalism
and efficient through the direction of professional officers and a
general staff.[13]

But America was not Germany and it was to an Englishman, Gen.

F.S. Roberts, that Wood turned for more practical advice.[14] The politico-military solution of the British hero of the Boer War was to create national reserve forces through extremely short-term universal military training, perhaps only six months with the army. In their public statements, both men emphasized the Swiss system as demonstrating that UMT could be compatible with democracy and a non-aggressive foreign policy. The major difference, of course, was that since Britain and the United States were much larger nations and active world powers, their larger reserve forces, unlike the Swiss Army, would play a significant role in international relations. Although Roberts failed in his campaign to obtain UMT&S in England, Wood adopted both his goal and his methods in America.[15]

As chief of staff, Wood sought to lay the groundwork for a change of policy. While Congress updated procedures for the U.S. Volunteers in 1912, Wood obtained from the General Staff's War College Division planners a recommendation for a wholly national army of 110,000 regulars and 650,000 reservists. Although they could not say so publicly, the planners assumed that such a sizable force would be obtained through national conscription, preferably UMT&S. There was little public response to this "Statement of a Proper Military Policy," and while the document gathered dust, Wood took the lead in forming what he hoped would be an effective civilian pressure group, the Army League of the United States. Copying the influential Navy League, Wood included distinguished citizens from important support groups. Unlike the capital-intensive navy, the army remained primarily labor-intensive; consequently, there were no pro-Army business groups comparable to the steel companies and shipyards which gave such support to naval expansion. Big business was not yet a major constituent of the army. Thus, although the Army League included representatives of the foreign policy elite, members of celebrated military families, and presidents of some of the most prestigious universities where reserve officers would be produced, it failed to become a major political force.

More successful was a program which Wood and several college presidents established in 1913 to offer military training to a few dozen students at army summer camps at Gettysburg and Monterrey. It was this program which became the model for the popular military training sessions for business and professional men who would become reserve officers and, Wood hoped, missionaries for preparedness. The summer military camps for the corporate elite began in 1915 at the army base at Plattsburg, N.Y., the source of the so-called "Plattsburg movement" for national reserve training. After the sinking of the *Lusitania* in the spring of 1915, the preparedness movement began to grow rapidly and Wood became its major

champion. In taking such an activist position, General Wood, who by
then was commander of the Department of the East with headquarters in New York City, aligned himself directly with President
Wilson's Republican rivals who criticized the administration's refusal to expand the army as well as the president's continual efforts
to mediate a compromise settlement to the war. The general's controversial role embittered the president, but endeared him to many
Republicans who eventually made him one of the two leading candidates for the GOP nomination for president in 1920.[16]

Focusing on Wood and Roosevelt provides an interesting narrative but an inadequate explanation of the preparedness movement
and the creation of America's mass army. It underestimates the role
played by civilian elites as well as the importance of structural and
attitudinal change. Wood's proposal for a national mass reserve
army based on UMT&S, unaccepted earlier, became persuasive to
many between 1914 and 1917 because an important segment of the
elite became receptive to such a program for its own reasons. As the
initial failure of the Army League demonstrated, it was not until
World War I that a significant group of influential civilian leaders
became convinced of the need for a drastic transformation of the
nation's military institutions. At that time, Wood spoke to an elite
which was already looking for a program of relatively inexpensive
and efficient expansion of America's military resources. It was this
civilian elite, rather than Wood or any other military officer, which
created and directed the major preparedness organizations and actually led the movement for a national draft army.

Collective biographical analysis shows that the civilian leaders of
the major conscriptionist organizations were predominantly members of the new corporate-oriented business and professional elite.
They included industrialists, financiers, railroad magnates, and major publishers, joined by corporation lawyers, university presidents,
and former diplomats. This was a confident and influential group.
Their interests and attitudes were linked to the evolving national
and international economy; and as a group they represented the top
echelons of power in the new social structure of urban, industrial,
corporate America.[17]

In the early 1900s, when the American elite was a great deal more
restricted socially and geographically than it would later become,
the leading figures were overwhelmingly white, Anglo-Saxon Protestants, with a few Catholics and Jews, who resided in the financial
centers of the northeast and north central regions of the country,
especially New York and Chicago. Conscriptionist leaders—those
who held leadership positions in the major preparedness organizations and who placed particular emphasis on compulsory national

military training and service—reflected a similar profile, since they came primarily from this corporate-oriented, business and professional class. Born into affluent and often enormously wealthy families that had long been resident in America, the majority of these "conscriptionists" had been raised as Episcopalians or Congregationalists, educated at private preparatory schools and graduated from Ivy League colleges. Generally they inherited their politics, like their religion, from their fathers. Linked by family and career to the business enterprises dominating the expanding national marketplace, they were for the most part social and political conservatives. With the exception of a handful of anti-Bryanite, eastern Democrats, the majority were loyal members of the eastern business-oriented wing of the G.O.P. Although a few had followed Roosevelt temporarily into the Progressive party in 1912, most were Old Guard Republicans who had stood by William Howard Taft. All were men; women were consciously excluded.[18]

The largest and most important of the preparedness organizations, the National Security League, illustrated the dominance of this corporate-oriented leadership. The league was formed in New York City in December 1914 at the suggestion of Rep. Augustus P. "Gussie" Gardner of Massachusetts, a Boston lawyer who had married the daughter of Senator Henry Cabot Lodge. Although the nominal head of the organization was S. Stanwood Menken, a southern-born Democrat and Wall Street lawyer, the real movers were Elihu Root, a leading corporation lawyer who had served as both secretary of war and secretary of state in the Roosevelt administration, and Root's former assistant secretary of state, Robert Bacon, investment banker and former partner in J.P. Morgan & Co. Also important in the league were Henry L. Stimson, a corporation lawyer who had served as Taft's secretary of war, and Herbert Barry, an attorney for half a dozen New York banks, insurance companies and other financial corporations, who had a life-long interest in the military.[19]

The governing committees of the other major conscriptionist organizations—the Military Training Camps Association (the Plattsburgers), Universal Military Training League, and Association for National Service—were made up of similar types of investment bankers and corporation lawyers, who were often former cabinet officers, together with publishers and university presidents and a few retired generals and admirals. This pattern extended beyond the national headquarters. By the end of 1916, the National Security League had 250 chapters with more than 100,000 members. Examination of the leadership of the state and local branches indicates that they were composed of a similar spectrum of elite members.[20]

The financial base of the league was linked to the new corporations. Between 1915 and 1917, the NSL received contributions totaling nearly $250,000 (a not inconsiderable sum at a time when the entire army budget was $300,000,000). One-third of the league's income came from only 150 donors, mostly New York City millionaires, including some of the richest men in America. Among these were Arthur C. James, a vice president of Phelps Dodge mining company, who had inherited $26 million, and T. Coleman DuPont who, after building the DuPont Powder Trust, had sold his holdings for $14 million. Joining them were financiers J.P. Morgan, and Mortimer and Jacob Schiff (directors of Kuhn, Loeb and Co., the largest investment banking house after Morgan), and Bernard Baruch, an independent investor. Industrialists included Henry Clay Frick, the steel magnate; William Hamlin Childs, coal tar manufacturer and director of a Cuban sugar company; and the Guggenheim brothers who controlled the American Smelting and Refining Company with mines and smelting refineries throughout the world. Joseph H. Choate, dean of the New York bar and former ambassador to Britain, was honorary president of the National Security League and was also a major contributor. After America entered the war, sizable contributions came from John D. Rockefeller, Jr.; and the Carnegie Corporation, under the leadership of Elihu Root, granted $100,000.[21]

In support of a mass conscript-reserve army, these influential members of the corporate elite were joined by a younger group of preparedness advocates, most of them also linked to the corporate world. The Plattsburgers who organized the Military Training Camps Association held similar views about international relations, national defense, domestic order, and a strong and responsible national government, yet they differed from their elders. Politically, these younger men tended to be more idealistic and less sceptical about reform; many of them were committed to Theodore Roosevelt and the progressive wing of the Republican party. Militarily, they desired personally to lead men in combat, to play a heroic role in the new national army. In the spring of 1915, at the Harvard Club in New York City, a group of young Wall Street lawyers and investors, including scions of the Astors, Jays, Carrolls, DuPonts, Roots, and Roosevelts, met to organize the Military Training Camps Association. Encouraged by General Wood and inspired by a sense of civic duty, these American "aristocrats" were guided by a spirit of class leadership and, for many of them, a personal need for physical challenge and self-sacrifice in pursuit of a higher goal than ordinary materialism. They sought to get the "natural leaders" of society out of their comfortable offices and clubs and into the training camps to prepare to lead the men of their country in wartime.[22]

They wanted to replace the old system of the National Guard and the U.S. Volunteers in which wartime citizen-officers were simply local notables, influential farmers or townsmen, ethnic group leaders, or machine politicians. Appalled at untrained, political generals like Benjamin F. Butler in the Civil War, or colonels like William Jennings Bryan in the Spanish-American War, the Plattsburgers must have shuddered at the possibility of union leaders like Samuel Gompers or socialists like Eugene V. Debs leading their own regiments or serving as field commanders. National standards would ensure a pretrained reserve officer corps of the middle and upper classes. Plattsburgers rejected requests from Gompers to include union leaders and others from the working classes in their officer training camps. The Plattsburgers were determined to prepare as officers only those who, in the words of MTCA organizer Grenville Clark, a 33-year-old Wall Street lawyer and heir to a banking and railroad fortune, were "our kind of people."[23]

Held on the shores of Lake Champlain, N.Y. in August 1915, the first Plattsburg encampment proved a smashing success. The urban professionals thrilled at spending a month in intensive physical exercise in the rugged, picturesque mountain setting. The sight of 1,200 members of some of the nation's most illustrious families—aristocrats like Saltonstall of Massachusetts, industrialists like William C. Proctor, the soap king from Ohio—staking out pup tents and hopping to orders barked by army sergeants proved irresistible to the press. Thirty-five days of military training could not produce an effective enlisted man let alone a qualified officer, but the immediate purpose of the encampment was less the preparation of a reserve officer corps than the promotion of the movement for a pretrained, national army of citizen-reservists. "My own view is that the training camp idea is simply a means to an end," Grenville Clark, the executive secretary of the MTCA, explained privately, "namely to get sane principles established. . . ."[24]

Preparedness leaders, whatever their age, advocated a new military format to bolster the U.S. role in foreign affairs; in their view, force played an inevitable role in international relations. As cosmopolitan men of business and public affairs, they had contributed to dramatic American commercial expansion and a more active international role by the U.S. government. Earlier, the older among them had supported the creation of a modern high seas fleet. Now they sought to expand the navy even further and to augment it with a "modern" army. The United States must have "a Navy powerful in every respect, and an Army in reserve visibly strong in numbers and visibly prepared for immediate service," former Harvard president Charles W. Eliot declared in 1916, adding that "the United States, having become an industrial and commercial World Power, needs to have all the seas and oceans of the world open for its foreign trade. . . ."[25]

In their attitude toward foreign policy, preparedness leaders differed from the majority of Americans. Isolationism remained strong among millions of agrarians and townspeople in the South and Midwest and among many ethnic Irish, Germans, Scandinavians, or Russian Jews who disliked the idea of joining on the side of Britain and Czarist Russia against Germany. Among the foreign-policy elite, predominantly English in ethnicity and sympathy, the overriding belief was in a liberal internationalism, in which American ideals and national interests were best sustained through economic growth, humanitarian principles, and international law. In contrast, few preparedness leaders remained sanguine after the outbreak of the world war in 1914. Although some of them had supported the prewar movement for peace through world law, virtually all of them believed that international relations were ultimately and increasingly, governed by force or the threat of it. While they recognized the role of idealism in mobilizing popular support for American expansion, preparedness leaders criticized "idealistic" crusades—like that to "free Cuba" in 1898—which could be disruptive unless skillfully guided and adequately supported by force. Americans, said Roosevelt, were too ready to "combine the unready hand with the unbridled tongue."[26] Thus far, the United States had acted in a highhanded manner with comparatively weak military opponents, such as Mexico and Spain, but it faced the eventual possibility of confrontations with major military powers like Germany and Japan.

As former Secretary of War Luke E. Wright of Tennessee explained at a conference sponsored by the National Security League in 1916:

> We have become a world power. We are not isolated any longer. American enterprise, American energy, is [sic] finding outlets all over Central and South America and all over the Orient. . . . [The Monroe Doctrine] is as prolific of fights as a barrel of red liquor, [for] we are constituting ourselves the inter-national policemen of the American continent.[27]

If the United States was not to suffer insults to its national honor and restriction of its expanding commercial and strategic interests, conscriptionists believed it needed a military force that would be taken seriously by other world powers. There was also a more immediate and pressing reason—aid to the Allies.[28]

As the European war continued, this "preparedness" element within the foreign policy elite began to favor U.S. entry into the struggle. Although they declined to say this publicly, preparedness leaders ardently championed Allied victory. From the beginning, Roosevelt, Root, and Bacon had argued that U.S. neutrality should be actively favorable to the Allies. By 1916, they privately endorsed U.S. entry if necessary to help Britain and France achieve a clear victory, believing that threats to the status quo, such as Imperial Germany posed to the Atlantic sea lanes and to the European balance of power, had to be curtailed to protect the expanding economic and strategic interests of the United States. Challenges to those interests could come from the colonial ambitions of aggressively expansionist nations like Germany, Japan, and Russia and from radical, nationalistic revolutions in areas of important markets or raw materials such as China and Mexico. Many preparedness leaders agreed with Roosevelt that the United States, Britain, and France should ensure the proper policing of the world by—and for—"civilized" nations. For such a role as well as possible intervention in the European war, America needed formidable military as well as naval forces.[29]

In the absence of direct military threats to the Western Hemisphere, preparedness leaders faced a difficult problem: how to overcome isolationism and deep divisions over the European war and mobilize public opinion behind a substantial prewar military build-up. Public discussion of American foreign policy continued to be couched primarily in traditional terms of the nation's ideals and unique moral mission.[30] Attempts to link military means with specific foreign policy goals were hampered by traditional suspicion of the military, by a lack of strategic thinking by decision-makers, and by bureaucratic rivalries, particularly among the Departments of State, Navy, and War. Consequently, foreign policy was usually developed by the president, the State Department, and civilian foreign policy elites with little if any coordination with army or navy officers who for the most part were viewed simply as implementers of policy. One of the major goals of the preparedness movement was to link the nation's military resources with its foreign policy needs.

This proved difficult in the American political arena. Despite a few attempts to explain the need for force to sustain bellicose policies like the Roosevelt Corollary to the Monroe Doctrine, some preparedness leaders fell back upon fantastic attempts to frighten the public through imaginary invasions of an increasingly prosperous America. Although the General Staff in 1916 had dismissed any possibility of invasion, General Wood advocated UMT&S because "we must have [a large army] immediately available for use at any moment on either coast."[31] Conscriptionists warned of the danger of seaborne raids on American coastal cities and military expeditions seeking to occupy particular regions. In one of their films, "The Battle Cry of Peace," spike-helmeted soldiers rushed up Long Island beaches and swarmed into Manhattan, robbing, raping and slaying. New York City was captured and its millionaire entrepreneurs held for ransom. Such fantasies surely eroded the credibility of the preparedness movement. Like similar predictions of postwar invasions or trade wars, such assertions deflected discussion from the real issues: the possibility of military intervention in the European war, the probable nature of long-term U.S. foreign policy, and the most appropriate military and naval forces for both of these.[32]

Instead of linking military resources with strategic goals, preparedness leaders concentrated largely on inherent problems in American military institutions, lack of prewar training, reliance upon localism, voluntarism, and amateurism. To impugn that tradition, they rewrote the history of America's wars. In a 700-page study, *The Military Unpreparedness of the United States*, Frederick L. Huidekoper, a Washington lawyer and a founder of the National Security League, updated Emory Upton's treatise and argued that the fact that the country had never lost a war had blinded it to the excessive casualties resulting from its inadequate wartime military institutions. It was only because it had never fought against a first-class power, wholly dedicated to victory, that the United States had not been defeated, he warned. Despite its many historical distortions, Huidekoper's massive polemic became the Bible of the preparedness movement, emphasizing the invincibility of a properly trained and organized national citizen army. Conscriptionists sought to destroy one myth about citizen-soldiers by creating another.[33]

The National Guard was a prime object of their contempt. Many future preparedness leaders had served as officers in the rejuvenated militia in the 1890s, but they had become disillusioned with it. Like the officers of the regular army, they saw the state forces as badly armed and poorly trained and with an officer corps often influenced by state politics. Organized labor had become increasingly hostile to the National Guard because of its strike-breaking activities, thus jeopardizing any sense of military obligation among the working classes. Extended strike duty became onerous for middle-class Guardsmen who themselves were kept from their civilian jobs. To control strikes or riots, several industrial states turned instead to a new, full-time professional force, the state police.[34]

Yet militia units retained considerable support, particularly among local elites in the South and West. Through effective lobbying, the Guard in 1903 had obtained congressional designation as the nation's primary ready reserve. The Army continued its opposition and the attorney general's 1912 opinion that the militia could not be required to serve outside the United States seemed to negate the Guard as an overseas force. Conscriptionists were also concerned that, as in the War of 1812 and the Spanish-American War, some of the state militia units, supported by their governors, would refuse to comply with presidential directives. The National Guard, declared former Secretary of War Stimson, was "a hopeless anachronism and a shackle on our progress both in the states and in the Nation."[35]

The U.S. Volunteers were even more inadequate, since they not only demonstrated the same flaws of amateur local leadership, but—even worse—had no prewar training or organization. Further, there was no predicting how many men would turn out. "There is not sufficient organization, there is no certainty as to who is coming. That is why we damn the [volunteer] system," General Wood exclaimed. "We do not know whether the men are going to be enthusiastic . . . whether they are opposed to the action of the President in calling out the troops. We have no certainty whatever [as] to the response; it is chance when we want certainty. . . . It's a kind of referendum in a crisis."[36]

To rely wholly upon voluntarism meant that national action would be limited to decisions made by hundreds of thousands, even millions, of individuals. The utilitarian concept that society and the economy would benefit when individuals were free to pursue their own interests had, of course, become widely challenged by the progressive era. As America was transformed through massive immigration, rapid urbanization, and sweeping industrialization, faith in natural development fostered by unrestrained individualism and an unregulated market place gave way to a fear that "blind social forces" were remoulding the country without regard to social goals and values.[37]

Earlier efforts in the first two decades of the 20th century had coalesced into a nation-wide attempt to bring these social forces under some control. A vital part of the "progressive movement" was a readiness to modify concepts of laissez-faire, unrestricted individualism, and an unregulated marketplace. It also included an unprecedented willingness to use governmental or other purposeful collective action, if necessary, to manipulate the social, economic, or international environment to achieve group and national goals and ideals. In regard to the military, conscriptionists sought to apply this "new interventionism" by replacing reliance upon decisions by thousands of individuals with coordinated direction by the national government.[38] Not the individual but the nation-State would decide who served and when.

Militarily, only conscription could ensure predictable numbers of recruits and replacements so the army could be assured of the viability of its plans for mass mobilization and strategic operations. World War I had not followed the pattern of "short total war," which had been the prevailing strategic doctrine in Europe since the Prussian defeat of France in 1871. By 1915–16, it was clear that on the Western Front the war had bogged down into grinding conflict of national attrition. Many of the leading commanders, Wood among them, considered this an aberration and continued to believe that future wars could be fought as "short total conflicts."[39] In the meantime, siegecraft on the Western Front required masses of soldiers and millions of replacements for those lost in frontal assaults upon entrenchments fortified with barbed wire and machine guns.

Americans learned from the British experience of 1914–16 that although the volunteer system could indeed raise millions of soldiers, it was highly unpredictable and inefficient. Dependent on highly emotional recruiting campaigns, enlistments increased dramatically when England came under aerial bombardment or when civilians were killed by German submarines. Furthermore, in economic terms, the wrong people often volunteered. Many of the early British volunteers had been skilled workers and supervisors from munitions factories or shipyards and their loss had impeded the increased production demanded by the extraordinary firepower of the navies and new mass armies.

Although conscriptionists advocated *universal* military training, most of them recognized that this would involve *selective* military service or, as a few extremists suggested, possibly even wartime *national service*. Theodore Roosevelt confided in November 1915:

> The great reason I wish universal service, which of course means compulsory service, is because I want to see each man put to work at what the country needs. The volunteer service *makes* the married man with children who could do invaluable work in turning out munitions of war go to the front and his unmarried brother stay in idleness at home. I wish to send the idle brother to the front and make the other man either go to the front or work in the munition factory, *as the country deems best*.[40]

The statement was typically Rooseveltian in its politically effective intertwining of moral and economic issues to rouse public support for government intervention. Although few would have gone as far as national service, virtually all conscriptionists agreed on the inadequacy of the volunteer system on social and economic as well as military grounds.

National UMT&S proved additionally appealing for its domestic benefits. Conscriptionists asserted that it could help to meld the disparate and contending interests which characterized heterogeneous America into a united nation. The idea of using the army as a "school of the nation"—to inculcate nationalism and particular behavioral norms—had been broached much earlier in America by Federalist Secretary of War Henry Knox, but its major development had occurred in Europe. In Revolutionary and Napoleonic France, governing elites had employed it to guide mass enthusiasm for popular government into acceptable channels. But the idea found its fullest development in late 19th-century imperial Germany where wealthy landowners and aristocratic officers employed UMT&S to build a mass conscript army for national power and simultaneously to stifle regionalism and radicalism by instilling nationalism and discipline among conscript-reservists. Copied by Austria, Italy, and other continental nations as well as regional powers like Argentina and Japan, the Prussian model of the nation-in-arms was not simply an instrument of military policy. As a "school of the nation," the mass army was seen by conservative elites as an antidote to the challenges posed by anarchism, socialism, and popular democracy.[41]

Members of the new corporate-oriented elite who led the preparedness movement in the United States had similar fears and saw UMT&S as a potential antidote for them. However, unlike the conservative European elites' direct expressions of preserving the interests of their class, these Americans spoke more typically of misunderstandings among people rather than of conflicting class interests. "Obviously the problems ahead are problems of labor and capital and in some degree of race," wrote Henry S. Hooker, a Wall Street lawyer and Plattsburger, to Woodrow Wilson in late 1916. "They appear to arise in very great part through misunderstandings created by rumors, newspapers, and lack of personal contact." Like many other Plattsburgers, Hooker predicted that universal military training, which brought together boys from Groton preparatory school and boys from the Bowery, would tend "to obliterate the so-called class distinctions. I really believe that nothing else will so surely aid in making us a united and understanding people."[42] With characteristic exuberance, Theodore Roosevelt claimed that "the military tent, where all sleep side by side, will rank next to the public school among the great agents of democratization."[43]

Such an observation reflected the concern of most of the corporate-oriented elite that industrialization in America had brought with it not only a great expansion of national wealth, but also attendant regional, class, and ethnic (what they called "racial") conflict which they believed threatened to destroy the basis of economic growth. The preceeding decades had been filled with agrarian protest, labor unrest, bloody strikes, and lockouts. In 1900 a socialist party that emphasized conflicting class interests began to win increasing numbers of voters until in 1912, its presidential candidate, Eugene V. Debs, garnered a million votes, 6 percent of the national turnout. In the same election, the winning Democratic candidate, Woodrow Wilson, also warned of an inequitable division of wealth and of curtailment of opportunity caused by the recent rise of "big business," although, unlike Debs, his appeal was to the traditional middle classes in small business and agriculture, particularly in the South and the West. Senator Henry Cabot Lodge voiced the fears of many conservatives in 1912 when he told Roosevelt that America's greatest danger came not from any foreign foe but from internal threats.[44]

The fear that the "genteel" world of the 19th century was sliding into the confusion and chaos of the 20th century was widely held in cosmopolitan sectors of society. Many suggested an antidote in increased national consciousness and control. Roosevelt and Lodge viewed a stronger national government as the cement to prevent fragmentation. Some progressives like the journalist Walter Lippmann saw nationalism and a bolder central government as means of overcoming impediments to progress posed by a parochial, agrarian society; "a nation of villagers," Lippmann called it, composed largely of isolated and local settlements. The larger forces of urban industrial society left individuals almost helpless to determine the conditions under which they lived. Despite their differences over particular programs, progressive intellectuals like Lippmann, Charles H. Cooley, Mary Parker Follett and John Dewey espoused a national loyalty as a new and larger sense of community to link individuals, despite America's diverse ethnicity and regionalism and its traditional emphasis upon individual rights, through cooperative functional and other associational groups into a more interdependent national community. Emphasizing scale rather than quality, the influential English social theorist Graham Wallas had called such an ideal the large or "Great Society." Dewey chose the term "Great Community."[45]

Such a vision helped to justify unprecedented expansion of the State in the progressive era. Particular increments to the power of the central government came about largely because of pressure from powerful new interest groups—manufacturers, shippers, carriers, bankers, labor, farmers and consumers—as well as lobbying from government agencies themselves. The expansion also reflected a change in the predominant political attitude among elites which in the late 19th century had distrusted the State as generally ineffi- cient, often corrupt, and potentially confiscatory. In the early 20th century, encouraged by the creation of non-partisan agencies and an ethic of public service, predominant elites came to accept, and some to advocate, a more powerful national government. Much of the middle and working classes also supported expanded government to protect workers, consumers, and natural resources. Nevertheless, Americans remained ambivalent about the growth of the national government, particularly the costs and the potential for abuse of power. From its beginning in the progressive era, strong, modern central government meant in America, as one historian termed it, an "uneasy State."[46]

Although the members of the corporate-oriented conscriptionists were nationalists who supported an expanded State to protect cor- porate institutions and economic growth, they also feared that such a State might be destructive if controlled by demagogues respond- ing to the masses. "Direct democracy" and popular government, rallying cries of reformers and radicals, sounded threatening to many conservatives who suspected that politicians might promise and conduct "ruinous" assaults upon capital accumulation in their desire for election and re-election. "If there is a weakness in repre- sentative bodies today," declared Charles Nagel, Taft's secretary of labor and commerce, "it is their too ready response to superficial popular demand"[47] Yet more enlightened conservative conscription- ists like Root recognized that industrialization, by its very nature, altered a social structure formerly based primarily on agriculture, and led in America as in Europe to increased demands for greater popular participation in government and for limitation of privilege. The United States, Root said, was "now witnessing the natural and inevitable struggle for a fair division of this new and rapidly in- creasing wealth."[48]

Pragmatic conservatives believed that if the people were to govern, then they must be taught to govern responsibly. Popular democracy must be accompanied by educating the masses to self- control and the necessity to subordinate class and regional interests to goals of national economic growth and prestige. Corporate elites need not fear popular government; rather it could be used to their advantage. As Root declared wryly:

Democracy turns again to government to furnish by law the pro- tection which the individual can no longer secure through his free- dom of contract and to *compel the vast multitudes on whose*

*cooperation all of us are dependent to do their necessary part in
the life of the community.*[49]

"Popular government is organized self-control," Root asserted.
Neither government nor society could rest primarily upon force or
even the continual threat of force. "There must be both the habit of
self-control and the dominating influence of the common ideal to
enable men so to act together, subordinating minor differences of
interest and opinion, as to make popular government possible."[50]
The common ideal, of course, was nationalism and the belief that in
the unique republican society all had the opportunity to benefit
from economic growth. Within the American elite in the progressive
era, neither conservatives nor progressives were willing to accept
the idea of permanently conflicting class interests. Responding to
what conservatives saw as Wilson's "capitulation" to the threat of a
national strike by railroad workers during the 1916 election, Frank
A. Vanderlip, president of National City Bank of New York and a
leading conscriptionist, told the American Bankers Association
flatly:

> It is the duty of everyone of us to do what we can to induce wage-
> earners to examine their relations to the industrial system as a
> whole and to be loyal to the industrial system as a whole rather
> than to any narrow mistaken opinion of class interest. *The whole
> idea of separate class interests is an illusion and, if cherished, fatal
> to the welfare of all classes.*[51]

American nationalism offered a device for reducing ethnocultural as well as class and regional divisions. Since the basic
unskilled and semi-skilled industrial workforce in the United States
was overwhelmingly composed of immigrants, the issues of class
and ethnicity became intertwined in America. Many believed that
recent immigrants were the radical and violent agitators among
industrial laborers. But as Root reminded conservatives, since the
children of immigrants accepted the dominant Anglo-American culture, such radicalism usually disappeared in the second generation.
"Our hope lies in education, in citizen participation in government,
and in a sense of the duty of citizenship."[52]

In their plan for eliminating class and ethnic divisions, preparedness leaders went beyond normal educational and naturalization
programs when they advocated national military training to help
"Americanize" immigrants. Drawing upon a popular new metaphor
for national assimilation, "the melting pot," former Assistant Secretary of War Henry Breckinridge, a San Francisco steel manufacturer, asserted in 1916 that through UMT the nation would become

"a real melting pot, under which the fire is hot enough to fuse the elements into one common mass of Americanism."[53]

In the public realm, the nexus between the nation's needs and the individual's loyalties and obligations is the concept of citizenship. Social and legal definitions of citizenship have been most dramatically expanded in periods of war and reform in America: notably the eras of the Revolution, Civil War, and World War I.[54] It has long been recognized that political and economic rights were expanded in the progressive era through direct primaries, referendums, women's suffrage, worker's compensation, union recognition, arbitration procedures, and regulation. At the same time, the prevailing concept of democratic citizenship excluded or placed in subordinate positions large numbers of non-whites and other minority groups. The rights of American citizenship were not granted, or in some cases only partly extended to native inhabitants of America's new colonial empire. This represented a resurrection for colonial purposes of the kind of legal differentiation earlier expounded in the *Dred Scott* decision—between full citizens and mere native residents or subjects.[55] During the progressive era, increased restrictions on citizenship were forced on blacks in the South, on Hispanics, Asians, and American Indians in the West; and on American women everywhere, in the legal finding that their national citizenship was totally dependent upon that of their husband.[56]

Leaders of the movement for UMT&S generally reflected such racial and anti-feminist attitudes. General Wood took a contemptuous view of most non-whites. When Roosevelt, who seems to have considered the possibility of some symbolic military units of educated blacks, suggested that a few qualified Afro-Americans be included in the Plattsburg camps, Wood quashed the idea of such officer candidates "with whom our descendants cannot intermarry without producing a breed of mongrels; they [the officer candidates] must at least be white."[57] Only whites were enrolled in the Plattsburg camps; and in regard to the proposed UMT camps for the masses of citizen-reservists, most conscriptionists apparently assumed that the South and West would find means to exclude their non-white minorities from the new military format, as they had excluded them from the polity.[58]

The massive influx of immigrants together with the acquisition of a populous island empire triggered the most extensive discussion of the nature of American citizenship in the nation's history.[59] Although a few influential Americans asserted the value of ethnocultural pluralism, the majority demanded conformity with Anglo-American norms. In the North, dominate elites did not exclude subordinate ethnic and racial groups from citizenship as did the South and West. However, they limited recent immigrants to a form of second-class or "apprentice" citizenship until they were deemed to have accepted prevailing Anglo-American norms and leadership. This situation was exacerbated by World War I when nationalists assailed so-called "hyphenated Americans," particularly anti-English ethnic groups like those of German, Austrian, and Irish descent; it was argued that these still retained divided loyalties and had not become adequately "Americanized."[60] As Woodrow Wilson told newly naturalized citizens in May 1915:

> America does not consist of groups. A man who thinks of himself as belonging to a particular national group in America has not yet become an American. . . . Americans must have a consciousness different from the consciousness of every other nation in the world.[61]

Wilson defined that American consciousness as an allegiance "to a great ideal, to a great body of principles, to a great hope of the human race . . . for liberty and justice."[62] It was a set of Enlightenment ideals and a sense of destiny which had served as the basis for nationalism among a people that lacked ethnic, religious, and cultural unity, and a rooted, common tradition. One sense of Americanism has been an emphasis upon personal rights, freedom, and opportunity, with a context of localism, egalitarianism, and limited governmental authority. Yet another sense of Americanism has been expressed in political terms of national unity, strength, and the supremacy of the federal government.[63]

The discussion of citizenship at the turn of the century sought to shape these social and political concepts of citizenship in the context of modern, urban, industrial corporate America. Formerly, America had been viewed as a democracy of producers, mainly farmers, tradespeople, and owners of small businesses. But by the turn of the century, the self-employed had been superseded by growing numbers of employees who worked for others for wages. Some radical progressive reformers, like Governor Robert M. La Follette of Wisconsin, proposed that Americans stop identifying with a vanished democracy of producers and accept a common politico-economic identity as consumers of goods and services. Such a new citizenship, identifying consumers rather than producers as the source of public virtue and rationality in a mass consumption society, would enable people of otherwise diverse interests and loyalties to unite behind programs to regulate corporations in the public interest.[64] The idea of a society of producer-citizens retained considerable support, however, and some farmers' and workers' organizations favored radical politico-economic action to achieve democracy by extending ownership of the means of production to all workers.[65] National progressives generally did not directly address this producer-consumer dichotomy, but rather focused on a new concept of citizenship and government which stressed the importance of subordinating selfish individualism to the larger public interest. Liberal progressives, like the editors of the influential *New Republic*, hoped to guarantee certain basic rights and protections for all Americans, while using the concept of the public interest to limit unrestricted freedom of action by owners of property, where such action was harmful to the community.[66]

There was another dimension to the evolving concept of citizenship in the progressive era—the emphasis, particularly by socio-economic and political conservatives, on the *obligations* of citizenship. By this was meant not simply the obligation to pay taxes (indeed many of the conservative conscriptionists like Joseph H. Choate had actively opposed the idea of a federal income tax),[67] but rather the obligation to be a "good citizen."[68] As General Wood put it:

> Real democracy rests upon one fundamental principle, and that is that equality of opportunity and privilege goes hand in hand with equality of obligation, in war as well as peace; that suffrage demands obligation for service, not necessarily in the ranks, but wherever it can best be rendered. The army to-day is the army of the people.[69]

This good-citizenship concept represented a mechanism for controlling the masses and establishing a self-disciplined political democracy. It could also contribute to industrial efficiency. Achieving higher productivity was viewed as a major problem at a time when most unskilled industrial workers arrived from rural cultures.[70] "We have everything . . . except discipline," an economist-conscriptionist expounded. "We have initiative, we have imagination, we have capacity, but one thing we have not got is capacity to steadily, day in and day out, for a period of months, stick to a definite job and do it under any conditions."[71] He predicted that UMT would make young men "far more desirable citizens and far more productive laborers."

There was some evidence that military training contributed to increased productivity. Many employers envied the position of their German counterparts with a more disciplined and productive workforce. Ignoring other aspects of German culture, American conscriptionists attributed these characteristics primarily to Prussian

UMT&S. General Wood estimated that six months in an army camp would increase a worker's productivity by 15 to 30 percent. An official of John Wanamaker's department stores in Philadelphia and New York boasted that the store's cadet training program had made employees "alert and taught them to think quickly and obey instinctively."[72] The director of the Ohio Association of Manufacturers predicted that UMT would teach new immigrants quickly to assimilate what he called *our industrial citizenship.*"[73]

"Our undisciplined youth," as Henry L. Stimson called them, posed an additional problem which could be rectified by UMT. Obsolescence of the apprenticeship system and the weakening of the family, church, and school had contributed to increased "juvenile delinquency" and "the youth problem." Liberal reformers and youth workers established playgrounds, youth centers, physical and vocational education programs and, for law violators, special systems of juvenile justice and rehabilitation. A number of conscriptionists had been active in these efforts, particularly in paramilitary youth programs like the Boy Scouts, which combined woodcraft and outdoor activity with uniformed drill, military training and organization. Because of the considerable success in teaching self-discipline and national patriotism, such organizations were cited as evidence of the domestic benefits of UMT&S. Writing in 1915, an enthusiast declared: "The Boy Scout Movement is a great national antidote for the devilish spirit of anarchy to the states and the nation that is now cropping up like rank and poisonous weeds all along the path of our nation's progress."[74]

Most clearly, it was the emphasis on force, coercion, and military training that set conscriptionists apart from the American liberal tradition. Progressives like Dewey, Lippmann, and Herbert Croly, author of the popular *Promise of American Life,* emphasized that it was in an individual's self-interest to support a democratic activist State. These liberals argued that "Americanization" could be accomplished more appropriately through civilian than through military institutions. They were unwilling to compel individuals to restrict their freedom and abandon their "pursuit of happiness" to serve in the military, unless it became absolutely necessary to defend the nation, its interests, and its ideals. Even then such coercive interrruption could be only temporary. As one of the contributing editors to the *New Republic* wrote in 1916:

> Military service is at once a necessity, a good and a danger. But it is primarily a necessity. By this I mean that it is justified only as a means to an imperative end. It is not to be undertaken for itself, nor is it lightly to be adopted as a means. Nothing short of national

safety or some higher design of international justice and order can make it reasonable to cultivate the art of destruction.[75]

Since the conservatives who dominated the conscriptionist movement sought to impose military training on virtually every male citizen, in peace as well as war, it was clear that the two groups differed over UMT&S and over the nature of citizenship.

Given the appeal of democracy in the progressive era, it was particularly important for preparedness leaders to portray conscription as democratic. They emphasized the relationship between citizenship rights and military obligations and belittled the idea of "hiring" a wartime army of paid volunteers. "A democracy must do its own fighting," Roosevelt declared.[76] They also sought to separate the image of conscription from its traditional association with tyranny, whether Napoleonic dictatorship or Prussian militarism. The Prussian army, they explained, was the instrument, *not* the cause, of militarism. They emphasized the origin of conscription in Republican France, where the nation-in-arms was an alternative to a monarchist professional standing army. Even more, they cited the example of tiny Switzerland as a non-aggressive republic which relied upon short-term UMT&S. European republics from ancient Athens to modern Switzerland and France had shown the compatibility of conscription and democracy. Indeed the one supported the other. "Far from being undemocratic," Grenville Clark declared, "such a system may well be the very salvation of our democracy."[77]

Actually the emphasis placed by preparedness leaders on the democratic nature of conscription represented less a commitment to democracy than their belief that UMT&S could not be adopted unless it was seen as democratic. As Henry L. Stimson explained to a rather slow-witted officer, conscription had to be "sugar coated" to have any chance of being adopted by popularly elected officials. This was partly why national conscription was advocated in the form of short-term UMT&S. When a senior officer and dedicated Uptonian complained in 1916 that the army neither needed nor desired the millions of soldiers that would be produced through national UMT, the former secretary of war patiently explained that, as the Civil War experience demonstrated, the American public would *not* accept conscription as a disagreeable necessity applicable only to a few unlucky men picked in a draft lottery. The public had to see it as "a democratic institution in which every man, rich or poor, shall bear his part in this obligation of citizenship." "If compulsory service is to come," Stimson continued, "it must come along the avenue of general universal training."[78]

Time would prove that the draft did not need to be universal to be adopted in America. In fact, it was selective service (although based on universal male *liability*) which was used to raise the nation's army in World War I and in subsequent wars. Preparedness leaders had reached their conclusion about the need for UMT in part because they misunderstood the public. It was true that Americans were not willing to accept a permanent system of universal conscription. But in wartime a majority was willing to accept a selective draft, if it were temporary, equitable, and in a worthy cause. Of course, preparedness leaders had also been guided by their desire to use UMT to build a sense of nationalism. As Stimson wrote privately to George Harvey Putnam, a conservative publisher, he considered UMT&S "both as a military necessity and as a highly important part of our education for civic duties."[79] On an earlier occasion he had stated: "The real need of the country is a change of ideals towards national duty in all respects—national defense being only one of its many phases."[80]

Examination of the outlook of conscriptionist leaders demonstrates that they were predominantly conservative in their views towards domestic and international affairs. In foreign policy, they were clearly *interventionists*, many favoring joining the Allies before 1917. All of them believed the United States would play an active interventionist role in international affairs for a long time to come. In their recognition of expanding U.S. economic and strategic interests, they were correct, but they were much less realistic in their assumption that permanent UMT&S was politically acceptable or that substantial military and naval forces would be necessary to protect U.S. interests in the immediate postwar period. At best they were partial-realists.[81]

Despite the fact that there was something of the *samurai* in Stimson, Roosevelt, and Wood, conscriptionist leaders were not the "militarists" portrayed by their adversaries. They did not seek a subordination of civilian considerations to the military, nor a massive standing army, nor the on-going, large-scale military imperialism which had characterized Napoleon III's France and late 19th century Prussia and which had given rise to the concept of "militarism."[82] It would be patently ridiculous to label as militarists sober-minded legalists like Elihu Root or Grenville Clark, who provided the real organizational leadership of the conscriptionist movement. Nor is preparedness adequately explained by attributing it to ambitious officers and greedy munitions-makers or simply patriotic nationalists.[83] Rather, it is more accurate to see preparedness leaders as *militant expansionists* who encouraged an active foreign policy for a burgeoning, industrial, world power, and who sought to establish a credible military reserve force for such a role and for national self-discipline and cohesion. Conscriptionists believed in the value of substantial military and naval establishments and sometimes military alliances, to protect the United States and its new overseas interests. In this they differed from isolationists, pacifists, and socialists. They also differed from liberal internationalists who accepted a limited military establishment, but who sought to restrict conflict through international commercial, legal, and political cooperation with the hope of banishing the use of military force from world affairs.[84]

Despite their proposal for a radical departure from America's preceding military format, preparedness leaders were overwhelmingly political *conservatives*. The progressives among them— Theodore Roosevelt, Henry L. Stimson, Grenville Clark, and George W. Perkins, a former Morgan partner—were as much a minority among preparedness leaders as they were among progressives. In this as on other important issues, the reformers themselves had split: the eastern corporate wing of progressivism followed Roosevelt, while the great majority of progressives, whether urban reformers or agrarian radicals, stood adamantly opposed to permanent UMT&S. And seemingly with good reason—the military format for a massive national reserve army raised through permanent UMT&S was not progressive, but profoundly conservative in its aims, focusing as it did on the use of force in international affairs, and the military socialization of youth in order to maintain the social and economic order in a corporate-dominated economy. These were not the goals of the majority of progressive reformers nor of most other Americans.[85]

But while permanent UMT was a conservative reform, in a predominantly progressive era even those seeking anti-progressive goals were led by political realities to employ the requisite political language of the day. Conscriptionists thus hailed the "equitable" and "democratic" nature of UMT, even though their use of these terms differed fundamentally from that by most progressives. Although progressivism was certainly not the only ideology available —democratic socialism or conservative constitutionalism were other choices—it proved to be the most politically influential. Conscriptionists were not the only conservatives to adopt progressive rhetoric to justify essentially anti-progressive goals.[86]

The position of conscriptionist leaders in society indicates that a significant relationship existed between changes in the social structure and new political attitudes and behavior. Urbanization and industrialization were accompanied by the rise of powerful new groups in society and it was from these groups—the new corporate elite and their professional allies—that the conscriptionist leadership emerged. Members of this corporate-oriented elite sought both to protect the interests of their group and to ensure national progress. In support of an expanded military and their vision of America's place in the world order, they issued appeals particularly to those in the new urban middle class of white-collar workers—salaried workers, professionals, and managers—who shared their vision of American growth and the means to sustain it.[87]

Like their conservative predecessors, the Federalists and the Whigs, these predominantly Old Guard Republicans feared challenges to their collective interests as threats to the social order. But the conscriptionists of the progressive era went beyond these earlier conservatives when they committed themselves to UMT&S.[88] Late 19th-century conservatives had feared a strong State might be used against capital, if dominated by democracy; early 20th-century conservatives in the preparedness movement had a greater willingness to accept and use an empowered State in their own interests. Many of the corporate leaders in the preparedness movement had become State-builders for conservative rather than liberal reasons, like the Federalists more than a century earlier.

Yet the conscriptionists remained rather reluctant State-builders. They did not want a continental style large standing army, nor a European style large bureaucratic State. Rather they sought greater efficiency through increased national coordination in mobilization of military manpower and through a reserve system. In the same manner, they sought increased planning and coordination in various aspects of industrial mobilization through combined public-private advisory bodies like the Council of National Defense. In all of these, including UMT&S, they sought devices which would increase national power through greater coordination and central direction yet at the same time preserve a balance of public and private interests.[89]

The military model that they proposed in UMT&S was very much a product of the times. These conservatives were frightened by the threats posed to the economic order by rapid urban and industrial change, by the massive numbers of immigrants coming to the nation's cities, and by the rise of socialism and other radical alternatives. The possibility of permanent divisions within society was especially disturbing to an elite which was also affected by the era's dominant ethos, denying the legitimacy of diverse and contending interest groups and stressing the ideal of a single, harmonious, national social order.

The U.S. Army was, of course, one of the oldest *national* institutions in a land which had emphasized localism and individualism. To a variety of Americans, the structure and values of the military seemed to offer a model for helping to achieve national goals. The

Union Army had been portrayed as God's terrible swift sword and the nation's strong right arm. In the 1880s, a utopia based upon a cooperative form of military organization had been prescribed by the nationalistic reformer Edward Bellamy.[90] Since the nationalistic 1890s the spread of military and paramilitary training in schools, youth organizations, and patriotic groups suggested that some Americans saw the self-discipline and intensive nationalism emphasized by the military as personally attractive and a valuable antidote for social ills.[91] For all the Jeffersonian antimilitarism that existed in the United States, many Americans could still believe in the value of widespread voluntary military training particularly on the local level. The popularity of the movement for UMT among certain groups showed that many were willing to carry such sentiment to the national level and make it compulsory as well.

In the half-dozen years between 1915 and 1920, the new corporate elite and their professional allies framed the issue of a new military format, including a military model of socialization, and sought to convince major segments of the public to support it and Congress to enact it. Yet in attempting this transformation of military institutions, this corporate-oriented elite directly challenged established institutions like the National Guard and the prevailing sense of the country's military tradition, the local citizen-volunteer. It also aroused the hostility of numerous groups already suspicious of the goals and leadership of big business. The fight over the new military format, like those over proposals for national regulatory agencies for business, banking, and the currency, was one of the important political struggles of the progressive era. Like these, it involved a dispute over definitions of public and private spheres, localism and nationalism, and ultimately, the relationship between the individual citizen and the State.

4

Resistance and Reform, 1914–1917

D ESPITE THE OUTBREAK of World War I and the creation of a powerful preparedness movement, most Americans, including President Woodrow Wilson, remained unconvinced of the need for any major change in military institutions. Consequently, few traditionalists took the preparedness groups seriously until late in the year. On Nov. 4, 1915 Wilson suddenly proposed a significant reorganization and expansion of the army and navy.[1] The conversion of the president, who had been a leading reformer and an outspoken critic of militarism, dramatically altered the context of the debate over the adequacy of the nation's armed forces.

The chief executive hastened to explain that he sought only "moderate" reorganization and expansion, an increase in the regular army by one-third (from 108,000 to 142,000) and, most importantly, creation of a strictly national ready reserve, a 400,000-man "Continental Army." These citizen-reservists would volunteer for two months of military training each summer for three years, and would be subject to emergency mobilization for an additional three years. The new Continental Army would replace the National Guard as the nation's ready reserve. Officers for it would be obtained from the Plattsburg camps and military training programs in colleges and universities as well as from former officers of the U.S. Army. Naturally, the Guard opposed such a threat to its position, but so did many Americans who were opposed to the idea of a large standing army and possible military intervention in Mexico, Europe, or Asia. There was considerable opposition to the cost of the defense buildup and the taxes necessary to pay for it. Even excluding the cost of proposed naval expansion, the addition to the ground forces would increase the federal military budget by 20 percent, approximately $200 million a year.[2]

There was much speculation about the reasons for Wilson's dramatic change of mind. It appears that international and political motives were more important than direct economic reasons.[3] Prominent Democrats advised Wilson that Roosevelt, Root, and other Republicans hoped preparedness could re-unite the GOP, which—if the 1912 schism over reform could be healed—would contain the majority of registered voters in the nation. Wilson also understood the influence of the preparedness movement, particularly in the urban East. He told his secretary of war in August 1915 that "the demand for reasonable preparedness is clear enough."[4]

Despite the opposition of many agrarian Democrats, workers, immigrants, and liberal pacifists, Wilson understood that many liberal internationalists, echoing the *New Republic*, had concluded by late summer of 1915 that given the provocative German submarine campaign, some military reorganization and expansion was necessary.[5] The president's most impelling motive seems to have been the course of international events. The timing of his action confirms the growing importance he placed on having credible military force to support his foreign policy.[6] Within four days after Berlin announced on Feb. 4, 1915 that it would unleash its submarines against maritime commerce, Wilson had met with his secretary of war to discuss suggestions ranging from increasing the National Guard to enacting some of General Wood's ideas about a Swiss-style system of widespread, short-term military training. Three months later, Wilson said privately he was willing to consider any plan to increase the army's efficiency or improve the military system.[7]

In May, 1915, the torpedoing of the *Lusitania* and the death of 128 Americans posed a direct challenge to Wilson's policy of holding Germany to "strict accountability" for American ships and lives lost in illegal submarine attacks. In a series of diplomatic exchanges, the president pressed a reluctant German government to abandon its terroristic submarine warfare. It was on July 21, 1915, the day he sent his third *Lusitania* note to Berlin, a virtual ultimatum that the sinking of a passenger liner without warning would be considered a "deliberately unfriendly" act, that Wilson also directed his defense secretaries to develop plans to enlarge the armed forces. Such a force would give Wilson more credibility with these world powers as he sought to avert American entry and mediate both a settlement of the war and a lasting peace.

Secretary of War Lindley M. Garrison, a former corporation lawyer and equity court judge from New Jersey, was more in sympathy with the views of the leaders of the preparedness movement than those of the president. At the same time, he recognized that divisions within the officer corps could be used by opponents to block any expansion and reform. Consequently, he issued a "muzzling order" prohibiting active duty officers from making statements on public policy, to prevent the army from "pulling in every direction and getting nowhere."[8] In his personal belief in UMT&S, he was joined within the administration by his assistant secretary of war, Henry Breckinridge, a San Francisco iron manufacturer, as well as by Assistant Secretary of the Navy Franklin D. Roosevelt of New York; Secretary of the Interior Franklin K. Lane of California; and Edward M. House, the Texas "colonel" who was Wilson's closest adviser in foreign affairs.[9]

The president, however, adamantly rejected *compulsory* military training in peacetime as well as any suggestion that the U.S. might prepare to intervene in the war. Garrison, therefore, directed the military planners to avoid such controversial issues as whether the army should be raised by voluntary enlistment or conscription and whether strategic planning should be for defensive or offensive action.[10] Despite the vigorous objections of "young Turks" in the General Staff's War College Division, most senior officers accepted the president's decision. In a meeting in Garrison's office, the only persons who voted for compulsory military training and service were the assistant secretary of war, the chief of staff, Gen. Hugh L. Scott, and the former chief of staff, Gen. William Witherspoon. The more cautious bureau chiefs, including Brig. Gen. Enoch H. Crowder, the judge advocate general, who ironically would later write the draft law and administer the draft in World War I, all voted against even a statement in favor of conscription, fearing that it would doom the entire proposal and might even lead Congress to slash the army's budget in retaliation.[11]

Although Garrison precluded any reference to compulsion in the administration's proposal, the General Staff was convinced that the public needed to be educated about the need for a mass citizen-reserve force based on compulsory training and service. Garrison therefore directed the War College Division to produce a "Statement of a Proper Military Policy," relegating the militia to purely local duty and recommending a wholly national army of 1,000,000. This would include a regular army of 250,000 with an additional 250,000 soldiers in a ready-reserve, in keeping with Uptonian and European thinking, and, in deference to General Wood's ideas, a second-line reserve of 500,000 citizen-soldiers prepared by nine months of military training.[12] Even though none of the planners believed that either the one million or half-a-million troops could be obtained through voluntarism alone, they studiously avoided any reference to conscription in their report. Nevertheless, by November 1915 it was an open secret in Washington that the General Staff viewed the Continental Army proposal as a step towards popular acceptance of compulsory military training and service, an opinion confirmed by the congressional testimony of several general officers in January 1916.[13]

With his amiable and kindly demeanor, General Scott quickly emerged as an effective advocate of conscription. A soldier-diplomat, he had joined the army as a replacement for one of the officers killed with Custer, and after learning Indian sign language, Spanish, and various Filipino dialects, served effectively as a negotiator rather than a combat leader. When Wilson was elected, Colonel Scott, whose brother was part of the Wilsonian faction on the Princeton faculty, visited the president-elect and urged him to support the army "progressives" like Leonard Wood against the bureau chiefs— "the political element"—who cooperated with the "little army" agrarians who controlled the House military affairs committee. Although Wilson did not support the arrogant Wood, he did appoint Major General Scott chief of staff from 1914 to 1917.[14]

In 1915–16, the president feared that Scott's advocacy of conscription might jeopardize the administration's proposal. Wilson's claim to a moderate centrist position had encouraged many other moderates to follow his lead, including those from groups previously opposed to any expansion of the army, such as immigrant ethnic groups, trade unions, farmers' associations, and progressive reformers. The *New Republic* endorsed Wilson's program for a stronger and truly national military establishment as a preliminary step to obtaining major national governmental programs of aid and direction for agriculture, employment, education, and public health—all under the banner of "real, industrial, community preparedness." Yet most Americans, and probably most progressives, refused to support Wilson's defense program.[15]

The national controversy over "preparedness" that erupted in 1915–16 demonstrates the newly dominant, issue-oriented, pressure-group politics which emerged in the progressive era. Traditional political parties had been assailed as "corrupt machines" and weakened by electoral reforms which disfranchised many recent immigrants and blacks. The result was a reduced, if more middle-class, electorate which was encouraged to participate more actively through "direct democracy" measures. This was an electorate of specific loyalties which could be drawn upon, often regardless of party identification, by charismatic candidates or through highly charged issues, emotionalized by the new mass media. The party system remained significant, particularly for the election and coordination of candidates in a political structure which was organized geographically. But national issues cut across such territorial boundaries, and modern means of group organization and communication facilitated the creation of a new means of political influence, the national pressure group.[16]

The National Security League and Military Training Camps Association were only two of dozens of such organizations formed in the wake of the successful lobbying of the prototype pressure group, the Anti-Saloon League, and the increased concentration of power in Washington. Like most national pressure groups, they viewed themselves as nonpartisan and rejected attempts to affiliate directly with a particular political party. Instead of relying primarily upon established parties to achieve their program, pressure groups, like the conscriptionist organizations, worked directly to mobilize public support and build a coalition of groups. Appeals to these groups were based on ideology or occupational self-interest, rather than on partisan political loyalties. Pressure group politics could work both ways, however. Those opposed to UMT and to the president's program also organized and sought in similar ways to mobilize public opposition. The public arena became a battleground in which contending groups contested over the nature of the American military format.[17]

Opposition to a major change in military institutions came from a wide variety of groups, who saw themselves as "antimilitarists," defending the American tradition. Among these were agrarians, immigrants, industrial workers, liberal pacifists, members of the women's movement, political and economic radicals, anarchists, and socialists. Opposition to expansion of the armed forces and to military intervention were virtually all that these groups shared. In fact, several were suspicious or overtly hostile to each other. But although antimilitarists failed to organize the kind of cohesive and sustained movement that characterized the preparedness movement, they still made an impact because they included several sizable elements. Agrarians formed the largest group, and the most influential, including as they did Jeffersonian advocates of individual liberty, local democracy, and the volunteer tradition. They felt they were facing a dangerous coalition of big business and the army; in Bryan's phrase, a "munitions-military conspiracy against democracy."[18] With more than half the American population living in rural areas of fewer than 2,500 inhabitants, particularly in the South and trans-Mississippi West, agrarian opposition was a powerful force. Both the National Farmers Union, with perhaps two million members, and the National Grange, with one million, took a stand against UMT&S and the Continental Army reserve. So did most representatives from rural areas on Capitol Hill. Together, they constituted an "antimilitarist" coalition of southern Democrats and Midwestern Republicans.[19]

In the South, race relations inevitably constituted part of the debate, for a UMT program might mean training blacks in the use of arms. Although most conscriptionists envisioned a program limited to whites, a few black leaders like author-diplomat James Weldon Johnson wanted to ensure that blacks were included in any military obligation as a step towards the full recognition of their rights as citizens. In their opposition, blatantly racist demagogues like Vardaman of Mississippi, Watson of Georgia, Blease of South Carolina, and Catts of Florida evoked memories of Reconstruction to bolster opposition to any national military program like UMT or Wilson's Continental Army reserve. They also tried, without success, to eliminate the four traditional black regiments in the regular army, but they did preclude the organization of such additional regiments in the prewar period.[20]

For a different reason, many union locals, city labor councils, and even a few national unions like the United Mine Workers urged Samuel Gompers, head of the five-million-member American Federation of Labor, to take a strong "antimilitaristic" stand. So bitter was labor over the use of the regular army and the National Guard to protect strike breakers that some unions denied membership to anyone serving in the military. Many workers feared that an expanded army might be used to break strikes. Radical workers' organizations like the socialist unions, the Socialist party, and the syndicalist Industrial Workers of the World staked their opposition on such grounds. Although the AFL leadership did condemn compulsory military training in peacetime, Gompers supported the president's proposal for a Continental Army reserve because he feared accusations of lack of patriotism and because he correctly viewed Wilson as a friend of the moderate trade unions and did not want to alienate him.[21]

Many ethnic groups wished to prevent the United States from joining the war on the side of the Allies and saw preparedness as a move in that direction. Millions of Americans of German or Irish descent felt considerable hostility towards Britain. Hundreds of thousands of Jews who had escaped Czarist pogroms had little desire to help Imperial Russia. Many immigrants had fled their native lands in part to avoid compulsory military service under authoritarian regimes and feared that similar programs were being advocated for America. Many refused to allow their children to join the Boy Scouts which held military-style drills. As one immigrant woman told a Chicago social worker: "This is what we came to America to get away from."[22] Despite such sentiment in the immigrant working-class settlements, many ethnic community leaders refused to oppose the president's proposal publicly for fear of giving nativists another chance to attack immigrants for divided loyalties and lack of assimilation.

Among the largely native-born American middle class, public opposition was led by liberal pacifists who were oriented towards social reform and social justice at home and abroad. They included social workers, labor lawyers, liberal publishers, "social gospel" clergymen, and feminists. It was in fact women of the suffrage and feminist movements who played the crucial role in organizing the new liberal pacifist organizations. In 1915, Jane Addams, prominent Chicago settlement-house leader and suffragist, founded the Women's Peace Party, whose affiliated groups represented more than 40,000 women.[23] Women pacifists and reformers, already experienced in organization-building and social causes, took the lead in the creation and direction of a new group designed to coordinate amorphous "antimilitarist" sentiment among farmers, workers, immigrants, radicals, and pacifists—the American Union Against Militarism (AUAM).

The AUAM was founded in November 1915 in reaction against the preparedness movement in general and President Wilson's proposal in particular. Its founders included social workers like Jane Addams and Lillian D. Wald, labor lawyers and feminists like Crystal Eastman and Amos Pinchot, liberal publishers like Paul U. Kellogg of the *Survey* magazine and Oswald Garrison Villard, grandson of an abolitionist and publisher of the *Nation* and the New York *Evening Post*, and clergymen like Unitarian minister John Haynes Holmes, Presbyterian minister Norman M. Thomas, and reform Jewish Rabbi Stephen A. Wise.[24] For operating expenses, they raised funds from among the executive committee and from affluent Philadelphia Quakers and the New York banking families including the Peabodys, Crams, Lewisohns and Schiffs. These families had "deserted" the corporate elite on this issue largely because of philosophical, religious, or ethnic differences. Like most other national issue-oriented pressure groups which developed in the progressive era, the core of the AUAM was its small but dedicated full-time staff. The director, in the New York headquarters, was Crystal Eastman, daughter of upstate New York Congregationalist ministers, graduate of Vassar College and N.Y.U. law school, committed social reformer, feminist and suffragist. She was joined by Charles T. Hallinan, a former newspaper reporter who had done publicity work for women's suffrage organizations and who now lobbied for the AUAM in Washington, D.C.

From their two offices came newsletters and scores of different printed items for allied organizations and the press; Eastman and Hallinan also coordinated speeches and congressional testimony. Through social and professional contacts among feminists, social workers, pacifists and others, AUAM leaders constructed a national organization with branches in 21 cities, with 6,000 members and an additional 50,000 sympathizers who could be called upon to write letters to Congress. With such capabilities, the AUAM was recognized on Capitol Hill as "the brains" of the "antimilitarist" movement.[25]

Structurally, the AUAM and National Security League were similar in several ways. Both operated through national headquarters which mobilized branches and constituent groups. The leadership of both organizations came from wealthy or economically-comfortable families in the northeast and had attended prestigious eastern colleges. Nevertheless, there were crucial differences between the two groups. While women were completely absent from the governing councils of the preparedness organizations, they played an important if not determinative role in the AUAM.[26] Furthermore, while conscriptionist leaders were linked to the new giant corporations or the military, the men and women of the AUAM had followed careers aimed at helping the less privileged and the oppressed—women, children, immigrants, blacks.

The eastern urbanites who led the AUAM had little in common with other "antimilitarist" leaders except their suspicion of big business. Unlike the Ivy League graduates of the AUAM, agrarian leaders like Bryan, Senator Robert M. La Follette of Wisconsin, and House majority leader Claude Kitchin of North Carolina had been graduated from state colleges. Most began their careers as small-town lawyers. With a different, often more limited, view of the expansion and role of the national government, they sought to protect the parochial agricultural interests of their predominantly rural regions. Actively "antimilitarist" socialist labor leaders like Eugene V. Debs; Joseph Cannon, organizer for the Mine, Mill and Smelter Workers of America; and James Mauer, head of the Pennsylvania Federation of Labor, were usually self-educated, former skilled workers. As socialists, they accepted a larger and more radical role for the State than most progressive reformers, but until such times as it was taken over by the workers, they believed the national government would be largely influenced by big business. "Antimilitarists" differed on foreign as well as military policy. Most agrarians from the South and Midwest were ardent isolationists while socialists and progressives held actively internationalistic views. Neither the agrarians nor the labor leaders felt comfortable or fully trusted the eastern social reformer leadership of the AUAM, considering them paternalistic and often unreliable. Their relationship remained a temporary coalition of convenience.[27]

The AUAM had considerable prestige and tangible financial resources as well as access to the media and to the president who knew and respected several of its leaders. Largely ignoring the reserve officer camps, the AUAM focused on the dangers of army expansion and UMT&S.[28] These would be tremendously costly to taxpayers and to America as a whole because of the loss to the economy of the labor and wages of millions of trainees. Rejecting conscriptionists' claims that military training built up both character and body, the "antimilitarists" quoted physical education instructors who claimed that the constricted movements of military drill were not physically helpful and could even prove harmful to adolescents if done excessively.

Nor did military training produce the right kind of citizens. "Antimilitarists" accepted the conscriptionists' claim that such an experience made young men more responsive to authority and more obedient workers, but they charged that this ran counter to American values of individual initiative and freedom. Conditioning the people to "blind obedience" would cripple their ability for self-government, Villard warned. "We have always valued the American's self-assertiveness—yes, his refusal to recognize masters, his independence of thought and action. . . . We hated the servile obedience of the foreigner. Universal conscription . . . drives men into intellectual slavery."[29] George W. Nasmyth, sociologist at the University of Wisconsin and author of the most extensive AUAM pamphlet, belittled the claim that UMT would foster democracy: "Those who believe that class distinctions can be broken down and democracy created by regimenting men and forcing them to drill together, have missed the central idea of democracy which is based on the principle of voluntary cooperation, of equality of opportunity, and the abolition of caste privileges."[30]

Max Eastman, editor of a radical journal, the *Masses*, challenged the claim that conscription would ensure equity of sacrifice, pointing out that while the rich lad simply deferred going to college for a year or two, the poor boy lost the wages he and his family needed to sustain themselves. He predicted that in actual practice, rich young men would obtain exemptions.[31] Skeptics suspected that fiscal conservatives were really trying to create a large but "cheap" army in which the poor would be forced to serve without adequate compensation. Even though it failed to do justice to the conscriptionist idea of the military obligation of all citizens, this suspicion was not entirely unfounded. Conscriptionists were cost-conscious and wanted to eliminate enlistment bonuses, competitive wages, or other financial inducements which would increase the cost of raising an army.

"Antimilitarists" also argued against the military need and value of UMT&S, maintaining that the United States could continue to rely upon its navy and coastal fortifications and a small regular army augmented by wartime volunteers. Former Civil War officers, like Nathan A. Miles, now retired commanding general, reaffirmed the value of volunteers as being more reliable than conscripts.[32] Voluntarism had provided more than adequate numbers to win the Mexican and Spanish-American Wars. Whatever else "antimilitarists" said against the army expansion and conscription, their primary argument was that such drastic changes were unnecessary. They ridiculed the suggestion that foreign forces were likely to invade the United States or anywhere in the Western Hemisphere. The Atlantic remained a formidable barrier and the U.S. Navy was the third largest in the world. The bloody failure of the British and Australian amphibious assault on Turkey's Gallipoli peninsula in 1916 had demonstrated the difficulty if not impossibility of a successful invasion against a properly defended coast. Furthermore, the war was depleting the major powers of Europe. As one "antimilitarist" declared, "The whole idea of a nation desiring to gobble up the United States is preposterous."[33]

In reality, neither the preparedness movement nor the Wilson administration feared an invasion of the United States; rather the largely unspoken rationale for a larger army was to support a more active U.S. role in the world. "Antimilitarists" suspected that an expanded army would give impetus to a greater readiness to employ military force and a more belligerent foreign policy. Recalling the intensification of national hatreds produced by the massive military build-up in Europe before the war, diplomatic historian Carleton J.H. Hayes reportedly told an "antimilitarist" student rally at Columbia University in 1916 that "universal military training is un-American and inhuman. It will lead in time straight to war."[34]

Many Americans agreed that conscription was ultimately interventionist. During 1915 and 1916, members of Congress, particularly those from the isolationist South and Midwest, received thousands of letters from constituents warning against military expansion and seeing it as a major step towards U.S. entry into the war. Even though few politicians said this publicly or privately, the existence of so many such letters indicate that the debate over preparedness and the proposed changes in the military format in 1915–16 was related in the public mind to the debate over the relationship of the United States to the war.[35]

Despite the many differences among them, "antimilitarists" expressed a common suspicion of the new national centers of power— the corporate and financial interests, the national government, and potentially, the army. Many farmers, workers, and social reformers feared the impact of a corporate-dominated, powerful State. Rep. George Huddleston of Alabama predicted in January 1917, that UMT would mean that ultimately the national government would investigate and intervene in people's residence, education, occupation, and marital arrangements.[36] Students of the progressive era, by focusing on strong nationalists like Theodore Roosevelt, have often neglected progressives like Addams and Villard, who remained deeply suspicious of the centralized power of the nation-State. Many continued to fear that business would corrupt politics, gain control of government, and use it against the interests of other Americans, a fear that made many progressives reluctant State-builders.[37]

The struggle in Congress over the president's proposal to expand the regular army and build a large national reserve force became the major battle on Capitol Hill during the winter of 1915–16.[38] It soon became clear that although the Democrats controlled both houses of Congress, the president's moderate preparedness plan could not muster a majority in the lower chamber, particularly in an election year. After public hearings in January 1916, Rep. James Hay of Virginia, chair of the House Military Affairs Committee, sought to fashion an acceptable compromise, one which would provide a reserve force, but would not alienate Democratic constituents and break up the winning political coalition of the agrarian South and West that had elected Wilson president in 1912.[39] The Hay bill accepted the increase of the regular army to 140,000, but replaced the proposed national Continental Army reserve with a plan nearly to quadruple the National Guard from 125,000 to 450,000 through vastly increased federal funding.[40] Hay's compromise would maintain the locally oriented militia units as the national ready reserve, but the Guardsmen would take a dual oath to the nation and their states and—as Hay confided to the president—in wartime the National Guard units could be drafted into federal service.[41] A response to American military traditions and the political influence of the National Guard Association, the Hay compromise sought to forestall more radical change by providing some additional military power to the national government.[42]

Within the halls of Congress, the National Guard Association proved more influential than did the AUAM, labor, or farm groups in shaping the military format.[43] Because it favored increased military preparedness, the Guard had been slow to mobilize against the president's proposal, but when its leaders realized that the War Department and the conscriptionist organizations sought to eliminate them as a national ready reserve, they launched a vigorous counterattack.[44] Although some of the eastern militia officers joined the national conscriptionists, the majority of officers in the National Guard Association were business and civic leaders from the South and West with considerable influence in state and local politics as well as with local members of Congress. "Under the cloak of 'preparedness,'" the National Guard magazine argued, "the real purpose of the effort that is being made is to change the military policy of the nation instead of perfecting the one established by the Constitution."[45] "National and professional," the editor warned, were not necessarily better than "local and amateur."[46] Some Guard officers proposed a nationally funded program of UMT&S in the militia instead of the regular army, a proposal greatly feared by conscriptionists because it had the political potential to derail their movement for a wholly national reserve force.[47]

Despite the president's position as leader of the agrarian-based Democratic party, Wilson personally favored a national rather than a dual military establishment. Publicly committed to his Continental Army reserve plan, he initially rejected Hay's personal entreaties. Instead, he took his case directly to the people. For an entire week in January 1916, the president toured a dozen major cities in the East and Midwest, urging support for "reasonable preparedness" in order to maintain American rights, honor, and the security of the Western Hemisphere. Despite the applause of the urban crowds, the attitude on Capitol Hill remained unchanged. Having made his appeal, and now in a position to blame an obstinate Congress if preparedness became a major issue in the fall election, Wilson accepted the political realities of the situation. Abandoning the Continental Army plan, he left the details of military preparedness to Congress. Disgusted, Garrison and Breckinridge resigned in protest.[48] When the president abandoned the Garrison plan, pressure for military reorganization hissed out of Congress like air out of a balloon. The collapse of congressional attention proved only temporary, for in the spring of 1916, a threat of war with revolutionary Mexico rapidly revived interest in ensuring an adequate American army. A party of Mexican irregulars from General Francisco "Pancho" Villa's forces raided several border towns, killing nineteen Americans. Responding to demands for action, Wilson dispatched 5,000 U.S. Regulars, under Brig. Gen. John J. Pershing, on a "punitive expedition" in pursuit of Villa.

The threat of war with Mexico drove Congress into action. With Wilson's approval, the House quickly passed the Hay bill. It was a close and sectional vote, with southern Democrats and midwestern Republicans supporting it against a bipartisan coalition of eastern nationalists. The Senate, however, favored a large, solely national army and by a narrow margin adopted a bill, patterned after the General Staff's proposals, which would have doubled the regular army to 175,000, and created an entirely national reserve, the entire force totaling nearly 1,000,000. Pushing this through was the chair of the Senate Military Affairs Committee, George E. Chamberlain, a maverick Democrat from Oregon, originally a Southerner, whose policy reflected his personal belief in UMT as well as West Coast fears about Japanese expansion.[49] A conference committee proved unable to reach a compromise on the two radically different versions of the proper military format for America.

Although they viewed the National Guard as "antidemocratic" and "militaristic" and even more politically influential than the regular army, AUAM leaders focused their attack on the Chamberlain bill as the more extreme proposal. Touring a dozen cities, they satirized "militarists" with a paper-mâché dinosaur exhibit, "All Armor Plate—No Brains."[50] Carefully, they avoided attacking the president, because they still considered Wilson a domestic reformer and a liberal internationalist and immensely preferable to bellicose Republicans like Roosevelt. On the afternoon of May 8, 1916, a delegation from the AUAM was ushered into the White House, where they reported that their tour had disclosed widespread opposition to "preparedness." They urged the president to reconsider his support for expansion of the army and navy.

In response, Wilson remained polite but firm, rejecting what he called the extremes of militarism or absolute pacifism. He agreed with the AUAM delegation on the importance of America's moral leadership in the world, but defended his program as "reasonable preparation" consistent with American traditions and the current circumstances. He maintained that the regular army, small and dispersed from the Atlantic seaboard to the Philippine Islands, was inadequate even to protect the border with Mexico. But there were larger matters on the president's mind, and he spoke candidly on the relationship between military force and foreign policy goals. The United States had undertaken to keep European influences out of the Western hemisphere. In addition, if it were to play an important role in the larger cause of world peace, it would need significant military and naval forces. In a postwar peace conference, he said, the major powers would rightly or wrongly regard as negligible the counsel of countries believed to be militarily helpless. He noted that there was a growing sentiment for a postwar "family of nations" to prevent wars, an idea supported by many pacifists and liberal internationalists. "Now, in the last analysis, the peace of society is obtained by force," the president declared. ". . . And if you say we shall not have any war, you have got to have the force to make that 'shall' bite. The rest of the world, if America takes part in this thing, will have the right to expect from her that she contributes her element of force to the general understanding."[51]

In contrast, the president seemed uncharacteristically imprecise on the subject of conscription, distinguishing between military "training" and "service," hedging about universal compulsory training ("I didn't say I believed in it. In my judgment, to use the phrase of a friend, my mind is to let on the subject. I would say merely that it is not contrary to the spirit of American traditions."), and differentiating between widespread military training and governmental organization of the people into a large army subject to the dictates of a particular group.[52] Three months earlier, in February 1916, Wilson had written unambiguously to Garrison that "I do not at all agree with you in favoring compulsory enlistment for training. . . . "[53] Yet, by May, he had become more open to universal military training, even though such training would presumably have to include compulsion in order to be universal. Even more discouraging to the AUAM, the president did not see a threat to democracy in either the movement for UMT or in the discipline involved in military training. He doubted that six weeks of such training would endanger the citizenry and he argued to skeptical "antimilitarists" that the widespread training he had in mind involved neither extensive discipline nor an obligation to serve in reserve units. As he put it, there would be "no authority over the man in training; he merely volunteers? Don't you see what I mean? He is not thereby bound to an organization in which he looks to some particular person to give him orders. That would be organization."[54] Discouraged, the delegates concluded that their only hope was that Wilson was, at heart, an "antimilitarist." A few weeks after the meeting with the AUAM leadership, Wilson announced his support for what he called "universal voluntary training," if the people wanted it, with volunteering compelled only by the force of public opinion.[55]

Only when a second raid by Villaista irregulars killed more Americans and escalated the possibility of war did Congress finally accept a compromise and enact the National Defense Act of May 13,

1916. Although essentially a political victory for the National Guard, this legislation offered something to almost every interested party. The General Staff obtained a near-doubling of the regular army to 175,000 in increments over a five-year period and, in case of war, a tripling to 298,000. "Antimilitarists" could draw some satisfaction that the Continental Army reserve had gone down in defeat and that the law did *not* authorize compulsory military training in peacetime. Bryanite agrarians also obtained authorization for the federal government to build and operate a plant to produce nitrates used in making explosives, a gesture to the idea that taking the profit out of munitions-making might curtail pressures for a defense build-up and war.[56]

Plattsburgers obtained federal funding for reserve officer training camps, to be run jointly each summer by the War Department and the MTCA, for men between the ages of 25 and 43, with graduates commissioned in a newly created Officers Reserve Corps (ORC). In addition, Congress established a Reserve Officer Training Corps (ROTC) on various campuses to tap the increasing college manpower pool as a source for reserve junior officers.[57] Through uniform national programs of appointment, training, and certification, these programs could produce large numbers of pretrained national reserve officers and replace the locally oriented officers of the traditional U.S. Volunteers.

As the primary ready reserve, the National Guard was to receive an influx of federal funding to enable it to expand incrementally over the next six years to a force of approximately 450,000—an enlargement many regulars feared would mean reduced appropriations for the regular army.[58] However, the Guard would be subject to close supervision and control by the regular army to ensure uniform standards of fitness, training and equipment. To guarantee the national government's supremacy over this reserve, each Guardsman would be required, for the first time, to take a dual oath of allegiance to both the state and the national governments, with the call of the commander-in-chief deemed supreme. In a sweeping assertion of national authority, the president was empowered to *draft* the National Guard—the organized militia—directly into federal service in time of war or other national emergency. In regard to other male citizens, the preamble of the National Defense Act of 1916 reasserted the principle of universal military *obligation* among all able-bodied male citizens between the ages of 18 and 45—the so-called unorganized militia. However, since the statement was not part of the substantive provisions of the statute, it had no effect in law.[59] Still, it indicated that even the agrarian-dominated, locally oriented House of Representatives was willing to recognize a relationship between the privileges and the obligations of citizenship and to assert, obliquely at least, the principle that all male citizens had a military obligation in wartime.

Mexico became the testing ground for the new reserve arrangements. Two weeks after the enactment of the law, further border raids led Wilson to employ his new powers. On June 18, he summoned 100,000 National Guardsmen into federal service to seal off the border. The border mobilization of the summer of 1916 provided a lesson for many Americans. For with 105,000 militiamen patrolling the Rio Grande and the regular army pursuing Villaistas deep into Mexico, the raids ended within six weeks. Yet, conscriptionists claimed the episode demonstrated the failure of the militia and the volunteer system. Extended patrol duty on the hot, dusty border was not simply frustrating and boring, it also showed clearly that military service had different impact upon urban and rural Guardsmen. Farmers were better able to sustain a long absence from the workplace than urban workers and managers. Loss of wages and salaries caused such distress to urban Guardsmen and their families that, under pressure from the Guard Association, Congress belatedly voted them compensatory pay for active military duty.[60] Eastern urban Guardsmen, conscriptionist organizations, and the metropolitan press stressed the "inequity" of placing the full burden of service on volunteers while the "less patriotic" (some emphasized recent immigrants) remained at home. In short, conscriptionists began to argue that it was more "equitable" and less socially and economically disruptive if society determined who should serve in the army and who should remain at home. Some conscriptionists began to argue publicly that the volunteer system should be replaced in wartime with *selective* compulsory national military service.[61]

This argument of the need to compel the "less patriotic" to serve in the army was reinforced by the decision of the British government in 1916 to introduce national conscription for the first time in the nation's history. Massive casualties led to seemingly endless demands for replacements. Furthermore, many of the early volunteers had been skilled munitions workers who clearly were more valuable to the war effort in the factory than in the trenches. Politically, there was a widespread, but disputed, belief that large numbers of able-bodied unmarried men had refused to enlist; the draft was adopted partly to force these "slackers" into the army. Despite a schism in the leadership over such a coercive instrument, the Liberal government, under pressure from Conservatives and the military, reluctantly adopted a national wartime selective draft in 1916.[62] Britain's experience helped legitimize the idea of national wartime conscription in America because it weakened the Anglo-Saxon volunteer military tradition.[63]

The irony of justifying national conscription on the basis of *both* equity and industrial efficiency was that, despite some attempts to reconcile them, the two were frequently in conflict. It was only rhetorically true that "the man at the lathe is just as much a part of the defensive organization of this country as the man with the musket [sic] on the firing line," as was claimed by Howard Coffin, vice-president of the Hudson Motor Car Company and chair of the Navy's Industrial Preparedness Committee.[64] Certainly the positions of the worker and the soldier were *not* comparable or equitable in terms of compensation or risk. It was not equity but economic efficiency and industrial productivity that was the goal of Coffin and other key advocates of selective conscription. A selective draft would mean that skilled workers and managers deemed vital to the economy and war production could be kept at work while "non essential" workers were forced into the army. This, Coffin concluded, was the only way "to raise an army upon a business principle."[65]

But the notion of a selective draft, like the idea of U.S. military intervention in the European war, was seldom addressed directly or publicly in 1916 because of the widespread public sentiment against both. Although many in the military and civilian elites privately saw a selective national draft as economically and militarily advantageous in wartime, the public debate on military format remained largely focused on the provisions of the National Defense Act of 1916 and the advisability of a permanent policy of universal military training.[66]

Conscriptionists made considerable strides in the summer and fall of 1916 in their campaign to educate the public and expand the coalition of groups behind UMT&S. Most important were business, financial, and industrial organizations—from the National Association of Manufacturers, representing medium-sized industry, to the newly formed U.S. Chamber of Commerce, which spoke for small businesses across the country, and whose branches endorsed UMT, 889 to 56, the opposition being primarily in the deep South.[67] Additional endorsements came from educators, the clergy, and physicians. UMT was particularly appealing to physicians and public health workers, not simply for national defense but because it might be a means of involving the federal government in national health care. Although many teachers and professors opposed peacetime compulsory military training, the National Educational Association ended its opposition in 1916 and UMT won a number of converts, particularly among educational administrators, school principals, and superintendents, who wished to develop a sense of patriotism and increased discipline among youth. Some college and university presidents emphasized the need for college-trained reserve officers to lead such a UMT-prepared citizen-reserve army. Many clergymen actively opposed the movement for UMT and no denomination endorsed it, but conscriptionists won influential support from several leading Protestant and Roman Catholic religious leaders, including the Rev. William T. Manning, rector of New York's Trinity Episcopal Church on Wall Street; the Rev. Lyman Abbot, pastor of the Plymouth Congregational Church in Brooklyn; and John Cardinal Gibbons of Baltimore, the senior Roman Catholic prelate in the United States. Under the leadership of Mayor John Purroy Mitchel of New York City, a National Defense Conference of Mayors from major cities adopted a resolution favoring UMT.[68]

The domestic aspects of UMT proved especially appealing to many of these groups. To those concerned with the increased juvenile delinquency, it would take up "the slack of idleness" during what one economist called "the hoodlum period" in late adolescence. "Businessmen are not afraid of compulsory military education," the U.S. Chamber of Commerce reported. "They believe it will develop a better balanced and more self-disciplined youth from which to build succeeding generations of American citizens." Cardinal Gibbons declared UMT would help restore order and respect among youth:

> [It will] instill into them the spirit of obedience to lawful authority, a virtue too often disregarded in our land of freedom. It will teach them the dignity of obedience, which they will regard not as an act of servility to man, but as a homage rendered to God since they will consider their superiors as His representatives.[69]

From his own observation of Japanese conscription, General John J. Pershing asserted that military training "inspires respect for constituted authority . . . demonstrates the necessity for obedience to law, and makes better and more useful citizens."[70]

Conscriptionists demonstrated the effectiveness of modern advertising and publicity techniques. They hired professionals to run the campaign. These drew upon the celebrity-endorsement system so effective in tobacco advertising, and obtained endorsements for UMT from figures as varied as former President William Howard Taft and Connie Mack, baseball manager of the Philadelphia Athletics. Each was promptly publicized in order to create the impression of a bandwagon effect. Similarly, their message was spread through the local press, pulpit, and political platform. In the spring of 1916, the National Security League launched a series of "preparedness parades," mammoth processions of flag-carrying residents led by prominent citizens. By the end of the year, most of the major newspapers in the country had endorsed UMT&S.[71]

Nevertheless, there was a surge of antiwar and antimilitary sentiment in the summer of 1916, perhaps stemming from intensified anti-British feelings generated by London's increased tightening of its maritime restrictions, including use of the "blacklist" against certain American firms, and its ruthless suppression of the Easter rebellion in Ireland. Furthermore, antiwar sentiment mounted with the daily news of additional Allied casualties in the unsuccessful Somme offensive, 600,000 killed and wounded between July and November, with the stalemated war seemingly endless.[72] Most politicians responded to this groundswell of American sentiment, especially in view of the November presidential election. Although conscriptionists included some of the major contributors to the Republican party, they were unable to get public commitments from the party's convention or presidential candidate, Charles Evans Hughes, former New York governor and associate justice of the U.S. Supreme Court. Caught in a quandary between the wishes of some of these major benefactors and the antipathy of large numbers of Republican voters, particularly ethnic Germans and Scandinavians in the Middle West, party leaders quailed. As a member of the platform committee reported bitterly: "They [the committee] all admitted readily enough that we must come to universal training, but they did not think the people were ripe for it, and they were afraid to risk it."[73] "Antimilitarists" easily obtained condemnation of UMT&S from the urban, labor-dominated Socialist party and the rural-oriented Prohibitionists, and although the Democrats avoided a direct statement, they claimed credit for averting militarism and avoiding U.S. entry into the war.[74] Virtually all the normally Republican AUAM leaders supported Wilson's re-election; however, their confidence was shaken in late summer by fear of a militaristic plot involving the so-called "Hayden joker."

A last-minute, little-noticed rider attached to the long and intricate National Defense Act of 1916 as it cleared Congress, the "Hayden joker" authorized the president, in wartime, to use a *draft* to fill reserve battalions of militia replacements if voluntary enlistment proved inadequate. Although most legislators dismissed it as inconsequential when the AUAM lobbyist discovered it, "antimilitarists" saw it as a surreptitious, possibly conspiratorial, attempt to authorize conscription; the liberal pacifists pressed Wilson to denounce it and press for its repeal.[75] Although expressing sympathy with their concern, Wilson was unwilling to see the issue of wartime conscription raised in the midst of his re-election campaign and at a time

when the stalemated war was entering such a desperate phase that
the United States might be drawn in by reckless German action.
After his electoral victory in November, as he began a major peace
initiative, Wilson steadfastly declined to seek repeal of this provision. Neither he nor his new secretary of war wanted to repudiate
the principle of wartime conscription which lay behind it.[76] Rep.
James Hay viewed the "joker" as a "legislative fluke" and rejected
attempts to repeal it. He reportedly told his colleagues that the
"draft was inevitable in war and Congress should recognize the fact
and give the military authorities the power they need. . . ."[77]

Neither the military nor the corporate-oriented civilian "preparedness" elites had been able to achieve all, or even the most
important, of their goals. Elected federal officials had been concerned with the economic and political costs of the military format
as well as its military effectiveness. Given the absence of military
necessity and the relatively high economic and political costs of the
conscriptionists' program, a majority simply could not be obtained
for such changes as elimination of the militia, complete nationalization of the military establishment, and UMT&S. Yet without the
"preparedness" movement, there probably would have been little
significant change in the military format before the United States
actually went to war. In 1915 and 1916, the business and professional elites which dominated the preparedness organizations put
the issue on the national agenda and framed the public debate. With
the help of Wood and Roosevelt, they put forward an alternative to
the old U.S. Volunteers and to the European model of a mass conscript-reservist force based on two or three years service with the
regular army. That alternative, a short-term UMT in peacetime and
a selective draft in wartime, had proven acceptable to a sizable and
influential minority of Americans.

In the 1915-16 debate over "modernization" of the military format, progressives had generally taken an obstructionist position,
the majority even opposing President Wilson's moderate proposal
for a limited national reserve based on voluntary short-term military training. Consequently, the format provided by the National
Defense Act of 1916 represented a compromise largely between
cosmopolitan urban conservatives and localistic agrarian traditionalists. When the United States entered the war in the spring of
1917, the Wilson administration (without time or occasion for an
extensive national debate) would turn substantially to the selective
wartime draft which had been advocated primarily by the conservative conscriptionists, modified somewhat by liberal-progressive
ideas and various interest groups. Because mainstream progres-

sives had not prepared a plan for a liberal democratic military format during the pre-1917 period, they were unable and, in fact, largely unwilling to develop a comprehensive proposal on such short notice.

If the progressives had so desired, they could have drawn on then current liberal and radical ideas about military institutions. One possibility was the proposal for a national defensive militia, a classless and defense-oriented "people's army," advocated by the French socialist leader Jean Jaurès. (For most of the period after the Second World War, the Israeli Defense Force resembled such a democratic, defensive-oriented format.)[78] In America, a few suggestions for a progressive army had been made in 1916 by former Secretary of the Interior Walter Fisher, a progressive Midwestern Republican, and Senator John D. Works, a California Republican. Fisher recommended eliminating the anti-democratic caste system between officers and enlisted men, replacing the harsh code of military justice and discipline, and increasing soldiers' wages, all in an attempt to make the army attractive to a broader socio-economic spectrum of Americans. Senator Works and some other westerners suggested that the peacetime army be employed productively to fight floods and forest fires and to help build roads, irrigation canals, and other public works projects, a role rejected by most professional military officers and, for entirely different reasons, by organized labor. A progressive army might encourage upward social mobility through specific educational and vocational programs to teach skills valuable in the civilian economy, as Garrison's successor, Secretary of War Newton D. Baker, former progressive mayor of Cleveland, later suggested when he established "the Khaki University" to keep the doughboys occupied in the months after the armistice. However, none of these suggestions won priority on the liberal agenda.[79]

No doubt progressives could have influenced the nature of the American military format considerably if they had concerned themselves with the fact that some kind of army would continue in peacetime and that a large military force would have to be raised in wartime. On the whole, however, progressives were influenced by the liberal, antimilitary tradition, particularly strong among certain elites in the North. In peacetime, that tradition had been largely to scorn the military as archaic and anti-liberal and war as generally a temporary aberration. Both were usually considered impediments to social progress, although occasionally war could be a worthy crusade.[80]

In a period of ascendent reform, the comparatively small effort of progressives to influence the shape of the modern American military establishment as it was fashioned through a combination of inherited traditions and new legislation in 1916, 1917, and, later 1920, was more than simply unfortunate. It represented a fundamental flaw in American liberal thought. For in the long run, this abdication of responsibility took on major significance, because the military format of the World War I era became the basis for the format the United States would use in the Second World War, the Korean War, the Vietnam War, and indeed for a considerable part of the 20th century.

CHAPTER

5

Decision to Draft the Doughboys, February–March 1917

THE DRAMA AND THE EVENTS of early 1917 which led to U.S. entry into the World War—Berlin's reckless decision to launch all-out submarine warfare, the intrigue evidenced by the Zimmermann telegram, and the torpedoing of American merchant ships with the death of their crews—are well known, even if Wilson's decision for war has remained the subject of debate. His subsequent decision for a selective draft has been much less studied, even though it led to the primary instrument for raising America's wartime armies for the rest of the 20th century. An examination of that decision provides new insight into the attitude of the president as he took the country into war, the nature of decision-making in the executive branch, and the relationship of liberalism to war and the military.[1]

Although Wilson did not openly espouse a wartime national draft before 1917, he had not been averse to the idea. In his *History of the American People*, first published in 1901, Wilson had seen nothing inherently wrong with national conscription during the Civil War draft; his main criticism was that the law was inequitable and inadequately managed.[2] During 1916–17, Wilson had come to see a selective wartime draft as the most effective means of raising a mass army without disrupting an industrial economy. Like most progressives, he opposed compulsory peacetime UMT, but as he had indicated privately in 1916, Wilson (while not seeking prewar authority for wartime conscription) was unwilling to do anything to undermine it as a prerogative of the national government.[3]

The idea of wartime conscription coincided with Wilson's increased willingness to use the powers of the federal government in an interdependent, national industrial economy.[4] The selective draft was a device by which the State could coordinate the extraction of manpower from the labor force. It fitted Wilson's belief that complete reliance on the market system was often harmful to the larger public interest, a belief reinforced in this case by the British experience with munitions workers who had enlisted in the army. "The idea of the draft is not only the drawing of men into the military service of the Government," Wilson later wrote on May 4, 1917 while Congress was still considering his proposal, "but the virtual assigning of men to the necessary labor of the country. *Its central idea was to disturb the industrial and social structure of the country just as little as possible.*"[5]

This appreciation of the industrial benefits of a selective draft over a system of haphazard voluntary enlistment was shared by Wilson's new secretary of war, Newton D. Baker, who had succeeded Lindley M. Garrison in March 1916. When appointed, the diminutive, bespectacled lawyer-reformer had a reputation as a pacifist because he had earlier denounced "preparedness" as based on a manufactured war scare and designed to stimulate a "militaristic" spirit. Professional soldiers were skeptical at first, but General Scott, the chief of staff, worked diligently to convert him to UMT&S. Although Baker was impressed by the improvements in physical stamina and general health produced by military training and by the batches of newspaper editorials General Scott forwarded to him, he understood that the president and the Democratic party were opposed to UMT&S. Despite his reputation as a "pacifist" and his postwar recollection that General Scott had persuaded him of the need for a wartime draft, Baker as early as January 1916 had privately expressed sympathy with the idea of a selective draft to raise a large wartime army with a minimum of social and economic disruption.[6]

While accepting the preparedness leaders' interpretation of the superior efficiency of a selective wartime draft over the haphazard, local-national Volunteer system, Wilson and Baker disagreed with conscriptionists' ideas about UMT and foreign policy. Permanent UMT&S was costly, disruptive, politically unacceptable, and unnecessary. Warfare was not inevitable and the role of the United States was to reform rather than police the international order. Neither Wilson nor Baker was a pacifist in the non-resistant sense, but, unlike Roosevelt, they saw force as a last resort. Although Wilson employed the armed forces on a number of occasions during his eight years in office, particularly in the Caribbean and Central America, he did so reluctantly, under pressure, and often with little faith in the ultimate effectiveness of military force.[7] Suspicious of "jingoes," Wilson had at least twice rebuked the military for allegedly trying to push the country into war.[8]

By 1917, Wilsonian foreign policy emphasized the end of isolationism and its replacement with the promotion of constructive international diplomacy and trade to achieve American interests and ideals. Within this context, Wilson maintained the policy of preserving the Western Hemisphere free from European incursion and helped enlarge the concept of the "Open Door" for U.S. interests in China to Latin America as well. In response to the European war, Wilson proclaimed U.S. neutrality, a policy reinforced by his concern about the war's effect upon America's ethnically diverse population. Wilson also endorsed neutral maritime rights. When both sides infringed them, the president agreed to subject British violations of property rights to postwar adjudication, but—particularly after the torpedoing of the *Lusitania*—he considered the loss of civilian lives from terroristic German submarine attacks to require immediate settlement and cessation. Through firm negotiation backed up by increases in the army and navy, Wilson had eventually obtained virtually a complete cessation of submarine warfare. Yet, the president realized that in desperation Germany might eventually force him into a choice between national humiliation or entry into an unpopular war. To avoid such a choice, Wilson made a number of determined efforts to mediate an end to the war, including an unprecedented offer of U.S. participation in a post-war league of nations as an immediate inducement to an early, negotiated peace and a long-term instrument to reform and stabilize the international order.[9]

In a desperate gamble, Berlin resumed U-boat warfare on February 1, 1917 and, as U.S. entry became increasingly probable, public debate over the American military format began to shift from the nature of a permanent military manpower policy to the proper method of mobilizing a wartime army, although conscriptionists still hoped to achieve both a permanent policy of UMT in peace and a selective draft in war. Even if they had not already endorsed UMT&S, most of the elites and the press, as well as the attentive urban public, endorsed the idea of a selective wartime draft.[10] Conscriptionist organizations launched a major drive against isolationism and antidraft sentiment in the South and Midwest, with former President Taft, Henry L. Stimson, and others touring the cities of these rural regions and appealing especially to the middle and upper classes there. A major attempt to convert Midwestern elites was made by the newly organized Universal Military Training League in Chicago under the direction of the chief executive officer of Sears, Roebuck and Company, the nation's largest retail merchandiser.[11] Led by J.P. Morgan's brother-in-law, conscriptionists also helped prevent the southern and western elements of the National Guard Association from blocking conscription into a *national* army.[12]

In reality, the major issue was not state versus national conscription, or the possibility of UMT, but whether the wartime army would be raised through a national draft or through the traditional U.S. Volunteers. Faced with such a choice, most cosmopolitan nationalists—whether Republican or Democrat, liberal or conservative—who supported U.S. entry and believed in nationally coordinated mobilization readily urged a wartime draft. And now even those conservatives who had opposed preparedness, like Nicholas Murray Butler, president of Columbia University and an Old Guard Republican, swung behind the draft if not behind UMT.[13] More significant was the support given to a wartime draft in February and March 1917 by influential liberal thinkers like John Dewey, Walter Lippmann and others, who in the *New Republic* and in personal correspondence with decision-makers and other moulders of opinion, emphasized the need for practical, "tough-minded" thought in the emergency. "Orderly and quiet," the selective draft would avoid the adverse impact of an intensive military recruiting campaign on a tight labor market and on ethnic relations, especially regarding German-Americans.[14]

At the same time, the amalgam of antidraft groups began to come apart. Within the Socialist party, an important minority among the leading intellectuals, including Upton Sinclair and Charlotte Perkins Gilman, argued against German militarism and repudiated the party's continued opposition to U.S. entry and conscription. Internal division also paralyzed the liberal leadership of the American Union against Militarism.[15] More importantly, Samuel Gompers, head of the American Federation of Labor, indicated privately that he personally favored a selective draft in wartime, because it would keep skilled workers on the job.[16] Since many workers continued to oppose compulsory military service, Gompers reminded them that national citizenship included recognition of the obligations as well as the rights of labor. In a statement co-signed by eighty union leaders, Gompers linked the military obligations of citizenship with the right to be protected against exploitation, the right to "industrial justice." These moderate union leaders hoped that the federal government, in return for labor's support, would sustain labor's rights to collective bargaining against any wartime anti-union efforts.[17]

In the War Department, General Scott, during the winter, had continued his efforts on behalf of UMT&S. At his direction the War

College Division, under Brig. Gen. Joseph E. Kuhn, former U.S. military attaché to Berlin, prepared a detailed "Plan for a National Army." Despite the mounting crisis, the General Staff had chosen to focus on a permanent format, not one for immediate use. The plan submitted to Scott on January 27, four days before Berlin's announcement regarding submarine warfare, called for producing over a five-year period, a National Army composed of a regular army of 310,000 supported by a first-line national reserve of 2,500,000 citizen-reservists prepared through a UMT program of eleven months of military training at 19 under the supervision of the regular army, followed by organization into reserve units which could be mobilized within a few weeks.[18]

The administrative agency proposed for this UMT program was more bureaucratized and militarized than the civilian conscriptionists had envisioned. All male citizens and declarant aliens 18 and over would be required to register at U.S. Post Offices and keep the postal staff informed of any change in residence or status. The country would be divided into 16 Army Division Areas; in each the Divisional Commander would be responsible for overseeing all military units and training camps in his area. Claims for exemption from compulsory military training and service on grounds of physical or mental condition, moral position, or dependency status would be heard by regional boards composed of three federal officials: an army officer, appointed by the Division Commander; and assistant U.S. attorney; and a specially appointed U.S. commissioner. Physical examinations would be given by army doctors. Evasion or falsification was a misdemeanor punishable by up to one year in jail. Any law enforcement officer was authorized to arrest an evader and take him to federal authorities.[19]

Despite Scott's enthusiasm, most senior officers on the General Staff, including Crowder, doubted that Americans would accept such a radical departure from tradition, especially without a declaration of war. Maj. Gen. Tasker H. Bliss, assistant chief of staff, suggested that it would be more effective and appropriate to recommend instead simply a *selective* wartime draft.[20] Nevertheless, General Scott insisted on submitting the plan regardless of its relevance to current circumstances or the political risk to the army. Secretary Baker held it until Senator George Chamberlain pried it out of his office on February 23, 1917. Although Baker said he was submitting it only for discussion, without any recommendation, some Washington journalists speculated that the administration might be testing the "winds of public opinion." But, as is now clear from the evidence, the journalists were completely wrong.[21]

The administration was *not* considering UMT&S, nor, more surprisingly, any other system of compulsory military training or service—not even a selective wartime draft. In fact, for nearly two months after the break in diplomatic relations with Germany on February 3, 1917, as the nation moved towards war, Wilson and Baker repeatedly rejected various recommendations from the General Staff for selective wartime conscription. Instead, throughout February and most of March, the president and the secretary of war insisted to the military planners that the wartime army by raised, at least until enthusiasm subsided, entirely by voluntary enlistment.

With the severance of diplomatic relations with Germany, the administration began to consider a wartime military format. Baker asked the General Staff on February 3 to prepare a plan for raising and training a force of 500,000 additional *volunteer* troops to augment the expansion of the regular army and National Guard to a wartime level of 500,000 men.[22] Although neither Baker nor Wilson was averse to the idea of a wartime draft, they were *not* willing to commit themselves to it before the traditional volunteer system had failed. Baker privately acknowledged the widespread support for "some form of universal service." But he quickly added that because of conscriptionists' efforts to use the emergency to establish a fundamental change in American military institutions, "there would undoubtedly be great suspicion aroused if compulsory service were suggested at the outset and before any opportunity to volunteer had been given."[23]

On February 7, Baker told the president that the General Staff was preparing plans and estimates in case it was decided to increase the regular army and National Guard to war strength and enlist and train "a large volunteer force . . . tentatively fixed at 500,000 men."[24] The president apparently concurred, because Baker proceeded on that course despite the opposition of the military planners on the General Staff. Responding to the February 3 request, the War College Division submitted an extensive confidential report on February 20 for raising and training a wartime army. In doing so, it drew greatly on its January 27 program for a "National Army" based on UMT&S. The military planners had emphatically recommended abandoning the volunteer system, relegating the National Guard to local defense, and relying upon a solely national army raised through conscription.[25] When Baker continued to insist on a force of 500,000 regulars and Guardsmen and 500,000 Volunteers, the planners on March 15 grudgingly submitted a proposal for invoking the Volunteer Act of 1914. At the same time, they continued to urge that the volunteer system be used only if Congress were unwilling to adopt national conscription.[26] Nevertheless, as General Scott confided to a friend on the editoral board of the *New York Times* on

March 7, the administration apparently would not seek to inaugurate a draft until volunteering had been exhausted.[27]

During February and most of March, Wilson continued his efforts to keep the United States out of the war, hoping that he could persuade Germany's leaders to modify or reverse their decision. Domestically caught between increasing pressure for resistance to German aggression and his own recognition that a majority of Americans still opposed U.S. entry, Wilson avoided provocative action, while secretly seeking a negotiated settlement of the conflict through the war-weary Austrian government. He would not allow the army or navy to make any major public preparations for war. By late February, with American shipping holed up and even a number of antiwar leaders suggesting armed neutrality as preferable to full-scale belligerency, Wilson decided to arm U.S. merchant ships as an alternative means of maintaining American rights, trade, and national honor without actually entering the European war.[28]

The lame-duck Congress would end in March and, since the new Congress was not scheduled to meet until December, Wilson was confronted with the possibility that he might have to react to German submarine attacks upon American ships with Congress out of session. He decided to prepare in advance for such an eventuality. On February 22, 1917, he made a surprise personal visit to the secretary of war and advised Baker that he wanted a bill drawn up which would give him broad legislative authorization for military and naval action. After the president left, Baker told Maj. Gen Enoch H. Crowder, the judge advocate general, that the chief executive wanted authority to arm American merchant ships and to raise an army of one million men as an emergency measure in case German submarines committed an overt act while Congress was in recess. It was this episode (which occurred on February 22, not on February 4 as the general mis-remembered it) that Crowder later asserted was the origin of the selective draft law of May 1917. This assertion was accepted by his biographer and subsequently by most historical accounts of the United States in World War I.[29] In reality, however, this was *not* the origin of the draft law. The truth is both more complex and more revealing.

Amidst coffee cups and cigar-filled ashtrays, Crowder and his staff of army lawyers worked through the night on February 22–23, 1917. Their key decision was to distinguish between "raising" and "using" an army. They prepared a joint resolution which would give the chief executive authority to *raise* an emergency army, but still require congressional approval to *use* it in war. To raise such a force, they cited three different pieces of existing legislation: (1) the National Defense Act of 1916 which provided for expansion of the regular army to a wartime level of about 300,000 as well as expansion and federalization of the National Guard; (2) the Volunteer Act of 1914 providing for calling out the U.S. Volunteers; and (3), surprisingly, the Hayden "joker," the surreptitious rider to the 1916 Defense Act which authorized drafting men into militia replacement battalions. The "joker" was the only existing statutory authority for conscription that Crowder could find. This wartime army, Crowder crowed to a colleague on February 28, would become "a Volunteer Army in name only." For after volunteering slackened, it could be maintained, through the Hayden "joker," by conscripting men into replacement battalions of the militia, which would already have been federalized into an integral part of the "national army," and then at the War Department's discretion into units of the regular army, National Guard, and the so-called "Volunteer" Army. As Crowder confided: "This is as far as the Secretary [of War] would allow me to go."[30]

Baker would not allow either immediate or exclusive use of the draft. Nevertheless, Crowder's proposal for creeping conscription was a particularly audacious, convoluted, and devious scheme, seeking as it did to draft a wartime army even before a declaration of war. The Hayden "joker" was, after all, a little-known last-minute addition to the 1916 Defense Act designed by its author simply to keep National Guard units up to strength in wartime. After examining the "joker" in January, the General Staff had dismissed it as amateurish and inadequate. Similarly, they now rejected the judge advocate general's proposal as vague and impractical.[31] Although Wilson's reaction to Crowder's suggestion is not recorded, he did *not* present the proposed resolution to Congress.

On February 26, 1917, the president went before Congress and, indicating his support for armed neutrality, asked the legislators, before they adjourned, to authorize him to arm American merchant ships against attack and "to employ *any other instrumentalities* or methods that may be necessary and adequate to protect our ships and our people in their legitimate and peaceful pursuits on the seas."[32] When Congress adjourned without giving him that authorization, despite publication of the Zimmermann telegram encouraging Mexico to invade the Southwest, the president armed the merchant ships by executive order. Between March 16 and 18, U-boats sank three American merchant ships without warning and with the loss of most their crews. Confronted with these German attacks and supported by the unanimous vote of the cabinet on March 20, Wilson reluctantly decided to take the United States into the war.

But his reluctance was tempered by the fact that he believed, like many of his contemporaries, that the war was in its final stages and that U.S. participation in the conflict and at the settlement would help achieve a just and lasting peace and a reformed international order.[33] On March 21 he summoned Congress into a special session to begin on April 2.

However, the president's decision for war did not initially alter his plan for relying on the volunteer system before any resort to conscription. On March 21, General Crowder had sent his proposed joint resolution of February 22 to the chief of staff for possible use after the declaration of war. On March 22, he told a friend that the War College Division had eliminated "the conscription feature" of his resolution, "under instructions from the Secretary of War."[34] On March 23, Baker created a board composed of Generals Scott, Bliss, Crowder, and Kuhn to prepare for submission to Congress "a draft of legislation necessary to provide an army of one million men to meet possible contingencies."[35] After visiting the War Department twice on March 24, the president returned on Sunday morning, March 25, to meet directly with Baker and the board. As Crowder reported to Henry L. Stimson the next day: "The President stated his mind on the question of raising an army" which included increasing the regular army to war strength, "federalizing" the National Guard and increasing it to war strength, and, most importantly, raising "500,000 in the first unit of additional forces, to be followed at such time as the President may deem advisable by another unit of 500,000—this additional unit being new and not yet published [thus making a wartime army of 1.5 million men]. . . . Under the scheme as it stands to-day," Crowder said, "we will resort to the draft only *after* the failure of the volunteer system." Then he added in a terse, handwritten afterthought: "The President's reasons for this are interesting but confidential."[36]

Crowder did not divulge the president's reasons, but undoubtedly— given the antiwar and antidraft sentiment in Congress and the country—Wilson considered such a course of action politically advisable, in the sense of the "high politics" of political management, as opposed to petty partisan politics. Wilson needed both a wartime army and national support for the war effort. As Baker had explained in February, the administration understood the widespread fear that big business and the military were conspiring to foist a permanent system of UMT on the country. Acting on such a fear, the Democratic agrarian leadership in Congress had been able to block his proposal for a voluntary Continental Army reserve in 1916. In 1917, opposition to the war and to compulsory military service remained strong in the Democratic constituency as well as in the isolationist, Midwestern wing of the Republican party.[37] Wilson apparently supported the initial use of the volunteer system because he believed it would help ensure that the recalcitrant isolationist wing of the Democratic party, with its dominant position in the House of Representatives, would accede to his leadership in the declaration of war, in the mobilization efforts, and in the important peace negotiations which would follow.

Having decided on raising the wartime army through voluntarism, Wilson told Baker and the generals on March 25 that he was anxious to move promptly. He wanted them to fill in the details and prepare the necessary legislation for submission to Congress after April 2. On March 26, Crowder had the proposed statute ready for what he expected would be the final conference of the board on the afternoon of Tuesday, March 27.[38]

But suddenly, unexpectedly, the president decided to abandon the U.S. Volunteers completely. Voluntary enlistment would be limited to the regular army and the National Guard. As a memorandum from Baker to the president on March 29 reiterated, the additional forces (500,000 to 1,000,000 men) were "to be raised and maintained exclusively by selective draft."[39] "[W]e have practically thrown out of consideration the Volunteer Act," Crowder told Stimson that same day, "and the new force to be raised in addition to the Regular Army and the National Guard will not be called volunteers at all. . . . "[40] For the preceding "two or three days," Crowder had been engaged "in writing and re-writing" the bill which the president would submit to Congress. On Wednesday night, March 28, Baker had called a meeting of the board of generals to consider Crowder's tentative draft of the new plan envisioning conscription, and immediately thereafter "went to the White House, where he was to go over the bill with the President section by section."[41] The evening meeting at the White House appears to have been concerned mainly with the details of the draft, and not the issue— which seems to have been decided informally by the president a day or two earlier.[42] Less than a week before the president was to deliver his war message, he decided that, despite antiwar and antidraft sentiment, the popular Volunteer tradition, and the political strain to the Democratic party and its leadership in Congress, he would abandon the old system of U.S. Volunteers and rely from the beginning upon a selective national draft. What had caused this sudden and dramatic change?

Baker later asserted that Wilson had made the decision in favor of the draft on the evening of March 28, as a result of the reasoned arguments that Baker had presented. The former secretary of war's recollection in 1921 was that, using some notes prepared by General Scott, he had sought to persuade Wilson that the bulk of the war-time army should be raised from the beginning by a selective draft instead of through the old U.S. Volunteers. According to Baker, the president had reacted instinctively against the plan, particularly since the idea of compulsory military service was so identified with General Wood, but that after questioning Baker thoroughly, he had become resigned to it. "That is the fair way; it is the democratic way," Baker recalled Wilson saying. "The experience of England with the volunteer system is a warning to us."[43] As Baker remembered it, the chief executive then ordered him to have appropriate legislation prepared. This account was repeated by Baker's official biographer and has been accepted by many historians, but while previously plausible, new evidence makes it no longer persuasive.[44]

To begin with, Baker was disingenuous in his recollection. Like the president, in February and early March of 1917 he had supported an initial reliance on the Volunteers. Based solely on contemporaneous documents, a careful reconstruction of developments prior to the declaration of war on April 6 demonstrates convincingly that in the postwar years, cabinet officers like Baker and Secretary of Agriculture David Houston as well as military officers like Crowder and Hugh S. Johnson retrospectively fabricated a consensus and decisiveness in the administration in favor of the immediate use of a wartime draft—which had not actually existed in early 1917.[45] There were obvious reasons for this fictive history. After the war, the draft was widely acclaimed, but there were also accusations—especially from former "preparedness" Republicans—that the Wilson administration had not made adequate preparations for war and that the result had been confusion, inefficiency, and waste. Thus, the postwar recollections of participants like Baker and Crowder sought to eliminate any indication of the hesitancy and indecision that had existed.

In his postwar account, Baker asserted that Wilson had been convinced of the need for a draft by his arguments on March 28, 1917. He implied that the president simply had not given serious thought previously to the issue of how the wartime army should be raised. But such an assertion does not stand up under scrutiny. Wilson had, in fact, given enough thought to the matter to reject several times the General Staff's recommendation for immediate and exclusive use of conscription in wartime. Instead, he had firmly ruled that the volunteer system must be tried first. Wilson had also heard, many times before, all of the arguments Baker allegedly used on March 28. Baker's account begs the question of why Scott's arguments, which the general had been making for months, would be more convincing on March 28 than they had been for the previous two months.

It might be argued that international circumstances had changed and that after the president's decision on March 20 to take the country into the war, the issue of raising a wartime army became essential rather than conjectural. From this perspective, the president may have adopted the idea of a draft when he first seriously turned his attention to the issue. Possible, but unlikely. War had been a strong possibility since February 1 and Wilson had discussed the matter of raising a wartime army with Baker several times since then. Contemporary evidence indicates that as late as March 26, six days after his decision to declare war, the president was still firmly committed to calling first for the U.S. Volunteers. That certainly does not suggest that it was simply the decision for war that led to the draft.

New evidence strongly suggests that, in addition to the decision for war, another—and separate—change in circumstances confronted Wilson between March 26 and 27 and played the determining role in his formal decision of March 28 to abandon the system of U.S. Volunteers and rely upon the draft instead.[46] The key to the change was Wilson's old political adversary, ex-president Theodore Roosevelt, who was now touting a military plan that Wilson considered dangerous and wished to forestall. Although 58 years old and blind in one eye, the old Rough Rider still itched for combat. Personally, he was eager to recapture the thrill he had experienced in 1898 on San Juan Hill. Strategically, he wanted to commit U.S. military power in a direct and extensive way to help the Allies defeat Germany decisively. Politically, the role of war hero might carry him again to the White House.

In part, the former president's hostility represented the jealousy of a political rival. But the depth of Roosevelt's anger is understood best by his bitterness at being replaced by Wilson as the moral leader of the nation. Viewing himself as a "realist" and a warrior, and increasingly bellicose in his foreign policy, the ex-president had expressed increasing contempt for Wilson. As he carped in December 1914: "If I must choose between a policy of blood and iron and one of milk and water . . . why, I am for the policy of blood and iron. It is better not only for the nation but in the long run for the world."[47] Contempt grew into loathing, and increasingly and maliciously, Roosevelt privately excoriated Wilson as insincere, shifty, utterly selfish, a physical coward, and a demagogic "peace prattler."

Roosevelt had been in the forefront of the minority urging Wilson to use force against Mexico and against Germany. In July 1916, he had offered to raise a division of Volunteers to punish Mexico.[48] After the diplomatic break with Germany, the ex-president feared Wilson might limit U.S. involvement to economic and naval support, a possibility he derided as a "limited liability" war, unworthy of a great power. To ensure that there would be an American expeditionary force across the Atlantic, and that the United States would play a major military role alongside the Allies, Roosevelt sought to raise a volunteer division and personally lead it to France. Unlike Wilson, who sought a compromise "peace without victory," Roosevelt agreed with the British and French governments that Imperial Germany should be crushed. Early in February 1917, the indefatigable ex-president wrote to the administration asking permission, in the event of war, to raise a division of Volunteers.[49]

Wilson was determined to prevent exactly the kind of politico-military challenges to presidential direction of the war that had emanated from political generals like Benjamin Butler in the Civil War and from Roosevelt himself in the Spanish-American War.[50] In 1898, the Rough Rider had frequently used his political connections and close relationship with the press to circumvent his military superiors, much to the embarrassment of the army and the McKinley administration. Wilson sought to avoid such political imbroglios, either from amateurs or professionals. On March 24, irritated by Leonard Wood's continued attacks upon the administration and with "no confidence either in General Wood's discretion or in his loyalty to his superiors," the president assigned the army's senior major general to a series of lesser posts and training camps which precluded him from any command in France.[51] Meanwhile, Roosevelt had obtained endorsements for his Volunteer division from the British and French governments, culled commanders for his units from the regular army, and on March 19 formally requested permission to assemble the division for training at Fort Still, Oklahoma. On March 20, the day of the cabinet's war meeting, Baker wrote to Roosevelt, rejecting his offer. He justified this decision on the grounds that Congress had not yet authorized a wartime army and, more directly because, as Baker put it, Roosevelt was ineligible for such a position because "general officers for all volunteer forces are to be drawn from the Regular Army."[52] Baker, however, had underestimated the irrepressible Roosevelt.

The ex-president refused to accept this rejection. On March 23, he wired back an immediate response, citing his heroic military experience in Cuba and reminding Baker exactly who he was in no uncertain terms: "I am a retired Commander in Chief of the United States Army and am eligible to any position of command over American troops to which I may be appointed."[53] Such impropriety must have startled the secretary of war, for Roosevelt implicitly challenged the authority of the administration to deny him a command.

The events of March 26–28, 1917 strongly suggest that the ex-president's challenge played the crucial role in Wilson's change of mind. On March 25, Wilson had spoken forcefully to the board of generals about the need to rely upon the volunteer system before any resort to the draft. On March 26, Baker sent the Rough Rider's telegram to the White House. On March 27, Wilson returned it, a covering note indicating his anger and amazement at Roosevelt's audacity:

> "This is one of the most extraordinary documents I have ever read! Thank you for letting me undergo the discipline of temper involved in reading it in silence!"[54]

One day later, on March 28, the president, in his evening meeting with Baker, formally approved the abandonment of the U.S. Volunteers and exclusive reliance upon the draft for raising the wartime army of citizen-soldiers (except for the regular army and National Guard, which would be initially raised through voluntary enlistment and which, it should be pointedly noted, already had their officers).[55] Thus, the crucial presidential decision occurred between March 26 and 28 immediately after Wilson had read Roosevelt's telegram. It seems obvious that the president's decision in favor of the draft resulted from Roosevelt's challenge.

Neither Wilson nor Baker made any explanation in March about the decision. Indeed, they never acknowledged the fact that they had first firmly supported the Volunteers and only rejected them late in March. The General Staff also remained mute on that issue and relevant documents of the War College Division remained classified for half a century. Therefore, until recently, the president's shift in March from support to opposition in regard to the traditional volunteer system remained unknown and undebated.

Once the shift is revealed, however, the presidential rejection of the so-called Roosevelt Volunteers emerges as the pivotal factor in Wilson's position on the draft. At the time, it had appeared a narrower issue. When the matter of the Roosevelt Volunteers became part of the public debate in April 1917, during congressional consideration of the administration's proposal for a draft, many believed that Wilson was simply rejecting the idea of the "Roosevelt Volunteers" as a supplement to the drafted wartime army. It was not publicly known that the president had initially favored the use of the U.S. Volunteers instead of a draft. For a variety of reasons that will be discussed later, when Congress finally approved the bill for the army and the draft, it authorized the president, despite his stated opposition, to accept the "Roosevelt Volunteer Divisions" in the wartime army.[56]

However, when Wilson signed the draft act into law on May 18, 1917, he declared that he had no intention of authorizing those volunteer divisions. Professional soldiers had advised him, he said, that the men most needed were of the younger ages and, more importantly, "we shall need all of our experienced officers" to train and lead the draftees. Roosevelt had picked the best of these, Wilson said, to lead the units of his force of two to four Volunteer divisions, and they simply could not be spared.[57] This became the major argument for rejecting the Roosevelt Volunteers. Baker had not used it in his rejection letter of March 20. It apparently originated with the president when Roosevelt came to the White House on April 10 and personally appealed to him on the matter.[58] Subsequently, Baker included it in a letter to Roosevelt on April 13 and reiterated it in his final and categorical rejection of Roosevelt's request on May 11.[59] Wilson first used the reason publicly on May 18, 1917, referring to his meeting with Roosevelt on April 10; he repeated the story two years later to the U.S. Ambassador to France, while attending the Paris peace conference.[60]

Indeed this was a good military reason for rejecting the Roosevelt plan, and it may well have been part of Wilson's motivation for refusing to appoint the ex-president or authorize his Volunteer divisions.[61] However, in determining Wilson's reasons for the draft, it is significant that the first contemporary evidence of this argument appeared on April 13, three weeks *after* the president had formally decided to jettison the entire system of U.S. Volunteers. The difficulty is that there were good politico-military reasons for either accepting *or* rejecting Roosevelt and his Volunteers. Most U.S. Army officers recommended against using amateur "political" generals and U.S. Volunteer units, as being counter to efficient military mobilization and operations. On the other hand, Roosevelt's ability to rouse public enthusiasm for engagement with the enemy and to organize and move his troops into battle on the Western Front as quickly as possible made the "Roosevelt Volunteers" attractive to interventionists, including a number of professional soldiers, on both sides of the Atlantic.[62]

Did Wilson reject the Roosevelt Volunteers strictly for military reasons, or did these reasons merely provide the justification (or simply part of the explanation) for a decision which he made on more political grounds? It is certainly a matter of record that Wilson did not always accept the recommendations of professional soldiers. He rejected permanent UMT&S; he turned down their pleas for exclusive use of the draft, until he changed his mind between March 26 and 28, 1917; he continued to use the National Guard despite the regulars' opposition; and, in November 1918, he would accept an armistice over the objections of U.S. and Allied military leaders who wished to push the attack into Germany. It seems he accepted the advice of the military when it coincided—or at least did not conflict—with his own deeply held view.

The argument that the Roosevelt Divisions would impede the regular army in training and leading the wartime citizen army was not the initial argument made by the administration against the plan. Furthermore, although the General Staff wanted the entire regular army to remain at home to train the levies of draftees, Wilson, under Allied pressure in late April, decided instead to send a division of regulars to France as soon as possible. When, despite the objections of the General Staff, the First Division and Gen. John J. Pershing and his headquarters staff left for Europe in the early summer of 1917, they took with them twice as many regular officers as Baker had insisted in his April 13 letter to Roosevelt could not be spared because they would be needed to train the draft armies at home.[63]

Doubtless, Wilson was even more concerned with the challenge posed to his leadership of the U.S. role in war and the peace settlement by having the insubordinate and unpredictable ex-president in partial command of American units in France. In a private conversation on May 18, 1917, the day he signed the draft act and publicly rejected the Roosevelt Volunteers, Wilson allegedly condemned the old Rough Rider's "intolerance of discipline" and his famous "Round Robin" appeal to the press from Cuba during the Spanish-American War.[64] Ten years later, Baker told Wilson's official biographer that he himself had made the decision to refuse the ex-president a command, because Roosevelt was "utterly unqualified," "impulsive and without discretion." It would, he said, have led to "no end of embarrassment to have an ex-President in the capacity of a subordinate commander."[65]

Thus, Roosevelt, the arch conscriptionist, played a pivotal role in obtaining a conscript army, but ironically he accomplished this inadvertently. At the crucial moment, he sought to utilize the traditional volunteer format for his own purposes, large and small. On March 22, 1917, two days after receiving Baker's first rejection and the day before he sent his audacious telegram, Roosevelt notified Senator Henry Cabot Lodge that he had already suggested to the French ambassador that, if the Wilson administration rejected his plan, he would be willing to "take an expeditionary infantry division to France under the American flag on my own account if the French government thinks it worth while to pay for us." He also made contingency plans to try the Canadian government, if the French turned him down. At the same time, he asked Lodge to have his friends begin to work in Congress to modify the legislation that would be submitted to raise the wartime army so that it would be "made proper to employ an ex-President—a retired Commander-in-Chief—in such a fashion."[66]

Roosevelt was indeed a potentially disruptive force, and Wilson apparently decided that the only way in which the popular ex-president, the nation's leading amateur soldier, could be denied a command was to eliminate the entire system of U.S. Volunteers. It was necessary to prevent Roosevelt—and others like him—from "politicizing" the army and the war. As Colonel House explained in May to a visiting British general: "In our efforts to bring about an effective army we must keep it out of politics and if TR is permitted to raise troops, dozens of politicians throughout the country will also insist upon doing so, to the consequent undoing of our regular army."[67] And, he might well have added, the disruption of the administration's leadership as well.

Wilson's re-evaluation was political in the larger sense of the term—political management rather than petty, partisan politics. In February and early March, he had supported the Volunteer system because he wanted the agrarian wing of the Democratic party, predominant in Congress, to give him a declaration of war and subsequently to support his efforts for wartime mobilization and for an active role in the postwar order. He could count on the Republicans because, except for their minority isolationist wing in the Midwest, the GOP was in this case the "war party." But when Roosevelt challenged the administration's right to deny him a command and, by implication, a leadership role in Europe, Wilson re-evaluated his initial decision to placate the agrarian Democrats (where else could they go politically?). The president recognized that his decision for the draft would be supported by the vast majority of the mass media, as well as by individual leaders of public opinion, already converted by the interpretations of the preparedness movement of modern warfare in general and the experience of Great Britain in particular. Thus Wilson decided on a moderate middle course, neither the U.S. Volunteers, nor permanent UMT&S, but rather a temporary, selective national draft for the duration of war.

It was not a difficult decision for Wilson because he, like the majority of cosmopolitan elites, considered a selective draft to be economically and militarily preferable to the Volunteer system. In private statements in April and May both Wilson and Baker placed major emphasis upon the economic efficiency of a selective draft. It

would avoid the "industrial confusion," Baker told Walter Lippmann in a provocative phrase, which would have resulted from
"promiscuous volunteering."[68] An orderly, selective process would
keep experienced industrial workers on the job. As Wilson wrote a
friend on May 4, "Its [the selective draft's] central idea was to disturb the industrial and social structure of the country just as little
as possible."[69]

The administration also stressed economic efficiency in its public
statements; but in these justifications, designed primarily to enlist
mass support, Wilson and Baker were understandably less precise.
Rather than emphasizing exemption of industrial workers, they
stressed universal liability to military service in national emergencies. "The principle of the selective draft, in short, has at its heart
this idea," Wilson explained, "that there is a universal obligation to
serve and that a public authority should choose those upon whom
the obligation of military service shall rest, and also in a sense
choose those who shall do the rest of the nation's work."[70] Wilson
could make such an assertion with confidence because liberal and
conservative nationalists had already agreed that there was a *national* military obligation in wartime.

General principles required specific implementation. Following
the president's March 28 authorization, Baker and General Crowder
had set to work on details of the draft. Initially, they planned to
provide statutory exemption for skilled workers in munitions
plants, shipyards, and other industrial facilities directly related to
the war effort.[71] Baker even considered awarding special badges to
these exempted "war workers" as an affirmation by the government
that these able-bodied men were not shirking their duty. The secretary of war quickly realized, however, that occupational group exemptions were publicly unacceptable. They would be seen as unfair
because there would be individuals within such groups who did not
warrant exemption. "In all the European countries, I am told," he
wrote to Walter Lippmann, "they have found it impossible to exclude industrial workers by general classification and have found it
necessary to release them for necessary industry after having first
caught them in their recruiting processes."[72] In early April he contemplated copying such a procedure of returning drafted workers
found essential to the economy.

In making plans for implementation of the draft, the administration had initially sought to exempt married men, for reasons of
fiscal efficiency as much as public support. By drafting only single
males, Baker explained to a closed session of the House Military
Affairs Committee, taxpayers would be relieved of the costs of car-
ing for wives and children through dependency allowances, pen-

sions, or death benefits.[73] But once again the administration soon came to realize that blanket exemptions and economic efficiency could clash with public demands for equity. Some husbands, and even fathers, would not be considered worthy of exemption, whether for reasons of desertion, infidelity, physical abuse, or marginal economic contribution to the family. Under Congressional pressure, the administration soon abandoned such a proposal and suggested deferments for those with dependency hardships. Local draft boards would determine who was qualified for deferments, whether on the grounds of dependency or occupation, or for the physically, mentally, or morally unfit.

The administration was greatly concerned about possible internal disorder caused among the large number of anti-Ally ethnic groups in the United States. Baker also justified the draft before Congress as a means of avoiding highly emotional recruiting campaigns of manufactured hatred which aroused communities and pitted members of different ethnic groups against one another.[74] In retrospect, such an argument, although appropriate enough, seems naïve and even ironic, given the subsequent use of intensively emotional propaganda campaigns to stimulate the purchase of war bonds. The conundrum of how to raise an army without raising emotions might be solved by the draft. The administration believed in the spring of 1917 that calm, logical, scientific selection could replace the excessive chauvinism. Responding to criticism from House members who argued that the enthusiasm of American volunteers had always made them better fighters than conscripts, Baker replied curtly that in modern war the soldier need no longer be enthusiastic. "Willingness to do his duty is enough."[75]

Although the administration did not emphasize it, part of the appeal of the draft, particularly to pro-Ally Americans, was that it could force the unwilling, the so-called "slackers," to go to war, and not place the burden of service exclusively upon those who volunteered. In a country already beset by nativist fears of lack of assimilation or divided loyalties among its multi-ethnic population, the fear that many members of anti-Ally ethnic groups would refuse to volunteer for the armed forces and might have to be compelled to fulfill their military obligation had been an underlying theme in the preparedness movement and was part of the appeal of the selective wartime draft. It was phrased in terms of the equity of distributing military liability, an equity that could be achieved better through compulsion than through voluntarism. The press and the preparedness organizations had already demonstrated how compulsory military training and service could be made to fit prevailing values such as equity, efficiency, national unity, and progress. It was the accom-

modation to political culture and political realities that could help
ensure that the public would accept such a change from the predominant American military format of the preceding century.

In a larger sense, the military reason was the main reason for the
administration's decision for the draft. Obviously, if the United
States had not entered the war, there would never have been a draft
in 1917–18, but that did not automatically mean that the war required a draft. As Wilson and, reluctantly, the General Staff understood, the Volunteer system could probably have produced a large
wartime force of perhaps 1.5 or even 2 million men, although undoubtedly it would have been more difficult to raise a force of 4
million soldiers, the size of the American army by the end of 1918.
Only the draft could produce an enormous mass army and do so at a
planned and predictable rate; only compulsion could maintain those
force levels with a steady flow of replacements for the extensive
casualties of war on the Western Front. But did Wilson think an
enormous army with regular replacements was necessary when he
made the decision for the draft?

A reconstruction of Wilson's thinking on the eve of the war indicates that calculations about domestic politics and political management weighed more heavily in his decision to advocate a draft than
did any prophetic insight that conscription would be necessary to
raise an army fast enough and large enough to save the Allies from
defeat. In February, March, and early April 1917, it was not clear to
Wilson and Baker, nor to many other knowledgeable Americans,
that the United States would need to raise an enormous army.[76]
Even in confidential conversations, the Allies had led the administration and informed elites to believe that Britain and France
wanted primarily additional credit and supplies, not troops from
the United States.[77] One of the main reasons Wilson was willing to
enter the war was his belief that it had entered its final stages, a
conviction which was widely shared. Some commentators believed
that war might end in stalemate or Allied victory by the fall of 1917,
after the Germans had failed in their desperate submarine blockade.[78] Wilson was primarily concerned with maintaining American
maritime rights and his credibility as a statesman, and of ensuring a
U.S. role in shaping the peace and the postwar order. Since the
second year of the war, he had realized that the European nations,
both Allies and the Central Powers, listened to other nations in
proportion to their military strength.[79]

The administration's initial plans in February and March 1917 for
the wartime army suggest that Wilson may have envisioned the kind
of military force and role recommended to him by Herbert Hoover.

The London-based administrator for Belgian relief privately proposed a large, but not enormous, defensive force, which would protect the Western Hemisphere and give the United States significant military status. If it became desirable, a smaller, offensive expeditionary force could be drawn from it and used at the decisive military moment ("when peace approaches," as Hoover put it) to help to bring the war to a conclusion and provide the United States with a place at the peace conference.[80] The projected goals for wartime force levels approved by the administration in February and March were commensurate with such a concept. They called for summoning a wartime army of 1 million, expanded in late March to 1.5 million troops.[81] Even after Wilson had decided to adopt the draft, this figure remained the same, as it did in the army bill Baker submitted to Congress on April 6. Furthermore, the nature and scope of the War Department's rather limited efforts in the spring of 1917 to obtain temporary new line officers also indicated that the administration and the General Staff were thinking in terms of such a large, but not enormous, wartime army.[82]

The size of the wartime army would be determined by two factors: its role and the available resources—men, money, clothing, equipment, training camps, and cadres. Restricted by hostile sentiment, the General Staff had not given much consideration in the prewar period to wartime planning.[83] But when they turned to it after the diplomatic break with Germany in February 1917, the planners of the War College Division predicted that, in case of war, American cooperation with the Allies initially would be solely economic and naval, although it might in a later stage of the war include joint military operations in some theater of war abroad. However, the planners and the senior officers of the General Staff recommended that until the United States could raise and properly train an army of 1.5 million men, no expeditionary force should be sent abroad. Existing forces were too small to have any influence in Europe, and, more importantly, the experienced regulars and Guardsmen were needed at home to train and command the new units of wartime citizen-soldiers. Only after the wartime army was fully trained (a process they estimated would take at least twelve months), would all or part of it be employed in Europe, "to exert a substantial influence in a later stage of the war." In February, Baker had approved this statement "in principle," but, he instructed the General Staff to take "no action until condition arises."[84]

The president's March 21 decision for war did not change either his or the General Staff's opinion on this matter. Not until April 13 did the War College Division make a brief and solitary response to an informal "personal memorandum" from Maj. Gen. Tasker H.

Bliss. When the assistant chief of staff asked about the time and shipping required to transport 500,000 soldiers to France, the planners estimated that an American army of 500,000 to 1,000,000 men could not be adequately trained and transported to France before the end of 1919.[85] This, of course, proved mistaken by more than a year.[86]

The decision for an American Expeditionary Force and eventually for massive reinforcement on the Western Front resulted from the dramatic appeals of the Allied Missions which came to the United States at the end of April 1917.[87] They helped to generate enthusiasm for the Allied cause and began to educate both the American public and government to a realization of the extensive mobilization involved in a war which had become a test of national stamina. Privately, in conversations with administration officials, they emphasized the desperate situation in Europe, which, since the Allies had kept it a secret even from their own people, was far worse than Americans had realized.

The gravity of the Allies' plight was now reinforced by reports from American military attachés and others in Europe. The German submarine campaign was succeeding in cutting off munitions and even food from the British Isles.[88] In France, manpower and morale were declining rapidly. Privately, French officials disclosed that 1.2 million soldiers had been killed and 2 million permanently disabled since 1914. The recent Nivelle offensive had failed miserably almost as soon as it started in mid-April (the French kept secret the fact that they had lost 120,000 men in ten days and that 40,000 soldiers had mutinied). British military and civilian leaders feared that without the official commitment of massive numbers of reinforcements by the United States, antiwar groups and declining morale might force the French and British governments into negotiating an unfavorable and therefore only temporary, settlement of the war. The Russian Army was in a mutinous state and the British feared that Russia might leave the war, freeing millions of German soldiers on the Eastern Front to join the attack in the West.[89]

The seriousness of the Allies' situation and the popular enthusiasm generated by the leading figures of the missions—Arthur J. Balfour, and especially Marshal Joseph "Papa" Joffre, the "Hero of the Marne," the one western commander who had captured Americans' imagination—convinced Wilson of the need to dispatch at least a symbolic expeditionary force to France. Although the British privately expressed their desire primarily for American economic and naval assistance, they too began to emphasize the need for American troops. Joffre and Lt. Gen. George T.M. "Tom" Bridges, head of the military section of the British Mission, agreed jointly to urge the immediate dispatch to France of a regular army division, followed as soon as possible by large numbers of volunteer and conscripted reinforcements, whose training could be completed in Europe.[90] They presented their appeals in meetings with Baker and the General Staff, beginning on April 26 after the key congressional vote for the draft, and subsequently in a meeting between Joffre and Wilson on May 2. But, probably to avoid indicating to the Americans how desperate they were, and therefore how vulnerable to U.S. influence as well as to German demands, Joffre and Bridges focused on the more limited immediate value of having a division of regulars dispatched to France for its effect on the morale of the Allies as well as the Central Powers. "The sight of the Stars and Stripes on this continent will make a great impression on both sides," Bridges emphasized.[91]

In his talk with Joffre on May 2, Wilson agreed to send an immediate token force of American regulars for its effect on morale. However, it is not clear that he committed himself at that time to send much more than that.[92] On May 8, Baker reported to the president on the status of plans for the expeditionary force. Major General John J. Pershing had been notified of his selection as commander, and he and a few officers would depart soon, followed (as shipping became available) by the expeditionary force which would consist of a division of 12,000 regulars. The Americans were to be supplied there with French rifles and artillery. As Baker said in a highly suggestive phrase, "the French Government having offered so to arm them and several other divisions of the same size *if we sent them over.*" This concluding phrase (emphasis added) suggests that neither the French nor the Americans were certain whether more troops would be sent abroad. "After this division is safely in France and is training," Baker continued, "General Pershing can advise us of conditions and of the wisdom of sending other divisions over to be trained in conjunction with the one already there, but my military associates here believe that it will be necessary to have a division of troops on this side ready to follow fairly shortly, so as to get the advantage of the training received by the first division and be able to supplement it should battle losses or sickness diminish its numbers."[93]

As late as May 8, Baker seemed to be following the idea of limiting the initial AEF to a division, perhaps followed by a replacement division, altogether about 25,000 men. Yet even the small expeditionary force of 12,000 regulars ran counter to the recommendations of the General Staff, which warned that there were differences between the military interests of the United States and the Allies. Although they grumblingly agreed to the dispatch of Pershing and his troops for moral effect, the General Staff recommended a delay in sending them. Generals Scott, Bliss, and Kuhn continued to advise against diverting the personnel of the regular army from their primary task of organizing and training the large wartime army of citizen-soldiers.[94] Nevertheless, on May 8, Baker asked Wilson to approve the AEF plan, indicating that it was as yet wholly flexible. On May 10, after speaking with Baker on the phone, Wilson put in writing his official approval of the program outlined by the secretary of war, "as it refers to the immediate despatch of General Pershing and the despatch as soon as possible thereafter of the Division which he is to command in France."[95] The president had formally authorized only the sending of one division of regulars to France; this was not yet the extensive commitment that it would become.

The open-ended commitment for American military reinforcement of the Allies on the Western Front apparently began at a meeting between Secretary Baker and Marshal Joffre on May 14, 1917. The two men reached formal agreement to dispatch immediately an American expeditionary force of one division of 16,000 to 20,000 combat troops to a camp in the French army zone, followed by other troops, "restricted only by transportation difficulties."[96] On May 18, 1917, the day he signed into law the army and selective draft act, Wilson issued the first public announcement that an American Expeditionary Force, the First Division of the U.S. Army, would go to France under the command of General John J. Pershing.[97]

Not until the last week in May, however, did the administration make a conclusive decision that the United States would send abroad not just a token American military unit, but considerable expeditionary forces. The Baker-Joffre agreement of May 14 seems only to have begun the process for this significant change in American military policy. Indeed, it appears that after his talk with Joffre, Baker initially thought of 500,000 troops as comprising the "great [expeditionary] force" in France in 1918. He later recalled that this idea had remained unchanged until Pershing went to France and reported in July 1917 "that we must send a truly great army."[98] In late May, without awaiting the results of a new study which he had directed the military planners to make as to "whether we are now to prepare for the dispatch of considerable forces abroad or to hold them for training at home," Baker concluded around May 24–25 that the United States simply could not stop with only a small, token force in France while Americans spent a year or more leisurely training their wartime army at home. Rather, as he wrote to Wilson

THE HEROIC BRONZE FIGURE of the "Minute Man" became the symbol of America's primary reliance upon citizen-soldiers in wartime, from colonial times to the present. The statue, sculpted by Daniel Chester French, was erected by the town of Concord, Mass., in 1875 in commemoration of the militiamen of 1775 whom Ralph Waldo Emerson had called the "embattled farmers" that "fired the shot heard around the world." *Photo © 1976 by Bernie Cleff*

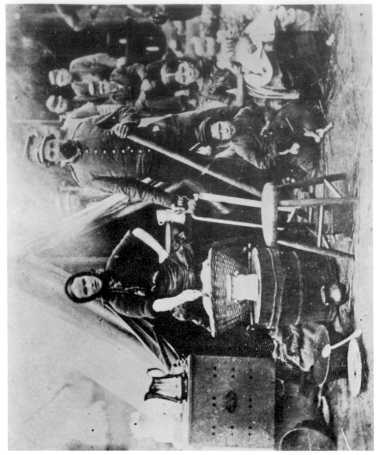

WOMEN AND CHILDREN sometimes accompanied the citizen-soldiers of America's wartime armies. Seldom depicted, they were until recently largely forgotten by history. As indicated by this rare photograph, entitled simply "Civil War tent life, 31st Pennsylvania Regiment," such women could earn extra income by washing laundry as well as mending clothes and cooking for the soldiers. *Collection of the Military Order of the Loyal Legion, bms Am. 1084, Box 38; by permission of the Houghton Library, Harvard University*

VOLUNTEER CITIZEN-SOLDIERS filled the ranks of both armies in the Civil War. Here a bearded lieutenant and two enlisted men, members of the commissary unit of the 4th Michigan Volunteer Infantry Regiment, pose for Matthew Brady's camera. A liberated black man crouches behind them. *National Archives Photo 111-B-5365*

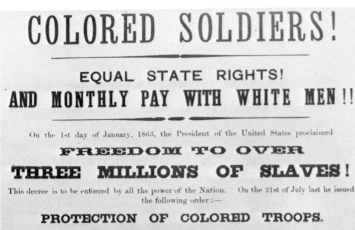

COLORED SOLDIERS!

EQUAL STATE RIGHTS!
AND MONTHLY PAY WITH WHITE MEN !!

On the 1st day of January, 1863, the President of the United States proclaimed

FREEDOM TO OVER
THREE MILLIONS OF SLAVES !

This decree is to be enforced by all the power of the Nation.   On the 21st of July last he issued
the following order :—

PROTECTION OF COLORED TROOPS.

WAR DEPARTMENT, ADJUTANT GENERAL'S OFFICE,
WASHINGTON, July 21.

"General Order No. 233.

RECRUITING BLACK SOLDIERS was part of the American wartime tradition. Although blacks had fought in every war in American history, southern whites in particular had feared arming slaves and, beginning in the 1820s, prohibited the recruitment of even free blacks by the U.S. Army. In the Civil War, faced with a shortage of recruits, a number of northern states engaged northern and southern black men to help fill their quotas in the Union Army. *Connecticut Recruiting Broadside, 1863*

ANTIDRAFT RIOTS IN NEW YORK CITY in July 1863 were the worst in American history. In the four-day rampage, rioters from the city's Irish ghetto burned the draft office, sacked a number of homes, and lynched several black men. Not until six regiments returned from the battle of Gettysburg and fired on the rioters was order restored. *Engraving from* Frank Leslie's Illustrated Newspaper, *July 25, 1863*

ROOSEVELT'S "ROUGH RIDERS," the 1st U.S. Volunteer Cavalry Regiment, pose victoriously around Lt. Col. Theodore Roosevelt and the American flag atop San Juan Hill in 1898. Although largely ignored by the press, the capture of this strategic position among the defenses overlooking Santiago Harbor in Cuba had been made possible in large part by two regiments of black regulars. *News photo by William Dinwiddie; Library of Congress LC-USZ62-7626*

WHAT UNIVERSAL MILITARY TRAINING CAN DO

AT ENLISTMENT   FIVE MONTHS LATER

These photographs should convince the most sceptical of the benefits of **Universal Military Training** to the individual.

The photograph on the left was taken at Morehead City, N. C., on August 15th, 1916, the day these two young men enlisted in Company K, First North Carolina Infantry. The other photograph is of the same young men, taken at Camp Stewart, El Paso, Texas, on Jan. 20th, 1917.

DURING THE WORLD WAR I ERA, advocates of universal military training and service, like ex-president Theodore Roosevelt, stressed the physical, attitudinal, and behavioral improvements which they argued would result from short-term military training. In this leaflet of the "preparedness" movement in 1917, two undernourished and dishevelled young men from North Carolina have been transformed into healthy, neat, upright citizen-soldiers. *Conscription File; Swarthmore College Peace Collection, Swarthmore, Pa. 19031*

U.S. ENTRY INTO WORLD WAR I in April 1917 led initially to some attempts
to convince young men to volunteer for the U.S. Army. Among the recruiting
efforts was this device to shame young men into enlistment. As part of the
recruiting campaign in 1917, Roger Perrott dressed half as a wealthy playboy and
half as an army doughboy and paraded the sidewalks of New York City urging
young men to doff their civilian clothing and pursuits and demonstrate their
masculinity and patriotism by getting fully into uniform. *National Archives*
165-WW 480 A-28

REGISTRATION FOR THE DRAFT was held nationwide on June 5, 1917 for 10 million young men aged 21 to 30. After eligibility had been extended in August 1918 to men aged 18 to 20 and 31 to 45, another national registration day was held on September 12, 1918, for 13 million men. Here the New World prepares to draft the Old World as women volunteers from uptown Manhattan neighborhoods register men from virtually every ethnic background in the immigrant ghettoes of the Lower East Side of New York City. *National Archives 165-WW 480 B-39*

PRESIDENT WILSON being blindfolded before drawing the first capsule in the third draft lottery held Sept. 30, 1918. Maj. Gen. Enoch H. Crowder, wartime head of the Selective Service System, faces him on the right. The national drawing determined the order in which qualified draft registrants would be called. *National Archives 165 WW 474 D1*

DRAFT OPPONENT Eugene V. Debs, Socialist party leader, assailed the war, the draft, and wartime conformity in a speech on June 16, 1918, to more than a thousand persons who had come to Canton, Ohio, to attend the state convention of the Socialist Party of America. As a result, he was indicted and convicted under the Espionage and Sedition Acts and sentenced to ten years in prison. *Photo courtesy of Eugene V. Debs Home and Museum, Terre Haute, Indiana*

WHEN 5,000 WOMEN antidraft protesters, most of them reportedly from the Lower East Side, demonstrated in front of New York's City Hall on June 16, 1917, more than a hundred policemen broke up the demonstration. In the melee that followed, several police officers had their uniforms torn, their shins kicked, and their faces scratched; a number were jabbed with hatpins. Three of the women were arrested. *National Archives 165-WW-481 A-6*

AMIDST SMILES AND KISSES, these unidentified draftees left for army camp in the fall of 1917. *National Archives 165-WW-476-24*

DRESSED IN THEIR BEST SUITS, draftees arrived at Camp Sherman, Chillicothe, Ohio, under the supervision of U.S. Army regulars who would turn the civilians into wartime soldiers. Photo taken 1917. *National Archives 165-WW-474B-28*

on May 27, 1917, it was necessary to send American military forces (including the new draftees after only three or four months training) to France as rapidly as possible, given existing shipping, and then to rely upon the judgment of General Pershing to decide when they had enough training to take them into the trenches.

Wilson seems to have been reluctant to accept such a change in policy, involving the progressive commitment of large numbers of American citizen-soldiers to the Western Front, for Baker, in his May 27 letter, defended the change with an unusual degree of forcefulness. "Our own country will not be willing to continue here a long drawn out process of training with the ultimate intention of doing fighting on a large scale at some later time," Baker wrote.[99] In addition to the wartime public mood, he also cited politico-military reasons for his decision. Allowing the Allied powers to be worn down by attrition, he explained, risked the danger that the French or Russians would break down, "thus immeasurably increasing the size of our own task later." The speediest way to bring the war to the earliest possible conclusion was to create an "immediate and overwhelming aggregation of forces, including our own . . . and not to feed nations to the German machine in detail [in segments]." Baker said he would delay until after the completion of the current War College Division study before he asked the president for "a determination of our general policy in the matter of dispatching troops overseas at the present and in the near future."[100]

In retrospect, Baker's letter of May 27 seems to have triggered the administration's decision to abandon its (and the General Staff's) earlier more cautious plans and to adopt a new policy of sending American troops to Europe as quickly as possible. Since Baker made this decision regardless of the president's lack of enthusiasm for it and in spite of a fervent last-ditch appeal against it by the General Staff, he must have been influenced primarily by the Allied missions, particularly by Marshal Joffre, presumably supported later by General Pershing.[101] On June 7, 1917, the War College Division delivered the report Baker wanted, including plans for "a program for progressive dispatch of troops to France," beginning the transport of soldiers to France on August 1 at the rate of 120,000 a month (the maximum given existing shipping), until there would be a million semi-trained men in the American Expeditionary Force by the spring of 1918.[102] Confirmation for this policy was provided on July 10 by General Pershing who recommended an army of one million American troops in France as the smallest force which could operate in modern war as a complete, balanced, independent fighting unit. He believed it could be ready for combat by the end of 1918. At the same time, he also recommended that the AEF be expanded to

3 million men by the end of 1919, which Allied commanders now hoped would be the concluding year of the war.[103]

While acquiescing in the decision to build a million-man AEF in France by 1918, Wilson continued to respond favorably to civilian suggestions for avoiding a massive American military involvement on the Western Front, with its concomitant high casualty rates. Throughout the summer and fall of 1917, it was obvious that Wilson had still not abandoned the idea put forward in February by Herbert Hoover (and independently by the General Staff) of building up a large American army at home and using it abroad at a decisive moment at the end of the war. As late as November 1917, Wilson was also favorably inclined towards proposals advanced by civilians, including Prime Minister David Lloyd George, for avoiding a continuation of the bloody assaults on the Western Front through possible indirect attacks upon the flanks of Germany or her allies. Baker, having decided in May to support the Western Front commanders' view of the war, firmly resisted the president's tendency to seek other military strategies that might be less costly but also less decisive. After politely rejecting the president's suggestions in May, September, and October, Baker grew uncharacteristically petulant with his chief in November 1917, reminding the president that the additional levies of American troops "are, in some sense, pledged for use on the Western Front in cooperation with the British and French forces there."[104] This ended Wilson's queries about alternative strategies, as the president too surrendered to the dominance of the war in France.

As a result of the military situation described by the Allied Missions and subsequently expanded upon by General Pershing from France, the administration largely drifted into what became an open-ended commitment to send American troops to the Western Front, restricted only by the number of training camps in the United States and ships which could transport them to France.[105] Wilson had not specifically envisioned this when he decided for the draft, nor even when he first authorized a token American Expeditionary Force. Rather, although Wilson had significant ideas about how to reform the international system to reduce the role of force and the likelihood of future conflicts, once the United States entered the war he was soon forced to send troops overseas, because the country's new position and the current nature of the international system required a large military force for it to have a significant effect.

A concurrence of the domestic and international structure, together with the arguments of the conscriptionists, led America to the modern national draft. The timing, however, derived directly from the president and his decision of March 28, 1917 to abandon the system of U.S. Volunteers in favor of the draft. It is clear that Wilson's calculations about domestic and international politics weighed most heavily in his decision. Theodore Roosevelt, arch conscriptionist, had played a pivotal role in obtaining conscription, but, ironically, at the expense of his own ability to lead U.S. Volunteers to France and attempt to usurp Wilson's control of the war. The impact of the Roosevelt-Wilson confrontation demonstrates that at least the *timing* of significant historical acts can sometimes hinge upon just such personal episodes and personalities. Despite his decision to draft, the president still had to convert a hostile majority in Congress. The stage was set for a dramatic confrontation on Capitol Hill.

6

Confronting Congress with Conscription, April–May, 1917

A RMED CAVALRY ACCOMPANIED THE PRESIDENT as he arrived at Capitol Hill on April 2, 1917, to ask Congress for a declaration of war. Secret Service agents flanked him as he walked into the House chambers. Entering the war was a solemn business. In his address, Wilson emphasized America's justification and its goal to make the world "safe for democracy." He merely alluded to the draft, saying simply that he would ask Congress for a wartime army based on the principle of universal liability to military service.[1] To avoid complicating the congressional debate over intervention, the administration withheld the details of its plan for military mobilization.

Not until the day after the declaration of war on April 6, 1917 did Baker formally submit the army bill to Congress. As drawn up the previous week, the statute authorized expansion of the regular army to 298,000 and the National Guard to 440,000 and would "federalize" the Guard into national service, all under the National Defense Act of 1916. These forces would be recruited through voluntary enlistment, although, in a departure from the 1916 legislation, the president could authorize use of the draft if necessary. The major departure was the abandonment of the U.S. Volunteers. Instead, the bulk of the wartime forces, later designated the "National Army," would be raised exclusively through a *selective* national draft. The administration asked for authority to draft immediately 500,000 men between the ages of 19 and 25, with the possibility of another increment of 500,000, making a total initial goal of 1.2 to 1.7 million ground troops. Junior officers for the National Army would come primarily from the Plattsburg-trained reservists and graduates of new wartime officer-training camps.[2]

Unlike the Civil War there would be no substitutions or commutations, and none of the enlistment bounties that had proved so costly in previous wars. All soldiers, whether draftees or volunteers, would be required to serve for the duration. To prevent disruption, government officials would be exempted from the draft; and, as Baker testified in closed session, the administration also wanted broad exemptions for persons engaged in industries essential to the war effort. He also asked for exemptions for men with dependent families, men judged physically, mentally, or morally unfit, and conscientious objectors from pacifist religious faiths. The administration sought broad powers to implement and enforce the draft. To prevent obstruction by state officials as occurred in some areas in the War of 1812 and the Civil War, state and local officials would be required to implement the draft as directed by the president. Refusal to obey the draft law was to be a misdemeanor, punishable by up to a year in prison.[3]

The administration's proposal for a wartime draft produced considerable hostility, particularly in the South and Middle West. In the wake of the declaration of war, members of Congress from those agrarian and isolationist regions received many letters against the war and the draft, both often described as instruments of "the monied interests." "If this war was to protect the free institutions of America, our homes, our women and children," the head of the North Carolina Farmers' Union wrote in a typical letter, "selective conscription might be justified; but in that case there would be no need of conscription; patriotic men would rally to the call of our country. . . ."[4] Many opponents continued to equate the draft with European militarism and tyranny and denounced it as a slur upon the individualism and patriotism of Americans.[5] Such vehemency frightened many legislators already concerned with entry into the war. The greatest efforts to modify the administration's proposal came from the agrarian Democratic majority in the House of Representatives which was particularly fearful of such a radical departure from isolationist and volunteer traditions. The House Military Affairs Committee held up the army bill for more than three weeks while holding a series of closed-door hearings to provide time to sound out public opinion and establish the basis for a compromise.

Traditional accounts which have portrayed these congressional agrarians as obstructionists trying to block the adoption of a modern draft are inaccurate and unfair. They sought not to prevent the draft, but to establish it in a more politically palatable format. Despite their public protestations, many of the rural southern Democrats and midwestern Republicans accepted the concept of a national wartime draft, but they wanted a measure acceptable to their constituents. They argued for either a trial of the volunteer system before the introduction of the draft, or at least allowing the raising of U.S. Volunteers during the months it would take to establish a conscription agency and to put the draft into effect. At worst, they sought to pin responsibility for abandonment of the Volunteers and reliance upon the draft solely upon the president.[6]

Although the agrarians on the House Military Affairs Committee needled Baker about abandoning the Volunteers before showing they had failed, the secretary refused to be intimidated and continued to return to his main point, that the selective draft was the best way to raise an army without impeding vital industrial production. He accurately predicted that local elites throughout the country would understand this:

> Modern war is so different, and its dependence upon industry is so obvious, that I think everybody who thinks about it—and *the leading people in every community will think it out and explain it*—will find there is less to be feared from that source than might seem likely.[7]

Critics emphasized the political and constitutional issues involved in a national draft, such as the age of the draftees. The administration had recommended 19–25 because the General Staff considered younger men better soldiers and because the administration believed it would limit the financial cost—there would be fewer married men, and therefore fewer dependency allotments.[8] However, many Americans, particularly in rural areas, believed that country boys of 19 and 20 were too young and to naïve to be exposed to the roughness of army life. Furthermore, since 21 was the age of legal adulthood in most states, it seemed inconsistent to draft boys who were not yet legally adults and to place the military obligation of citizenship upon those who did not yet qualify for one of its major privileges—the right to vote. Also troubling to some critics was the "specter" of power centralized in the hands of national military and civilian authorities. The proposed statute provided a vague, blanket delegation of power to the War Department to write and administer regulations for implementation of the draft, which upon presidential approval would have the force of federal law. Concerned about such a mixing of legislative and executive functions, particularly since military authorities would be involved, many members of Congress, including those who supported the draft, wanted to know what the rules would be and who would administer them.

Agrarian lawmakers were particularly concerned with protecting farm labor from the draft. Since the administration emphasized the exemption of key *industrial* workers, it appeared that the drafted army might be composed primarily of young men from the agricultural areas, as were most mass armies in Europe. The agrarians' solution was to designate agriculture as an "essential industry," qualifying for special protection and exemption from the draft. American farmers had expanded production to feed the Allies, it was argued, and they would now have to feed American armies as well. Already farmers were experiencing a shortage of labor for spring planting because many young men had left for more lucrative employment in the cities. Farm state representatives argued that, without adequate safeguards, the draft would exacerbate the shortage and result in reduced production of cotton and foodstuffs.[9]

Southerners debated the impact of the draft on race relations as well as on the agricultural workforce, which was composed primarily of Afro-Americans. Since southern states had only in recent years completed their program of black disfranchisement and segregation, comparatively few white southerners wanted federal intervention in race relations, even indirectly through a wartime draft. Some southern racists denounced the draft as a direct threat to the white South. It would, Senator James K. Vardaman told a crowd of Mississippians, place "arrogant strutting representatives of the black soldiery in every community."[10]

The black community was divided. Most of its leaders wanted Afro-Americans to be included in the draft to reinforce their claim to equal citizenship. W.E.B. Du Bois, a Harvard-educated sociologist and editor of the magazine of the National Association for the Advancement of Colored People (NAACP), *The Crisis*, demanded that blacks be included in the draft. Seeing a chance, as in the Civil War, for blacks to obtain their rights by fighting for the nation, Du Bois and others urged them to participate willingly in the armed forces.[11] However, many blacks were skeptical of the chance for racial equality under a southern-dominated Democratic party which, since it regained national power, had expanded segregation in the federal civil service. Florida-born James Weldon Johnson, author and columnist for a black newspaper in New York City, accused the administration of seeking selective rather than universal military service in order to select only whites—at least for combat. If blacks were drafted at all, Johnson predicted, it would be for menial service, such as in labor battalions, which would not help their claim to equal citizenship.[12]

The NAACP decided not to lobby on the draft bill unless southern whites raised the race issue in Congress and sought to exclude blacks from the army. Although this failed to occur, a commotion did erupt in the House, when a white representative from upcountry South Carolina warned heatedly against the possibility of racially integrated units. "If you put a [white] boy from Mississippi in a negro regiment from Massachusetts, you won't have to go to Germany to have a war," he declared. "You will have it right here."[13] The chamber rang with a chorus of rebel yells from southern congressmen. Although the black press reported such incidents, the NAACP did not challenge the issue directly in the southern-dominated Congress. Rather, it tried to persuade the executive branch to include blacks in the draft and in the officer-training camps.[14]

Northerners in Congress suspected that southern members of Congress might attempt to remove blacks from the calculation of draft quotas, a move which would give southern states smaller draft quotas than their total population warranted. To avoid this, Rep. Martin Madden, a Chicago Republican, amended the administration's bill to require that draft quotas be based on total male population, not simply the number of men actually eligible for the draft. Thus, if southern whites did succeed in excluding blacks, they would be required to conscript more whites to fill their quotas.[15] However, in an unforseen quirk of fate, Madden's amendment produced the opposite effect of what he and his northern supporters had intended. Blacks were not excluded, but undeclarant aliens who were still citizens of other nations were. Therefore, the amendment applied in practice mainly to northern cities filled with such unnaturalized immigrants, increasing the burden on U.S. citizens in such districts, including Madden's.

Responding to the agrarian leadership in Congress, the president agreed that farmers, like munitions workers, could be considered an important part of the war program. Baker privately assured the House Military Affairs Committee that the administration planned to exclude essential farm workers from the draft.[16] Although some agrarians remained skeptical, many were gradually won over. They were already disinclined to wrangle openly with the president for fear of being denounced as disloyal. The champion of rural America, William Jennings Bryan, summarily abandoned his longtime opposition to conscription, and following the declaration of war, declared that "whatever the government does is right."[17]

Southern members of Congress were assured by the administration, and by General Crowder, that the draft would not adversely affect race relations or their agricultural labor supply. The ratio of blacks and whites in the South would not be disturbed, Baker promised the committee. Under pressure from Senator Kenneth D. McKellar of Tennessee, General Crowder became even more specific, developing tentative regulations which would keep Afro-Americans working in the cotton fields. House Majority Leader Claude Kitchin of North Carolina told a concerned white employer that under the proposed draft regulations, "few of them [the blacks], if any, will be taken." The white southerners were also assured that there would be no integrated units. Black soldiers who enlisted or were drafted, Secretary Baker told committee members, would serve only in racially segregated units.[18]

Afro-Americans were neglected until the NAACP appealed directly to the president and the secretary of war, and threatened to embarrass the administration's claim to be fighting for democracy. At issue was not the desegregation of military units, which not even the NAACP demanded, but rather whether members of the black middle class would obtain officerships and whether black enlisted men would receive fair treatment in the army and in training camps in the South. In response, the administration appointed Emmett J. Scott, an associate of the late Booker T. Washington, as a special assistant to Baker to deal with complaints of racial discrimination from the black community. Despite hostility by regulars, the administration also established a special training program at Fort Des Moines, Iowa, which ultimately graduated 639 black officers.[19] Since the draft was extended to Puerto Rico, an officer training camp there graduated 700 Puerto Rican officers.[20]

As regards white ethnic groups, the administration won the support, or at least the acquiescence, of most of their important leaders with relative ease. In several ethnic communities, especially those of German, Irish, and Russian–Jewish background, many people continued to oppose conscription into an army which might fight alongside Britain and Russia, but many also proved willing to fight, either out of enthusiasm or fear of repression.[21] Since the nation's 17 million Roman Catholics comprised nearly 20 percent of the American population and a majority in the industrial workforce, the administration welcomed the endorsement of leading prelates like James Cardinal Gibbons of Baltimore. Cardinal Gibbons led a delegation of archbishops to Washington and publicly assured the president of the church's support. For its part, the administration affirmed that there would be Roman Catholic and Jewish as well as Protestant chaplains for the armed forces. Seeking to counter vociferous opposition to the war and the draft by some lay Catholics, especially within the ethnic Irish and German communities, Gibbons declared that "the members of both Houses of Congress are instruments of God in guiding us in our civic duties."[22]

Regardless of their religion, many industrial workers who had opposed U.S. entry continued to object to compulsory military service. Especially strong opposition came from union locals and city labor councils in the urban centers of New York, Ohio, Wisconsin, California, Maryland, Missouri, and Louisiana and from radical national unions like the United Mine Workers and the International Union of Mine, Mill, and Smelter Workers. Samuel Gompers and other moderate leaders of the A.F. of L. effectively contained such sentiment, however, and negotiated directly with General Crowder to protect the trade unions' interests. In particular, Gompers obtained assurances that the draft would not be used against the unions, but rather Crowder would attempt to defer skilled industrial workers and include representatives of organized labor on the district draft boards which would assess the labor needs of each region. To convert the rank and file of the A.F. of L., Gompers invited representatives of British labor unions to explain why American labor should support both the war and the draft [23]

Radical labor and liberal antidraft organizations split over the proper course to take. At the grass-roots level, members of the Industrial Workers of the World condemned it as a policy of the "dominant capitalist exploiters." Yet William "Big Bill" Haywood and the executive council refused to go on record for fear that this would give the I.W.W.'s enemies a weapon with which to crush it.[24] Among the liberal pacifists of the American Union Against Militarism, more conservative leaders like Lillian D. Wald and Paul U. Kellogg accepted the draft as inevitable and blocked proposals by radicals like Crystal Eastman for public denunciations and mass meetings. Instead, AUAM leaders sought to convince the president to recognize the right of conscientious objection on secular humanistic as well as religious grounds. In mid-April, a delegation led by Wald and Jane Addams obtained assurance from the secretary of war that the administration would try to avoid prosecution and widespread harassment of conscientious objectors, such as had occurred in England.[25]

Despite the adminstration's attempt to mollify some of the dissenters, a core of organized opposition remained. A few days after the declaration of war, the majority of delegates at the Socialist party convention in St. Louis officially condemned the conflict as a capitalists' war and advocated active public opposition to it. When several prominent socialists—including Upton Sinclair, Charlotte Perkins Gilman, and the 1916 presidential candidate Allan Benson— quit in disgust, opposition to the war and the draft was left to centrist and left-wing elements of the Socialist party, led by New York labor lawyer Morris Hillquit, Milwaukee editor Victor L. Berger, and Charles E. Ruthenberg of Cleveland. Fiery anarchist Emma Goldman founded the small Harlem Union against Conscription. Crystal and Max Eastman, journalist Louis P. Lochner, and others founded the People's Council for Peace and Democracy in opposition to the draft and imperialism. Recognizing that most of these groups were small and radical, the administration neither negotiated with them nor particularly opposed their suppression.[26]

Within two weeks after Congress had received the draft bill, the House Military Affairs Committee had come up with two alternatives. Both accepted expansion of the regular army and National Guard, but differed over the president's plan to draft the National Army. Rep. Daniel R. Anthony (Rep.-Kan.), a smalltown newspaper publisher, proposed a five-month trial for raising the wartime army under the Volunteer Act of 1914, with a turn to the draft only if not enough Volunteers were obtained.[27] A more popular alternative came from the chair of the Military Affairs Committee, Rep. S. Hubert Dent, Jr. (Dem.-Ala.), a lawyer from Montgomery, who proposed simultaneously raising the Volunteers and creating the mechanism for the draft. The Dent bill authorized the president to establish a Selective Service System, to conduct registration for the draft, and, when and if the chief executive determined that voluntarism had failed, to induct young men into the armed forces.[28] Dent's proposal offered something to both sides, those who favored the Volunteers and those who wanted the draft. Politically, it was also designed to enable the legislators to avoid directly coercing unwilling constituents. As an agrarian representative on the Military Affairs Committee confided, it "puts the responsibility on the President to determine whether the volunteer system is a failure."[29]

The Dent plan may have also been designed to avoid sending draftees to Europe.[30] It created two types of forces, one volunteer, one conscripted, which raised at least the possibility that any overseas expeditionary force might be composed solely of volunteers with the drafted army for home defense. Such a two-tier force would not have been unique. Continental European nations had maintained mass armies of conscripted citizen-reservists, liable for service only in Europe against other major powers, and separate professional armies, raised by long-term voluntary enlistment, which served primarily to fight overseas expeditionary wars and perform constabulary duty in the colonies. The distinction was made during the World War in overseas British dominions like Australia and South Africa with substantial anti-English minorities, composed of Irish and Dutch. Because of the large ethnic Irish and German populations, as well as agrarian isolationism in America, there was considerable sentiment for such a two-tier force in the United States, coming from sources as varied as the *New Republic* and the Hearst press. As a New York Republican on the House Military

Affairs Committee explained privately, "many Democrats want a volunteer system for foreign service as well as many Republicans."[31]

The House Military Affairs Committee finally put the proposals to a vote on April 18. Rejecting both Anthony's recommendation for an exclusive five-month trial of the Volunteers, and the president's proposal for exclusive reliance on the draft for the wartime army, the majority adopted Dent's bill for simultaneously raising the Volunteers and preparing for the draft. The 13–8 vote on the Dent bill showed a split along urban-rural and regional lines rather than along party lines, a division also reflecting attitudes on American entry into the war. The conscriptionist minority behind the president was composed primarily of Republicans but included several Democrats, all of whom represented internationalist metropolitan districts in the Northeast or on the West Coast. The majority that supported the Dent compromise included Democrats and Republicans from isolationist, agrarian districts of the South and Midwest.[32]

Ironically, the fight in Congress for the Democratic administration's army plan was led in the House by a Republican, and, as many newspapers emphasized, one born in Germany. A native of the Grand Duchy of Baden, Julius Kahn had arrived in the United States with his parents when he was five years old. Settling in California, he later became an actor, then a trial lawyer, and finally, a politician, representing San Francisco in Congress since 1898. The German-American community was divided over the concept of conscription, with antimilitaristic south Germans and descendants of the liberal exiles of 1848 vigorously denouncing it as an autocratic, Prussian institution, while others like Julius Kahn, who had previously taken considerable pride in Imperial Germany's accomplishments, endorsed UMT&S as well as a wartime selective draft for the United States.[33]

In the Senate Military Affairs Committee, the situation was reversed. On April 18, Senator Chamberlain had gotten a 10–7 endorsement of the president's proposal. The split once again pitted urban-internationalists against rural-isolationists, regardless of political party, but this time in the Senate.[34] The rural minority, led by Senator McKellar, dissented and introduced a two-track compromise similar to the Dent bill, although in McKellar's case this seems to have been for the benefit of antidraft voters in Tennessee where he would face re-election in 1918. On March 24, he had confided to a friend that although he was opposed to compulsory military service in time of peace, "I do believe in drafting in time of war or when war is imminent. Such a time is now."[35]

During the two weeks that the military affairs committees had been considering the draft, conscriptionist organizations and the press had mobilized a massive publicity campaign in support of the president's proposal. None outdid the Hearst press in pumping up nationalism and the martial spirit. The New York *Journal-American* carried daily stories, editorials, and political cartoons endorsing what it called the president's plan for "universal military service." It also bombarded the city with leaflets scattered from airplanes, sponsored "Wake-up America" parades, and secured more than two million signatures on petitions supporting the draft. With fewer theatrics, the draft was endorsed by *The New York Times, The New York World*, the Boston *Transcript, The Chicago Tribune*, and most other urban dailies.[36]

The press and the preparedness organizations focused on the inequitable burden which the volunteer system placed on patriotic citizens who enlisted while "slackers" escaped their duty, the fear of which apparently afflicted many already concerned about the loyalties of so-called "hyphenated Americans." The problem with voluntarism, one Hearst editor declared, was that:

> Those who are most patriotic and most intelligently loyal are necessarily sacrificed in the defense of the least patriotic and least loyal—so that in the very process of defending the land we automatically lower its future standard of citizenry and leave its destinies in the hands not of the brave and freedom-loving but in the hands of cowards and those fit only to be slaves.[37]

Conscription, it was argued, would distribute the military burden more intelligently and equitably. Mingling terms like "selective draft" and "universal service" as if they were synonymous, editors hailed the president's proposal as "democratic," "scientific," and "modern," whereas the volunteer system was "flintlock" legislation, as useless "as a leaky bucket." The National Security League alone sent out nearly 100,000 pieces of literature on behalf of the draft and supplied speakers for over 400 meetings. A new umbrella organization, the Conference Committee on National Preparedness, attempted to mobilize local elites to pressure "voluntarist" members of Congress, sending wires which began:

> Does your district by silence now want to be a party to the injustice of permitting its representative in Congress to jeopardize American liberty and waste American lives by voting for a military policy that sent George Washington to his knees at Valley Forge?[38]

Tactically, the conscriptionist organizations and the prodraft press concentrated on the majority on the House Military Affairs Committee, castigating those who voted for the Dent bill as giving "aid and comfort to the enemy."

Like a summer thunderstorm, a deluge of letters and telegrams battered Capitol Hill. Half a million came from the 300,000-member Navy League alone. Except for the declaration of war, the draft led to more constituent mail than any other issue in 1917. Although the letters indicated that considerable opposition remained, they also showed that a large number of articulate people, particularly in business and the professions, clearly supported the draft.[39] As more than one member of Congress noted, this prodraft mail came from "the most substantial citizens" in their community. Many of them praised UMT for its ability to improve the physical condition and social attitudes of young men; at the same time, they liked the selective draft because it would leave key workers at home while forcing those who were not essential to the economy to serve in the army.

Furthermore, the appeal to class and ethnic prejudices against groups considered "slackers" had been highly effective. Many of the local elites had concluded that the volunteer system was not only inefficient and unfair, but that it also "works a hardship on the best element," and makes an "unequal sacrifice of the educated classes."[40] Those with more specific ethnic prejudices concluded that the selective draft was necessary to ensure that the unskilled, the unacculturized, the "loafers," "slackers," and (some added), "radicals" went into the army. "I implore you [to] vote for conscription," a Chicago business executive wrote to members of Congress, "and let the loafers and unsympathetic *naturalized foreigners* do their part."[41] From Wisconsin, a local civic leader demonstrated an anti-Semitism and general xenophobia as he urged his congressman to support the draft:

> We have in this country over two million Jews of military age and many more millions of pacifics [sic] and pacifics [sic] sons of like age, none of whom will volunteer. Compulsory service will make good American citizens of these classes. My ancestors fought in the revolution and rebellion and I can assure you this is the feeling of the intelligent men of this section.[42]

Faced with a mobilization of local elites and pressure from the president, from conscriptionist organizations, and the press, many members of Congress had begun to waver even before debate on the army bill began on April 21. Prodraft newspapers reported that the legislators had "heard from home," and unofficial tallies suggested that support in the House for the president's proposal had increased from 138 to 200, only 18 votes short of a majority. Wilson had lined up some powerful southern committee chairmen and convinced Majority Leader Kitchin, who remained opposed, not to participate in the debate. To strengthen the resolve of sympathetic representatives who wanted to support the administration on the draft, but feared the opposition of their districts, the president summoned them to the White House in a symbolic gesture to help them assuage their constituents.[43]

The week-long debate on what everybody recognized was a historic measure elicited both eloquence and political positioning. Behind the words and postures, however, lay fundamentally different visions of the nature of America and its role in the world: an urban industrial internationalist vision superseding an older agrarian, isolationist view. Those who led the congressional battle for the immediate draft reiterated most of the arguments praising the efficiency and equity of the draft compared to the volunteer system.[44] The most repeated and apparently most persuasive argument, however, was that under the traditional format "slackers" would evade military service. "The volunteer system," a Minnesota Republican declared, "takes those who had not ought to go, and . . . exempts those who ought to go." "If we depend upon the volunteer system, we shall let our good men go to war and our slackers stay at home," warned William C. Adamson (Dem.-Ga.), chair of the House Interstate Commerce Committee, "We shall have to keep an army at home to protect the country against the men left alone when the best men go to war."[45] Thus the "equity" of the draft was seen as doubly important.

Although few discussed the military use to which the American wartime army would be put, some supporters argued that the Volunteer system was inadequate for modern warfare. "This is not a war which any nation can 'muddle through,'" asserted Senator Joseph S. Frelinghuysen (Rep.-N.J.), "Cincinnatus would not have been an effective soldier in this war, and the Minute Men of '76 would have survived about a minute on the bloody slopes of San Quentin."[46] In contrast, agrarians argued that volunteers made better soldiers and that the Volunteer system could raise a million troops faster than the draft, which would first require the establishment of a widespread bureaucracy. The draft was denounced as inequitable, as class legislation, and as a means by which American draftees would be sent across the Atlantic to help the Allied nations achieve "their selfish goals." Young men from Georgia, Senator Thomas W. Hardwick declared, should not be forced into the trenches "for European squabbles . . . to decide who shall have

Alsace or Lorraine or Bosnia or Herzegovina, or some other outland-
ish country over there."[47]

The most dramatic moment of the debate came when the Speaker
of the House, James Beauchamp "Champ" Clark, stepped down
from his rostrum and for two hours on April 25 expounded in favor
of "a fair, reasonable trial of the old volunteer system which has
gained us victory in all our wars." The sage of Bowling Green,
Missouri, explained the appeal of what a historian would later call
the "island communities" of agrarian America:

> Missourians wish to serve shoulder to shoulder, elbow to elbow,
> heart to heart, with their neighbors, friends, and kindred and do
> not desire to be broken up into small squads and distributed
> among strangers from distant localities. Wounded, their neigh-
> bors would tender first aid. Sick, their friends would minister
> unto them. Dead, their friends and neighbors would bury them
> Homesick and discouraged, their comrades would cheer them up.
> All history teaches that men fight better under such circum-
> stances.[48]

In what proved to be a major mistake, the Speaker declared
with rhetorical flourish: "I protest with all my heart and mind and
soul against having the slur of being a conscript placed upon the
men of Missouri. In the estimation of Missourians there is precious
little difference between a conscript and a convict."[49] Because the
metropolitan press focused on this last sentence in an attempt to
discredit voluntarists, it became the most controversial statement
made against the draft. However, Clark's actual intention and deliv-
ery may have been somewhat different. One prodraft member of
the House recalled that Clark had been referring to the Civil War,
had said it only to brighten his speech, smiling when he did so, and
that everyone there knew he was speaking facetiously.[50]

Finally, three weeks after the administration had introduced the
draft bill and following a full week of debate during which emotions
had grown heated, the measure reached a vote in the House on April
28. Agrarian voluntarists controlled the procedure, so the first—
and crucial—vote was on Congressman Dent's two-track proposal
for simultaneously raising the Volunteers and creating conscription
machinery, which would also shift responsibility for declaring voluntarism a failure entirely onto the president. As House members
filed past the tellers (in a vote which tallied numbers but did not
record names), the count registered only 98 for and 279 against the
Dent bill. The president had won and, with success assured, pent-up
tension broke. An exuberant demonstration erupted on the floor
and several members began a snake-dance down the aisle. Brus-
quely the Speaker gavelled them back to order, but with the eventual

outcome clear, the bandwagon began to roll. In a roll-call vote putting members on record, the Dent bill was defeated by an even larger margin, 109 to 313. Finally, half an hour before midnight, the president's draft bill came up for a vote at last. It was adopted 397 to 24, only a handful holding out against it.[51] The Senate voted the same day, defeating the McKellar amendment (similar to the Dent bill), 18 to 69. Then, learning of the House's adoption, the Senate enacted the draft bill by a vote of 81 to 8 only a few minutes before midnight.[52]

Coming after weeks of congressional opposition and delay, the administration's overwhelming victory—particularly in the House—came as quite a surprise. It meant that within three weeks the House of Representatives, pivoting like a weathervane in a windstorm, had completely reversed itself. The Washington press corps could not remember another such rapid and complete reversal.[53] Advocates of the "voluntarism first" compromise, who had constituted a majority in the House in early April, had found themselves a beleaguered minority by the end of the month. This erosion had been largely concealed by the fact that the press had focused on the continued public opposition expressed by the House leadership; behind these leaders, a large number of members had buckled under enormous pressure.

Antidraft legislators complained that the pressure came from several sources—the administration, the press, local elites mobilized by the conscriptionist organizations, and the British and French Missions which had arrived in late April. Marvin Jones, a rural Texas Democrat serving the first of his twelve terms in the House, later recalled that the Allied Missions had helped bring home to many in Congress that the United States was being catapulted into an active international role: "The whole picture of this country was changing all at once. . . . [You] could almost feel the process of change, a transformation from an individual nation into an important position in the family of nations. One could almost see it unfolding just like one may almost see corn grow when the season's just right, at least you can actually hear it crackle."[54]

Even if the major battle over the draft had been won by the administration on April 28, the legislative skirmishing was far from complete. Although both Houses of Congress had approved the president's proposal for an immediate draft, each chamber had made different amendments to the army bill. Both had rejected the idea of drafting 19- and 20-year-olds, establishing draft eligibility at 21 instead. The House, in an attempt to curb enthusiasm for the draft by bringing the threat of induction to a broader age group, included males from 21 to 40 years of age. The Senate, with an eye on keeping costs down and skilled workers and managers at work rather than in the army, limited the ages of eligibility to 21–27.[55] In regard to compensation, the administration, influenced by conscriptionist organizations and the General Staff, had suggested that wartime citizen-soldiers should serve out of patriotic duty and, therefore, need not be compensated with wages in addition to their sustenance. Rejecting this, Congress decided to double the current pay for soldiers and to provide allotments for their dependents (eventually, Congress also voted War Risk Insurance). In addition to food and housing, a private would now receive $29 or $30 a month (the House and Senate versions differed), plus domestic allotments sent directly to dependents. This was not an inconsiderable sum since civilian laborers responsible for their own living expenses earned only $80 a month.[56]

In the Senate version, reformers had obtained a provision for the prohibition of alcohol and the suppression of prostitution. It would make it illegal to sell liquor to soldiers in uniform and it would empower the president to exclude, from the vicinity of any army base, saloons or other establishments selling alcoholic beverages, as well as "houses of ill fame, brothels, or bawdy houses." Reflecting the growing prohibition movement as well as the continuing unfavorable public image of career enlisted men in the regular army, these provisions were adopted over the opposition of the General Staff which saw them as irrelevant to the military mission and an aspersion on the Army's reputation. This attempt to prevent the "corruption" of young draftees was adopted largely as the result of an active campaign by prohibition groups, led by the Anti-Saloon League, by youth and moral reform organizations such as the Young Men's Christian Association, and by an influential combination of rural evangelical Protestants and cosmopolitan urban social reformers. Prohibition for the wartime army became an important step towards postwar national prohibition.[57] A conference committee from both Houses soon settled most of the differences in the Senate and House versions of the army bill. They agreed on age limits of 21 to 30, a monthly pay of $30 for privates, and the prohibition of liquor and brothels near army camps. But the committee could not reach agreement on what proved to be a thorny issue—the "Roosevelt Volunteers."[58]

Theodore Roosevelt was never easily suppressed. Although the administration had refused his offer to raise and lead an expedition of Volunteers to France, there were many in Congress and the country who wanted to let him do so. During the congressional debate, a group of Senate Republicans, led by Henry Cabot Lodge, had amended the army bill to allow the president to accept the

"Roosevelt Volunteers." By limiting this authorization to four divisions, a corps of 100,000 troops, the measure was designed as an addition, not a substitute, for the president's plan for a drafted army. These Old Guard eastern Republicans did not want to reinvigorate the system of U.S. Volunteers with its locally raised and led companies, battalions, and regiments. Rather, reflecting the views of their conscriptionist constituents, they were working simultaneously to get a wartime draft enacted by a Democratic Congress. They wanted the "Roosevelt Volunteers" primarily for partisan purposes—to help give the GOP a heroic role in the war.[59]

The idea of the "Roosevelt Volunteers" caught the public imagination. The old Rough Rider was the nation's most popular amateur soldier. He sought to make his Volunteers a symbol of America. For officers, he had selected descendents of families with illustrious military histories like the Lees, Jacksons, and the Grants, as well as a number of prominent citizens. As one of the initiators of the "politics of ethnic recognition," Roosevelt also intended to have a variety of ethnic regiments, including Americans of Irish, German, Polish and other European ancestry, and a black regiment (under white officers), all symbolically fighting under the flag of the United States.[60]

Both isolationists and interventionists could support this volunteer force. Pro-Ally interventionists applauded it in April because it would ensure a U.S. expeditionary force to France and would help involve Americans emotionally in the Allied cause. Conscriptionist newspapers that had been flaying the inequitable and archaic volunteer system saw no inconsistency in supporting the "Roosevelt Volunteers." They argued that an exception should be made for Roosevelt, because no other single individual could stir the country's martial spirit like "Teddy."[61] Many opponents of the war and the draft also supported the "Roosevelt Volunteers," because they believed that it might mean that only volunteers would be sent overseas. Especially after Congress rejected the Dent bill on April 28, support for the "Roosevelt Volunteers" grew among isolationist, antidraft forces in Congress and the country, particularly in the rural South and Middle West.[62]

On April 28, the Senate had adopted an amendment to the draft bill to *require* the president to authorize four divisions of U.S. Volunteers. A solid phalanx of Republicans was joined by a considerable number of voluntarist Democrats from the South and Midwest who refused to be swayed by administration lobbying against the amendment. Indeed, the day after Senator McKellar had spoken on the Senate floor in favor of sending the ex-president and his unit to France, the president came to Capitol Hill and told him that "it would be a mistake to send Col. Roosevelt over there."[63] The House, however, proved unwilling to support the "Roosevelt Volunteers," for the prickly ex-president had alienated many anti-interventionist representatives, Republicans as well as Democrats, when over the previous two months he had denounced them as obstructionists. Now this anti-Roosevelt coalition defeated his proposal.[64]

It was this disagreement over the "Roosevelt Volunteers" that the Senate and House conference committee found impossible to resolve. For nearly two weeks, Senate conferees supported Roosevelt, while the House delegates, backed by the administration, stood firmly against him. As the days dragged by, however, conscriptionist organizations and the press became increasingly impatient and hostile, arguing that Roosevelt's personal ambitions were blocking the nation's mobilization and goals. The New York *World* complained that Roosevelt's position was that "the volunteer system is vicious and indefensible except when he personally wishes to raise a division of volunteers."[65] More importantly, Republican party leaders began to turn against him, for they feared that the GOP might be blamed for obstructing the war effort. Some of Roosevelt's admirers advised him to save face by accepting an appointment to head a national campaign to spur enlistments into the regular army and National Guard, but the ex-president refused to budge.[66] As a way out of the impasse, some Senate Democrats appealed to Wilson to appoint Roosevelt a brigadier general in the U.S. Army, but the president declined.[67] Unexpectedly, Senate Republicans gave in first, with three GOP delegates agreeing on May 10 to jettison the Rough Rider and his Volunteers. Privately furious at such "treachery," the ex-president publicly announced that he was ending his campaign for command because he realized that continued delay of the draft and army bill might hurt the Republican party, and the American war effort. Sadly, the "colonel" pulled his helmet out of the ring.[68]

In a final irony, however, the issue of the "Roosevelt Volunteers" took on new life, despite its apparent demise. For after previously rejecting the idea, the House of Representatives now turned around and endorsed the "Roosevelt Volunteers." This final bid for some trial of the volunteer system was led by Kansas Republican Daniel R. Anthony, whose bill for exclusive reliance on volunteers had already been defeated. Behind him now in mid-May was a coalition of anti-administration Republicans and voluntarist Democrats from the South and the Midwest. Angry conscriptionists blamed the House flip-flop on partisan politics, but it was more than that. Considerable sentiment from throughout the country continued to favor the "Roosevelt Volunteers," even if there were to be a draft. For another week, the conferees debated in private until, on May 16, they reached a final compromise which *permitted* but did not require the president to authorize the four Volunteer divisions.[69] Members of Congress could, therefore, vote for the ex-president's unit, while passing full responsibility for quashing the idea to the president. Both Houses quickly adopted the administration's army bill, which now included amended sections involving age limits, wages, liquor, and the authorization for the "Roosevelt Volunteers." The vote was 397 to 24 in the House and 81 to 8 in the Senate.[70] Before signing the draft act on May 18, 1917, Wilson announced that he had no intention of authorizing any Volunteer divisions. It would, he said, interfere with the orderly process of the draft. The days of the U.S. Volunteers were over; Roosevelt would miss his last chance for glory. "The business now at hand," Wilson concluded, "is undramatic, practical and of scientific definiteness and precision."[71]

After signing the draft bill into law, the president proclaimed that a nation-wide registration of men aged 21–30 would be held on June 5. In a speech prepared by Major Hugh S. Johnson of General Crowder's office, Wilson spoke of the task now facing the country:

> It is not an army that we must shape and train for war; it is a nation. . . .
>
> The whole Nation must be a team in which each man shall play the part for which he is best fitted. . . . Each man shall be classified for service in the place to which it shall best serve the general good to call him.[72]

This new venture in American history represented a landmark of progress, the president explained, a new manner of vitalizing the people's duty through devotion to the common purpose. In a soaring peroration, the presidential message concluded: "It is in no sense a conscription of the unwilling. It is rather, selection from a nation which has volunteered in mass."[73]

Of course, the nation had not at all volunteered in mass. In fact, it was a lack of faith in mass volunteering which had contributed substantially to interventionist support for the draft. And Wilson's March 28 decision to turn immediately to conscription had been based largely upon his desire to block Roosevelt and his Volunteers. Hence, the draft was adopted in a nation which clearly remained divided both over the wisdom of U.S. entry into the war, and the necessity of a draft.

The heated debate at the time indicates that the draft was problematic rather than inevitable in 1917 and that neither its specific nature nor the timing of its implementation was irreversibly preordained. Athough international conditions indicated the appropriateness of a mass army for a major power, a variety of military formats had been available for a large-scale force. The General Staff and civilian conscriptionists wanted to abandon the National Guard as well as the U.S. Volunteers and, although they differed over details, to replace both of these with a permanent system of UMT&S. Alternatively, the traditional U.S. Volunteers were still highly popular in rural America. In the Volunteer Act of 1914, Congress had sought to reform the system to avoid the military deficiencies disclosed during the Civil War and to accommodate it to the economic needs of a more specialized and interdependent, industrial society. Extensive enlistment of U.S. Volunteers could easily have produced an army of 1.5 million men in 1917, as army officers admitted in postwar analyses.[74] This figure represented the initial goal of the General Staff planners and the Wilson administration between February and May, 1917 and was nearly as large as the ultimate size of the AEF which reached 2 million by the Armistice in November 1918.

There had been other alternatives available. Besides the traditional U.S. Volunteers, there was also the possibility of a two-tier system of a drafted home defense army and a voluntary expeditionary force. A few progressive magazines had gone further and advocated a form of national service.[75] Theoretically, the United States could also have augmented its wartime army by actively encouraging recruitment of units from American colonies such as Puerto Rico and the Philippines, or from among subordinated groups in the United States: immigrant aliens, non-whites, and women. Although European nations tapped all such sources, including women for auxiliary military roles, predominant American opinion precluded any significant recruitment of colonials or women. Offers of European ethnic or American Indian units were generally refused due to fears of cultural fragmentation and "Balkanization." Afro-Americans served in segregated units. The Army and the administration rejected thousands of black volunteers and sought initially to limit them to the four traditional black combat regiments. Later, although hundreds of thousands of blacks were drafted, the majority were assigned to labor battalions—no more than two divisions were composed of black combat troops.[76]

Considering the militarily feasible alternatives available at the time, the particular format chosen by the United States—the *Nation-State Model*, employing a wartime selective draft—resulted from a conducive context of international and domestic circumstances and from the actions and attitudes of particular individuals and groups. The debate over the proper military format was substantially shaped by an articulate, well-organized, and amply financed effort, the "conscription crusade," and by the reaction to its program. But the power of the leaders of the preparedness movement to achieve their entire military program was limited by political realities— they could neither get rid of the National Guard nor win the establishment of UMT&S. Nevertheless, they had initiated effective reserve officer programs and, more importantly, had helped convince many Americans of the unsuitability of the old U.S. Volunteers and the appropriateness of the draft, at least in wartime. When the United States entered the war, preparedness organizations and their allies in the press generated significant public support for the president's plan for a wartime draft. Contemporaries and a number of subsequent scholars have correctly credited them with playing a major role in the adoption of the Selective Draft Act of 1917.[77]

"When Mr. Wilson cracks the whip I imagine, judging from past performances, they [the antidraft Democrats] will vote as he desires," a prodraft, Republican congressman from New York wrote in mid-April 1917. And this assessment was echoed by an aide to an antidraft Republican congressman from Wisconsin: "No one can appreciate the enormous influence the President has in Congress, unless he can actually see it working right here in Washington. . . . What he wants he gets."[78] It was not inherent presidential power, but rather the change in circumstances that came with U.S. entry which provided an unusual degree of power to the chief executive. Wilson used it with consummate skill and effectiveness. While remaining firmly committed to the draft after introducing it in Congress, he proved willing to negotiate the details of implementation. Most importantly, he realized that while the majority of Americans would not agree to permanent UMT&S they would accept a temporary, selective national draft, if it were seen as necessary for the achievement of a worthy and progressive goal. Wilson established that lofty wartime goal—not simply the response to U-boat attacks on a few American merchant ships, but the defeat of German aggression and militarism so that the international system could be reformed and the world made "safe for democracy."

The draft was made more palatable to Congress through modifications in the War Department's original proposal, instigated or agreed to by the administration during April 1917. In a most significant move, General Crowder and Secretary Baker had rejected the War College Division's plan for a highly federalized and somewhat "militarized" draft agency.[79] In view of American suspicions of the army and of a powerful central government, the administration adopted lines that had been largely suggested by Crowder and his staff, and proposed a much more "civilianized" and decentralized "Selective Service System." State and local officials would be used to carry out the national program that would be "supervised" by a national Selective Service Headquarters. The president would be authorized to create a system of local draft boards, one in each county, and one for every 30,000 persons in major cities. The board members were to be appointed by the president from among local citizens or authorities, the law stating specifically that "none of [the board members] shall be connected with the Military Establishment."[80]

Local draft boards would have the power to determine questions of induction and deferment under regulations prescribed by the president, through Selective Service Headquarters. In addition, the administration's plan, as finally adopted, created an appeals procedure (absent from the General Staff's original plan) by which decisions of the local boards could be appealed to district boards, one in each federal judicial district, and ultimately to the president. As in the General Staff recommendation, failure to comply with the act was a misdemeanor, punishable by up to one year in federal prison.[81]

Congress also modified some of the provisions defining who would be exempted from the draft, but accepted most of the administration's suggestions. It agreed to exempt officers of the executive, legislative, and judicial branches of the federal and state governments, but it also gave the president the authority to exclude county and local officials. For religious purposes, ordained ministers and theological school students were exempted. But in regard to conscientious objectors, the law authorized noncombatant military service solely for members of "any well-recognized religious sect . . . whose principles forbid its members to participate in war in any form. . . ."[82] Of more concern to Congress was safeguarding the economic interests of their constituents. The lawmakers agreed with the administration's desire to maintain industrial production, but added agriculture as well. Congress agreed that such large categories could not be specifically exempted by statute, but instead gave the president, and through him the Selective Service System, authority to exclude (through individual deferments) or discharge from military service "persons engaged in industries, including agriculture, found to be necessary to the maintenance of the Military Establishment or the effective operation of the military forces, or the maintenance of national interest during the emergency."[83] Congress also provided for deferments for those who were "physically or morally deficient" and for "those in a status with respect to persons dependent upon them for support which renders their exclusion or discharge advisable."

Yet in the final analysis, the ability of the president, the press, and the preparedness organizations to force a reluctant majority in Con-

gress to abandon the volunteer system and adopt a wartime draft
was possible, even predictable, for several larger reasons than simply effective pressure groups and an able wartime president. Among
these were the growth of an industrial economy and a heterogeneous, multi-ethnic society, the development of intensified concepts of nationalism and national citizenship, and the emergence
of a modern and more acceptable activist State in the progressive
era.

For all its divergent and sometimes contradictory elements, progressivism proved an effective political ideological construct, particularly for middle- and upper-class Americans in this era of challenge and change. In foreign policy, for example, the majority of
progressives were clearly internationalists who believed in an active U.S. role in the world and who, like Woodrow Wilson, favored
the reform of the international system. Progressives did differ from
most conservatives in their world view and in the relationship of
their attitudes on foreign and domestic policy. Regardless of differences among them, progressive reformers believed that in all
areas of public policy it was necessary to use moral criteria rather
than simply conventional notions of stability, national security, and
prestige.[84] While they often differed over means, progressives took
their idealism and their evangelical moralism seriously. The majority of progressives supported U.S. entry into the war in April 1917
on Wilson's terms—to halt German militarism and enable liberal
democracy to move ahead in the world—and, as a result, most of
them were willing to accept the military draft to help achieve that
goal. Such a constraint on individual freedom and such extensive
governmental coercion, however, was acceptable to most progressives only as a *temporary* expedient to achieve the worthy goal.

Was the draft a progressive reform?[85] A number of pro-interven-
tionist, prodraft progressives, like the editors of the *New Republic*,
supported it as an efficient military instrument, but cautioned that
it was also inherently inequitable and undemocratic and thus not in
itself progressive. As the editors declared on May 5, after it was
clear the measure would pass: "The engine of conscription is autocratic, unfair, and ruthless. It gives some men the power to select
other men for terrible sacrifices. . . . It would be mere cant to
sentimentalize this as democracy or equity." Yet as pragmatic liberals, they endorsed the wartime draft because, as they said, "conscription is a weapon, like the machine gun and the torpedo," and in
wartime a nation had to select the most effective weapons available
to it.[86]

In order to achieve worthy ends, many liberals who prided them selves on their practicality and tough-mindedness were willing to use some means, like compulsory military service, which they otherwise considered objectionable. "It is better to submit to a little so-called militarism here at home than to be subject in the future to the most horrible of all institutions, Germany['s] militarism," wrote progressive Republican Senator Knute Nelson of Minnesota to an antidraft constituent in late April 1917.[87] A few days before the president delivered his war message, Colonel House had advised Wilson that he must be prepared to conduct "a brutal, vigorous and successful war." "In my argument," he noted in his diary, "I said that everything that he had to meet in this emergency had been thought out time and time again in other countries, and all we had to do was to take experience as our guide and *not worry over the manner of doing it.*"[88]

The efficiency of wartime conscription also fit into the emergent trend—from private to public responsibility, from haphazard individual voluntarism to governmental coordination—that had appealed to many of the more nationalistic, State-building progressives. The argument that had won passage of conscription, explained Joseph Tumulty, the president's long-time private secretary and a shrewd political observer, was that the government, rather than the individual, would be the more effective judge of where a man could best serve his country, on the farm, the assembly line, or the firing line.[89] The draft could not have been adopted in 1917 without being justified in liberal terms and without support from the majority of progressives. They supported it because they saw it as an effective instrument, on military, economic, and social grounds, for helping to win in a worthy cause. Most progressives accepted it as at least somewhat equitable and democratic, especially when the military format was modified with some liberal provisions for due process and appeal, conscientious objection, increased pay and dependent allotments, war risk insurance, and some opportunities for members of minorities and the working classes to become officers. For these reasons, the wartime draft can be seen as a *quasi-progressive* measure. With the decision for war, interventionist progressives adopted a key part of the conservative-led preparedness program—abandonment of the U.S. Volunteers and their replacement by a drafted force—but they adjusted it to liberal values to make it acceptable to various influential groups, then used it as an effective instrument to help achieve progressive international goals. Nevertheless, the American military format of the World War I era—the *Nation-State Model*—was as much a creation of political conservative "modernizers" in the preparedness movement as of the progressives and others who helped adopt and legitimate it during the war.⁹⁰

Significantly the crucial division in Congress over the vote on the wartime draft was not between conservatives and progressives. The correlation in Congress in the spring of 1917 was largely between support for U.S. entry into the war and support for the draft. Progressives who endorsed the American role in the conflict also endorsed the draft as a wartime measure. So, of course, did conservatives. Those reformers and non-reformers, largely agrarians, who opposed U.S. entry also voted against the draft. For the primary division in Congress and in the country, over the draft, as over U.S. belligerency, had not been between progressives and conservatives, nor between Democrats and Republicans, but rather between urban and rural America, between isolationists and internationalists, between ethnic groups, and to a certain extent between the conscriptionists of the most urbanized areas of the nation in the East and along the West Coast against the voluntarists of the predominantly rural regions of the country in the Middle West and the South.⁹¹

American entry into a major European war came at a time when long-established customs and views were being altered as a result of disruptions caused by the forces of industrialization, immigration, and urbanization. With the agreement of the majority of progressive and virtually all conservative leaders in American society, the federal government broke with prior practice and established a national draft at the beginning of a war and as the exclusive means of raising the wartime National Army. The New York *Tribune*, which spoke for the eastern corporate wing of the Republican party, correctly assessed the nature of the battle a few days after the crucial vote in Congress in favor of the draft:

It has been an up-hill fight to overcome the tradition of voluntarism. The idea that one may serve the State or not, as he pleases, had taken deep root in our easy-going American individualism. It fitted in with the loose structure of our national organization and with our frontiersman habits of thought. In young and sparsely settled countries volunteering is in harmony with popular temper. . . . But in a country which has attained, or is attaining, its growth, where economic and industrial conditions are complex, volunteering handicaps efficiency. It hampers national effort, because it prevents unification and scientific selection. It is a policy of muddling and waste.⁹²

Most "modernizers," whether conservative like the *Tribune* or progressive like the *New Republic*, agreed. It was not, however, the opinion of agrarian America, particularly in the South and Middle West, where traditions of localism, voluntarism, and isolationism remained strong. The wartime replacement of the U.S. Volunteers by a National Army of draftees in 1917 is, therefore, best understood as a victory for the values of a cosmopolitan urban-industrial elite over rural-agrarian traditions.

CHAPTER

7

Uncle Sam Wants You!
1917–1918

T HE WHITE-BEARDED UNCLE SAM who pointed with determination
at millions of Americans from James Montgomery Flagg's famous World War I recruiting poster for the U.S. Army was sketched
to appeal to powerful feelings of national patriotism. Yet the nation
which girded for war in the spring of 1917 was still very much a
nation in transition. While a national economy and a strong central
government were rapidly emerging, the United States was still a
large and diverse land in which local ties remained important.
Would the U.S. government in World War I be able to avoid the
turbulence which accompanied the draft during the Civil War?
Would it be able to implement successfully this much more ambitious conscription program of 1917–18, to draft a large army with
a minimum of disruption in a much more industrial and interdependent economy?

Unlike the Civil War experience, the World War I draft proved
quite successful in its major goal of raising the wartime army. The
Selective Service System was administered successfully during the
war precisely because it combined central direction from Washington with local administration under civilian authority. The way
in which the selection process operated in the United States was far
less mechanistic and militaristic than the Civil War draft or the
European conscription systems, and harmonized with a number of
American values and traditions.

Achievement of the secondary goal, withdrawal of large numbers
of workers from the labor force with minimal disruption of the
economy, was somewhat less successful. In large part this was due
to traditional attitudes which limited the power of the central government over the economy. In implementing the draft, particularly

in relationship to civilian manpower and occupational exemptions and deferments, Selective Service was anything but a relentless, monolithic, bureaucratic machine, making decisions based on the most objective consideration of the military and economic requirements.[1] Rather, the interest-group politics of the progressive era continued during the war and helped to influence Selective Service policy. Although the army remained its major client, the draft agency also responded to pressures from competing economic groups expressed directly or through representatives in the legislative or the executive branch. Those who directed Selective Service, like those who led the Wilson administration and its other wartime mobilization agencies, were not autocratic centralizers but rather often hesitant State-builders who sought—indeed were forced—to coordinate rather than dictate to the influential interest groups in American society. Even in wartime, America maintained an "uneasy State."[2]

Well aware of the disastrous experience with conscription in the Civil War, Wilson, Baker, and General Crowder concluded that the draft in World War I must be tailored to minimize conflict with local loyalties and to win popular acceptance. In addition to being the army's chief legal officer, Enoch Crowder had long been a student of wartime conscription. In 1889, while a young cavalry officer at one of the lonely forts in the Dakota Territory, he had read a copy of the report on the Civil War draft by its administrator, General James Fry, and a more perceptive commentary by Brevet Brig. Gen. James Oakes, a West Pointer who had been in charge of the draft in Illinois. In his 1866 report, Oakes had made several prescient recommendations in case the government decided to use a national draft again in the future.[3]

When in 1917 the Wilson administration decided to turn to conscription, General Crowder dusted off Oakes' 50-year-old report and drew heavily upon it as well as on his own understanding—as a bureau chief—of Congress, the American political culture, and civil-military relations. Although the military planners of the War College Division, members of Congress, and Baker and the president all exerted some important influence, it is Crowder, more than any other individual, who created the modern American Selective Service System.[4] With congressional and presidential encouragement, the judge advocate general proposed a decentralized administration and primarily local civilian implementation. Confronted with the task of conscripting 1.5 million men and sending them to army training camps by the end of September, less than six months away, Crowder and his associates decided that they did not have the time to erect an extensive new federal bureaucracy. More, they believed such a bureaucratic machine would be counterproductive. Instead Crowder sought to use local officials to carry out the national program through a concept he called "supervised decentralization."[5] These officials included state governors and adjutants general as well as local sheriffs and county clerks, who served ex-officio as Selective Service System representatives for their areas. Like other wartime agencies, Selective Service was seen from the beginning as a temporary wartime agency and consequently, instead of building up a large staff of civil servants, it relied mainly on people from the private sector serving temporarily and without pay to handle many of its specific tasks, particularly on the local and district draft boards.

Even before passage of the draft act, Crowder and Baker for reasons of speed had ordered the secret printing and mailing of millions of registration forms to 40,000 sheriffs throughout the United States. The sheriffs had kept the secret, and when the draft was adopted were ready to begin registration almost immediately.[6] To enhance the legitimacy as well as efficiency of draft registration, Crowder—inspired by a recommendation from at least one member of Congress—then decided to use the voter registration machinery to register the 10 million young men between the ages of 21 and 30. It would, he saw, be a symbolic demonstration of the connection between the right to vote and the obligation of military service. Although the voting precinct would be the primary registration place, he selected the county, as "the principal minor unit of political administration throughout the United States," to be the working unit for draft registration and eventually selection as well (except in cities with a population of more than 30,000, where wards were grouped together into a registration district, under a city-wide "board of control"). Registration in the voting precincts was under the supervision of newly appointed "county boards of control." The governors would appoint these "boards of registration" for each county-district. When he confidentially informed the executives of the details, Baker urged that these registration boards be composed of the local sheriff as executive officer, the county clerk as custodian of records, and the county medical officer as the person in charge of physical examinations. The purpose was not only to save time in creating the registration system but also to link the draft system with local government and the local community. As Crowder later said, he envisioned administration by "friends and neighbors," operating through familiar agencies, speedily, fairly, yet easily controlled. It followed "the democratic doctrine of local self-government," yet "the guiding star of which was a uniform national policy, nationally defined and nationally directed."[7]

In addition to stressing the decentralized and civilian characteristics of the conscription machinery, the administration also emphasized the voluntarism and public service involved in the draft. Members of the more than four thousand local and regional draft boards served voluntarily; only the clerical staff received compensation. As Secretary of War Baker explained to Congress, the administration sought to improve the image of the procedure, by avoiding the use of negative-laden terms like "conscript," "conscription," and even the "draft." Instead, it sought rhetorically to emphasize positive concepts of "selection" and "public service." Thus conscripts became "selectees" and "servicemen," and the conscription bureau became the "Selective Service System."[8]

Although General Crowder had hoped that the registration boards would continue as the agencies which would actually select the draftees, Congress required that the boards that made the actual selection decisions be appointed by the president, not by the governors. Thus the ad hoc registration boards were replaced by local draft boards. In keeping with the local focus, however, the governors were given considerable influence through the recommendation of appointees. There was a local draft board for every subdivision of approximately 30,000 persons—4,647 boards in all. Thus, local boards made the crucial decisions of whom to induct and whom to defer from among the eligible young men in their district. As with the registration boards, there were three members on each draft board; they too served without pay, emphasizing their civic duty. A small clerical staff helped them. On these boards, one member was required to be a physician who would conduct medical examinations. Twenty percent of the other members were local officials (a demonstration of the carryover of sheriffs and county clerks who had been members of the registration boards), 18 percent were lawyers, and 12 percent were business people. This was an indication of the predominant influence of local commercial and professional elites. John P. White, president of the United Mine Workers Union, was justified when he complained that labor was significantly under-represented. In fact, fewer than 10 percent of the board members considered themselves members of labor.[9] Women, blacks, Hispanics, and Asians were absent from the boards.

Supervisory regional district boards were created for each federal judicial district, 155 in all. Their primary function was to monitor and respond to the economic situation and labor requirements of their area. Eventually, they established advisory bodies of representatives of industry, agriculture, commerce, and finance to help them. In addition, they heard appeals from individuals who were dissatisfied with the decisions of the local boards. To chair these bodies and add legitimacy to them, the administration sought such notables as Charles Evans Hughes of New York City, a former Supreme Court justice who had been the Republican nominee for president in 1916.

Despite the civilian local and district boards which dealt with the public, the Selective Service System was directed by a National Headquarters in Washington, D.C., composed of military officers. Although Selective Service used state and local officials and other members of local elites to implement the draft, national policy emanated from the provost marshal general's office in the War Department. Regular army and reserve officers there shaped guidelines that were transmitted through civilian or sometimes military channels to the district and local boards. However, rather than administer by rigid governmental bureaucratic fiat, Selective Service recognized the need for input from the influential economic groups: industrialists, bankers, retailers, farmers, and to a lesser extent, organized labor. Consequently, Selective Service officials conferred informally with representatives of these groups at the national level and eventually set up a system of representative advisory committees to assist the district boards which were responsible for occupational deferment policy in their regions.[10]

Brigadier General Crowder had continued to be judge advocate general until a few days after the passage of the draft act, when the president named him provost marshal general and administrator of the Selective Service System. A longtime military bureaucrat, Crowder had never taken part in military combat, but he was a veteran of many battles with Congress over appropriations. As bureau chief he had learned how to sustain a military agency within the various conflicting pressures of American society. As late as January 1917, his sensitivity to the antimilitary sentiment in Congress had made him unwilling to recommend UMT&S. Once given the assignment of preparing and administering the Selective Service System, however, Crowder proved an effective choice, for he combined an understanding of law and politics with an intimate knowledge of the military. Because Crowder was more aware of civilian political pressures than most career officers, he was able to adapt the draft agency both to political realities and to military needs.

He was helped in this by some extraordinarily talented assistants. These included Captain Hugh S. Johnson, a career officer who in the 1920s became an adviser to financier Bernard M. Baruch and in the 1930s was selected by Franklin D. Roosevelt to head the National Recovery Administration. He was joined by several reservists: Major J. Rueben Clark, later Hoover's assistant secretary of state and author of the "Clark Memorandum" which repudiated the Roosevelt

Corollary so that the Government could proceed to the "Good Neighbor" policy; Major Charles B. Warren, a leading Republican attorney and president of the Detroit Chamber of Commerce; and Colonel John Henry Wigmore, dean of the Law School at Northwestern University and author of the definitive treatise on the rules of evidence. This staff of legal experts reinforced Crowder's own proclivities and contributed to a cautious, undoctrinaire approach which was as successful as it was undramatic.[11]

To get millions of young Americans to register for the draft, the national government turned primarily to fostering enthusiasm rather than to direct coercion. The Committee on Public Information, aided by local Councils of National Defense and the press, stirred up national sentiment and appealed to Americans to demonstrate their patriotism by registering for the draft. There was also the threat of social and governmental coercion. Selective Service announced its intention to publish the names of registrants so that each community would know who had *not* registered. To encourage community rivalry, it would also publish comparative achievements among cities and states. Of course, this was accompanied by some efforts at intimidation.

Four days before registration, President Wilson declared that anyone failing to report or seeking to dissuade potential registrants faced arrest and up to one year in prison. In New York City, local police and off-duty servicemen broke up a protest meeting of the embryonic No-Conscription League and the People's Council. Several speakers were arrested for denouncing the draft, among them the famous anarchist and feminist, Emma Goldman. Nevertheless, the registration drive, like the later liberty bond drive modeled on it, was one of the first successful exercises in mass compliance through propaganda, hoopla, and peer pressure. With less disturbance in most cities than at an ordinary election, 10 million men reported on June 5, 1917 in what the press hailed as "like a battle won." It was, the *Wall Street Journal* declared, "the first real step to a spiritual realization of the fact of war by our intensely individualistic people."[12]

To determine the order of selection, Crowder turned to a lottery. In justification, he spoke in favor of "an atavistic appeal in the wager of hazard which springs perhaps from some lurking idea of divine intervention."[13] But he was also following precedent. Some colonial militia levies had been conducted by lot and, in the Civil War, draft authorities had used the same jury wheels that were used to choose prospective jurors, thus symbolically joining these two obligations of citizenship. Because there had been so many charges of favoritism and fraud in the locally held Civil War draft lotteries, authorities in 1917 decided to hold one central lottery in the capital, both to demonstrate its impartiality and to maintain Washington's control over the procedure.

Draft quotas came from the General Staff which determined how many soldiers it needed and how many could be supplied and trained at existing facilities. The first quota was for 687,000 draftees by September 1, 1917, when the new cantonments were to be ready. This represented only 60 percent of the 1.2 million additional troops needed by the military. Some 40 percent had already enlisted voluntarily in the regular army and National Guard. In an attempt to ensure sectional fairness, Selective Service apportioned to each state credits for residents who had volunteered. This credit was deducted from the state's total quota of servicemen based upon its population. As a result, states which had supplied proportionately larger numbers of recruits to the National Guard, the regular army, the navy, or the Marine Corps—such as the states in New England—received low draft quotas in this first call. On the other hand, southern states, where the war was unpopular and volunteering had been relatively low, received high draft quotas in 1917.[14]

Between July 20 and August 25 local board members heard almost a million cases (an average of seventy cases per board each day). Claims for dependency deferments posed the hardest decisions. With the onset of the draft, thousands of young men had rushed into matrimony, some at least in the hope of avoiding service in the army. However, draft boards had been given extremely wide discretion in determining whether military service would create undue hardship for a soldier's dependents. The increase in a soldier's pay to $30 a month made it comparable to the monthly earnings of an unskilled laborer and the War Risk Insurance Act made it possible for doughboys to allot considerably more than their monthly pay to their families. This represented a liberalization of the conservative concept of serving without pay, but it still avoided the controversial concept of an enlistment bonus. Thus the economic hardship of military service was somewhat minimized. In some case, such as among the urban poor and agricultural laborers, the combination of military pay and dependency allotments provided a greater and more regular income than they had ever been able to earn in irregular civilian employment. Consequently, there were instances of wives bringing their husbands to the draft boards for induction in order to guarantee a regular income for the family. Despite all this, however, most of the married men in the first draft who claimed dependency hardship were able to obtain military exemptions, as sympathetic draft boards decided, with public approval, that on the whole bachelors should be sent first. The first draftees were dispatched to camp on July 25; in the next six months, draft boards examined 3 million men, certified one million of these for military service, and sent 516,000 draftees off to camp.[15]

These first draftees were given a rousing send-off by their local communities in spectacles reminiscent of the departure of the U.S. Volunteers, except that no local officers accompanied them (in the new National Army, all officers were selected and trained separately according to standards set by the national government). In the heart of the Pennsylvania coal mining region, for example, members of the local draft board in the little community of Dickson City led the 88 draftees to the train station accompanied by veterans of the Civil and Spanish-American Wars and volunteer firemen with their fire engines, all moving to the martial music of the local marching band. Red Cross volunteers handed out box lunches to the young doughboys and the townspeople cheered as their train pulled out. In varying degrees, such celebrations were repeated throughout the country. In New York City, General Crowder joined the mayor and governor on the reviewing stand to watch the first 2,000 inductees march down Fifth Avenue. The national draft appeared to be a tremendous success. Ex-president Roosevelt congratulated Crowder for "one of the best specific bits of work our Army has done in my time."[16]

How well did the Selective Service System really achieve its military goals? In practice, it proved quite successful in filling substantially increasing demands for soldiers during the 18 months that the United States was an active belligerent, even though the American military role in the war grew unexpectedly in the summer of 1917. That occurred when, after consultation with the Allies in France, Brig. Gen. John J. Pershing, commander of the small force of regulars and Guardsmen sent to France in June 1917, suggested a much larger AEF, one of three million troops by the end of 1918. Wilson accepted these force levels and, under the prodding of Baker and Pershing, agreed gradually and reluctantly to commit a massive American effort to the Western Front.[17]

By the end of December 1917, Selective Service had met the initial goal of 1.5 million troops authorized under the draft act. At the time war was declared, the U.S. Army had 128,000 men and the National Guard 164,000. Within three months, voluntary enlistment produced 301,000 recruits in the regulars and the militia; in both cases the enlistment contracts were equalized at 3 years, later converted to service for the duration of the war. An additional 109,000 men joined the navy, which was the first service to see action in a war initiated by German U-boat attack. After drafting began in July, the enlistment rate in the Army and the Guard dropped slowly from approximately 100,000 to 25,000 a month, except for a spurt to 141,000 just before the government on December 15 prohibited voluntary enlistment into these services by draft-eligible men.[18]

The prohibition of voluntary enlistment was a clear break with tradition and surprised the public, but the managers of the draft considered voluntarism inefficient within the larger mobilization picture. Since enlistment swung upwards whenever a draft call seemed near, Crowder concluded that many men preferred to enter military service as volunteers rather than as draftees. In some regions and subcultures, the old stigma of the conscript remained. But no matter how popular the idea of voluntary service might be with the masses, it was increasingly unpopular with the men in charge of raising America's armies. Like the leaders of the conscription crusade, Crowder and his aides concluded that many of the volunteers were more useful to the nation in their civilian occupations, particularly since many volunteers were skilled factory workers. Furthermore, voluntary enlistment hindered the ability of the government to allocate manpower with maximum efficiency. It allowed the individual to choose the service he wanted, and in practice forced the army, navy, and marines to compete for recruits. The army usually suffered as a result. On July 27, 1918, draft-eligible men, 21–30, were prohibited from enlisting in the navy or the marines. In August 1918, when draft age limits were extended, voluntary enlistment was prohibited by men of any age. Thus, by the end of the war, the Selective Service System had become the sole dispenser of the nation's military manpower. As the *Chicago Tribune* put it: "the citizen's personal desire and judgment cannot put him where he is of greatest service."[19]

Like the civilian regulatory agencies of the progressive era, the Selective Service System was given relatively little statutory guidance by Congress or initial direction by the administration in its most difficult task—determining the public interest, in this case the proper balance between extracting men for the army and maintaining essential services and industries.[20] As a result, at least in the first draft, local boards made their own decisions with widely different outcomes. Increasingly, however, Selective Service Headquarters and the Wilson administration recognized the need for more central guidance, for the sake of efficiency as well as protection of the draft agency itself. Consequently, but only under pressure, they moved gingerly towards more coordination, and the expansion of government's control over the work force.

Unlike the navy which was more technologically oriented and capital-intensive, the army had not been much accustomed to working with industrialists. But with the rapid military expansion brought on by the war it quickly became clear that the army's relationship with the economy was hopelessly outdated and inadequate. As former cavalry and infantry officers, few of the U.S. Army's senior commanders gave the kind of thought the navy did to complex weapons systems. Their main concern, outside of certain branches like artillery and engineering, had been with the acquisition of large numbers of relatively unskilled or semi-skilled civilians and their training and retention as soldiers. The army's supply system had been designed for the limited purchases made by the small constabulary of the nineteenth century; its decentralized bureau structure and policies for procurement did not fit into the new national system of business. By the winter of 1917–18, the situation, especially in regard to purchasing of supplies, weapons, and munitions, had become so confused and chaotic that corporate leaders, the press, and many congressional leaders demanded greater centralization and coordination to meet the various needs for matériel and transportation. Although refusing to employ as much coercion as European governments, the Wilson administration created a temporary central agency, the War Industries Board, in which wartime administrators encouraged cooperation within industry and with the military to allocate material resources more effectively.[21]

Similarly, in regard to manpower policy, the government came under increased pressure from corporate and other groups to meet the labor needs of industrial and agricultural production. This became particularly important as the armed forces grew towards their ultimate strength of 4 million men, when they absorbed nearly 12 percent of the work force. Those who thought in terms of national economic groups, such as the industrialists, labor leaders, and others on the Council of National Defense, recognized even before the United States entered the war that certain groups of skilled industrial workers were more important to the country at their civilian jobs than in the army.[22] The Wilson administration considered asking for exemptions for such groups—railroad employees and munitions workers, for example—but decided that such blanket statutory exemptions might undermine popular support for the draft system.

In fact, very few statutory exemptions were made. To prevent disruption of government, Congress had specifically exempted federal and state legislative, executive, and judicial officers. It also exempted clergymen, seminarians, and divinity students on religious grounds. Beyond that, the legislators gave the president discretionary authority to exclude county and local officials (which the administration later expanded to include fire-fighters and members of the police force) and pilots and mariners actually engaged in sea service. As citizens of other countries, aliens who had not declared their intention to become U.S. citizens were exempt from being drafted into the U.S. armed forces, although theoretically they could still be conscripted by their home countries. Americans deemed physically, mentally, or morally unfit for military service were also exempted.[23]

Civilian members of local draft boards had even less idea than professional soldiers how to balance the needs of industry and of the military. They were therefore reluctant to recognize particular individuals as being indispensible to the economy; few employers in the summer and fall of 1917 were willing to assert that such men could not be replaced by others. Although dependency hardship deferments were granted to most husbands and fathers, the local boards in the first draft were unwilling to grant most claims for agricultural or industrial deferments. Under pressure to get draftees to training camps by September, the boards (as General Crowder later admitted) had simply drawn the 687,000 most available men from among the 3 million registrants whose lottery numbers made them subject to immediate draft.[24] Selective Service produced its quota of troops, but in ignoring the manpower needs of the economy, it inadvertently irritated a number of politically powerful economic groups. These began to press for protection of their interests.

Initial pressure in late summer 1917 came from agricultural interests concerned about a labor shortage for the approaching harvest season. Arguing that increased agricultural production was necessary to feed and clothe the armies and to win the war, their champion Herbert Hoover, head of the U.S. Food Administration, urged a blanket exemption for farmers and agricultural workers.[25] A few spokespeople from the farm belt even recommended that the government force young men from the cities into an agricultural reserve force and compel them to work on the farms during the planting and harvesting seasons.[26] Quite naturally, the Wilson administration ignored such a radical idea.

The administration never seriously considered compelling urbanites to work on the farms, but it did seek to ease the farmers' complaints in other ways. Under congressional authority, the army gave brief furloughs to several thousand trainees from labor-scarce regions so that they could help with the crops during planting and harvesting seasons. In addition, under a compromise worked out in 1918, Selective Service Headquarters directed local boards to expand their acceptance of agricultural deferments. Consequently, the rate of rejection of those claiming deferment on agricultural grounds dropped from 64 to 48 percent.[27]

As the agricultural experience demonstrated, Selective Service's response to powerful pressures took the form of modifications in policy guidelines rather than of blanket exemptions. In the spring of 1917, Secretary of War Baker had already turned down requests for group exemptions from teachers, students, technical industrial workers, mine workers and railroad employees. As he explained to the president, " . . . it was deemed wiser, indeed seemed necessary, rather to let the draft fall where it will and make exceptions after the men are drawn, than to create classes, and the consequent *class feeling*, by exemptions in advance."[28]

President Wilson supported Crowder and Baker in opposing blanket deferments, although he wavered—but did not yield—in response to pleas for exemptions for railway workers from William G. McAdoo who was secretary of the treasury, head of the Railroad Administration, and also his son-in-law. In the end, Wilson made only one major exception: men working in shipyards and on the merchant marine. He overrode Crowder's objection because the shortage of shipping had become the primary obstacle to supplying the Allies and rapid enlargement of the AEF in France. In two other industries—coal mining and the railroads—Crowder and Baker successfully fended off efforts by interest groups. Coming under pressure from the Fuel Administration and the Railroad Administration in 1918 to ease labor shortages in those industries, Crowder first held an investigation and then denied that Selective Service had contributed materially to these crises. At the same time, he admitted that some boards had been overzealous in drafting workers, and he sent out directives telling board members to exercise their discretion more broadly.[29]

As the war economy heated up in the fall and winter of 1917–18, industry spokespeople began to warn of a broader and more critical labor shortage, a "man-power famine." European governments had dealt with the wartime contraction of the normal labor supply in several ways. They had increased national coordination and control of labor turnover and supply, especially in defense industries, and they had expanded the labor force through the use of large numbers of women and, in the case of Germany, of forced labor from occupied countries. Various proposals to ease the labor shortage were put forward in America, the most common being the expansion and coordination of the labor pool. While there was some increased coordination, the primary result was that employers did hire more women workers and also large numbers of southern rural residents, blacks and whites, as well as—from the Southwest—Hispanic-Americans and Mexican immigrants.[30]

The federal government came under such intense pressure to ease the labor shortage of skilled industrial workers that it sought to make the Selective Service System more attuned to the needs of industry.[31] Thus in late September 1917, after the first draft was completed, Crowder and his staff began to develop a system for classifying every draft registrant according to his occupational and marital status. Patterned after the system in Britain, the classification system approved by the president was designed to ensure, in Crowder's words, that men would be taken from "the civic, family, industrial, agricultural institutions of the Nation . . . in the order in which they best can be spared."[32]

Through an extensive questionnaire, local boards conducted an inventory of the 10 million draft registrants, classifying them into five different categories by eligibility. Those in Class I were eligible for immediate military service. They included unskilled workers and those engaged in industrial or agricultural enterprises not considered essential. Class I also included bachelors, and husbands and fathers who either habitually failed to support their wives and families or who were not usefully employed. "Unmarried men not needed in industry," was the way Baker explained Class I to the president, thus nicely making clear the occupational emphasis.[33] Those temporarily deferred until after Class I men had been drafted, Classes II and III, included married men usefully employed, and skilled industrial and agricultural workers engaged in necessary enterprises, such as technical and mechanical experts and assistant or associate managers. Class IV, not to be drafted until after the other classes, included married men whose dependents had no other means of support and the heads of necessary business or agrarian enterprises. Class IV also included those men exempted by statute. During the twelve months that the classification system was in operation only Class I men were drafted. Thus the classification system protected the others.[34]

Few programs could coincide better with the progressive era's emphasis upon social efficiency than this idea of classifying much of the nation's manpower. This systematic approach was presented as being both a businesslike and scientific inventory of national resources, including impartial data-gathering and analysis. Selective Service officials encouraged support for their new procedure by linking it with the public confidence in the scientific method, an unbiased search for facts.[35] However, the fact that the classification plan was systematic did not mean that it was unbiased. In reality, the classification system was open to considerable partiality at the local level in the determination of particular cases. As for the system as a whole, the categories established by the national headquarters of Selective Service reflected normative judgments about the value of particular occupational and social groups, judgments that mirrored the prevailing notions of upper- and middle-class Americans.

Wartime labor shortages also led some economic and political figures to offer extreme solutions for maintaining essential agricultural and industrial production by using the coercive power of government. These included proposals for conscripting essential workers into the army and then returning them to their jobs under military discipline, using the draft as a clout to curb strikes and labor turnover, and compelling civilians to work at particular jobs, either through "anti-loafing" laws or an extensive system of national service.

With increased willingness to use the power of government to encourage and coerce conformity with the goal of victory, legislators saw compulsory work laws as both good politics and good business. Employers pressed for such legislation not only to expand the work force but also as a means of curbing preindustrial work patterns such as the penchant of some people to work in the winter months and live on their savings during the summertime. By the spring of 1918, nearly a dozen states had adopted compulsory work laws, a response by state and local authorities to demands for action against idlers and for expansion of the work force.[36] The national government came under similar pressure.

State "anti-loafing" laws were aimed primarily against the poor and the marginally employed. However, at the national level, suggestions for the U.S. government to *conscript labor* were directed mainly against skilled labor and unions. Some editors and employers proposed drafting certain groups of workers into uniform and then returning them to work under military discipline. Some recommended making the draft deferments of essential workers contingent upon their staying on the job, thus effectively precluding them from changing to another employer in the same industry for higher wages, or going out on strike. These suggestions were justified as a means of maintaining essential production. The Wilson administration rejected proposals to put railroad and shipyard workers in uniform,[37] but by February 1918 the president was willing to use the threat of revocation of draft deferments as a club to force striking shipyard carpenters in New York City to end their strike. It proved effective in getting the men back to work.[38]

The idea of expanding military service into *national service* had its roots in the experience of warring European nations, like Germany, who used it to compel work in particularly crucial industries. At the time of U.S. entry into the war, several Rooseveltian progressives and a few conservatives had made such suggestions. By the end of 1917, production problems caused by overlapping purchasing, transportation tie-ups, and increased labor militancy (triggered particularly by inflationary leaps in prices) had led several business and political figures also to advocate national service. Indeed, bills for national service were introduced in Congress in early January 1918 by Republican Senators Joseph I. France of Maryland and Porter J. McCumber of Oregon. The legislation would authorize the federal government to place men between the ages of 18 and 45 wherever they were most needed, in civilian or military positions. Neither the Democratic majority in Congress nor the leaders of the Republican minority were enthusiastic about such proposals and the bills died in committee after President Wilson denounced the idea of compulsory labor as a radical and unwise departure from the policy of a free state.[39]

The idea of "industrial conscription" was anathema to unions who recognized it as a device which could be used to restrict labor's advantageous bargaining position in the wartime boom. At the outset, Samuel Gompers had decided to support the Wilson administration's mobilization program and to seek government support for labor in return. He refused appeals by pacifists and antiwar socialists to cooperate in opposing the draft after it was enacted. Instead he lobbied to obtain labor representation on the district boards which would rule on occupational deferments in the various regions of the country. Some business-oriented reservists in Selective Service Headquarters, like Major Charles B. Warren, former head of the Detroit Chamber of Commerce, opposed such a concession, but Gompers wrote directly to the president. Subsequently Secretary of War Baker announced that there would be a person "who is in close touch with labor" on each *district* board and that Selective Service planned to keep interference with industry to a minimum.[40]

Throughout the war, union leaders sought to avert the use of the draft against labor. Gompers argued that business was over-emphasizing the scarcity of workers. The problem, according to the A.F. of L., was maldistribution, not overall lack of labor. Union leaders blamed this on difficulties in the market system and urged better coordination of labor supply and demand to ease it. They also called for alleviation of inadequate wages and working conditions which they argued caused most work stoppages. "Industrial conscription," Gompers declared, "means loss of freedom to wage-earners. It is incompatible with American institutions and with the spirit and purpose of the war."[41]

The famous "work or fight" order issued on May 17, 1918, was the Selective Service System's response to the mounting pressure for effective action to maintain agricultural and industrial production. Under this new Selective Service regulation, any deferred registrant found by the nearest draft board to be an idler or engaged in a nonproductive occupation would be liable to immediate loss of his deferment and induction into the army. "Duty to work, and to work effectively, was the foundation of the measure," Crowder later explained. "There was no other alternative."[42]

Of course, there were other alternatives—some of them more extreme—and these were exactly what Crowder and the administration sought to avoid. Although it was touted as a highly forceful measure, "work or fight" was much more moderate than proposals for national service or the conscription of labor. It was Selective Service's gesture to reduce pressures from business and agricultural interests and opposition Republicans for dramatic action, while at the same time seeking to avoid disrupting the support of the A.F. of L. leadership for the draft system.[43]

The original proposal put forward by the Selective Service System on March 20, 1918, had included not only the "work or fight" order but also extension of registration to men between the ages of 18 and 50. It asked for authority to induct men not usefully employed, to designate certain priority industries, and to identify certain classes of registrants who must find work in these priority industries or face induction into the army.[44] The War Council of senior military officers and the secretary of war agreed, but the Wilson administration was not so easily persuaded. Gompers and other labor leaders vehemently denied that there was a shortage of workers and denounced the proposal as an insult to American labor. The A.F. of L. chief predicted that it would not get past the White House where, indeed, it was pigeon-holed for quite some time. Although the memo was pried lose from the White House with the aid of the venerable former Speaker of the House, "Uncle Joe" Cannon, it came back "disapproved."[45]

But Selective Service was not finished with the idea and the irrepressible Johnson leaked the proposal to the press. As he recalled: "it provoked such a storm of editorial approval that no politician could stand against it."[46] The *Washington Post* hailed it as a "purification" of the deferred classes. The editor defined a draft deferment as a privilege, not a right. The *New Republic* approved the proposal as a compromise measure, a substitute for the conscription of labor. Vociferous criticism, however, came from socialists, liberals, pacifists, and others who had opposed the draft. Also speaking out against it were many local union officials who feared that the measure would be used to thwart strikes and to reduce wage scales by forcing thousands of the unemployed to compete for jobs in the work force.[47] Publicly, the head of Selective Service belittled the fears of organized labor, asserting that any wage cuts would be offset by reduced prices stemming from increased production. He did not mention that most of the increased production would be in military-related industries. More importantly, Crowder assured labor that "work or fight" would not be used against strikers. Not long after Baker returned from France in mid-April, the secretary of war recommended approval of the "work or fight" order. However, he deferred expansion of draft registration to those aged 18 to 50 until such time as it became necessary for military rather than economic reasons. When Crowder finally issued a somewhat restricted "work or fight" order in May, he did so with presidential authorization.[48]

Politically, the "work or fight" order proved to be a tremendously popular measure with some influential elements of the population. It reflected the desires of business and agriculture for expansion of the labor pool and greater discipline over the work force, as well as the desire of millions of Americans, especially those with someone of importance to them in the service, to force the unemployed to do something society wanted done in the national interest.

To avoid unduly antagonizing organized labor, Selective Service Headquarters took special precautions in drawing up the first guidelines for implementing "work or fight." Although Crowder's office did not offer any rationale for the initial list of jobs that would be vulnerable, an examination indicates that the military planners were guided by cultural and economic assumptions about the value of particular occupations, and political assumptions about the power of the A.F. of L. Significantly, not one of the occupations listed as non-productive was an organized trade in the A.F. of L. Only relatively low-income, unskilled or semi-skilled urban service jobs were listed: bartenders, soda fountain workers, waiters, doormen, bell boys, porters, elevator operators, chauffeurs and other such attendants. In addition, there were office and sales clerks in semi-skilled white-collar occupations who could easily be replaced. A class bias may have been responsible for deeming as productive men in the theater, the motion picture industry, and the opera while those in amusement parks or arcades and professional sports were declared to be in non-essential fields.[49]

The decision to draft baseball players aroused a furor that caught the administration off base. Despite much pressure from the fans, the clubs, and the press, however, the president refused to reverse the decision and exempt the ballplayers. Nevertheless, he acceded to a postponement, for Secretary Baker delayed induction of key players until after the end of the baseball season, and by the time the "World Series," as it was just beginning to be called, had been held, the war was over.[50] Hotels, restaurants, luncheonettes, and retail stores had none of the influence of baseball clubs and they lost many of their male employees. But many of these employers had already begun to replace them with women, and thus the industry's complaints went largely unheeded. Bankers, on the other hand, afraid of losing experienced clerks and tellers, proved successful in their appeal to Crowder through the American Banking Association and the Federal Reserve Board. Selective Service subsequently declared banking an essential industry and exempted its clerks from the "work or fight" order. In the implementation of the order, the burden not surprisingly fell most heavily on unorganized and unrepresented workers.[51]

While Selective Service was expanding its powers to deal more effectively with the civilian work force, it was also under increased pressure to obtain many more soldiers for a dramatically expanded American army. Although the goal of a 3-million-man force had been set in July 1917 for the following year, events during the winter of 1917–18 led military officers to call for an even larger American force. The Italians had been routed at Caporetto. The British offensive ground to a bloody halt at Passchendale. When Lenin took the Soviet Union out of the war, Germany shifted its eastern armies from Russia to France, negating the Anglo-French numerical superiority of 250,000 which had existed since 1917. The Allies looked desperately for an American army to replace the Russian forces and bolster their own plummeting morale. When the Germans launched their "win-the-war" offensive in the valley of the Somme in March 1918, Prime Minister Lloyd George sent his famous "crisis telegram" to Wilson pleading for waves of American soldiers to come in immediately to prevent a German victory.[52]

To supplement the 200,000 troops already there, the United States sent 300,000 additional soldiers right away. At the same time, Wilson went to Congress and obtained approval to draft as many troops as might be needed. By July 1918, when the German offensive had failed, the American Expeditionary Force had reached 900,000 men. The Allies now counter-attacked in force and planned an enormous offensive for the spring of 1919 to carry them into Germany. At the request of the General Staff, Wilson agreed on July 18, 1918 to triple the size of the AEF by the spring of 1919 to nearly 3.2 million men and to have an American army of 5 million men in France by the time the war was expected to end in late 1919.[53]

Such a mammoth army, which would have been by far the largest in American history, would require a dramatic expansion of the military manpower pool. Since less than 100,000 men were left in Class I, the group which could be most readily taken for service, the more than 2 million additional soldiers would have to come either from men between 21 and 30 who had received occupational or other deferments or from men outside these age limits originally set by Congress. Crowder recommended that, rather than take men from the currently deferred classes, the eligible age limits be expanded to 18–50. Since congressional elections were coming up in November and there was much public opposition to drafting young men under 21 who were not even legally adults, it was a difficult choice for Congress and the administration.[54] The controversy which ensued highlighted the difficulty presented by conflicting military, economic and political pressures and the administration's search for a compromise policy which would placate the most pressing interest groups and also achieve the government's mobilization goals. The army had always wanted younger men (18- to 20-year-olds) because they were, in Crowder's words, "the soundest and most pliable military material"—physically more fit, easier to train, and more willing to take risks than older men.[55] Congress, however, had in the past refused to *require* men below the age of legal maturity—21 in most states—to serve in the military. Furthermore, the upper age limits (31–50) frightened many industrial and labor leaders by raising the specters of both compulsory labor and the possible conscription of managers.[56]

In weighing its decision, the Wilson administration sought to sustain a majority political coalition behind the war effort, maintain industrial production, and play a major role in the defeat of the Kaiser's army. Given the widespread popular opposition, both Baker and Wilson had been reluctant to accept the drastic expansion of the draft age limits advocated by Crowder, particularly since this expansion of the draft was cheered on by advocates of permanent UMT&S, and by the administration's critics in Congress, especially the eastern Republicans.[57] The administration's policy here was apparently to follow rather than to attempt to lead public opinion, and to wait and see whether national interest groups and the press would be able to build enough political pressure that they would have to be at least partially appeased. By July 27, 1918, Baker came out in support of extension but said he had not decided what the age limits would be. Public debate then shifted largely to the age limits instead of the legitimacy of extension itself. On August 3, Baker announced the administration would seek extension to 18 and 45.[58] He and the president also assured labor that there would be no compulsory work; and to improve the handling of occupational

deferments among the older workers and managers, Crowder created a system of industrial advisory committees.[59]

Once the administration had given its support there was little
chance that the age extension would be defeated in Congress.
Crowder then urged Congress to swift action, warning that if authority to register men in the broader age brackets was not received
by early September, Selective Service would exhaust the resources
in Class I and be forced to dip into the deferred groups, beginning
with Class II.[60] The political leaders were now confronted with a
choice of either drafting husbands, fathers, and those with occupational deferments, or extending the draft to younger men; reluctantly they decided that youth would have to go. On August 31, 1918,
Congress approved the new age limits.[61]

Preceeded by what was probably the most intensive publicity
campaign of the war, the third national draft registration (the second was held on June 5, 1918 for those who had become 21 since
June 5, 1917) was held at the nation's polling places on September
12, 1918, and was hailed as a great success when 13.4 million men
signed up. When the lottery was held on September 30, the president himself drew the first number from the glass bowl. In the next
month and a half, Selective Service drafted 143,000 men, although
most of the new registrants were still being classified when the
armistice ended the fighting, and the draft, on November 11, 1918.[62]

Despite the Wilson administration's reluctance to alienate the A.F.
or L. or any other "influential part of the public," as Wilson expressed it to Baker, the federal government did in fact increase its
intervention in the labor market during the war through the Selective Service System.[63] The "work or fight" order represented an
increased use of coercion over labor beyond what the administration had been willing to exert in 1917. The president and most of his
mobilization agency managers had sought to coordinate through
public-private cooperation rather than to attempt directly to coerce
their sectors of the economy. But under pressure in the spring and
summer of 1918, the government had somewhat increased its use of
coercive power over management and labor to ensure maximum
production of war materials and to ease pressure for more extreme
measures such as conscription of labor. Under the authority of the
Overman Act, the administration commandeered a few recalcitrant
defense firms whose production was blocked in labor disputes, such
as the Western Union Telegraph Company and the Smith and
Wesson arms plant in Springfield, Mass. Later in 1918, in response
to public pressure and its own procurement needs, the government,
despite initial hesitation, began to increase the use of the army and

the draft to curb work stoppages and ease labor shortages in crucial sectors of the economy. For example, the army furloughed soldiers to help bring in the crops in response to agricultural complaints about labor shortages at harvest time. The program was a tremendous success and the potential it demonstrated did not escape notice in Crowder's office. Indeed, one of his aides suggested that "the practice will not have to go much further before it reaches the stage of being in effect an industrial draft."[64]

Unknown to the public, Selective Service Headquarters was actively considering plans to expand the use of the "work or fight" order in October 1918, in conjunction with the new 18–45 age limits, to ensure that men channeled from nonproductive to productive employment would be forced to remain on their new jobs. This was aimed specifically at what one of Crowder's assistants called "labor's conscious and willful avoidance of a full or fair measure of exertion," a complaint similar to that of management and echoed in the press as "industrial slackerism." The proposal under consideration called for penalties for men who had occupational deferments but were not working a 44-hour week. Withdrawal of deferment and induction into the army was the ultimate penalty. The original suggestion had been made by a member of the Shipping Control Committee as a means of eliminating "slackerism" among longshoremen. General Crowder's official reaction to the proposal was not recorded, but he believed the "work or fight" order could be expanded to increase industrial production by at least 35 percent.[65] Since the plan was submitted to Crowder only a month before the armistice, it was never seriously considered by the Wilson administration. But the president had clearly become more willing to use the draft as a club against strikers in defense industries. In October 1918, he warned striking machinists in defense plants in Bridgeport, Conn. that if they failed to return to their jobs, they would be barred from any war-related work for twelve months, in effect threatening a government "blacklist" of excluded workers. Even more ominously, he declared that, during that time, "the draft boards will be instructed to reject any claims of exemption based on your alleged usefulness on war production."[66] Faced with the threat of blacklisting and induction into the army, the machinists went back to work.

Less than two years after the armistice, military officers studying the draft experience concluded that only the termination of hostilities prevented further extension of federal control of labor through expansion of the Selective Service regulations.[67] While this was probably an accurate appraisal, it must be remembered that the president and his top advisers were reluctant to alienate one of their main constituents—organized labor—and moved in such a direction only gradually and with much caution.

By the time of the armistice, the authority of the Selective Service System in the military area was far beyond what it had been when it was created eighteen months earlier. As an instrument of military procurement, Selective Service had been extended to a majority of the adult male population, those aged 18–45. With the prohibition of voluntary enlistment, the draft agency had become the sole dispenser of manpower for all the armed services. General Crowder sought both of these extensions of authority, and with the support of the army, influential civilians, and the urban press, when enough pressure had built, he was able to push the Wilson administration and many reluctant members of Congress into such action.

The primary goal of the Draft Act of 1917 had been to raise large numbers of soldiers regularly and predictably with minimal disruption to the national economy. It achieved the military part of this goal with considerable success. In all, Selective Service delivered 2.8 million men to the army. By the end of the war, its draftees made up 72 percent of the 4 million Americans who had put on khaki uniforms since the war began, and more than half of the American Expeditionary Force in France.[68] In addition, another million draftees could have been obtained for the anticipated offensives in 1919. Compared to the effort of the European nations, American mobilization was quite small (the United States mobilized 20 percent of its male population, 18–45, in contrast to 60 percent in Britain). Still the 18-month achievement was unprecedented in the United States. Never before had the national government raised such an enormous army and never had it obtained nearly three-quarters of that army through a national draft.

The draft and the mass army it provided also enabled Wilson to carry out the kind of large-scale military intervention in Europe which would have been impossible for presidents like John Adams or Thomas Jefferson who had faced conflicts with European powers a century earlier.[69] Although he did not choose it for that reason, once having adopted a draft and then later decided to send an expeditionary force to France, Wilson was easily able to expand the size of that force. Without much difficulty he was able to increase the draft calls and ultimately the size of the draft pool. Indeed, the draft could have easily produced an army of 6 or 7 million men if the war had continued into 1919 and 1920.

Similarly, the expansion of the economic role of the Selective Service System was also an evolutionary and increasing process. By the end of the war, the agency had classified most of the adult male population and, through the manipulation of deferments and inductions, had taken a step towards a national policy of labor allocation and the maintenance of production in priority industries. Pressures for such policies had come from industrialists, cash-crop farmers, the press, and federal military procurement and economic mobilization agencies. Yet, once again the administration was also faced with opposition from significant segments of its coalition and its own reluctance to overcentralize and be too coercive.

This gradual rate of expansion of the use of Selective Service helped to mollify some powerful interest groups, and to keep some other skeptical groups in the wartime coalition. The administration saw that classification could be a way of keeping skilled workers in crucial industries while inducting replaceable unskilled workers. Through the classification system and the direction from Selective Service Headquarters to be more responsive to regional labor requirements, local boards granted a higher percentage of claims for deferments in 1918 than they had in 1917. Approvals for industrial deferments rose from 43 to 54 percent of applications while those for agricultural deferments jumped even more, from 36 to 52 percent.[70] Nonetheless, despite Gompers' protests, the threat of induction was used as a club against strikers by local boards on a number of occasions, and, in a few instances by the president himself.

The most coercive labor action taken by Selective Service, the "work or fight" order, seems to have had only a negligible positive economic effect. After the war, Crowder boasted that through it Selective Service had forced 137,000 men into more productive employment; however, in a work force of more than 35 million, this is an insignificant figure.[71] Furthermore, there is no evidence that these men (waiters, porters, bartenders and clerks) went into essential industries. Crowder failed to mention the negative impact of the "work or fight" order. In many cases, it actually increased unemployment among men. Often registrants in "non-productive" occupations were dismissed by their employers and replaced by women or older men. Unemployed, they did not have the experience to be hired as skilled workers and because they were subject to immediate draft, they found themselves unable to get work or credit. Bitterly they blamed the Selective Service for their dilemma. As one jobless clerk wrote to Crowder: "If the government is going to stop me from earning a living in the only way I know, why should I worry what happens to the Government? They [sic] care nothing for me."[72]

From the standpoint of the Selective Service System and the administration, the "work or fight" order was most successful on a political rather than economic level. At a time when important segments of society demanded governmental action to ease the labor shortage and to force so-called "slackers" to do their part in the war effort, the order seemed to indicate decisive action by national authorities. This is certainly the way it appeared to many members of Selective Service. Soon after the armistice, one Kansas draft board concluded that the "work or fight" order had "showed all the people that the Government was driving with a 'tight rein' and was on the job with a thoroughness and determination which we had not, till then, understood."[73]

Part of the successful acceptance of the Selective Service System during the war and its ability to respond to the needs of its primary client—the army—was the flexibility demonstrated by its chief, General Crowder, and his advisers, and indeed by the system as a whole in responding to contending pressures particularly from employers—industrial, commercial, and agricultural—and balancing the manpower needs of the armed forces against the needs of the nation at large.

Faced with pressures from a variety of sources for more effective military and economic mobilization for war, the Wilson administration had responded with a variety of policies and programs, but despite some expanded bureaucratization and additional coercion, the result was nowhere near the "dictatorial" centralized State that some critics feared.[74] True, the degree of governmental intervention in the economy was unprecedented and certainly went beyond that of the Civil and Spanish-American Wars. But it was neither autocratic nor, with a few exceptions, excessive, especially compared to the centralization of control and government direction of the economy established in various degrees in France, Britain, and Germany.

Rather, the extension of federal power, even while moving beyond older traditions of unrestricted individualism, laissez-faire, and an unregulated marketplace, maintained connections with important beliefs in voluntarism, pluralism, and limited government. In facing the task of total war mobilization, the United States differed especially from the continental nations in the nature of its elites, its traditions, and its ordering mechanisms. Despite the changes of the progressive era, the national government did not have an extensive and experienced bureaucracy, civilian or military, capable of directing such a massive national effort. Nor, given continued widespread distrust of bureaucracy, would such ordering mechanisms have been readily accepted.

The president and his mobilizers were ambiguous and often hesistant about the degree of expansion of federal control over the economy and the nation's manpower that was required.[75] In many cases, they were impelled to enlarge the powers of the government because of the dynamics of their wartime goals as well as pressures from Republicans like Roosevelt for more centralized and effective efforts to aid the Allies; sometimes these pressures came from the Allied governments as well. When the Wilson administration made the choice for enlargement, it always represented a compromise among conflicting interests and goals. Hardly power-hungry autocrats, they were rather reluctant State-builders.

The nature of the role of the State in the overall American mobilization of World War I, as well as the consequences of the wartime structure of the relationship of public to private groups, remains controversial.[76] This study of the Selective Service System explains the evolving structure and operation of the wartime mobilization agencies as attempts to create an American substitute for the expanded, modern, bureaucratic State. Most of the wartime mobilization was done not by pre-existing permanent governmental bureaus or regulatory agencies, but rather by the temporarily created public-private coordinating machinery which fell far short of Statism. This wartime system represented a massive and temporary elaboration of the kind of public-private coordinating structures that had begun to appear in the prewar period, including, most prominently, the Federal Reserve System.[77]

The Selective Service System was a temporary mechanism created to deal with the conflicting aims of recruiting a mass army while maintaining a civilian work force adequate to sustain vital production and services. Although it had legal authority to conscript by force, in practice it developed a structure of interlinked public-private as well as national-local authorities. Overall policy was set at the organization core, at Selective Service Headquarters, but implemented with considerable variety at the local and district level. In addition, the whole decentralized system of draft boards, made up of local citizens, not federal officials, provided a means not only of implementation of registration, classification, and conscription, but an apparatus for fostering community spirit and building social consensus. Despite its awesome legal authority, Selective Service operated to a surprising degree like the other wartime mobilization agencies (food, fuel, transportation, foreign trade, labor, and finance). It somewhat expanded the power of the State but did so without Statism. No matter how intensive it was perceived to be at the time, its "new interventionism" into the economy and the lives of the citizenry was only a temporary wartime expedient.[78]

Thus the organizational experience of the Selective Service System in World War I illustrated a particularly American type of State-building, and one that in some ways was particular to the first third of the 20th century. Like other aspects of mobilization, the draft marked an important break with older traditions of unrestricted individualism, laissez-faire, and the unregulated marketplace. On the other hand, although it built upon it, the Selective Service System also represented a shift away from the progressive ideology of permanent regulationism that characterized one wing of the progressive coalition. This alternative, the associative State, with its emphasis upon a partnership of public and private interests at certain important intersects in society and the economy, had important public goals, yet at the same time it attempted to maintain continued emphasis upon private and local community units. To call it complete business domination would be too simple. Nor was it corporatist (formal, institutionalized cooperation between the State and the major economic power blocs).[79] Pluralistic, individualistic, and antitrust traditions remained too strong, and elements in the American political culture remained too suspicious of the associative idea and of the regulatory and bureaucratic State (and downright hostile to any outright business domination) for there to be a corporatist State in America. Although it clashed with the ideals of complete individual liberty and of limited central government, the Selective Service did harmonize with many of the nation's traditions and values, including localism, civilian control of the military, and widespread use of citizen-soldiers only in wartime. It became the politico-military formula for raising America's wartime armies for the rest of the century.

CHAPTER

8

Critics, Dissenters, and Resisters, 1917–1918

DESPITE THE INCREASED MILITARY AND ECONOMIC EFFICIENCY of Selective Service, not all Americans were integrated smoothly into the new national wartime mobilization system. Although there was no repetition of the widespread rioting and other antidraft violence of the Civil War, the World War I draft caused much psychological strain and generated considerable social, cultural, and political tensions.[1] Challenged by opponents of the draft as well as critics of its operation, authorities in 1917–18 curtailed disruption and achieved a degree of public acceptance that legitimized the draft and the Selective Service System.

Pressure for conformity and outright repression helped fragment and suppress opposition. Recognizing the danger of being branded disloyal, virtually no nationally recognized spokesperson for immigrant ethnic groups publicly denounced the war or the draft.[2] After the declaration of war and enactment of the draft, agrarian leaders and the Democratic party leadership generally united behind the war and the implementation of the draft. So did the Republican party except for a few mavericks such as Senator Robert M. La Follette of Wisconsin. Otherwise, organized agrarian opposition to the draft was limited to a few local or regional, ethnic or radical politico-economic organizations, such as the Non-partisan League which was soon labeled disloyal and destroyed by incumbent Republican officials in Minnesota.[3]

In the South, alienated economic groups continued to oppose the war and the draft. Lower-income whites in upcountry Georgia and South Carolina were roused by denunciations of a "Wall Street war," by economic populists and race-baiters like Tom Watson and Cole Blease. "Men conscripted to go to Europe are virtually con-

demned to death and everybody knows it," Watson wrote in his
weekly newspaper before the government suppressed it. Federal
agents reported from the South in July 1917 that many believed "the
poor people have been hoodwinked by conscription and should unite
to proclaim their active opposition to its enforcement."[4] The North
Carolina Farmers' Union and similar groups of dirt farmers in west
Texas proclaimed similar isolationist sentiments, before all were
suppressed by local and federal authorities, including Attorney
General Thomas W. Gregory and Postmaster General Albert S.
Burleson.[5]

Disfranchised blacks were also skeptical about supporting a war
to make the world "safe for democracy." But although a small group
of black socialists like A. Philip Randolph and Chandler Owen argued against black participation, the majority of black leaders
urged Afro-Americans to aid the nation's war effort. W.E.B. Du Bois,
the Harvard-educated historian and editor of the NAACP's magazine, predicted that out of the black soldiers' contribution to victory
would arise "an American Negro with the right to vote and the right
to work and the right to live without insult."[6]

The largely middle-class peace movement faced internal dissen-
tion and external repression. Oswald Garrison Villard, leading pacifist and Harvard-educated publisher of the *Nation* and the New York
Evening Post, following stinging rebukes for his continued criticism
of the war and the draft, decided to limit his activity to private
efforts on behalf of conscientious objectors. Suffering similar ostra-
cism and vilification, Jane Addams, head of the forerunner of the
Women's International League for Peace and Freedom, felt "adrift in
a surging sea" and abandoned her peace work until after the war.[7]

Within the American Union Against Militarism (AUAM), the upper-
middle-class social reformers on the executive committee divided
over the proper policy. The majority refused to confront the administration over conscription once it was enacted. Instead, they put
their trust in the president and his liberal assistants, Secretary of
War Newton D. Baker and Assistant Secretary Frederick P. Keppel,
former dean of Columbia College, to withstand pressures for harsh
policies against conscientious objectors. Ultra-nationalists like Theodore Roosevelt and General Wood denounced conscientious objectors as cowards and traitors and urged that they be imprisoned with
alien enemies, deported as soon as possible, or, in cases of open
sedition or mutinous action, be executed by a firing squad.[8]

In the spring of 1917 the AUAM created the National Civil Liberties Bureau to provide free legal advice for conscientious objectors,
over the objections of conservative board members like Lillian D.
Wald and Paul U. Kellogg. Even moderates like Villard dissented

from attempts by radical board members like Crystal Eastman to commit the AUAM to opposing the draft actively and pressing for its repeal. Consequently, instead of seeking to mobilize antiwar, antidraft sentiment among its constituency of urban liberals and the woman's movement, the AUAM sought to convince the administration to protect conscientious objectors, and to support the goal of a liberal peace.[9]

The People's Council for Peace and Democracy, an attempt by left-wing progressives and socialists to form an activist, confrontational antidraft, antiwar organization among liberals, women, farmers, and labor, was curtailed by local authorities and the direct opposition of Samuel Gompers. The A.F. of L. president formed the American Alliance for Labor and Democracy to discredit the People's Council's claim to speak for American workers, and he denounced the People's Council as composed of dupes or traitors who were aiding the enemy. The press and many public officials agreed with him. Woodrow Wilson privately described Amos Pinchot, the Eastmans, Rabbi Judah Magnes and other leaders of the People's Council as "eminent cranks and others who have sense in normal times."[10] Mass meetings of the Council were prohibited or broken up in several cities and its speakers denounced, threatened, and sometime physically assaulted.[11].

Even greater repression was used against prewar politico-economic radicals like the anarchists and syndicalists. When anarchists Emma Goldman and Alexander Berkman formed the No-Conscription League and held rallies in New York City and San Francisco, federal marshals and local police raided their offices and seized their files. Shortly before the draft registration day in June 1917, police arrested them for "conspiracy to induce persons not to register."[12] The leadership of the Industrial Workers of the World avoided outright denunciation of the draft, concentrating instead on increasingly successful organizing drives among the low-paid agricultural, lumber, and mining workers in the West. Nevertheless, the antiwar, antidraft stand of the rank and file helped their enemies brand them as disloyal and they were harassed and arrested, and at least one organizer was lynched. Pressured by western governors and several cabinet members, the president concluded that the IWW was hindering essential production through its labor stoppages, and authorized its prosecution on charges of impeding the war effort by inducing young men to refuse to register for the draft or encouraging them to desert from the army. After a mass trial of 166 IWW leaders, the majority were sentenced to terms of one to fifteen years and the Industrial Workers of the World was ended as an effective organization.[13]

The most important organization opposing the war and the draft was the Socialist Party of America, which continued its dissent even after the declaration of war. At a national convention in St. Louis, the majority of delegates had voted for a resolution which called for "continuous, active, and public opposition to the war [and to military conscription, sales of war bonds, and taxes on the necessities of life], through demonstrations, mass petitions, and all other means within our power."[14] Despite the loss of a nationalistic minority who refused to accept this stand and bolted the party, the Socialist party offered the major electoral opportunity for the expression of popular discontent against the war and the draft. In numerous municipal elections in the summer and fall of 1917, Socialist candidates garnered a dramatically increased share of the vote, often polling between a quarter and a third of the balloting, and electing scores of local officials in several major cities like Cleveland, Buffalo, Chicago, and New York City.[15] Disruption and suppression of socialist antiwar, antidraft activities had begun in late May 1917 as local police and gangs of civilians and servicemen broke up meetings and harassed speakers; in several districts, U.S. attorneys arrested socialists for violations of the Draft and the Espionage acts, and for speaking out against the war and the draft. Postmaster Burleson excluded all the major socialist newspapers from the mails, arguing that "nothing can be said inciting people to resist the laws. There can be no campaign against conscription and the Draft Law, nothing that will interfere with enlistments or the raising of an army."[16] In the spring of 1918, armed with the sedition act, and under considerable pressure for action, the federal government indicted and sent to prison a number of prominent socialists, including the unsuccessful Socialist candidates for governor and U.S. Senator from Minnesota, and, most importantly, the party's presidential candidate of 1900, 1904, 1908, and 1912—Eugene V. Debs.[17]

The harassment and repression of dissenters in 1917–18 was too widespread and varied to be centrally directed or conspiratorial. The major impetus came not from the president, who frequently sought to limit such repression, nor primarily from his administration, but rather from a variety of private and public sources, particularly at state and local levels.[18] It was entwined with the fabric of American society as well as with the wartime nationalism and mobilization which encouraged it. Quite clearly there were strains of anti-foreignism and anti-radicalism involved in such a mass phenomenon. Xenophobia had flourished as a result of massive new immigration from southern and eastern Europe since the 1890s. Now the anti-foreignism and the demand for "100-percent-Americanism" was turned specifically upon particular ethnic and politico-economic groups that were considered unsympathetic to what had now become the American cause. Examples of some German espionage and sabotage in the United States before 1917 enabled wartime chauvinists to exaggerate the danger of internal subversion.[19] By 1918, some commentators warned of "thousands" of spies and saboteurs in America. Such unwarranted assertions exacerbated wartime hysteria and undoubtedly contributed to the violence against those who for ethnic, economic, or political reasons opposed U.S. entry and conscription, and were consequently labeled German sympathizers or traitors.

Organized ultra-nationalists included the political and economic conservatives of the National Security League and other existing preparedness and patriotic associations as well as newly formed quasi-public "law and order" bodies, such as the American Protective League. A citizens' group of some 250,000 volunteer amateur citizen-sleuths, the APL worked with the Department of Justice to enforce draft registration and maintain surveillance on persons thought to be unsympathetic or subversive to the war effort.[20] Among the most vociferous and unrelenting chauvinists were Theodore Roosevelt and Senator George E. Chamberlain of Oregon. "American pacifism," Roosevelt declared, "has been the tool and ally of German militarism, and has represented, and always will represent, deep disloyalty to our beloved country." He suggested sending conscientious objectors to clear minefields to prove that they were not cowards but merely opposed to killing others. By early 1918 Roosevelt had concluded that civilian legal procedure was too slow to be effective in wartime and called for the use of martial law in America. Even the normally judicious William Howard Taft criticized the Wilson administration for inadequate counter-espionage and publicly urged that spies be found and shot.[21]

Drawing upon the examples of England, France, and Germany, Senator George E. Chamberlain in March 1918 introduced a bill which would have declared the United States to be within the "zone of war" and provided for the establishment of military courts throughout the country.[22] Classifying as a "spy" every person who published anything "endangering the success of the military forces" of the United States, it would have authorized the government to avoid the civilian legal system, with its substantial protections for individual rights, and take such dissenters directly to a military tribunal which operated under less stringent rules of evidence and procedure and which could conclude trials quickly without bail and delay, and mete out punishment swiftly and severely. Indeed, conviction could result in execution by firing squad. Progressive and conservative civil libertarians denounced the bill and, when the president himself quickly condemned it, the measure died. But the fact that many editors and local officials had hailed it demonstrates the considerable support that existed for even greater suppression of wartime dissent.[23]

Moderate Americans also sought to deal with the limits of acceptable dissent and the nature of good citizenship in wartime. Most pragmatic progressives considered liberty to be an ethically neutral concept and believed that excessive use of it would hinder national efficiency in pursuit of worthy wartime goals. John Dewey sought to discredit the pacifist ethic and convince pacifists and other non-interventionists of the efficacy and "compelling moral import" of the American cause. Viewing suppression of dissenters as historically ineffectual and even counterproductive, Dewey advocated toleration of critics of the war effort and lenient treatment of conscientious objectors.[24] But pragmatism was generally not conducive to absolutist moral stands and antiwar critics were ostracized and suppressed and many of their publications banned from the mails.[25] The predominant position on civil liberties in the early part of this century was that they were only to be protected for those citizens who had demonstrated by their attitudes and their behavior that they were prepared to utilize those freedoms in positive and constructive ways. Although a few liberal intellectuals began to assert the constructive social value of dissent, the right to exercise freedom of speech and other civil liberties was generally considered to be relative to the circumstances. In practice, that meant such rights were frequently denied to minority or other subordinate groups, blacks, Hispanics, politico-economic radicals, and (in World War I) German Americans and other isolationist ethnic groups.[26]

Prosecution of dissenters in World War I occurred primarily at the local level, but there was increasing pressure for the federal government to establish national norms and limitations on dissent. Wilson and the Democratic Congress did enact legislation to limit espionage and significant obstruction of mobilization in a divided nation. Eventually the government prosecuted antiwar leaders of the anarchists, socialists, and the I.W.W., and denied many of their publications the use of the mails. Nevertheless, the administration took far less drastic action than was advocated by American ultra-nationalists like Roosevelt or was enacted by the coalition government in Great Britain.[27]

With the specter of the Civil War draft riots recalled by a number of anti-conscriptionists, federal and local authorities awaited Registration Day—June 5, 1917—with considerable concern. Compulsory

draft registration of an estimated 9 to 10 million young men between the ages of 21 and 30 would be the first major test of the new
law. General Crowder and his aides gambled that the drama of
holding registration on a single day rather than an extended period
would focus public attention and help make it a success. They
emphasized patriotic duty, but they also reminded the public of the
penalties for failure to register. A headline in the *Los Angeles Times*
declared "Anti-Draft Agitators To Be Treated With No Leniency" and
"Death For Treason Awaits Anti-Draft Plotters." In the week before
registration, local police in various cities arrested a number of
persons for denouncing registration, and Secretary of War Newton
D. Baker secretly wired governors asking if they needed regular
army troops to ensure an orderly process. They did not. Between 7
a.m. and 7 p.m., some 9.6 million young men registered quietly for
the draft at their local polling places. Although there were a few
protest demonstrations such as one by some 600 Irish-American
miners at Butte, Montana, they were quickly broken up by police.
Registration Day was universally hailed as an enormous success.[28]

Behind the hoopla, however, the administration suspected that
thousands of young males of military age had failed to register. Over
the next five months, nearly 6,000 young men found without registration cards were arrested by the Justice Department for failure to
comply with the law, but General Crowder confided to the attorney
general's office that Selective Service had no way of knowing how
many had actually evaded registration.[29] Over the course of the war,
the number of men who failed to register for the draft may have
reached three million. Given Crowder's own working estimates of 10
to 15 percent evasion on the second registration day—June 5, 1918—
it can be assumed that perhaps two million men, aged 18–20 and 31–
45, failed to sign up on the third registration day, September 12,
1918. Adding the 150,000 of June 1918 and another 200,000 to
900,000 from June 1917 (2 to 10 percent in 1917) it appears that
although 24 million men registered during the war, an additional 2.4
to 3.6 million may have successfully avoided draft registration.
Most were never discovered. Some fled to Canada or Mexico (authorities knew of a temporary colony of young American middle-
and upper-class liberal pacifists and socialists living in Mexico
City).[30] The majority of the non-registrants, however, remained in
the United States but outside of the Selective Service System.

But it was not cosmopolitan, young, middle- or upper-class radicals who made up the bulk of the draft registration evaders. Rather,
arrest figures suggest that most were poorer men: agricultural or
industrial laborers, isolated and alienated from the larger society or
the national war effort because of geographical location or their

economic, ethnic, or racial status. Of the 5,870 arrests in the summer of 1917 for failure to register, most were in the Appalachian Mountain regions of Virginia, the Carolinas, and Mississippi; the rural backcountry areas of Louisiana, Missouri, southern Illinois, Oklahoma, and Texas; and the lumber, farming, and mining regions of Minnesota and Colorado. There were also numerous arrests in urban areas with heavy concentrations of unskilled ethnic immigrant populations such as Boston, New York, Jersey City and Paterson, N.J., Cleveland, and Detroit.[31] If the U.S. Attorney's Office in Mobile, Ala. was typical, the types of men reported to authorities by middle-class townspeople as registration evaders were usually members of minority groups, not regularly employed, or as one informant put it: "he is always loafering [sic] around town, never seeming to have any thing to do. . . . " But the evidence also showed that some non-registrants were simply too alienated or confused to deal effectively with the bureaucratic processes of the Selective Service System.[32]

Induction, not registration, was the true test of the draft. On July 20, 1917, Secretary of War Baker, blindfolded, drew out of a large glass bowl the first of 10,500 numbers (the most registrants in any district) which determined the order in which draftees would be called before their local boards. At that time, board members would question the young men about claims for deferment; if these were rejected and the young man passed a medical examination by the board's physician, he was ordered to report for induction into the army. This process began in late July and went on into September, until the new training cantonments were filled with the first wave of draftees.

When induction actually began, it triggered some antidraft violence in isolated rural areas of the country. In the largest episode, the "Green Corn Rebellion" in eastern Oklahoma, more than 500 tenant farmers gathered in the hills for a protest march on the nation's capital. A sheriff's posse surrounded and arrested them. These sharecroppers, and a few Appalachian mountaineers and western Indians who engaged in shoot-outs with local lawmen over their resistance to the draft, posed little threat to the enforcement or legitimacy of Selective Service. Most incidents involved only a handful of resisters and their uncoordinated actions were generally quickly suppressed. In scrimmages between individual draft resisters and local police in the mountains of Arizona, Nevada, Arkansas, and North Carolina, between 20 and 25 persons were killed, a sharp contrast to the scores, perhaps hundreds, of deaths resulting from armed draft resistance during the Civil War.[33]

Evasion, not open resistance, was preferred in World War I. In

1919, the provost marshal general reported that 337,649 men had taken the overt step of either failing to report for induction when summoned by their draft boards, or of deserting after arrival at training camp. Both offenses were classified as "desertion" in World War I because the registrant was considered to be in the armed forces from the date he was due to report for induction (in subsequent wars, a draftee did not become part of the military until he actually reported and took the oath of service). Although General Crowder sought to minimize the importance of the 338,000 draft "deserters" by reporting them as only 1½ percent of the 24 million registrants, it would be more accurate to portray them as 12 percent of the 2.8 million men who were actually drafted.[34] Fragmentary evidence suggests that these draft "deserters," like the non-registrants, were disproportionately members of lower-income ethnic groups in the northern industrial areas, or poor whites and impoverished blacks or Hispanics in the rural South and Southwest. However, the most famous "draft-dodger," Grover Cleveland Bergdoll, was the son of a wealthy German-American brewing family in Philadelphia.[35]

By mid-1918, the Justice Department had prosecuted 10,000 men for failure to register for the draft, but it was widely and accurately believed that thousands more remained undetected. In the spring and early summer of 1918, as the German Army launched an enormous offensive in France, public hysteria soared in the United States. To direct such activity into legal and more constructive channels and to overcome criticism that Washington had been lax in pursuing draft avoiders, Attorney General Gregory, supported by General Crowder, decided to launch a series of "slacker raids."[36] These nationally coordinated sweeps in a dozen cities rounded up draft delinquents in a dragnet in which hundreds of thousands of people were stopped on the street by federal and local lawmen, questioned, and, if suspect, interned until they could prove they were not draft delinquents. The raids showed chauvinists that federal authorities supported forceful action against slackers, but the illegalities and violations of civil liberties involved in such massive random interrogation, and the temporary detention of men without warrants or formal charges, raised serious issues about extensive violations of due process of law. When it was learned that only about 5 percent of the several thousand detainees turned out to be draft evaders, even the efficacy of the dragnet process was sharply questioned.[37]

A week before the draft registration of September 12, 1918, authorities staged the largest "slacker raid" of the war in New York City. For three days after the Labor Day holiday, 2,000 armed soldiers and sailors joined federal agents, local police, and APL auxiliaries in stopping tens of thousands of men of military age and forcing them to show their draft cards. Of the 50,277 who were detained, a thousand were inducted into the army and 15,000 were turned over to their local boards as delinquent in some manner. The New York raids produced a major outcry against the dragnet method; particularly offensive was the role of the armed forces. Even normally ardent champions of the administration, like the New York *World*, denounced the seizure of thousands of men merely on suspicion as "a shameful abuse of power" and a "rape of the law."[38]

Although, outside New York, a number of editors and politicians praised these "slacker raids," anti-Wilson Democrats and Republicans in the Senate, with an eye to the congressional elections in November, denounced the administration for this violation of civil liberties. The president launched an investigation under John Lord O'Brian, a progressive Republican and the most respected civil libertarian in the Justice Department. O'Brian obtained from Attorney General Gregory a statement which, although it defended the need for "slacker raids," claimed that overzealous subordinates had ignored his orders against using military personnel and members of the American Protective League, and that arrests by such persons were illegal and "ill-judged." Another result was that the Federal Bureau of Investigation was temporarily reduced and reorganized immediately after the war.[39]

By mid-1919, roughly half of the 337,649 draft "deserters" had been apprehended, or their cases had otherwise been settled. In regard to the others still at large that year, the government simply published their names. In 1920, the army sought an extension of the statue of limitations so that draft delinquents and other non-combat-zone "deserters" might still be prosecuted despite the end of the war. President Wilson, however, turned down the request.[40]

During the war, large numbers of Americans sought to evade military service by fraud or other illegal methods. When it was learned in the spring of 1917 that Selective Service intended to draft single men before drafting husbands, thousands rushed to the altar. Unfortunately for them, this did not prevent some 123,000 of the anxious new bridegrooms from being put into the most eligible category, and many of these were indeed drafted. Other men lied about their marital status; some lied about their age, their health, or their employment. Some sought to corroborate their claim with false documents or perjured witnesses. A physician at a New York City board reported that the most common physical subterfuges were simulation of deafness, poor eyesight, and hemorrhoids. Some took drugs to affect their health, or to increase their heart rate or blood pressure. More dangerously, some took opiates, primarily morphine or heroin, so that they would be rejected for narcotic addiction. Since convicted felons were excluded on moral grounds, some bungled a burglary so that they would go to prison rather than to the trenches. Even more desperate were young men who deliberately cut or shot off a finger or toe or blinded one of their eyes to keep out of the army. Such cases of self-mutilation, Crowder reported to the FBI, were "rather frequent."[41]

Whatever the motivation of those who sought to evade the draft by flight or subterfuge, some young men formally and directly challenged the authority of the government to force them to fight. A number of religious and liberal pacifist organizations—Quakers, Mennonites, the Fellowship of Reconciliation, and the AUAM—had sought to convince the government to grant such freedom of conscience. They argued that the British experience of 1916–17 had shown that the clash of wills between committed conscientious objectors and the administrative apparatus of the State, particularly the military, could result in miscarriage of justice and severe, even fatal, brutality.[42]

The problem in World War I as in the Civil War was that the national government was afraid of charges of inequity and of providing a sizable escape route which would impede raising the wartime army. Upon the recommendations of Secretary of War Baker, Congress limited conscientious objection to members of traditional pacifist faiths and exempted them only from combat, not non-combatant military service. John Nevin Sayre, a young Episcopal minister and leader of F.O.R. whose brother was married to one of Wilson's daughters, wrote to the president in April 1917 asking that the exemption be determined according to individual belief rather than organizational membership; but the chief executive rejected his suggestion, stating that "it has seemed impossible to make the exceptions apply to individuals because it would open the door to so much that was unconscientious on the part of persons who wished to escape service."[43]

It was clear that the administration felt caught in cross-pressures in regard to the conscientious objectors, the concern of some liberals for the preservation of individual conscience, and the demands of others—like Roosevelt—that it was morally unfair and militarily inefficient to allow some draftees to refuse to serve.[44] Yet at the same time, Baker's policy—designed to avoid encouraging conscientious objection—contributed in practice to unfair and often harsh treatment of the objectors. Selective Service did not determine or inform local boards which denominations qualified as bona fide pacifist sects; consequently, board members often ruled arbitrarily on such claims. Moreover, even certified conscientious objectors were sent to training camps until it was determined what to do with them. Not until October 1917 did Baker direct army commanders to segregate the conscientious objectors and place them under military officers who would treat them with "tact and consideration."[45] The results depended largely on the local commanders. A considerate officer, like Maj. Gen. J. Franklin Bell at Camp Upton, New York, succeeded in persuading a majority of the conscientious objectors to serve in the army. Conversely, hostile critics like Maj. Gen. Leonard Wood, at Camp Funston, Kansas, who branded conscientious objectors as "enemies of the Republic, fakers, and active agents of the enemy," contributed to the tensions and brutality that led to the imprisonment of many and the death of perhaps 17 conscientious objectors.[46] Some 64,700 men filed claims for conscientious objector status (undoubtedly many other objectors either evaded the draft, or claimed deferment on dependency, occupational, or physical grounds). Local boards certified 56,800 as conscientious objectors; of the 30,000 who then passed the physical examination, 20,873 were inducted into the army. After a period in camp, nearly 80 percent of these (some 16,000 men) decided to abandon their objection and take up arms.[47]

Nevertheless, 3,989 drafted objectors continued to assert their scruples against war and the military. They were not recent immigrants as was commonly believed. Rather, 90 percent were native-born Americans, although many had immigrant parents. The majority belonged to historic pacifist religious faiths, especially the Quakers, Mennonites, and Moravian Brethren. Two small millenial groups would grow by World War II into the most numerous religious objectors to war—the Seventh Day Adventists and the Russellites, later known as Jehovah's Witnesses. The majority of these religious sects maintained a literal view of Biblical injunctions against killing and they resisted compromise with their principles and integration into the army even as (except for the Quakers) they and their elders resisted integration into secular society at home. Their faith and the strong support of their ethno-cultural religious communities sustained them against the intense pressure to accept military service. From his cell in the military prison at Fort Leavenworth, Kansas, one young Mennonite farmer wrote to his parents in stumbling English: "You cant emagen how it is to be hated. if it wasent fore Christ it would be empossible."[48] Although objectors from the historic peace churches made up probably three-quarters of the c.o.'s in the army camps, there were also other individual objectors.[49] Perhaps 15 percent were religious objectors who came from non-pacifist churches, mostly young, well-educated, middle-class liberals committed to domestic and international reform and concepts of love and compassion for humankind. Among them were "social gospel" ministers like John Nevin Sayre and Norman M. Thomas and former social workers like Roger N. Baldwin.[50] About 10 percent were non-religious, "political objectors," including active socialists, syndicalists, and anarchists as well as some young men of anti-Ally ethnic descent who challenged the Allied and American war aims.[51]

Reassured by early signs of the success of his policy, Baker took a more liberal step and on December 19, 1917 gave official recognition to the non-religious objector opposed to wars in general. Nevertheless, they would have to perform non-combatant service, which in the spring of 1918 was designated as serving in the support branches of the army.[52] Although 1,300 of the 4,000 conscientious objectors ultimately agreed to serve in the Medical Corps or other non-combatant branches, the rest would not. The National Civil Liberties Bureau urged that such "absolutists," who refused to comply with any military order, be allowed to perform "essential" civilian jobs in industry or agriculture, but Baker lost patience both with the absolutists and the NCLB. He did, however, establish a Board of Inquiry which interviewed all conscientious objectors remaining in the camps. By the end of the war, 1,300 had accepted non-combatant service in the military; 1,300 had been furloughed for civilian work; 940 remained segregated in the training camps objecting to combat or non-combatant service; and 450 "absolutists" had been court-martialed and incarcerated in military prisons.[53]

To young men conscientiously opposed to war, the draft and the training camp posed a crisis of conscience to which each reacted in his own way. Evan Thomas, a religious objector and brother of the activist Presbyterian minister who would later become the Socialist candidate for president, refused to cooperate with the military in any manner on the grounds of complete Christian pacifism. Subsequently in protest against conditions in the military prison, he participated in a hunger strike which contributed to the permanent impairment of his health. Ernest Meyer, a student at the University of Wisconsin, took an "absolutist" position on secular political grounds and also went to prison. He later recalled that the Board of Inquiry had asked him what he would do if a burglar tried to rape his mother, then ignored his attempt to differentiate between indiscriminate mass warfare and individual self-defense. The board also rejected his argument that the United States had alternatives other than war. Most conscientious objectors gave up their pacifism in the training camps, among them Alvin C. York, a semi-educated Tennessee mountaineer and deacon in the fundamentalist, pacifist

Church of Christ and Christian Union. When his draft notice arrived, York with the support of his pastor had sought exemption as a conscientious objector, basing his claim upon his belief in the Bible and the Sixth Commandment: "Thou Shalt Not Kill." When his claim was rejected, the troubled young man reported to the training camp as ordered. There, however, his battalion commander persuaded him that the Bible sanctioned righteous war. A second conversion experience convinced him that God wanted him to fight. During the Meuse-Argonne offensive a year later, the former conscientious objector and mountaineer marksman shot and killed 25 German soldiers in a single day and captured 132 more, becoming, as "Sergeant York," the most renowned doughboy hero of World War I.[54]

In the fall of 1918, the director of the National Civil Liberties Bureau, Roger Baldwin, confronted with his own induction, refused to cooperate with his draft board and challenged the entire conscription system. An extreme individualist, this affluent, Harvard-educated New Englander believed in the right of every person to exercise his or her own free will. Government was useful in protecting individual rights, but if it turned to arbitrary control of the individual, it should be resisted. In his widely reprinted statement made to the court on October 30, 1918, the 34-year-old Baldwin went beyond refusing to kill and denounced the principle of "conscription of life by the State, for any purpose whatever, in war-time or peace. [It is] a flat contradiction of all our cherished ideals of individual freedom, democratic liberty, and Christian teaching."[55] Since he was tried in a civilian court, Baldwin was sentenced to one year in the local jail, an imprisonment he readily accepted because of his belief that his action was an important statement against unwarranted encroachments by the State. This, and the end of war, led liberals—including many who had supported the war—to consider him a martyr to the principle of individual conscience and to begin, over the opposition of many ultra-nationalists, to seek leniency for all imprisoned conscientious objectors.[56]

For all the anguish and mistreatment caused by the government's early policies and delays, the Wilson administration did eventually move to a policy which was more liberal than Britain's and certainly more humane than that of France and Germany, where such objectors were imprisoned or shot. Most of the mistreatment and suffering could have been avoided if the objectors had kept out of the army and assigned to alternative civilian service, but uncertainties and ultra-nationalists like Roosevelt made such a course difficult. Nevertheless, the experience of 1917–18 was painful enough to lead Franklin D. Roosevelt in World War II to respond to the suggestions of religious organizations and many liberals and to offer certified conscientious objectors alternative civilian public service work from the beginning.[57]

More important to the government than the issue of conscientious objectors was the legitimacy of the draft. Since the legal authority of the national conscription had not been adequately upheld by the judiciary in the Civil War, the administration moved quickly in 1917 to validate the draft before the Supreme Court of the United States.[58] In the principal cases, the *Selective Draft Law Cases* (Arver et. al., *v.* United States), several Minnesota socialists, Joseph F. Arver, Otto H. Wangerin and a number of others, had refused to register for the draft on June 5, 1917. Within a month, they had been tried and convicted in a federal court in Minneapolis and sentenced to one year in prison, to be inducted into the army following their incarceration. In New York City, several other draft resisters were similarly convicted. All were in prison when the Supreme Court of the U.S. grouped together all of these appeals by persons who had refused to register. At the same time, the justices also heard direct appeals on two other sets of cases which concerned the constitutionality of the draft act. Emma Goldman and Alexander Berkman, both Russian-born anarchists and aliens, were serving two years' imprisonment for conspiring to counsel resistance to the draft law. Three prominent socialists from the Midwest, including Charles E. Ruthenberg a leader of the party's left wing and co-author of the St. Louis antiwar proclamation, had been convicted in Cleveland and sentenced to one year in jail for encouraging a young man not to register for the draft. All of these cases involved political radicals, socialists, or anarchists, either aliens or native-born citizens most of whom were of German descent, who had challenged the legality of the draft law, primarily as an assertion of power not granted to federal government by the Constitution and also as a direct violation of the Thirteenth Amendment's prohibition against slavery and involuntary servitude.[59]

By a unanimous vote, the Supreme Court upheld the constitutionality of the Draft Act, announcing its decision in the *Arver et al.* case on January 7, 1918. Chief Justice Edward D. White wrote the opinion in what was one of the most important decisions in his long career on the bench. White's opinion upheld the right of the U.S. government to draft citizens directly into a national army through a broad construction of the constitutional provisions granting Congress the power to declare war and to raise and support armies, combined with the necessary and proper clause. He quickly dismissed the plaintiff's contention that the framers intended only a limited power to raise national armies by voluntary means while the states alone had the power of compulsory military service because, they had argued, state citizenship was primary and national citizenship only derivative. As White put it:

> As the mind cannot conceive any army without the men to compose it, on the face of the Constitution the objection that it does not give power to provide for such men would seem to be too frivolous for further notice. . . .[60]

The chief justice emphasized the principle of national self-defense and of reciprocal rights and duties of citizens. As he phrased it: "It may not be doubted that the very conception of a just government and its duty to the citizen includes the reciprocal obligation of the citizen to render military service in case of need and the right to compel it."

In an interpretation speaking to a 20th-century audience rather than the majority of the nation's Founders, who undoubtedly would have rejected it at the time, White claimed that the constitutional clauses regarding the militia and the power to raise armies meant that the states controlled their militia only to the extent that that control was not taken from them by the federal government. In a single page, White cavalierly dismissed as manifestly unsound the appeal to the Thirteenth Amendment, to which White devoted his concluding, and stridently patriotic, paragraph:

> Finally, as we are unable to conceive upon what theory the exaction by government from the citizen of the performance of his supreme and noble duty of contributing to the defense of the rights and honor of the nation . . . can be said to be the imposition of involuntary servitude in violation of the prohibitions of the Thirteenth Amendment, we are constrained to the conclusion that the contention is refuted by its mere statement.[61]

The convictions of Joseph Arver and the other young men for failure to register were affirmed and the constitutionality of the conscription act upheld in these *Selective Draft Cases*. A week later, the chief justice announced the results of the other two sets of draft law cases. A unanimous court upheld the convictions of Emma Goldman and Alexander Berkman for conspiracy to violate the draft law and of Charles Ruthenberg and the other Ohio socialists for encouraging young men not to register for the draft.[62]

There never was any doubt that the Court in 1917 would declare the wartime Draft Act constitutional, for the jurists were part of a dominant majority among cosmopolitan elites in support of both the war and wartime measures like national conscription. In upholding such statutes, the high tribunal simply extended during the wartime emergency the expansion of national authority which it had generally upheld during the domestic reforms of earlier phases of the progressive era. But though the *Arver* decision settled the issue of the constitutionality of national conscription for the courts, it did not completely end the matter. In subsequent years, challenges to different aspects of compulsory military service and of conscientious objection to it reappeared periodically and dramatically—in the 1920s, in World War II, and particularly in the Vietnam War. Although the Supreme Court in later periods modified the definition of conscientious objection and also some of the procedures of the Selective Service System, it saw no reason to re-examine *Arver* or alter White's conclusion that national conscription was constitutional, even though by the late 1960s there had emerged a strong body of legal and scholarly opinion which held (irregardless of attitude toward the correctness of the opinion) that Chief Justice White had written a weak opinion and too easily dismissed various challenges to the constitutionality of national conscription.[63]

Despite the considerable accuracy of subsequent criticism of the historical and legal weaknesses of much of White's written opinions in the selective draft cases, these decisions upholding national conscription even for overseas service were products of their time and of the growth of the national government and the United States as a world power. In 1917–18, the Court was clearly ready to help legitimize the Draft Act, particularly in a divided society with a sizable minority opposed to conscription, especially for service in Europe. Opposition to conscripting Americans for overseas service, although primarily related to isolationism, also stemmed in part from a continuing strain of American thought—the common militia idea that compulsory military service was only appropriate when one's home or homeland was directly threatened. In this dissenting view, the militia concept, and the State's power to compel service, was not appropriate for the expeditionary military forces of a world power; those forces should be composed of volunteers. Among the predominant cosmopolitan elites, a majority disagreed and favored broad national control over the raising and deployment of America's military forces. As Justice Oliver Wendell Holmes muttered to a colleague while constitutional lawyer Hannis Taylor was vehemently arguing against the legitimacy of compelling the common militia to serve outside the United States: "Taylor is a pig-headed adherent of an inadequate idea."[64] The Supreme Court, like the majority of the legal community, dismissed such ideas and instead maintained the myth that the Framers and the original intent of the

Constitution approved of conscription by the national government in support of its legitimate purposes. Actually, as more dispassionate recent historical research had indicated, this probably was not the intent of the majority of the Founders in 1787–88, but in the context of 1917–18 that was not greatly relevant, except in the perpetuation of a myth and the largely fictive history enunciated by the Court.[65]

Politically, the most important challenges to the draft were not assertions from a minority that it was unconstitutional, but rather criticism about unfairness or illegality in the operation of conscription. Despite the administration's efforts, charges of favoritism and sometimes corruption in granting exemptions or deferments were levied against local board members or the staff during the war. Investigations by the Justice and War Departments found several to be correct. As a result, a small number of board members were dismissed for irregularities (including, two members of the Lawton, Oklahoma board and ten of the nearly seven hundred board members in Illinois, for example). Furthermore, a few were imprisoned for taking bribes. The early and quick conviction of two doctors from a New York City board, who confessed to taking $4,000 to exempt able-bodied men as physically unfit, and their sentence to two years in federal prison was widely applauded.[66] The honesty of the vast majority and the government's action against the dishonest helped maintain the image of the integrity of the system.

Inevitably in such a racially divided society, "the color line" became an issue in regard to the operation of conscription (and the organization of the army). In the first draft call for 687,000 men, during the summer of 1917, blacks—who composed 10 percent of the total population—made up 14 percent of the men selected for military service. Since 80 percent of American blacks lived in the South, so would most of the nearly 100,000 black draftees, and the most efficient policy would be to train them there. Yet during the summer, some southern members of Congress began privately to express concern about the impact of conscription and the training of black troops in the South, as well as the role of black soldiers in the army. Baker wanted them to serve in the conscripted National Army, yet he accepted the military segregation common since the Civil War era, and agreed to stop accepting black volunteers in April when the four regular army and eight northern National Guard black units had been quickly brought up to full strength.[67] As the War Department was considering the questions of conscription, training, and use of blacks, a bloody race riot occurred in Houston,

Texas on the night of August 25, 1917: after police beat up two soldiers unfairly, black regulars from the 24th Infantry Regiment stationed nearby marched into town and shot to death sixteen whites, including five policemen. An entire battalion was arrested and, after court-martial, nineteen of the black soldiers were executed by the army.[68] In October, a near repetition occurred when black militiamen in the Harlem regiment of the New York National Guard bridled at the southern racial code in force near the training camp they were sent to at Spartanburg, South Carolina.

Coming just as the draft calls were beginning, the Houston riot rocketed the race issue to the front pages of the nation's press. Southern representatives in Congress exploded, many of them seeking to have all black soldiers removed from their states. The black community was stunned by the Army's swift and sweeping retribution in arresting the entire battalion for the crimes of some of its soldiers. At the urging of white philanthropists and black leaders, Secretary Baker held a conference on August 31 of "men interested in the Negro question" and attempted to placate black spokespeople by appointing Emmett J. Scott, a former assistant of the late Booker T. Washington, as his special assistant for Negro affairs and by agreeing to establish a black combat division (the 92nd Division, composed mainly of black units from the regular army and National Guard).[69] Nearly 75 percent of the blacks in the army and almost all of the black draftees, however, were relegated to labor units. Although they comprised one-tenth of the American population and one-eighth of its military strength during the war, blacks made up one-third of the military laborers and only one-thirtieth of the American combat forces. Viewing blacks mainly as laborers and field hands, the Army relegated most black draftees to digging ditches, building roads, unloading ships, loading trucks, burying the dead, and performing other menial and unpleasant tasks.[70]

Bowing to southern pressure against sending nearly 100,000 black draftees to camp and training them in the use of arms, Baker at an emergency conference with some of his generals on September 9 decided "to defer for the present, the calling out of the colored draft."[71] This decision not only disrupted General Crowder's plans for filling the first draft quota, but greatly upset many southern whites because it meant that Selective Service had to draw on excessive proportions among whites to meet state quotas in the South. Southern members of Congress received numerous letters from white constituents expressing anxiety over the racial inequity (and the danger to "our sisters and daughters") if the black men were left at home when the white men went off to war. As one white man from

a heavily black county in North Carolina wrote to Rep. Claude
Kitchin:

> None of them [the Negroes], so far, have [sic] been taken or at least
> sent on [to] camp. This makes it fall heavily on our white boys.
> Many of them are leaving and most of them at big sacrifice, many
> leaving considerable business interests.
>   . . . They feel and others feel that these negro bucks should be
> put into service. I fear that unless they [the War Department]
> make some arrangement for them soon there will be complaint.[72]

Three weeks later, on September 22, 1917, the War Department
announced it would soon resume induction of blacks, but that Afro-
Americans would be carefully segregated during their journey and
at the camp and would not exceed one-third of the training population at any of the cantonments. In fact, large-scale induction of
blacks did not begin for nearly six months. General Crowder also
had to assure southern governors that whites would not be drafted
disproportionately in 1918 the way they had been in 1917. Although
the draft law provided only for basing draft quotas on the population of a state, Selective Service now prepared separate "white and
colored quotas" for each state and made these retroactive. Registrants were designated "colored" or "white" by local boards and
draft quotas for the district were assigned accordingly; as Crowder
put it, "apportioning the *burden of the draft* between white and
colored persons . . . substantially in proportion to the number of
each race as liable."[73] Thereafter, blacks were summoned in separate draft calls and sent in all-black troop trains to segregated
training camps. Given the racial tensions and the hostility of many
southern governors, the War Department decided not to send any
out-of-state (i.e. Northern) black troops into training camps in the
South (at least until the closing days of the war). Throughout the
war, induction of contingents of black draftees was repeatedly delayed as priority in the training camps went to preparing combat
units for the American Expeditionary Force. It was not until the
spring of 1918, after the first divisions of drafted whites had been
trained and sent to France, that blacks were inducted and began to
be mobilized in significant numbers, a delay criticized by many
whites and by black leaders as well.[74]
    But the delays meant that when the government finally did issue
induction orders in the spring of 1918, it was necessary to call what
even General Crowder later privately admitted were "unduly large
percentages of negroes . . . in order to even the account."[75] Black
and white civil rights leaders formally protested to the War Depart-

ment that Afro-Americans were being declared eligible for military service and drafted far in excess of their percentage of the population. The discrepancies varied in 1918 and in differing reports, but indisputably blacks, who comprised 10 percent of the population and 9 percent of the draft registrants, made up 13 percent of the draftees. Selective Service drafted one-third of the black registrants, but only one-quarter of the whites.[76] It was clear that blacks had been drafted disproportionately, but did that represent deliberate discrimination within the Selective Service System or rather a larger discrimination in society?

The issues of the fairness of the draft in World War I in regard to black Americans has been controversial ever since it was first raised. General Crowder and Secretary Baker responded to such criticism in part by noting that the government's limitation on black volunteers in the U.S. Army, Navy, Marine Corps, and National Guard meant that 650,000 draft eligible whites enlisted and only slightly more than 4,000 blacks were allowed to join these forces (in addition to the 20,000 blacks already in the Army and northern National Guard when war was declared). Thus, compared to the whites, the pool of able-bodied black men was relatively undepleted by voluntary enlistments.[77] While mathematically accurate, this explanation minimizes the conscious policy of discrimination in enlistment by the armed forces and neglects the importance of such policies in subjugating most black soldiers to menial tasks and thus hindering their claim to equal rights of citizenship. In all, 92 percent of the approximately 400,000 blacks who served in the wartime army were draftees. The claim that blacks were disproportionately drafted because more whites had enlisted voluntarily, while partially correct, does not stand the test of non-discrimination, nor does it fully explain the discrepancy between races in classification into Class I or in actual induction into the army.[78]

There is also considerable evidence of widespread and deliberate discrimination within the Selective Service System against black Americans. Despite the fact that the life expectancy of a black man was ten years less than that of a white man, a result of inadequate health care and a greater incidence of malnutrition and disease due to impoverished status, a significantly larger percentage of black men than white men were declared physically qualified for military service (75 percent as compared to 70 percent).[79] Local draft boards, particularly in the South, regularly inducted blacks who were physically unfit (to the consternation of training camp commanders) while excluding whites with similar disabilities. Black labor leader A. Philip Randolph, complained of the irony that "the Negro is tubercular, syphilitic, physically inferior for purposes of degrading him; but physically fit and physically superior when it comes to sending him to the front to save white men's hides."[80] Randolph, of course, was speaking for effect: although blacks were overdrafted compared to whites, comparatively few were allowed to serve in combat units. Most were deployed in labor battalions behind the lines.

Many blacks entitled to occupational or dependency deferments were also denied these by their local draft boards which certified them Class I, eligible for military service, at a significantly higher rate than whites. General Crowder and Secretary Baker argued that this was a result of blacks being largely unskilled and holding an inferior position in the American economy.[81] Yet, attributing the disproportionate classification and induction to impersonal structural differences in society (and asserting that army pay improved the economic position of many blacks) neglects the conscious, deliberate, personal discrimination shown by many local boards which also contributed directly to the discrepancy and hardships imposed on blacks.

There was conscious discrimination against blacks within the Selective Service System. Their lower rate of exemptions for family dependency or occupation was not solely the result of the economic system. In Fulton County, Georgia, around Atlanta, a local draft board was so flagrantly discriminatory (exempting 526 of 815 whites but only 6 of 202 blacks) that in this and two other cases, Baker replaced the entire boards. Emmett Scott also responded to individual complaints and obtained reclassification of hundreds of Afro-Americans who had been unfairly put in Class I eligibility. Yet these actions had to be triggered by black protests; countless other blacks were unfairly drafted without a challenge being made to Washington. In some regions of the South, black sharecroppers were exempted if formally requested by the planters whose land they worked. Without such a request, they were sent into the army, as were independent black farmers, even those with large families. As one student of the subject has concluded, it appears that many blacks who had sufficient claim for exemption were drafted and sent away to camp.[82]

The urban North also complained about certain aspects of the draft. One was the method of determining population estimates in 1917 which resulted in a disproportionate burden on northern urban industrial states.[83] The most unpopular aspect of the draft in the North, however, was the provision which exempted nondeclarant aliens—resident aliens who had not begun the process of naturalization by officially declaring their intention to become

American citizens. A sizable group, they included some 1.6 million immigrants, aged 21–30, according to the draft registration of June 5, 1917. Only the 800,000 declarant aliens were liable to the draft. By the end of the third registration in September 1918, with the expansion of military age to 18–45, the number of non-declarant aliens reached 4 million (16 percent of all registrants).[84] Since they were simultaneously part and yet not entirely a part of American society, these non-declarant aliens posed particular problems in regard to conscription.

The most obvious problem and complaint was that as originally written the Selective Draft Law penalized the citizen and declarant alien population of cities and states in which there was a large alien population. In the emotional debate over conscription, it had been particularly the unassimilated non-declarant resident alien who had so often been portrayed as the "slacker." Now conscription seemed to allow such "slackers" to escape and, even worse, increased the burden upon American citizens and would-be citizens. The problem was that by law draft quotas were based on total population. Thus citizens in a community or neighborhood in which there were many aliens had to furnish not only their own proportion of conscripts, but supply the quota assessed against the considerable numbers of non-declarant aliens who were legally exempt. In protest, Senator Henry Cabot Lodge cited a Chicago district with 70 percent of its registrants exempted because of foreign allegiance, while in one Brooklyn district, he said, the first draft call took "every eligible American."[85]

In addition, it seemed unfair to many American citizens for non-declarant aliens to be allowed to remain at their jobs while millions of citizens and prospective citizens either volunteered or accepted military conscription, often at considerable financial sacrifice. A quarter of the registrants of one Brooklyn district were exempt non-declarant Russian immigrants. As the frustrated local board complained to President Wilson:

> The major part particularly defy us, while many of them shrug their shoulders, laugh at us and say, 'What are you going to do about it?' . . . While the flower of our neighborhood is being torn from their homes and loved ones to fight, [these] miserable specimens of humanity . . . remain smugly at home to reap the benefits of the life work of our young citizens.[86]

With intense anger growing against the so-called "alien slacker," almost all major newspapers endorsed proposals to make aliens of military age subject to conscription. The New York *Morning Telegram* echoed the sentiments of many when it declared epigrammatically: "The country that is good enough to live in is good enough to fight for."[87]

Although hundreds of thousands of otherwise exempt aliens volunteered for military service or decided not to claim exemption when drafted, the discontent over the non-declarant aliens generated enormous pressure for amelioration upon Congress, the Selective Service, and the Wilson administration. The most popular reaction was to advocate making all aliens of military age, whether declarant or non-declarant, liable to conscription. In August 1917, Senator George E. Chamberlain introduced a bill to make all except enemy aliens liable for military service under the American flag. Those who claimed exemption would be required to leave the United States within 90 days or be forcibly deported. Chamberlain claimed the bill would add a million aliens to the ranks of potential troops and the proposal was widely acclaimed by the press.[88]

Regardless of its popularity in the United States, the idea of America forcing foreign nationals to fight in its army raised major legal and diplomatic problems and threatened to create an international crisis. After a number of Allied and neutral countries vigorously protested such a unilateral disregard for them and their citizens, Secretary of State Robert Lansing persuaded Congress to drop the bill and avoid embarrassing the governments of friendly nations while he negotiated treaties for reciprocal conscription, during the war, of non-declarant aliens, at least those from co-belligerent nations. "The idea of giving a foreign government the right to draft one's nationals came as rather a shock to conservative minds," recalled the British brigadier in charge of recruiting English subjects in America, but London quickly agreed.[89]

Under pressure from northerners, Congress in May 1918 revised the original draft law and declared that quotas would no longer be based on total population, but would be assessed only on the basis of men in Class I, the most eligible category, in each district. Non-declarant and enemy aliens and others exempted by statute were no longer counted in determining drafts.[90] At the same time, anti-immigrant sentiment—exacerbated by increasing demands for American troops in the spring and summer of 1918—led Selective Service and other agencies of the U.S. government to try to get exempted aliens into the armed forces. At the end of the war, General Crowder's office estimated that some 200,000 non-declarant aliens had been illegally listed as Class I, most eligible. Thousands of these exempted non-declarant and enemy aliens were illegally drafted by their local boards, since Selective Service operated on the principle that every registrant was eligible to be drafted unless he proved that he was not (an assumption upheld by the courts which required only that a full and fair hearing be held when exemption claims were made). With the burden of proof on the alien himself, the complexity of the process and the unfamiliarity of many aliens with the English language, most of the illegally drafted aliens served in the army, except for those who directly, or through their immigrant protection associations or local lawyers, were able to obtain release through formal appeals to Selective Service or to their diplomatic representatives.[91] On the other hand, as of September 12, 1918, General Crowder reported that 191,000 non-declarant aliens (in the 21–30 age group) had waived their exemptions. Including both legally and illegally conscripted aliens, and the legally drafted naturalized citizens, it is not surprising that, given the massive immigration to the United States in the preceding decades, perhaps 20 percent of the wartime draftees were foreign-born and perhaps 9 percent of the people serving in the military were not U.S. citizens.[92]

At the same time, the government also took positive steps to encourage the foreign-born, including those who were still legally the subjects of foreign governments, to enlist or willingly accept conscription into the wartime American army. To a very limited extent, the army created ethnically segregated units, such as the experimental companies of non-English-speaking Italians and Slavs, with officers familiar with their languages, at Camp Gordon, Georgia. Because of the desire of many Czechs, Slovaks, Yugoslavs, and other ethnic minorities to fight for independence against the Austro-Hungarian Empire, and the support of the British and French for the formation of such nationalist ethnic units, President Wilson supported the idea of a Slavic Legion as part of the American wartime army. In July 1918, Congress authorized the creation of a Slavic Legion of volunteers from these ethnic groups, now legally redefined as "oppressed races;" they had previously been ineligible for either voluntary enlistment or conscription because as part of the Austro-Hungarian Empire they had been considered enemy aliens. Although the bill authorized 250,000 volunteers, the Legion was just beginning to be recruited when the war ended. The Polish Legion, authorized in 1917, had raised a force of some 18,000 officers and enlisted men.[93]

However, the Polish and Slavic Legions had been authorized by the government over the objections of the American military which opposed such units of ethnic officers and enlisted men as militarily inefficient, even though some officers recognized the moral effect "of large, powerful, nationalistic units fighting for the freedom of their compatriots. . . . "[94] It can also be presumed that the regular army officer corps objected to alien officers even more than they did to the locally elected officers of the old U.S. Volunteers. In the anti-

immigrant climate of the period, Congress in the National Defense
Act of 1916 had restricted the granting of officers' commissions to
noncitizens by limiting the appointment of aliens. Not surprisingly
the General Staff also rejected a proposal by three civilian radicals,
after the Bolshevik Revolution in 1917, to raise a unit of American
Socialists, a "Red Guard," to help defend the Soviet Union against
Germany.[95]

The major effort of the War Department in regard to alien draftees or volunteer enlisted men was to integrate them into the American wartime army. This was done to make them more effective
soldiers through an understanding of English-language commands,
and only secondarily to acculturize them to American norms of
attitude and behavior. As a staff report to the army's chief of staff
concluded: " . . . we are not in this war to make more American
citizens, we are in to win the war. . . . "[96] Nevertheless, the army
came under increased public pressure for programs to improve the
intellectual as well as physical condition of its new soldiers when
the draft examinations and intelligence tests indicated significant
deficiencies among young men in America. The draft examinations
had shown a shocking degree of illiteracy. The War Department had
authorized psychologists to administer newly developed intelligence quotient (IQ) tests to classify draftees according to mental
ability. The testers and the public were startled to find that apparently 20 to 25 percent of the inductees could neither read nor write
in English or any language (Crowder's office was suspicious of the
validity of these figures, but they were reported so widely in the
press that they came to be commonly accepted). The culturally
biased tests also "revealed" that immigrants from southern and
eastern Europe scored disproportionately in the "inferior" mental
category.[97] It also disclosed an extraordinary degree of ill health. Of
the 2.5 million men between 21 and 30 given physical examinations
for the draft by December 1917, nearly one-third (29 percent) had
been rejected as physically unfit for military service.[98] Faced with
the exclusion of so many potential soldiers and under public pressure for improvement, the War Department established remedial
"development battalions," to improve the health, literacy (and in the
case of aliens their understanding of American institutions) of those
who had limited or remedial defects, in order to enable them to
perform some service in the military; for several thousand, this
involved duty as clerks in the Selective Service System.[99] In the
summer of 1918, Crowder expanded the idea by creating volunteer
boards of instruction for virtually each draft board to offer lessons
in personal health, the English language, and the nature of patriotism and American citizenship.[100]

The idea of granting U.S. citizenship to aliens and other non-citizens primarily as an inducement for wartime military service dates back to the American Revolution.[101] This tradition was dramatically expanded in World War I. With the demand for American troops and the popular pressures to conscript the "alien slackers," Congress in May 1918 provided for the immediate naturalization of aliens who enlisted in the armed services. The law waived proof of residence and there was no need to have made a prior declaration of intent. As a part of the "Americanization" movement, Congress moved on behalf of aliens already serving in the military, and waived the requirement of an official certificate of arrival in the United States. Thus the U.S. government in World War I established the precedent for waiving lawful entry for wartime military personnel who wished to become citizens. Special concern was shown for alien soldiers already serving overseas in the American Expeditionary Force so that they could take the oath of allegiance as soon as possible. In all 155,000 alien soldiers were granted U.S. citizenship through military service during the war.[102]

The need for troops and public demands for distribution of the military obligation also led to the conscription of a number of American nationals—Indians and Puerto Ricans—who were not yet full and equal citizens of the United States. Before 1924, in which year all Indians born in the United States were admitted to full U.S. citizenship, most were legally considered wards of the U.S. government. Only those were considered citizens who had left their tribes and settled on separate land received under the Dawes Allotment Act of 1887, or who otherwise lived independently for more than 25 years. Under the Selective Service Act, Indians who were citizens were eligible for conscription, but local draft boards often failed to make the distinction. Generally, the boards considered an Indian a citizen and thus subject to the draft if he or his parents lived apart from the tribe, even on the reservation, and had adopted "the white man's ways." The Bureau of Indian Affairs established draft boards and enlistment posts on Indian Reservations to facilitate enlistment of Indians into the army. Some 6,500 Indians were drafted, 55 percent of the 11,800 who registered, twice as high as the overall average induction rate. Almost none claimed deferment or exemption. Indeed, another 6,000 Indians, many of them non-citizens, enlisted voluntarily in the army; they included numerous Choctaws, Creeks, and Apaches who served in largely Indian companies, primarily under non-Indian commissioned officers, in the 36th Division from Oklahoma and Texas. Under a statute passed in 1919, non-citizen Indians who had served in the armed forces during the war were retroactively awarded U.S. citizenship from the moment they entered military service.[103]

The draft was also applied to Puerto Rico, a U.S. territory since its conquest from Spain in 1898, where 18,000 men were inducted out of 237,000 registrants. The War Department had originally contemplated a Puerto Rican division for the wartime army; instead, on October 1, 1918, more than 10,000 Puerto Rican officers and men were organized into a Provisional Tactical Brigade; it was, however, disbanded following the armistice a month later.[104] Puerto Ricans had been considered American "nationals" but not U.S. citizens until March 1917 when Congress extended U.S. citizenship to them *en masse*. Since the Selective Service Draft Act of May 1917 followed so closely, many Puerto Ricans concluded that the grant of citizenship was dictated by the strategic goals of the United States in World War I and its desire to draft Puerto Ricans into the American army. Although this "citizenship for conscription" interpretation has continued in popular as well as scholarly histories of the island, it is simply at odds with the facts, as a legal historian has recently demonstrated.[105] The United States did not have to confer citizenship upon the Puerto Ricans in order to draft them (as "nationals," who owed allegiance to the United States and were entitled to its protection they were even more subject to conscription than aliens); and the citizenship act had been adopted a month before the United States entered the war. Rather than being connected to the war, the action was directly linked to Congress' decision in late August 1916 to liberalize the territorial government of the Philippines and promise independence to the Filipinos as soon as a stable government was established. By subsequently extending U.S. citizenship to the Puerto Ricans, Congress intended to do little more than proclaim the permanence of Puerto Rico's political links with the United States. When the draft was imposed on Puerto Rico, even those who had declined to accept U.S. citizenship because they favored independence for the island were held to be liable for conscription if they were of military age, because they were still American "nationals."[106]

One of the major dangers to public acceptance of the draft in the United States in World War I would have been the belief that conscription was inequitably applied. Selective Service and the press were well aware of the need to show that the rich also served. Editors praised the enlistment in April 1917 of Marshall Field III, scion of the wealthy Chicago merchant family, as a private in the Illinois National Guard.[107] The press grumbled over the widely publicized draft deferments obtained by the sons of Detroit automaker Henry Ford, Chicago meatpacker Edward Morris, and newspaper-chain owner E.W. Scripps of Cleveland. All three young men had been ordered into the army by their local draft boards but had won occupational deferments through successful appeals to their district board, or in some cases to Selective Service Headquarters in Washington. The *cause célèbre* of Edsel Ford and the others led to criticism in Congress as well as in the press.[108] Since young men 18 to 20 were not liable to the draft until the legislative amendment of August 1918, only a few months before the end of the war, the issue of deferments for college students did not arise in World War I.[109] Throughout the country, people kept their eyes on what happened to the wealthy. As a member of the district board in Helena, Montana recalled: "In every community there were a few rich farmers or ranchers and their sons whose production of foodstuffs for the war effort was of more value than their service as a soldier. Yet the people watched these cases carefully and when we deferred such men we had echoes of waves of discontentment and dissatisfaction."[110]

In regard to class discrimination, there was also a belief, not without foundation, that the officers of the wartime army were being drawn almost exclusively from members of the upper and middle classes. They were volunteers who often owed their initial appointments to officer training school to personal connections. Some reformers and radicals and leaders of labor and ethnic groups argued that there should be more open access to wartime officership, that a democratic society should have a democratic army. While the wartime officer corps was at first obtained primarily through the Military Training Camps Association, their bias towards selecting members of the elite contributed to pressure to take officer selection away from such a private group and also to broaden the range of eligibility. General Crowder, for example, urged that a number of qualified draftees be sent to Officer Training School so that the National Army did not appear to be composed of conscripts led by regulars or a "ready-made" set of officers. Secretary Baker accepted Crowder's suggestion and also brought the selection and training of officers entirely under the control of the War Department.[111]

The majority of the 200,000 new wartime officers came from local or national elites—college graduates, in a society in which these were not yet common—and with certification of "good character" approved by the divisional commander in their region or, in some cases, directly by the War Department. To a lesser extent, temporary officers were drawn, because of their military expertise, from experienced non-commissioned officers from the U.S. Army or National Guard. Only a few rose from other socio-economic groups among the ranks or draftees. Upon graduation from Officer Train-

ing Camp, the "ninety-day wonders" were assigned to units of draftees and together they went into the line with only six months military training because of the urgent demand for troops by 1918.
Unlike previous American wars, generals were not appointed from
among civilian members of the elite (except in the National Guard),
but were nominated from the regular army by committees of the
General Staff, and were approved by the president and confirmed
by Congress. The replacement of voluntarism with conscription had
eliminated the need for "political generals" to induce reluctant
groups to enlist and to inspire citizen-soldiers, or to challenge presidential and professional direction of the war.[112]

Opposition to the draft in World War I had been effectively
blunted by a number of factors: the influence of the federal government and the conscriptionists over the national media, the identification of dissent with political and ethnic anti-Americanism in a
highly xenophobic era, and especially by the argument by both
progressives and conservatives that citizenship (and even prospective citizenship) carried with it a military obligation to serve in
wartime, and that the national government had the authority to
compel that emergency service. As the owner of a national flour-
milling company in Minneapolis wrote to the governor of Minnesota: "My attitude towards the boys at the front has been this:—
You must serve cheerfully just as long as our Government needs
you,—in fact we have got to learn in this country that there are
certain things that we must do for our country, and we must learn to
do them cheerfully."[113]

Because it was a national draft army, popular sentiment at the
time demanded that the federal government ensure a degree of
equity—and even purity—in a wartime army of citizen-soldiers, that
it be an army more in touch with predominant civilian attitudes,
that it be, in some ways at least, a progressive army.[114] The popular
image of the old peacetime regular army—with aristocratic arrogance among the officers, drunkenness among the enlisted men,
who were widely viewed as lower-class idlers, aliens, or second-
class citizens, and a harsh code of discipline designed to maintain
strict obedience within what was virtually a caste system—was
quite simply unacceptable for an army of millions of temporary
citizen-soldiers in a progressive society at war. The result by the end
of the war had been a renovation which ranged from educational
and entertainment facilities to an entirely new and more liberal
Code of Military Justice. The chief psychiatrist of the American
Expeditionary Force called it "the *sanest, most sober,* and *least
criminalistic* body engaged in the great war, under any flag. . . ."[115]

Like most bureaucracies, even a temporary, decentralized one, the Selective Service System expanded its role, and consequently the scope of government intervention, during the course of the war in ways often unanticipated when it had been created. Since verification of a man's age became crucial in determining draft eligibility, the national government developed a new interest in accurate birth statistics. In 1917, only 22 of the 48 states—primarily the urban, industrial regions—kept such records. In the South and the West there were generally no such official records, birth being recorded, if at all, in family Bibles or in the files of the physician, if one was present. Pressure for "modernization" from the Selective Service, the Census, and the urban press led a number of rural states to require official registration of births and deaths. Dramatically, the draft also led to the first mass serialization of Americans. Each of the 24 million registrants received a draft number and a federal draft card which they were required to keep in their possession. Suggestions for European-style national identification papers for every man and woman in American were rejected.[116] In February 1918, a version of the draft's serialized identification system was extended to soldiers in the American army, when the War Department, copying the European nations, ordered the doughboys to wear around their neck, aluminum tags (quickly derided by the soldiers as "dog tags"), whose seldom mentioned purpose, of course, was to ensure accurate identification of the dead.[117]

Because of the nature of their task, local draft boards often probed deeply into the personal lives of their "friends and neighbors." While some board members obviously enjoyed learning such confidential information (Selective Service Headquarters did seek to preserve the confidentiality of answers regarding health, dependency, and financial status), some members were frankly embarrassed by the need to investigate the most personal matters and, of course, many registrants and their families resented such investigations. To alleviate their consciences, board members often crammed their psyches into their official roles, or as one of them put it, they "buckled on the armor of impersonality" and plunged ahead. By the end of the war, the 14,000 local draft board members had been joined by 179,000 others (staffers, members of various legal, instructional, medical and other advisory boards) to give the Selective Service System a total complement of 193,000 volunteer workers and paid employees. General Crowder continually assured them that they were doing their duty for their country in its hour of need, and while Selective Service personnel were sometimes targets for much animosity from their neighbors, most board members were able to reassure themselves and continue the conscription of local residents, through their own sense of the importance of their role. As one of them said, they felt they had the approval of "the best people in the community," and they shared the conviction that they too (like the men they were conscripting) were helping to achieve national victory, serving, as they liked to put it, in "Crowder's Army."[118]

Listening to the people of their district, the board members became, as one of them said, "father confessors" to millions. They heard young men plead for a chance to join the service even though underage or physically unfit. They listened to mothers urge them to draft rebellious sons, wives ask them to draft loafing or unemployed husbands, people urging them to draft neighbors against whom they had long harbored grudges. On the other hand, board members found registrants trying to fool them and escape service by bringing in spurious wives or borrowed babies as their own. A carpenter who was chair of a board in Philadelphia was shocked: "I learned what confounded liars I had among my neighbors."[119]

As local offices of the U.S. government with greater knowledge of the individuals of the community than any other federal agency, some of the draft boards were called upon to do more than their original assignment of deciding who would be drafted and who deferred. Because they had quasi-judicial as well as quasi-executive functions, they often served as a form of domestic relations court and clearing house for family troubles. Constables and court officers used them to locate spouses involved in litigation. Some people tried to have local boards collect debts owed by registrants. Disgruntled wives sometimes brought troublesome or abusive husbands to the board, urging (and often obtaining) their induction and the monthly family allotment. Despite the supposed privacy of the financial data disclosed in the classification questionnaire, with the extension of the draft up to 45-year-old men in September 1918, agents of the Internal Revenue Bureau began to examine the draft questionnaires for evidence of income tax evasion by affluent individuals (then the only class subject to federal income taxation); this violation of previous guarantees of confidentiality brought cries of outrage from wealthy taxpayers and their attorneys. Given their position in the community, many boards also felt a sense of responsibility for bolstering patriotism, encouraging purchase of war bonds, and providing aid and advice to draftees. The staff helped arrange for appropriate flag ceremonies and a farewell parade to the train station for the conscripts (in the South, these parades were often led by aged Confederate veterans in faded uniforms), and for food to take on the trip to camp. They advised inductees on disposition of business interests, assisted in arranging marriages of their servicemen in distant parts of the country, and sought to protect "worthy" dependents from eviction. Some of these boards wanted registrants and their families to see them, as one board member declared, "not only as the embodiment of the Government, but also as their personal friend."[120]

When a deadly influenza pandemic from Europe, called the "Spanish flu," struck the United States in the fall of 1918, overwhelming local public health agencies and killing more than 500,000 Americans, many urban residents turned to their draft boards, as the most effective local agencies of the federal government, to mobilize emergency relief. In the working-class ethnic districts of south Philadelphia, where 5,000 cases of influenza were reported in a single week, local boards established temporary hospitals, including one in the draft board offices, raised donations from local business people, and hired and coordinated physicians, nurses, and senior medical students to tend to the ill. The board also supervised crews of volunteers as they distributed food baskets and took new patients to the infirmaries. Despite calls from the provost marshal general's office for more inductees, the epidemic was so extensive that at least in Philadelphia the draft came to a halt in October 1918 while local boards took on an entirely new and temporary function of coordinating the battle against the pestilence.[121]

The major result of the World War I draft experience and the preceding debate over military manpower was, of course, to provide a new general military format for the United States. In this *Nation-State Model*, the regular army remained comparatively small, although, as usual, incrementally increased from its prewar size. The soldiers of the states, the National Guard, were brought totally, if temporarily, under federal control. The U.S. government could "federalize" the National Guard, make it part of the national army, and even send it overseas. American military federalism had now ended, at least during wartime.[122] Most importantly, the source of America's wartime armies of citizen-soldiers had been transformed from the state and local loyalties predominant in earlier systems, such as the U.S. Volunteers, to a direct and predominant military obligation to the nation.

The national draft had come to America and had been widely, although not totally, accepted during the war.[123] In the concept of national military obligation and the nationally "supervised decentralization" of the Selective Service System, cosmopolitan American elites had found an effective politico-military mechanism for raising mass armies in an urban, industrial society and for projecting American military power overseas, at least in time of major war in support of American interests and ideals.

CHAPTER

9

The Legacy of the Draft, 1919–1987

T HE STILLNESS OF THE ARMISTICE brought a halt to both the fighting and the draft. Even though some U.S. troops remained on occupational duty in the Rhineland for several years, not one American was drafted after the cease-fire on November 11, 1918; indeed, troop trains turned around and took draftees home. Selective Service was not forgotten, however. It became the accepted mechanism for mobilizing America's manpower for every subsequent war. But this acceptance of Selective Service was neither simple nor complete. Rather, the subsequent expansion of the World War I military format was part of the complex process by which America became a world power.

With the end of the war, the future of the Selective Service System was, at best, uncertain. General Crowder developed a plan for using the local draft boards to muster out soldiers systematically as jobs became available. In addition to maintaining the agency, the proposal was designed to avoid the unrest which would result if the army suddenly discharged more than three million soldiers into an economy already plagued by layoffs. Crowder suggested that draft boards could discharge men according to local economic needs, while also keeping track of veterans in case a new call-up was necessary.[1] Despite the lobbying by Crowder and a few industrialists and labor leaders during the winter of 1918–19, the Wilson administration rejected the plan. When Congress and the public pressed for a speedy return of the veterans, Secretary of War Baker declined to perpetuate the draft agency. The idea, he said, was to terminate federal and military wartime responsibility, control, and expense and to return to normal as quickly as possible.[2] Such a demobilization policy was philosophically and politically understandable, but within ten months it increased unemployment and accelerated the decline in wage rates. Undoubtedly, it also contributed to the depression and widespread labor unrest of 1920–21.[3]

"The whole demobilization process has been flabbily handled," Col. John Henry Wigmore reported scornfully from Crowder's office.[4] Selective Service came to an end and, despite a terror of public speaking, Crowder went on tour for several weeks, personally congratulating, and dismissing, his draft boards. Closing their offices, they shipped 9,000 tons of records back to Washington for storage. The headquarters staff also left for other jobs; Crowder himself retired from the Army, and served as U.S. ambassador to Cuba until 1927.[5]

After demobilization, the debate over the nature of the postwar military format came amid uncertainty over the Treaty of Versailles and the League of Nations, the labor strikes and Big Red Scare of 1919, and the presidential election of 1920. As with the prewar preparedness controversy, the postwar debate over an appropriate format was linked not only to foreign affairs but to the nature of America society and the State. Planning for a permanent military format had begun even before the armistice, with the leadership coming, not from the Army—which was more concerned with current operations—but from the civilian conscriptionist elite. Public acceptance of the military obligation of citizenship had encouraged corporate-dominated conscriptionist groups—including the National Security League, the Universal Training League, and the Military Training Camps Association—to redouble their efforts to achieve permanent UMT&S during or after the war.[6]

Within the General Staff, some of General Wood's followers continued to advocate a postwar citizen-reservist army based largely on UMT&S.[7] But Gen. Peyton C. March, who had become chief of staff in 1918, remained an Uptonian, distrustful of "instant" soldiers as compared with "reliable" regulars. Encouraged by Baker, March also focused mainly on immediate needs rather than permanent military policy. Consequently, he proposed a large standing army of 510,000 regulars (compared to 175,000 before the war), who could be reinforced in an emergency by 750,000 veteran-reservists, including members of the National Guard. In peacetime, this large volunteer standing army would be raised by a combination of economic and educational inducements, including expanded academic and vocational training programs, in what Baker called "the Khaki University." To make it politically palatable, the proposed format specifically excluded compulsory military service in peacetime and stated explicitly that a selective national draft would be put into operation only after a congressional declaration of war.[8]

Although the Baker-March bill was prepared in January 1919, it was not introduced until the new Congress met in August 1919; by then, in response to pressure from civilian conscriptionists, the War Department had added a brief provision for universal military training for 19-year-old males. Apparently, this was simply a coalition-building gesture, for it provided for only three months training and the trainees were not required to serve subsequently in reserve units. Nevertheless, General March later defended it as an attempt to establish at least the principle of national compulsory military training.[9]

Despite the War Department's attempts to build enthusiasm for a large standing army, the idea had few supporters. Even Baker admitted that he saw it only as a temporary program, designed primarily to ensure an occupation force in the Rhineland, but leaving the determination of the ultimate peacetime size of the army to "less troubled times."[10] President Wilson, busy at the Paris Peace Conference during the first half of 1919, paid scant attention to military policy.[11]

The Baker-March proposal came under vigorous attack. Conscriptionists wanted permanent UMT&S. A coalition of liberals, pacifists, and groups interested in reducing taxes and government spending, wanted the regular army and the reserves kept small and inexpensive. In the public debate over the postwar military format, it was once again the well-connected, effectively organized civilian advocates of UMT&S who seized the initiative. But the postwar conscriptionist movement lacked effective leadership and a conducive international context. Theodore Roosevelt died at 61 in January 1919 and Leonard Wood had turned his primary attention to trying to win the Republican presidential nomination in 1920. Less able and more lackluster leaders succeeded them. Charles Lydecker, a conservative Wall Street attorney, became president of the National Security League, which had already been weakened by congressional disclosure of its corporate contributors. In charge of the Military Training Camps Association (the Plattsburgers), was Tompkins McIlvaine, a direct descendant of the vice president under James Monroe and an arrogant as well as aristocratic corporation lawyer.[12]

"A large Standing Army is not only the most expensive system but it is uneconomic, undemocratic and un-American," McIlvaine wrote Baker.[13] For a detailed plan for a citizen-reservist army based on UMT&S, the civilian conscriptionists turned to one of General Wood's disciples, Lt. Col. John McAuley Palmer, a slight, bespectacled, scholar-soldier, who had already converted Gen. John J. Pershing from Uptonian to citizen-army principles. Returning to Washington from France, Palmer confirmed the Plattsburgers' worst fears about the plans of the War Department, writing to Grenville Clark: "Your suspicions are completely justified that the policy here is predicated not only on the idea that we are not to have universal military training, but that it is definitely aimed at killing the idea if practicable."[14]

When Baker and March rejected the Plattsburgers' appeal to join behind a single bill for an army based primarily on UMT&S, the various civilian conscriptionist organizations united behind a piece of legislation of their own—the Chamberlain-Kahn UMT bill. Introduced in July 1919, it provided for a regular army of between 200,000 and 300,000 troops, supported by a national citizen-reservist force produced by six-months initial UMT, followed by ten years service in the reserves. The National Guard would be relegated to purely local functions.[15] Conscriptionists obtained endorsements from the new American Legion, which the Plattsburgers had helped to create; from many corporations and business and professional groups; from editors and additional influential individuals, including ex-President Taft; Nicholas Murray Butler, the president of Columbia University; Assistant Secretary of the Navy Franklin D. Roosevelt; and the victorious commander of the AEF, General Pershing.[16] With the Republicans in control of Congress after the 1918 election, the new head of the Senate Military Affairs Committee, James W. Wadsworth, Jr. of New York, began a major effort to enact UMT&S.[17]

Conscriptionist leaders believed that "the war had demonstrated clearly our unpreparedness and that now was the time, in connection with the necessary reorganization of the Army, to push the adoption of the principle of Universal Military Training."[18] Unlike supporters of Wilsonian liberal internationalism, conscriptionists never thought that the world war had terminated warfare or that a liberal League of Nations could prevent such conflicts. Pessimistic about human nature and the stability of the international system, UMT advocates warned that the general postwar hope for lasting and universal peace was being used to mislead the American public into a false belief that wars could be avoided without much effort or cost. "Our duty in the future," proclaimed the Plattsburger magazine, "is to guard ourselves against unreasonable idealism."[19]

Already conscriptionists saw real threats to U.S. national interests throughout the world. Bolshevism threatened to spread through Eastern and Central Europe. Revolutionary nationalism challenged American oil interests in Mexico and other concerns in China. In a longer perspective, U.S. interests could face disruption at the hands of an expansive Japan in Asia and the Pacific, and a reindustrialized and rearmed Germany in Europe.[20] Few conscriptionists endorsed the League of Nations because, as Root and Lodge explained, its Covenant imposed a universal commitment "to preserve as against external aggression the territorial integrity and existing political independence of all Members of the League." Most conscriptionists considered this commitment too inclusive and unnecessary. Instead, many of them favored a defensive alliance among the United States, Britian, and France directed specifically against future German expansion. In the debate over ratification of the Versailles Treaty, most conscriptionists either supported the League of Nations with the nationalistic "reservations" drawn up by Henry Cabot Lodge, or opposed the League entirely, believing like most senior military officers that the United States should rely upon its own strength and follow its own independent interests.[21]

"As we have made the world safe for democracy, we now must make democracy safe for the world," Charles W. Martin, former division commander and ardent nationalist, told a reunion of the 90th Infantry Division in October 1919. Even more than before, conscriptionists in the postwar period defended the need for national UMT in terms of its domestic advantages in addition to its international efficacy. This emphasis resulted both from the lack of any immediate foreign threat to the United States and the conscriptionists' real concerns about internal disorder. Labor militancy and political radicalism—especially the threat of communism which they saw in current demonstrations, strikes, and bombings—challenged their economic interests and their vision of national unity and strength. The Universal Military Training League recommended UMT particularly to "unify our citizenship and wipe out the red flag. . . ."[22]

While Bolshevism at home and abroad was the new scare that conscriptionists sought to exploit in 1919, the primary domestic advantage of mass military training continued to be the inculcation of a sense of citizenship and nationalism, to create "good citizens" and "good workers." UMT advocates bolstered their case with the evidence of widespread illiteracy and ill-health revealed by the Selective Service examinations. Arthur F. Cosby, executive secretary of the Military Training Camps Association, in a memo to his predecessor, Grenville Clark, emphasized the economic and social value of the proposed military training program: "The educational and Americanizing features of the plan are alone worth far more than its total cost, to say nothing of the increased health, industrial efficiency and social discipline of the men trained. Apart from these social benefits, the plan provides for an adequate system of national defense."[23]

But the traditional postwar reaction in America, combined with resurgent "antimilitarism" and a powerful drive to cut government spending and reduce taxes, ensured that there would be significant opposition to any plan for major expansion of the military.[24] An amorphous coalition of anti-UMT, anti–big army groups exerted substantial influence on Congress and the press. Once again they included liberal pacifists, like the American Union Against Militarism, and women's groups, such as the Women's Peace party (now the Women's International League for Peace and Freedom), churches, farmers, and organized labor, as well as southern whites afraid of arming large numbers of blacks.[25] However, the coalition now included representatives of small- and medium-sized businesses interested in cutting taxes. House Majority Leader Frank Mondell (Rep.-Wyo.) claimed that UMT would cost one billion dollars a year.[26] Furthermore, many progressives, liberal internationalists and isolationists alike, feared that a Wall Street–dominated Republican administration might use a large army and UMT&S to curtail industrial unrest at home and invade Mexico to protect American investments.[27] Many liberals who had supported the wartime draft now took a position against UMT&S and a large standing army. Reflecting the new directions among military thinkers, the *New Republic* advocated a large modern air force, efficient navy, and a well-equipped and trained volunteer professional army. Such a program emphasized reliance on technology rather than on masses of troops.[28]

Aside from this proposal for a small mobile military establishment equipped with the latest weaponry, the only other innovative comprehensive alternative to a large standing army, national UMT&S, or a return to previous tradition, was put forward by the National Guard. With its local roots and the glory its units had won in France, it rejected attempts by regulars and Plattsburgers to relegate them to a purely local role. Vowing "to build up the Guard and smash the regular army," the new president of the National Guard Association, Col. Bennett Champ Clark of Missouri, helped mobilize a counter-attack.[29] The militia's proposal, introduced by Republicans Sen. Joseph S. Freylinghuysen of New Jersey and Rep. William I. Hull of Iowa, sought to maintain the National Guard's dual status as state militia and national ready reserve guaranteed under the 1916 legislation, as well as to require that the War Department's Militia Bureau be headed by a member of the militia rather than by a regular. Eventually the Guard won on both points. It was, in fact, so influential with Congress that conscriptionists and anti-conscriptionists feared it might obtain a nationwide program of universal military training in the local militia. The Guard enjoyed

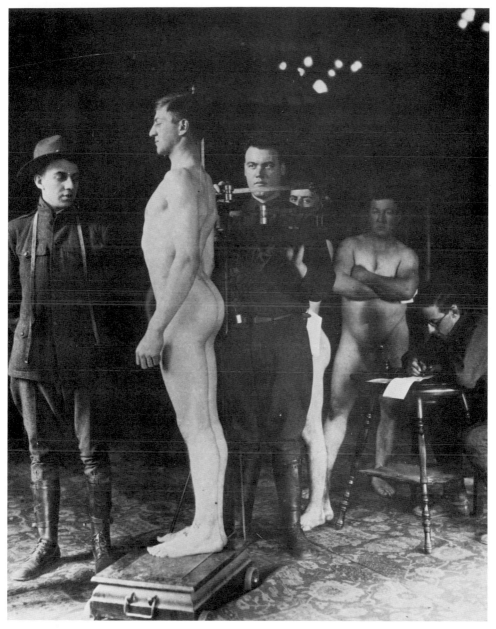

STRIPPED OF THEIR CIVILIAN CLOTHING, new recruits were measured up to be temporarily reclad and remolded as wartime citizen-soldiers. Boston, Mass., 1917. *National Archives 165-WW-479A-7*

JUBILANTLY, YOUNG DOUGHBOYS wave goodbye in 1917 as a lighter takes them from the docks at Hoboken, N.J., to the troop transport which will carry them across the Atlantic to the Western Front. *National Archives 165-WW-289C-7*

U.S.S. *LEVIATHAN*, camouflaged to deter effective submarine attack, heads out of New York Harbor on August 3, 1918. America's largest troopship could carry several thousand soldiers; on this trip it took the entire 56th Infantry Regiment, 7th Division, to France. *U.S. Army Signal Corps Photo. National Archives 111-SC-15633*

AMERICANS IN THE ARGONNE FOREST. Amidst smoke and shattered trees, doughboys move forward in the Meuse-Argonne offensive of late September to November 1918. Here a gun crew from the regimental headquarters company of the 23rd Infantry Regiment fires a 37 mm. gun during an assault on entrenched German positions. *U.S. Army Signal Corps. Photographer unknown. National Archives 111-SC-94980*

"Hell, when they run we try to ketch 'em. When we ketch 'em we try to make 'em run."

A STOIC MOOD characterized "Willie" and "Joe," the two G.I. characters made famous by combat cartoonist Bill Mauldin. Cartoon from France, Nov. 1, 1944. *Reprinted by permission of United Feature Syndicate, Inc.*

HEROIC STANCE dominated this World War II poster for the United States Army Infantry. *U.S. Army, 1942. Courtesy the George C. Marshall Research Library, Lexington, Va.*

THREE BRAVE BUT HAUNTED servicemen from the Vietnam War. Draftees supplied the majority of American citizen-soldiers who fought in Vietnam between 1965 and 1973; the draftees, black and white, fighting in a racially-integrated army, also made up the majority of American casualties. The "Three Servicemen" statue, sculpted by Frederick Hart, was erected at the Vietnam Veterans Memorial in Washington, D.C., in 1984. It faces a somber black stone wall inscribed with the names of the more than 58,000 Americans who died in the Vietnam War. *Photo by Mae Scanlan. Reproduced by permission of Frederick Hart and the Vietnam Veterans Memorial Fund.*

THE VIETNAM WAR led to an end to the draft in the United States, a result of widespread opposition among Americans to the war in Indochina. Here an anti-war, antidraft demonstration on the University of Wisconsin campus in the fall of 1967 included a protest by students and veterans. *Photo by J.D. Patrick. By permission of the Iconographic Collections, the State Historical Society of Wisconsin. WHi (x3) 36346*

"For me, learning about electronics is the first step to where I want to go in life."

SP4 Rich Parsons, HAWK Missiles

"When I was a little kid, I dreamed about being an astronaut. Or working with space-age technology. Now the Army's preparing me for a future, in high technology. All I have to do is go for it.

"I work on the HAWK high-power radar. Talk about complicated. It's like a puzzle made of circuit boards. It takes a really experienced technician to figure it out, fit the puzzle together and make it work. Since I'm the supervisor, I need to know it. Inside and out.

"Right now, I feel I'm standing tall on the mountain. With my electronics experience— real, hands-on experience—my future can go in a lot of different directions. All of them point up."

The Army could be your connection to a high-tech future. **ARMY.**

For more information, contact your local Army Recruiter or call toll free 1-800-USA-ARMY.   **BE ALL YOU CAN BE.**

THE END OF THE DRAFT in 1973 and the shift to an all-volunteer army led the U.S. Army to initiate advertising campaigns, including this 1986 ad, which sought to attract young recruits through appeals to enlistment bonuses, recreation, self-fulfillment, and valuable skills, such as expertise in electronics. *By permission of NW Ayer Inc.; "BE ALL YOU CAN BE" courtesy U.S. Government, as represented by the Secretary of the Army*

WITH THE END OF THE DRAFT in 1973, the Army reserves, including the National Guard, also found it necessary to increase their appeal to obtain enlistments for part-time soldiers. Like the U.S. Army, the National Guard increased its recruitment of women and members of minority groups. It also appealed to material self-interest by emphasizing economic rewards and valuable skills, like electronics or engineering expertise. Unlike the regular army, the Guard also made another powerful appeal, drawing upon the American tradition of wartime citizen-soldiers and their symbol, the Minute Man, as shown in this 1974 advertisement. *By permission of the W.B. Doner Advertising Co. and the National Guard Bureau, Department of the Army*

considerable popularity after the war, and it, rather than the regular army, was the true representative of the citizen-soldier tradition which derived from the colonial militia. Faced with the troubled domestic and international situation in 1919, four states had authorized militia drafts, if necessary, to bring their units up to strength, even in peacetime. As a compromise, many members of the Guard Association endorsed a nation-wide program of UMT supervised by militia officers rather than by regulars, in which reservists would have the choice of serving in the National Guard or the U.S. Army Reserve. However, because of divisions within the National Guard Association, the Freylinghuysen-Hull bill remained vague on this point.[30]

The winter of 1919–20 was a momentous time in Washington, with attention focused on the Senate debate over the Treaty of Versailles before its final rejection in March 1920. Congress was at the same time considering the postwar military format. Most of the civilian conscriptionists supported the League with the Lodge reservations, which in effect would create a tacit entente among the former Allies to contain Germany and would require an easily mobilizable mass army (probably through UMT) to sustain the U.S. commitment. On the other hand, Wilsonians asserted that full membership in the League of Nations was the way to achieve peace and disarmament. Indeed, Wilson went so far as to argue that if the United States did not join the League, it would be forced to act alone internationally and, given the disturbed state of the world, it would become necessary to turn the country into an armed camp. The United States would be forced to become a despotism, its manpower conscripted and its industries directed by a national government in which the general staff and the chief executive had become co-dictators, as in Imperial Germany in the World War.[31]

As always with highly emotional issues, members of Congress were influenced by conflicting pressure groups and by their own sense of proper policy and political self-interest. The latter became increasingly important with the approach of the 1920 election, as neither party wanted to expose itself to charges of fostering "militarism." Wilson was suddenly disabled by a severe stroke in September 1919. Congressional Democrats, influenced by the party's southern leadership, looked skeptically at any substantial, costly military expansion in the postwar period, and they were joined by many isolationist Midwestern Republicans. Yet there was considerable pressure for change, not from the administration, whose large standing army bill had no support, but from the UMT advocates who continued to speak for many of the major financial and industrial

interests of New York and Chicago. Since the Republican majority in both houses of the 66th Congress was split almost evenly
between conservative eastern internationalists and progressive
western isolationists, the struggle to obtain legislation for a national army based on UMT in the winter of 1919–20 was an uphill
battle.[32]

With the assistance of Colonel Palmer and advice from the civilian
conscriptionists and from the GOP Old Guard, Senator Wadsworth in January 1920 annnounced his own bill for military reorganization. Replacing the earlier Chamberlain-Kahn UMT bill, the
Wadsworth-Kahn UMT legislation included all of General Pershing's
main suggestions, including a regular army of 300,000 troops, but it
reduced the UMT requirement from six to four months to increase
its political appeal. It would cost $500 million annually, but
Wadsworth estimated that by providing two million trained reservists within five years, the UMT program would reduce the cost per
trained soldier from $500 to $176.[33]

With the enthusiastic support of conscriptionists, Wadsworth and
Kahn obtained favorable reports from the military affairs committees. But then Wadsworth made a major tactical mistake. In seeking
to create a bipartisan coalition between the Democratic administration and Republican Congress, he obtained Baker's public support
for the UMT bill by including some of the secretary's pet ideas about
vocational education. But the scheme backfired and further politicized the issue.[34] Once Baker had committed the Democratic adminstration to the UMT bill, dissident western Republicans in the
House, led by Majority Leader Frank Mondell, publicly denounced the Wadsworth UMT bill as radical and extravagant. Mondell's open assault showed a dramatic regional split in the GOP
ranks, for he was attacking eastern Republicans as well as the
Democratic administration. It made front-page headlines for days.
Fearing that the western Republicans planned to blame the Democratic party for the UMT proposal in the 1920 election, House Democrats bolted. Ignoring an appeal from the ailing president to avoid
taking an inflexible stand, Democrats in the lower chamber cau-
cused on February 9, 1920 and voted 106 to 17 to commit themselves
against any proposal which included general compulsory military
training.[35] Not to be outdone, Mondell and other Republican leaders
refused to allow the Kahn UMT bill onto the floor. On March 18,
1920, totally ignoring UMT, the House approved by 245 to 92, an
Army Reorganization bill which provided essentially for a return to
the format of 1916—a regular army of 220,000 supported by the
National Guard. Bitterly, Wadsworth complained to a friend: "The
House, as you know, is in a very Bolshevistic frame of mind concern-

ing the Army. It is almost impossible to get them to consider the Army sensibly and quietly."[36]

The Senate was also squeamish. When debate began in April 1920, it quickly became apparent that few members of either party would vote for UMT. As the Democrats openly assailed such "militarism," the Republican Old Guard found itself backed into a corner. As Wadsworth explained privately a few days later, the Democrats were maneuvering so that they might charge that "the Republicans had defeated the League of Nations which would have given us peace and now wanted Universal Training so as to be prepared for the wars that would come."[37] With the primaries approaching and Republican ranks crumbling, Lodge, Wadsworth, and other GOP leaders sought to avoid a direct vote and defeat on UMT, which would prove a great embarrassment, since many Republicans who privately supported it would be forced by public opinion to vote against it. To save face with the wealthy conscriptionists who were the party's primary financial contributors, the GOP leaders turned instead to a substitute—a plan for *volunteer* military training for youths, aged 18 to 21. It was adopted, 46 to 9 with 41 abstentions. Eastern Republicans could then tell conscriptionists they had established a preliminary framework for UMT, while explaining to the electorate that they had voted for voluntary rather than compulsory military training.[38]

For five weeks in the early summer of 1920, House and Senate conferees wrangled over different versions of the Army Reorganization Act. When Wadsworth finally agreed to a compromise, the regular army was set at 298,000 the General Staff was moderately strengthed, and the dual status of the National Guard was maintained. The bill continued the ROTC and Plattsburg-style summer camps and established an Officers and Enlisted Reserve Corps as a national army reserve, but the final version did not establish any system of widespread voluntary military training for enlisted men. Only days before it adjourned for the summer, Congress adopted the National Defense Act of 1920.[39]

Even more significant than the demise of UMT was the last-minute elimination of any provision for wartime Selective Service. The Baker-March proposal and every UMT bill since 1918 had included authorization for the president to initiate a *selective draft* following congressional declaration of a state of war or national emergency.[40] As late as February 1920, the lobbyist of the American Union Against Militarism reported that, unlike permanent UMT, the wartime draft was considered by most legislators "to be a very popular affair per se."[41] But with increasing fears that conscription might be used against strikers and with growing public concern over charges of "militarism," legislators of both parties facing re-election in November deleted all mention of the draft from the final version of the act. Gone were both the authorization and the statement of the principle that male citizens had a military obligation to the nation.[42]

So disappointed was the president that he seriously considered vetoing the bill. As the president's proposed veto message put it:

> It seems clear, quite beyond question, that the Selective Service
> Law by which the Congress provided for raising the great army re-
> cently disbanded was sound in principle, effective in operation,
> and just in distribution of military duty among the people of the
> country; and it is equally clear, both from our own experience and
> that of the great nations which participated in the World War, that
> some such element is an indispensable part of any fundamental
> military policy.[43]

Despite the validity of this statement, Baker warned Wilson that as a practical matter a veto would throw the future of the army in doubt by returning the military establishment to its prewar status, thus increasing the postwar demoralization among career and reserve officers. It might, he suggested, also interject the issue of conscription "into the pending political campaign" and "prevent it from centering upon the League of Nations and Treaty questions." On June 4, heeding this advice, Wilson signed the National Defense Act of 1920.[44]

Despite the limitations of the legislation, for the first time in peacetime the army had, at least on paper, a modern tactical and territorial organization. Each component—the U.S. Army, National Guard, and Organized Army Reserves—was assigned to contribute its share in war. To raise the citizen army in wartime, the country was divided into nine corps areas, each to contain one skeletal division of regulars, two of Guardsmen, and three of the newly organized Army Reserve. Although in theory a large citizen reserve force had been established, in practice no means were provided to create it. By 1923, the National Guard had less than half its 435,000 authorized personnel, and since Congress for racial and political reasons had severely restricted the enlistment of blacks and aliens, two groups which might have supplied large numbers, there were also few enlisted men in the Army Reserve. By the 1920s, there were nearly 100,000 reserve officers, but the national army reserve remained largely a force of officers without the soldiers to follow them.[45]

Surprisingly, as the army and the conservative conscriptionist business elites abandoned their hopes for peacetime UMT&S and

statutory recognition of wartime conscription, a "radical conscriptionist" movement emerged in the 1920s and 1930s. Non-elite groups
proposed that in the next war, capital as well as workers and soldiers should be conscripted. This idea of a "universal draft" in
wartime stemmed primarily from the veterans of the American
Legion. Angered by revelations of wartime profiteering and thousands of new "war millionaires," veterans sought to ensure equity
of sacrifice in future wars. Joining them were an odd assortment of
liberals, conservatives, socialists, pacifists, and isolationists who
hoped that eliminating war profits would eliminate war. Although
several such bills were introduced in Congress in the 1920s and
1930s, business feared "war socialism" and unions worried about
the conscription of labor. Bernard Baruch, the financier who had
headed the War Industries Board, channeled such sentiment into
government authorization to set up joint committees of industrialists and military officers to begin planning for the procurement of
industrial materials in wartime.[46]

By the early 1920s conscriptionists abandoned efforts to have a
peacetime Congress authorize Selective Service as a wartime policy.
Military leaders concluded that elected lawmakers could deal with
the issue after a declaration of war and that attempts to achieve
more than that would only hurt the Army. Furthermore, senior
officers believed that politically the draft could be employed only in
major wars. Militarily, they considered the draft necessary only in
conflicts against large nations which would involve general national
military and industrial mobilization.[47] Cowed by a hostile and par-
simonious Congress, intimidated by adverse public opinion, the
military declined to press Congress or the executive for any form of
preparatory draft legislation. This remained Army policy even after
the outbreak of World War II in Europe.[48] Responding to a question
from an officer at the Army War College about the possibility of
establishing a prewar draft a month after Hitler's invasion of Poland
in September 1939, Hugh S. Johnson offered the following blunt
advice:

> If you are asking for my opinion as a mechanical question as to
> whether you could get it through without being chewed up, I
> would say 'by all means, no.' *Get it ready but keep it in the dark.*[49]

Actually, the Army had been doing precisely that. Throughout the
interwar years, military planners had worked quietly, under somewhat questionable authority, to build a framework for wartime
Selective Service. They prepared updated legislation and regulations which could be submitted to Congress as soon as war was
declared. They also recruited and trained several hundred regular

and reserve officers as "selective service specialists" to provide a skeletal framework for a future draft agency.[50]

Beginning in 1926, the two defense secretaries facilitated this work by creating a Joint Army and Navy Selective Service Committee with a staff which could work effectively with state officials and local elites. Maj. Lewis B. Hershey began his long association with Selective Service when he was appointed secretary of the Joint Committee in 1936. The son of a rural Indiana sheriff, Hershey had been an artillery officer with the National Guard in France during the war, then obtained a regular army commission in 1919. He was recommended to head the Selective Service Committee because of his ability to manage people and to work with civilians, including adjutants general in the states. One of Hershey's major strengths, his biographer later noted, lay in appearing to be "more a Scout leader than a martinet."[51]

Throughout a long career with Selective Service lasting until he was removed by President Nixon in 1969, Hershey remained committed to the politico-military formula established in World War I. That meant a selective national draft, based—as the Joint Committee stated in a declaration of principles in 1933—upon "the right of the State to choose from its citizenry those who are best fitted to bear arms by reason of their individual status." It also meant that the decisions about particular individuals would be made in a decentralized system of local draft boards, "by a man's neighbors on the ground of economic and social necessity."[52]

Both the expanded concept of the obligation of national citizenship and the idea of using state and local officials to carry out a national policy such as the draft were emphasized during the 1920s and 1930s in a variety of attempts to expand the power of the federal government in civil as well as military areas. The courts upheld the extension of military obligations among certain classes of people. They sustained the right of a legislature to compel able-bodied young men at state colleges to complete ROTC training as an obligation commensurate with society's funding of their education. In addition, the U.S. Supreme Court approved the Immigration Service's denial of naturalized citizenship to aliens (men or women) who, as secular conscientious objectors, refused to swear to serve in the armed forces if called upon in wartime, a position maintained by the Court until after World War II.[53]

In the legislative arena, a number of groups sought to apply the concept of mass compulsion behind the draft—the principle that, in the larger public interest, government could limit the freedom of millions of individuals—to obtain social reform legislation. In order to stem the decline in voter turnout, reformers sought to amend state constitutions to define suffrage as an obligation rather than simply a right of citizenship. However, even in Massachusetts, where compulsory voting legislation was authorized by the Constitution of 1918, it was never implemented. More successful were efforts in a number of states to require physical examinations, vaccinations, and physical exercise for schoolchildren in order to combat the widespread ill-health indicated by the draft statistics.[54] Reformers tried with less success to create a major role for the *national* government in education, based upon the wartime demonstration that illiteracy was a national problem (7 percent of the draftees had been unable to speak English, and 25 percent could not read or write in any language). Arguing that the war experience also demonstrated the effectiveness of national policies, advocates of federal aid to education drew upon the draft model as they submitted bills to Congress for a variety of programs to combat illiteracy and to "Americanize" immigrants. None was enacted. Instead, the unfavorable image of alien residents contributed to the adoption of restrictive legislation curtailing immigration.[55]

In some important ways, the successful administration of the draft in World War I foreshadowed elements of the "new federalism" of the 1920s and 1930s and Washington's use of state and local administrative structures. The registration of 10 million Americans in a single day in June 1917, for example, was to retired general Hugh S. Johnson:

> One of the most remarkably efficient efforts in administration that this Government has ever made—remarkable not alone for the clear-cut result but also as a point of departure in our political history. No new and expensive federal machinery was created but the States were called upon—and for the first time—to perform a task that was distinctively federal.[56]

In 1920, General Crowder had endorsed the applicability of the system he called "supervised decentralization" in his book, *The Spirit of Selective Service*. Like many others during that period, Crowder believed that social problems could be alleviated largely through proper organization. Crowder went further than recommending this form of mobilization as a palliative for national problems of illiteracy, public health, and lack of acculturation among immigrants. He proposed it as a means to prevent labor-management conflict from leading to class warfare and socialist revolution. He had in mind industrial boards composed of representatives of workers, employers, and the public, with the power to impose settlements through binding arbitration. Crowder told a friend that a reinvigorated federalism, stimulated by national spirit, might make possible "the prosecution of national policies and the attainment of national efficiency without the surrender, in the form of government ownership, of the right of private property."[57] Although several industrialists, corporate lawyers, and engineers hailed Crowder's idea of applying to society the spirit of Selective Service (one advocate of scientific management called it "the greatest feat of organization of the ages"), most commentators dismissed the general's proposals as hopelessly naïve. Few believed Americans would accept such a degree of governmental intervention in peacetime.[58]

Nevertheless, the Selective Service model proved instructive. The Coolidge administration adopted a policy of employing state officials as federal officers to help enforce Prohibition.[59] Later, in the social and economic crisis of the 1930s, Franklin D. Roosevelt and others applied the metaphor of mobilizing the nation for a "war" against the Depression as against a foreign invader.[60] Several New Deal agencies were modeled after wartime agencies. The National Recovery Administration stemmed largely from the War Industries Board; the Civilian Conservation Corps came in part from the idea of socio-economic benefits from UMT, of which F.D.R. had been a great admirer in World War I. In these and several other federal regulatory programs, Congress and the executive experimented with applying various aspects of the Selective Service administrative model. In the CCC, for example, the U.S. Department of Labor delegated to existing state relief agencies responsibility for the selection of young participants in the program. The executive director of each state agency was designated an official representative of the federal Department of Labor for this purpose. Even more directly, the National Recovery Administration, headed by Hugh S. Johnson, copied the draft experience. As with the wartime draft registration campaigns, Johnson employed massive demonstrations, widespread publicity, and sheer hoopla in an attempt to build a sense of national purpose and common support for the NRA program. In addition, the local NRA compliance boards were modeled after the old district draft boards.[61]

A different approach, but one still influenced by the Selective Service style of federalism, was taken during the New Deal in the Motor Carrier Act and Public Utilities Act. When Congress passed this legislation in 1935, it provided for joint federal and state regulatory boards in these two areas to deal with matters of common interest. Federal officials were to be provided with the benefit of state officers' knowledge of local conditions, while the national government sought to maintain uniform standards across the country.[62] In the New Deal era, these experiments were viewed largely as alternatives to the growth of an extensive federal bureaucracy and excessive control by the national government. Fearful of the effect of an expanded national government, particularly one increasingly influenced by organized labor and urban interest groups, a number of rural and conservative commentators advocated a revival of federalism, a few suggesting that the administrative model of the draft might point the way.[63]

The experiments with the civilian application of the draft's administrative model and the Army's cautious planning for a wartime Selective Service should not be misconstrued: what was most significant about the draft in the immediate post–World War I period is how quickly America abandoned it. Not a single induction order was sent out after the armistice on November 11, 1918. Within six months, long before the last draftees came home from Europe, the Selective Service System had closed down. By the spring of 1920 Congress had rejected any kind of compulsory military training in peacetime and reduced the wartime army from nearly 4,000,000 citizen-soldiers to a force that numbered only 200,000 regulars. In some ways, the postwar military format looked quite traditional: a small regular army supported by the National Guard as the primary ready reserve. Yet for a variety of reasons several important changes had been made, and the United States actually had a new general military format for wartime, together with specific changes even in the peacetime army. Some, like the creation and expansion of the air service, resulted from pressure by military and civilian elites to rely upon new technology. Others, like the enlargement of the General Staff and the creation of ROTC and joint industrial-military planning, stemmed from the desire of such elites for greater centralization and national standards.

What then was the lesson of America's experience with a national draft in 1917–18? During and immediately after the war, the draft and Selective Service System were hailed as major successes by most leaders of public opinion, including some who had initially opposed them. Retracting his earlier skepticism, Ernest Gruening, then managing editor of the *New York Tribune*, called Selective Service "the greatest single achievement of America's participation in the war." Felix Frankfurter, a Harvard law professor then serving on the National War Labor Policies Board, proclaimed the draft to be "one of the most signal contributions towards victory." Most historians have concurred.[64]

What most impressed these contemporaries and subsequent policymakers and scholars was the compatibility of the wartime Selective Service System with American ideals—localism, individualism, civilian control of the military—and with the economic and military

needs of the nation in modern mass warfare. The popularity of the
politico-military formula came from the fact that, while it rested on
a "universal" national obligation, it was implemented on a *selective*
basis, and further that the national military policy was temporary
and was exercised through local civilian authorities. "When it was
necessary to separate an individual from his fellows, it was done by
his neighbors in the community," Hugh S. Johnson explained to
students at the Army War College in 1922. Then he waxed into
characteristic hyperbole:

> Neither state nor nation had one iota of power in this selection. It
> was the method of the Norman fief. It was the method of the
> Saxon Hundred. It was a method that went so far back toward the
> racial springs from which flow the genius of our Nordic political
> institutions, that it was accepted like an ancient Suabian song—
> with intuitive recognition and approval.[65]

Besides illustrating "old iron-pants'" reputation for florid oratory,
such an explanation suggests the powerful ethnic as well as political
appeal of "localism" in an America undergoing rapid demographic
and economic change in the first decades of the 20th century.

Despite the popularity of wartime Selective Service among dominant social groups, the national draft was *not* made an official part
of the postwar policy, either on a peacetime standby basis or as a
statement of principle. The army and dominant civilian elites saw
the wartime experience as evidence of popular acceptance of this
kind of national draft, but only in a major war. During most of the
interwar period, political realities kept any other assertion of conscription carefully circumscribed. But the fact remained that the
national draft and the Selective Service System in World War I had
been politically acceptable as well as militarily and economically
successful. Regardless of the unwillingness of the public and elected
representatives to put it into law in the 1920s and 1930s, and the
return to a small, traditional military establishment during the
interwar period, the positive assessment meant that Selective Service would surely be used in the next major war fought by the United
States.[66]

With the outbreak of World War II in Europe, and particularly
after the unexpected collapse of France in the spring of 1940, remaining conscriptionists launched another educational and lobbying campaign for a draft even before U.S. entry into the war. They
eventually obtained the support of a Democratic reform administration which, although it had resumed the domestic interventionism of
the progressive era and had increased the scope and expenditures of
the federal government, remained cautious in regard to controver-

sial military and foreign policy decisions, particularly in a presidential election year. Despite substantial isolationist opposition, old Plattsburgers like Grenville Clark and Henry L. Stimson (who had recently been appointed secretary of war by Franklin D. Roosevelt), were able to obtain a *prewar* draft in 1940. They succeeded in large part by portraying this expansion of the military format as necessary for the defense of the Western Hemisphere, in the wake of the dramatic shift in the balance of power in Europe.[67]

Once the United States entered the Second World War after the attack on Pearl Harbor, Americans supported the conflict as necessary for national defense and for the survival of democracy against nazism, fascism, and militarism. As a result, the public accepted the selective draft for the duration of the war. The World War II experience, in which 10 million servicemen were drafted, demonstrated the success of the 1917–18 military format and politico-military formula of Selective Service.[68]

The size of the army and the power of the State was again reduced in postwar 1946. Despite the objections of the military, the nation terminated the draft and reverted to a comparatively small peacetime army. Circumstances had changed, however, because of the expanded U.S. leadership in international affairs, the sense of vulnerability of American strategic and economic interests in a world of unprecedented turmoil and upheaval, and escalating tensions with a powerful Soviet Union. Consequently, political and economic elites—including a number of old conscriptionists—joined the military in seeking a larger army, navy, and air force to support a sustained, extensive American involvement in international affairs.[69]

Aware that the public would support such an expanded military, including compulsory military service, only in times of national emergency, they described the international situation as a "Cold War" in which American interests and ideals of freedom and democracy were at stake. After an unsuccessful attempt to expand the military format through permanent UMT&S, they were able—in the crisis atmosphere following a communist coup in Czechoslovakia and the beginning of the Soviet blockade of Berlin—to obtain a "temporary" draft based on the World War I selective draft format.[70] For political reasons the draft was not made legally permanent; instead, the enabling legislation for induction authority was adopted for four-year periods, renewable in the politically safer years that follow a presidential election. The Cold War era's national security managers used the formats of the two world wars as the basis for providing the expanded ground forces used for garrison duty in Europe and Asia, and for combat in the limited expeditionary wars in Korea and Vietnam.[71]

Administered through the Selective Service System, the draft worked successfully in the Korean War, 1950–53. It won considerable public acceptance even though it was used in a limited war, because that war was seen as a conflict against a Soviet client-state at a time when communist Russia was portrayed as posing a threat to American ideals and interests comparable to the earlier challenges of Nazi Germany and militaristic Japan. Furthermore, in the Korean conflict, despite the absence of a declaration of war, the U.S. government drew upon its World War II model of total mobilization, including wage and price controls and wartime rhetoric and taxation. However, in a departure from the format of 1941–45 and despite the opposition of the military, civilian authorities decided that draftees would not serve for the duration but only for two-year terms, and would be rotated through the battle zone. Civilian policymakers modified the concept of military efficiency by choosing short-term service for draftees and precluding the kind of veteran units of World War II, because they were searching for a military format which would be publicly acceptable in an era of continual mobilization and periodic limited wars.[72]

From World War I to the Korean War, the draft had been dramatically expanded. By the 1950s, it included prewar mobilization, use in an undeclared, limited expeditionary war, and auxiliary recruitment of sizable U.S. overseas garrison forces during the "Cold War." Bipartisan support depended upon public perception that the draft was temporary and was necessary to sustain American security and ideals. After the Korean War, the army was again reduced. A Republican administration, dedicated to limited and less expensive government, significantly lowered levels of conscription as well as taxation, and pursued a foreign and military policy designed to avoid committing U.S. troops to combat. Comparatively few Americans were drafted during the Eisenhower presidency and none of these was killed in combat. Consequently, the peacetime draft was largely tolerated as a gesture of America's military readiness against the Soviet Union.[73]

In the Vietnam War, President Lyndon B. Johnson and his national security managers overextended the use of the draft beyond the consensus established in the world wars and early Cold War. Beginning in 1966, opposition to massive U.S. combat involvement in Indochina spread through American society. Questions arose concerning the morality of the war, its peripheral relevance to U.S. security and other national interests, the growth of American casualties, and the lack of clear progress towards victory. By 1968, bipartisan and public support for such military intervention and for the draft had broken down and large numbers of liberal Democrats and Republicans were openly challenging the legitimacy of the war and the draft.[74]

As the war became increasingly unpopular, the draft became a major focus of dissent. The Selective Service System had maintained its basic decentralized format since it was first created. While its most extreme opponents wanted to eliminate the draft entirely, a few liberal Democrats sought to make the draft more equitable as well as socially constructive through expansion of the draft to national service, civilian and military. Moderate critics sought simply to reform Selective Service in line with recent developments in American society, to make it politically acceptable. Endorsing the greater power of the national government under the Democratic administrations of the 1960s, these liberal reformers argued that the importance of localism had been superseded by demands for equity which could better be established through national policy and standards. Reflecting this liberal position, a presidential commission headed by Burke Marshall, former assistant attorney general for civil rights and subsequently general counsel for the IBM Corporation, proposed replacing the autonomy of local boards with more equitable and uniform national standards. It also suggested the elimination of student and occupational deferments, and the establishment of an annual national draft lottery for all 18-year-olds to determine once and for all their relative liability to induction so that they could go on with their careers.[75]

In contrast to the political sophistication and flexibility that Maj. Gen. Enoch H. Crowder had shown in World War I, Lt. Gen. Lewis B. Hershey, the head of Selective Service from 1942 to 1969, became inflexible and stubbornly resisted modification of the draft system during the Vietnam War. In this he was supported by a number of civilian and military conservatives. To counter the liberal-reform impulse of the Burke Marshall commission, the House Armed Services Committee under Rep. L. Mendel Rivers (Dem.-S.C.), created its own advisory committee, headed by retired Gen. Mark W. Clark, which reported in favor of retaining the Selective Service System with only minor adjustments. With both sides staking out firm positions, the bipartisan coalition which had previously sustained the Selective Service System fragmented.[76]

Following the conclusion of the American combat role in Vietnam, the draft was eliminated in 1973 and the country shifted to a new military format, an All-Volunteer Armed Force, for a publicly acceptable *World Power Model*. The system of local draft boards was dismantled, although the National Selective Service Headquarters remained primarily for record-keeping and as a cadre for future reactivation. The Nixon administration favored these actions largely for political rather than military reasons. In fact, although it has been recently argued by one historian that General William C. Westmoreland, the chief of staff, supported the ending of inductions, neither he nor most other senior military officers favored the termination of the draft before the end of the war, nor the elimination of the military obligation and the complete abolition of the Selective Service System.[77] The draft was ended because its increasing unpopularity made the promise of its elimination a political asset in 1968 and 1972, to presidential candidates like Eugene McCarthy, Richard Nixon, and George McGovern. Since the draft had proven disruptive in maintaining support for an active American international role, a majority of the civilian foreign policy and national security elites agreed to its substantial modification or termination.[78]

Opposition to the draft had been part of the widespread popular distrust of the executive and of foreign policy and national security elites during the Indochina war. Consequently, through the War Powers Act of 1973, Congress also limited the power of the president to commit troops to combat abroad. In the conversion to an all-volunteer armed force in 1973, the legislature had directed that the president would have to obtain specific congressional authorization before resuming induction, a requirement which would assure a broad national consensus before such action was taken. In the 1970s, the U.S. government had dramatically curtailed the expansion of the draft system which had occurred in the preceding years, but this was done without abolishing the potential for using the draft in wartime and thus—it was hoped (although not demonstrated)—without impairing the credibility of the American means of raising a mass army when necessary. Since 1973, the U.S. military format, an attempt at an acceptable *World Power Model*, has included a large professional volunteer standing army, closely linked to smaller but allegedly upgraded volunteer reserves (the Organized Army Reserves, Individual Ready Reserves, and the National Guard) which are integrated in planning and training with the units of the so-called Active Army.[79]

Resumption of a relatively minor aspect of the draft—compulsory draft registration—was obtained by the Carter administration in 1980. Put forward as a response to the Soviet invasion of Afghanistan, it represented a rather meaningless gesture in foreign policy, but it had some domestic political and military importance. Consequently, it received enough bipartisan and public support to be enacted. The step also reflected resurgent attitudes within the foreign policy and national security elites that the United States should begin to expand its military establishment, so as to demonstrate its willingness and ability to meet increased threats to American interests and ideals, and its commitments to its allies.[80]

Two years later, in 1982, the Reagan administration decided to continue compulsory draft registration and also to begin to prosecute a number of young men who had refused to register. The Republican administration had been caught in a particular dilemma: Ronald Reagan had campaigned on a program which included opposition to a peacetime draft as an unnecessary infringement upon individual liberty, yet once he was in power, his administration sought to send evaders of compulsory draft registration to prison.[81] In part, the explanation for this apparent contradiction was political: the Republican administration took office having pledged to build a stronger national defense establishment, and so could not appear to take a weaker defense posture than its Democratic predecessor. (The primary emphasis of the Reagan administration was heavily on capital-intensive weapons systems and munitions, rather than on labor-intensive policies involving personnel.) But there was also an important principle involved: citizens should not be allowed to flout the authority of the national government. Such dissent was particularly objectionable to the president and his supporters when it came from the same type of people—pacifists, college students, liberals, and radicals—who had sought to force the United States to withdraw from Vietnam even if such action failed to preclude a communist victory there.

Furthermore, although it sought to cut taxes and domestic programs, the conservative Republican administration never intended to dismantle the State. Rather its purpose was to reorient the focus of the national government towards military and international affairs and away from domestic social services. Despite objections to the peacetime draft which were philosophical, economic, and political (as Secretary of Defense Caspar Weinberger declared in 1981, "we know what the draft did to the social fabric of this country in the '60s"),[82] the administration proved unwilling to relinquish the right of the State to compel young men to register for the draft. Among other reasons, it wanted to ensure it would have the power to draft in wartime. As part of a new conservative concept of citizenship and the relationship of citizens to the State—which reduced the idea of "entitlements," for example—conservatives in Congress and the Reagan administration required young men applying for federally-supported loans for college students to demonstrate that they had complied with draft registration. In addition to enforcing the draft registration law, the U.S. government in the 1980s thus also began to link benefits with obligations of citizenship.[83]

Given the expanded strategic goals of the Reagan administration, a national debate began in the mass media in the 1980s over the adequacy of the All-Volunteer Armed Force after approximately a decade with that military format. As far as manpower was concerned, the media focused on such problem areas as the declining pool of 18-year-olds; the quality of the recruits (in terms of mental ability and educational achievement); and the socio-economic composition of the enlisted personnel, particularly the increasing percentages of non-whites, especially in ground combat units. The latter revived issues of inequitable distribution of the burden of military service as well as of the reliability of such a force if used in domestic riot duty or in predominantly black or Hispanic countries in the third world. Some concern was expressed about the increased cost of a military format which relied on enlistment bonuses and civilian-level wages to maintain high force levels. And questions were raised as to the ability of the all-volunteer format to produce either a sufficient number of soldiers to provide a credible deterrent against Soviet invasion or intimidation of central Europe, or an adequate fighting force if an invasion occurred.[84]

As the concerns with cost, quality, social composition, and the burden on minorities indicate, more was involved than whether the All-Volunteer Force had been a failure or a success in simply filling recruiting quotas—a phenomenon once linked in peacetime largely to demography and the unemployment rate. Issues of equity, economic costs, obligations of citizenship, and foreign policy goals also played a crucial role in the shaping of military formats.[85]

In the 1980s, the debate was revived over whether the U.S. military format should remain all-volunteer or whether it should return to some kind of mixed force of draftees and volunteers. Some critics have even suggested that there should be a program of national service requiring young men (and possibly also women) to spend a few years in either the armed forces or civilian public service jobs.[86] Combat readiness to meet strategic goals naturally became the immediate focus of the public debate, but in fact, in the 1980s and 1990s as in the past, the controversy over how to raise the nation's army also reflected issues about the nature and direction of American society as well as the international position of the United States.

CHAPTER

10

Conscription and America

Like shadows of soliders on a parade field, military institutions are shaped by the society that creates them. The military format is particularly influenced by prevailing attitudes about the relationship of the citizen to the national community, to the State. Because the army is an institution of organized violence, designed to wage or deter war, it is also affected by the realities and predominant perceptions of power in the world. More than the soldiers themselves, larger domestic and international forces determine the nature of military institutions.

In the 400 years since the first permanent English settlement, the manner in which Americans have raised and organized their armies has been characterized by long-term patterns reflecting historical forces. In the short run, reacting to proximate events and goals, individuals and groups have through the political process frequently altered the size and nature of the army. This has been particularly true in regard to types of recruitment and terms of service, and the mix between career regulars and temporary citizen-soliders, between draftees and volunteers, national forces and militia, standing army and reserves. In contrast to short-term variations, long-term general military format models—sustained over several decades or even a century—have been linked to larger changes in the nature of American society and the international system.

After experimenting with several formats in the colonial and revolutionary periods, the United States established a format model, beginning hesitantly in the 1790s, which would last throughout the 19th century. It was the *New Nation Model: the local-national military*, a small regular army and some militia units, but most importantly, with wartime armies filled by ad hoc, locally raised, nationally directed, previously unorganized units of U.S. Volunteers. A dramatic change occurred in the World War I era, however, when the United States adopted its modern wartime format: the *Nation-State Model: wartime national mass mobilization*. The substitute for the U.S. Volunteers was an almost entirely nationally raised wartime army composed mainly of drafted citizen-soldiers and temporary or reserve officers. America employed this format successfully in both world wars. Variations were used with decreasing success in the Cold War and to raise troops for limited conflicts in Korea and Vietnam. Since the end of American involvement in the Vietnam War in 1973, the United States had experimented with a different format: a *World Power Model: a large professional volunteer standing army* which has been closely linked with expanded and supposedly upgraded volunteer reserves. The success of this latest experiment, untested in war, remains unproven.

The forces shaping these military formats have *not* been primarily military technology and theory, which although important, are seldom the determining factors by themselves. In the American Revolution and the Civil War, where each side used the same types of weapons and held generally similar military views, differences in formats reflected not simply different strategic situations, but also variations in society and political culture. Since World War II, even that most startling development in the history of weaponry, the atomic bomb, for all its effect upon the strategic nuclear arms race, has not dictated a particular military format for the ground forces. In a majority of the world's military nations, conscription remains the primary means of raising armies. When the United States ended the draft in 1973, it did so for reasons which had little to do with atomic weaponry. Indeed, the impetus for the decision involved neither military technology nor doctrine and in fact was made, over considerable opposition in the military, by civilian policymakers largely for political reasons. Military effectiveness is but one criterion in the choice of a military format and American soldiers have repeatedly demonstrated that they can use whatever format is authorized by civilian leaders. Just as war is too important to be left to the generals, so, because of the significance of the direct demands upon American citizens, the military format is too important to be left to the military.

The most significant continuous, long-term trend among format models has been the shift from local to national military institutions and systems of military service. This nationalization of the American military, which reached full fruition only in the 20th century, reflected a larger transfer of power and direction in society from the local and state communities to the national level. Indeed, the monopolization of military power by central governments over rival parochial elements has been a historic part of the growth of modern States. Despite the encumbrance of a dual federal system, the U.S. government eventually gained a clear supremacy in military affairs, in order to prevent state militia from refusing to follow central government directives, as occurred in the War of 1812, the Civil War, and the Spanish-American War. Even the Republican administrations of the 1970s and 1980s, despite their emphasis on a "new federalism" and a return of many national government programs to the states, had no intention of relinquishing national supremacy over the state militia, nor of diminishing Washington's ability to protect expanding American economic and strategic interests overseas.

The military has had a reciprocal relationship with the State. While in most countries the maintenance of the army has always been required for *raison d'état*, most Americans traditionally chose to ignore or deny this fact. Nevertheless, even in the United States, the growth of the central government has enabled it to enlarge the military establishment. Reciprocally, the expansion of the military, particularly in wartime, has contributed to the growth and power of the State. The armed forces have normally been the largest single expense in the national government's budget and, therefore, have been a major factor in the State's need to obtain revenue. Although the largest and most dramatic expansion has been during wars, and more recently during the "Cold War," postwar demobilization has seldom meant that either the military or the State shrank to their prewar levels.

With the national government's unprecedented growth in the 20th century, Americans showed a greater willingness, at least until the present period, to sustain governmental intervention in the economy and society. Successful national conscription, which came to the United States only in this century, was a part of that new national interventionism, and for some time had the backing of the liberal coalition. When that coalition was shattered in the 1960s, a return to solely voluntary enlistment took place in the 1970s during a period of extensive criticism of active interventionist policies at home and abroad.[1]

In the 1970s and 1980s a neo-conservative movement contributed to a reduction of the federal regulatory and redistributive role. At the same time, however, the national government dramatically increased its spending on defense, particularly for new weapons systems. This was not accompanied by increased demands upon the citizenry for military service. Instead, the Reagan administration made greater use of automated equipment as well as private contractors and civilian personnel to provide support services to the military. Voluntary enlistment, not compulsory service, fit within a new emphasis upon the market system rather than on governmental intervention in the economy and in mobilization of the citizenry.[2]

National conscription in the 20th century can also be viewed as part of an expansion and intensification of national citizenship. Beginning in the progressive era, reform administrations and later the judiciary increased the rights and privileges of Americans. This enhanced the importance and benefits of national, as opposed to state, citizenship and forged a more significant linkage between the population and the central government. Increased federal benefits and defense spending were, naturally, usually accompanied by increased taxation. In a similar vein, although usually at different times, the government also broadened the national military obligation of American citizens and alien residents. Liability to compulsory military service was expanded from the World War I concept of service when needed in major wars, to prewar mobilization in 1940, then to training and garrison duty during the Cold War, and to combat in limited, undeclared expeditionary wars in Korea and Vietnam.

The turmoil that began in the late 1960s led to a re-evaluation of the expanded State. Challenges to the legitimacy of its major extractive powers were posed by extensive evasion of taxation and conscription. By eliminating the draft, the Nixon administration took a politically popular step and also terminated a significant source of disorder and challenge to the government's authority. Important ramifications, however, went largely unnoticed. Since liability to military service was one of the few duties of citizenship in the liberal State, its elimination further reduced the symbolic importance of American citizenship. "Whatever its merits," two recent students of American citizenship have concluded, "this policy [of eliminating the draft] diluted a preeminent feature of political membership—the sense of shared sacrifice and patriotic commitment to a common goal."[3]

Dominant conservative attitudes in the seventies and eighties, however, also contributed to some increases in governmental authority. In the sixties and seventies, welfare benefits had become justified as "entitlements," rights enforceable against public resources by individuals residing in America, whether they were U.S. citizens or not.[4] In the 1980s, several state governments linked some of these entitlements to requirements that recipients actively seek, train for, or obtain paid employment. In regard to the military, the national government first required young men to register for the draft (even though the induction authority had been terminated and the Selective Service System largely dismantled) and then required that these young adults be denied federal student aid if they failed to meet this limited military obligation.[5]

In the evolution of general military formats in America, some traditional restrictions and other inequities have been diminished—a result of the need for more personnel combined with popular and ideological pressures for equity. This was evident in the use of blacks in the War of 1812 and the Civil War; the elimination of compulsory militia training in the North in the Jacksonian era; and the prohibition of hiring substitutes for draftees in the 20th century. Since World War II, this movement led to desegregation and the opening up of the armed forces, first the ranks and then the officer corps, to racial minorities and to women.[6] And during the Vietnam War, demands for equity led to an end to the educational and occupational deferments that had been used as an inequitable avenue of escape from military service by more privileged youths.

Military format models have coincided with changing realities in the international system and particular attitudes towards the appropriate U.S. role in the world. Until the end of the 19th century, the predominant American foreign policy was one of economic and territoral expansion, but of political and military isolationism in regard to events outside the Western Hemisphere. Then, in the closing decades of the century, industrialization, expanding empires and world trade, the growth of popular nationalism and continental militarism, all stimulated Americans to play a more interventionist role in the world. Beginning sporadically at the turn of the century, interventionism replaced military and political isolationism as the dominant American tradition at the end of World War II, when the United States assumed a continually active international leadership.

Despite the substantial use of military force in various times, Americans have generally been unwilling to pay the personal costs of a large army, except in time of national emergency. That reluc tance has been sustained by a heritage of comparative geographical security as well as a tradition which emphasized individual liberty and relatively restricted government. The popular military ideal has not been the career enlistment man—frequently caricatured as an unmotivated misfit—but rather the temporary citizen-soldier. First personified by the homespun "Minutemen" of the American Revolution, this popular figure included the blue- and gray-clad "Boys of '61" in the Civil War, the khaki-clad "doughboys" of 1917–18, and the "GIs" of World War II in olive drab.

Yet the American ideal of the citizen-soldier is more limited than often believed. At its core, from the time of the American Revolution has been the belief that a virtuous, self-governing republic should rely for protection upon patriotic citizens rather than on the hired regulars of professional standing armies. Americans adopted this belief for ideological as well as material reasons. Theoretically and legally, the government had the authority to create such a large standing army, but the dominant national political elites chose not to exercise this power. In practice, the United States has had a two-army tradition, of different peacetime and wartime forces. A small professional army served in peacetime as a frontier constabulary and a repository of technical knowledge, augmented in wartime by a larger temporary army of citizen-soldiers. Although officers in both armies tended to come from the upper and middle classes, the rank and file differed dramatically. Career enlisted personnel came disproportionately from lower socio-economic groups. The temporary citizen-soldiers of the wartime armies generally represented the various classes, ethnic groups, and regions that made up America, although representation often reflected the popularity of the war. From the original obligation to train and serve briefly in the colonial or state militia for *local* defense when necessary, Americans eventually derived the concept of temporary *national* wartime armies composed largely of amateur citizen-soldiers.

But not every male citizen was obligated to be a soldier. Unlike contintental European nations, in the 19th century, the United States did not adopt a mass conscript-reserve army based on UMT&S. What the ideal of the citizen-soldier meant to Americans in practice was that every young adult male citizen or declarant alien might be *liable* to the military obligation for temporary service in what was agreed by public authorities to be an emergency. Initially and briefly, this service was in the colonial militia; by the 20th century, it was in a national wartime army. While Americans have honored the ideal of the citizen-soldier, they have generally relied in peacetime upon career troops recruited primarily from lower-income groups. Thus, most of the time, the military burden has rested only lightly on the bulk of the citizenry, particularly the middle and upper classes.[7]

Despite the historic complexity of the nation's military tradition, it has been possible for Americans to make dramatic sustained changes in military institutions and, indeed, to adopt modified systems of national conscription. One of the pivotal changes was the World War I adoption of a new general wartime military format—the *Nation-State Model* of wartime national mass mobilization. Although hardly inevitable, the U.S. government chose a wartime army raised by a temporary selective national draft. Debate over the proper military format in the World War I era was substantially shaped by an articulate, well-financed, largely civilian group—the "conscriptionists" in the preparedness movement—and by the reaction to their proposals for a reserve officer corps, a solely national and conscripted army, and a permanent system of UMT&S. Coming mainly from the new national business and professional elites which had emerged in the urban, industrial North, the conscriptionists included leaders of the giant new corporations, supporters in the professions, and leaders of the political and foreign policy elites. This corporate-oriented elite viewed the traditional military format as antiquated, unresponsive, unpredictable, and inefficient. To them the National Guard and the U.S. Volunteers seemed partisan and parochial. Because of its need to offer competitive wages, the regular army was both small and expensive. Worst of all, America's traditional reliance upon wartime volunteers could cause massive disruption of the work force and of essential production. Instead, this business-minded elite sought a more rationalized, nationally directed system of military manpower which would also take into consideration the labor needs of a modern, interdependent national economy.

These conscriptionists were interventionists who believed that the United States should be prepared to aid the Allies with military force. But that was not the foundation of their advocacy, for Britain and France could also be assisted just by a temporary expansion of the army. What led the conscriptionists to advocate a *permanent* format of UMT&S was their belief that, regardless of the outcome of the European war, the United States had begun a new and continuing role as world power. Protection of expanding American interests required a military system with greater capability and credibility in the new international arena.

While significant, the power of this economic and professional elite to achieve its military goal was limited by the political realities of the time. Among these were active opposition by other groups, traditions of individual liberty, the primacy of private interests, lack of demonstrable need for a gigantic permanent program of UMT&S, and the sheer inertia of the national political system. Opposition to permanent UMT&S came for varying reasons from a number of groups which otherwise had little in common: upper- and middle-class pacifists, liberal reform internationalists, and—at the other end of the socio-economic spectrum—isolationist agrarians, trade unionists, and urban immigrants. The majority in the National Guard and Congress opposed national UMT&S, as did President Wilson. Consequently, although the conscriptionists obtained their lesser goals of producing reserve officers and introducing a selective draft in wartime, they failed in their primary quest for permanent UMT&S.

When the United States entered World War I in the spring of 1917, power flowed to the commander-in-chief. After privately deciding first to try out the traditional volunteer system, largely to mollify ethnic and agrarian isolationists in the Democratic party, Wilson changed his mind a week before the declaration of war. He decided to abandon entirely the U.S. Volunteers and rely instead upon a temporary and selective draft to raise the national wartime army. The primary, but largely unacknowledged, reason for Wilson's switch was the challenge by former president Theodore Roosevelt, who sought authority to raise and lead an expedition of U.S. Volunteers to France. In his irrepressible desire to repeat his triumph at San Juan Hill on the Western Front, the old Rough Rider dragged the U.S. Volunteer system down with him.

Conscription is usually best understood as a means to an end. Those who support a war will generally accept a draft if it is seen as the most effective means of achieving victory. In World War I, although the majority of progressives had opposed permanent UMT&S, most of them supported the temporary use of a selective draft because they accepted Wilson's progessive war aims. A century earlier, in the darkest days of the War of 1812, some anti-Statist Jeffersonians had endorsed temporary national conscription to preserve the republic. During the Cold War, 150 years later, most Americans accepted a limited draft to demonstrate national resolve against threatened Soviet expansion in Europe, but they turned against the draft in opposition to the Vietnam War.

The nexus between a nation's needs and an individual's obligations is the concept of national citizenship. In the World War I era, the new American military format was part of an intensified and expanded concept of national citizenship which increased the obligation of the citizen to the nation-State as contrasted to family, local community, or ethnic group. Progressives and conservatives agreed that citizenship (even anticipatory citizenship of declarant aliens and 18- to 20-year-old minors) carried with it a military obligation to serve in the wartime armed forces if necessary. As Ralph Barton Perry, a Harvard philosopher and disciple of William James, wrote in 1916:

> Nothing short of national safety or some higher design of international justice and order, can make it reasonable to cultivate the art of destruction. But since military service is so justified, as a painful necessity like surgery, capital punishment or self-sacrifice, it is reasonable that it should be done well, and soberly undertaken as a function of the state. In a democracy this means that it should be acknowledged and assumed as an obligation by

all citizens. For democracy implies that there shall be neither privilege nor immunity.[8]

In a just cause, Perry concluded, compulsory military training and service was compatible with liberty. "If we are to be free, we must be safely and effectively free. There must be a place secured for freedom, and to secure that freedom, free men may be soldiers."[9] That expanded concept helped to make the national draft acceptable to the majority of Americans. The successful implementation of the national draft during the war added to an intensified concept of national citizenship.

The expanded role of the State and of modern reformist presidents during the progressive era contributed to the success of the new military format. Identifying themselves as champions of the people and the nation and employing the new mass media, Theodore Roosevelt and Woodrow Wilson developed latent powers inherent in the presidency and showed their ability to mobilize widespread popular support for their programs. In addition, the expansion of the federal regulatory functions and bureaucracy during the reform period gave the national government the institutional ability to help coordinate manpower and other aspects of the economic and military mobilization of World War I. State-building and increased national sentiment and standards helped legitimate the replacement of local, volunteer military traditions with a drafted national army.

The draft system in the United States harmonized with a number of American traditions and values and functioned in a far less mechanistic manner than European systems of conscription. A temporary, wartime phenomenon, America's conscription bureau—the Selective Service System—was highly decentralized, and in World War I used only interim local volunteer workers rather than long-term federal civil servants in its nearly five thousand local draft boards. In addition to the inherent appeal of local civilian autonomy, the system of "supervised decentralization" diffused, at the local level, discontent about decisions involving particular individuals, and discouraged disaffected elements from coalescing into a consolidated attack on overall national draft guidelines established in Washington.

It was the new politico-military formula, its structure and procedures, along with intensified concepts of national citizenship and the expanded role of the State, which proved so important in the success of the new wartime format. Afterwards, in the 1920s and 1930s, although the United States returned to a small regular army, the selective draft was accepted as the means of raising the citizen-soldiers in the next major war. In 1940, after heated controversy, it was adopted before a declaration of war, as a prewar defense measure following the unexpected defeat of France and the shift in the balance of power in Europe. After Pearl Harbor, the nation unified behind the war and the draft. Selective Service proved a successful part of America's total mobilization in World War II.

During and after the Second World War, presidents Franklin D. Roosevelt and Harry S. Truman and internationalists in the business and foreign policy elites sought popular and institutional means to sustain the new U.S. role as an active and continuing world power. With continuing emphasis on economic and diplomatic policy, they created bipartisan support for the United Nations, the International Monetary Fund, and the World Bank. Both presidents also drew upon old conscriptionist assertions (reiterated by Secretary of War Henry L. Stimson, Gen. George C. Marshall and others) of the need for a permanently strong military format, including UMT&S, to back up extended international commitments. Given foreign policy divisions among Americans and the lower priority assigned to the military by most liberals and many conservatives, the Democratic administration proved much less successful in this latter task. Although Truman achieved bipartisan support for containing the Soviet Union, he failed to obtain UMT and settled, after 18 months without the draft, for a compromise that included a mixed format of volunteers and two-year draftees, the latter obtained through the re-established Selective Service System. For the next twenty-five years, Washington adjusted induction rates according to demography, economic costs, and foreign and strategic needs.

In the wake of the world war experience and under the impact of the early crises of the Cold War, Americans accepted some use of the selective draft on a temporary basis. Limited draft calls from an expanding population during the non-war years supplied short-term draftees and draft-induced volunteers as part of a larger than normal peacetime force. When the nation mobilized for the Korean War, draft calls were escalated rapidly. Despite the introduction of the rotation system of short-term tours of duty, public disenchantment with what soon became a bloody and static war of attrition offered a prophetic warning against the future use of the draft in limited and inconclusive wars.

Nevertheless, in the late 1960s, President Lyndon B. Johnson, supported by many in the national security elite, used the draft as the primary device to obtain troops for massive U.S. military intervention in Vietnam. With a complete victory still elusive after three years of increasing effort and mounting casualties, bipartisanship collapsed and a divided American public demanded an end to the war, some by withdrawal, others by greatly increased use of air and naval power. Stretched far beyond the limits of public acceptance, the American consensus on the use of conscription broke down completely as a result of the war in Vietnam.

Because it is so closely tied to its origins in the anguished debate over the disastrous American experience in southeast Asia, the current military format—the large, volunteer standing army—will probably be seen as transitional rather than as a long-term general model. The all-volunteer force, like other formats before it, represented a choice among options and resulted from political more than purely military decisions. This suggests that domestic and global changes in the years ahead may lead to a re-evaluation of current federal institutions and policies, including the means of raising and organizing America's armies.

What is the meaning of the continuing debate over the American military format and the kind of model which might be adopted for the United States in the final years of the 20th century? The present course reiterates the nation's traditional reliance upon the navy, now augmented by the air force—the more technological and less manpower-oriented services—as the first line of defense. Historically, concepts of sea power and strategic air power have been put forward as alternatives for costly and extensive land warfare.[10] Although expensive, the navy and air force, unlike the army, make fewer demands for personal service by the citizenry, a fact that enhances their popular appeal. Americans have generally been more willing to spend money on weaponry than to impose widespread military service. Sea and air forces will probably continue to be the primary defense components for some time. But, as has been repeatedly demonstrated, air and naval power alone have usually failed to provide a decisive substitute for effective ground forces. Even in an age of nuclear weapons, the numerous wars which have occurred in various areas of the world since 1945 have continued to confirm the importance of effective ground units, whether guerrilla, militia, or conventional troops.[11] Since there is no evidence that the United States intends to reduce its extensive economic, strategic, and ideological interests nor its role as a global leader, it will undoubtedly continue to rely in some part upon military forces to maintain those interests and responsibilities. Unless non-violent means of defense replace them, substantial and effective ground forces will continue to be used as a deterrent and possibly—given the belligerence of recent U.S. foreign policy—as an instrument of combat, probably in the Third World[12]

Yet although the nation has maintained extensive global commitments since World War II, it still lacks a durable military format for its role as an active world power. Since 1945, it has experimented with one format after another, and the period of improvisation has not ended. Continuing charges are being made that the current U.S. Army is in trouble in the quality and representative nature of its recruits, and that its 16 divisions are understrength, under-ready and stretched too thin around the world; these charges suggest that the present untested, all-volunteer standing army of 780,000 may not be an adequate or even proper model in the long run.[13] In part, the inability of the United States to achieve a durable military format as a world power has resulted from confusion about the nature of war and the military. For years it was believed that nuclear weapons would be decisive instruments of war and diplomacy. But given the understandable reluctance to use them, particularly after the U.S. atomic monoply was broken, it became clear that they had not obviated the need for an army. But what kind of army?

In Vietnam, the United States tried without success to use an army composed largely of short-term draftees to fight a long-term expeditionary war in a region unrelated to American security. Largely as a political consequence, the United States abandoned the draft and turned instead entirely to voluntarism and a large professional standing army. Yet it appeared to some that the mistake of using draftees to fight a counter-guerrilla war in a peripheral area like southeast Asia had, for political reasons, precluded using a draft to maintain a conventional deterrent force in a vital area like Western Europe.[14] Supporters of the volunteer system, however, argued that elimination of the draft had helped to prevent large-scale American military intervention in other Third World countries after Vietnam.[15]

Currently, perhaps the most widely discussed alternatives to the all-volunteer force are proposals for two kinds of armies for two kinds of wars, or for a return to the unified mixed force of the Cold War era. Two-tier advocates suggest that a rapidly deployable professional force of specially equipped, volunteer career regulars— similar to the old British colonial army or French Foreign Legion, with modern weaponry—would be most effective militarily for so-called "low-intensity," counter-guerrilla conflicts. To provide a credible conventional deterrent against "high-intensity" conventional wars among major powers, such as those in Europe, these civilian and military thinkers recommend an army composed of a mixture of regulars and short-term citizen-soldiers obtained through compulsory military training and service, perhaps UMT&S, and channelled into the active army or the army reserves.[16] In opposition, many officers and civilians object to such notions of a two-tier army with a separate elite force. Those who favor a single, unified army generally desire a return to the mixed army of volunteers and selected draftees of the 1950s and 1960s, although with a reformed and more equitable draft system which would prevent members of the privileged classes from escaping military service.[17]

A number of liberals recommend some form of national service that could provide governmental public service and job training programs for young people (especially urban minorities) as well as help to provide the quantity and quality of manpower needed by the armed forces. The main type advocated would require all young men to perform some military or civilian duty for the government.[18] On the other hand, some secular or religious pacifists call for total abolition of military weaponry and the armed forces, and the substitution of a system of massive non-violent civilian resistance as a defense against invasion of Western Europe or the United States.[19]

For the present, however, the all-volunteer force retains considerable support as well as the advantage of already being in place. Some supporters believe that it is more efficient militarily and that, politically, the close linkage between reserve and active units avoids the kind of creeping escalation that characterized President Johnson's interjection of the American military into southeast Asia. Unlike the Vietnam War, at the beginning of any future major U.S. military intervention the president would have to take full political responsibility and be able to mobilize public support for it. Legally, the War Powers Act requires congressional approval for such military action. More practically, the integration of active duty and reserve units means that few combat outfits could be deployed without mobilizing the National Guard and the Army Reserves, with all the political costs involved in calling up and dispatching the husbands and fathers included among these reserves of citizen-soldiers.[20]

To be politically acceptable as well as militarily effective, a two-tier army format probably could *not* include a near or wholly universal draft as most of its advocates suggest. Indeed, a universal draft, like universal national service, is highly improbable in America because of its great economic costs, its divergence from traditions of individual liberty and limited government, and the fact that it would far exceed the personnel needs of the military. On the other hand, a reformed selective draft, operating under uniform standards, might be militarily adequate and politically acceptable. It would have even greater chance of acceptance if it were applied equitably to all races and socio-economic classes, and if it also included liberal allowances for alternative public service.[21] Such *selective civic service* could allow those selected by the draft to choose from a range of civilian and military options. They might agree to serve in the active or reserve military forces, or they could opt to participate, perhaps for a longer period, in civilian public service. The latter could include a variety of options: foreign or domestic, local or national, through governmental agencies like VISTA or the Peace Corps, or non-governmental programs run by religious, humanitarian, or civic improvement groups.

Some kind of broad obligatory service would probably benefit society as well as the armed forces. Militarily, a selective civic service program could provide the army with adequate numbers and quality of soldiers. The service of draftees could be legally limited to use in clearly defined areas of direct vital interest such as Western Europe. Politically and socially, it could also help to instill an ethic of community service in the pursuit of America's ideals in place of the current driving emphasis on individual self-interest. As William James recognized long ago, a system of civic service could emphasize the aspects of life that unify Americans rather than those that drive them apart.[22] Internationally, it could bolster the credibility of conventional forces as a deterrent to aggression and intimidation in Europe, thereby reducing the threat of nuclear war.

As the postwar experience has shown, the difficulty of achieving a durable American format is more than military. It is directly related to the larger reasons why Americans have been reluctant to pay the kind of military costs generally sustained by world powers. Until recently, the nation had a tradition of geographic security. Even now, the Soviet nuclear threat poses simultaneously both a lesser and a greater menace than the kind of brutal invasion and oppressive occupation which has characterized much of the history of warfare, but which has seldom threatened the United States. Nor has this country ever been a major colonial power, with world-wide colonies requiring overseas forces to conquer and maintain the empire.[23]

Without militarily strong and aggressive neighbors, without a far-flung colonial empire to govern, Americans have generally been free to avoid sustained military mobilization. Traditionally, they remained largely unprepared for major war. However, once war arrived, they mobilized with an intense sense of retaliation. Rather than coordinating military force to foreign policy on a long-term basis, they engaged sporadically in impetuous, highly charged crusades. Such a pattern of intermittent mobilization was commensurate with a national emphasis upon individual, private interests, and upon a limited State, as well as an international position based primarily upon active economic rather than sustained political and military involvement.

In the two world wars, the *Nation-State Model* of a temporarily drafted army, first adopted and accepted in 1917–18, proved to be a legitimate and effective answer to the problem of intervention in those titanic conflicts and of the total national mobilization of society that accompanied them. But the international position of the United States since World War II as an on-going world power has not been commensurate with such an intensive mobilization of society. As shown by the limited, expeditionary conflicts in Korea and Vietnam and by the current debate, the temporarily drafted army of the world wars was linked to intense, temporary socio-political mobilization. It is neither an effective nor acceptable answer to the problem of the new U.S. role as a continuing world power in a quite different international system.[24]

Although the nation's traditional isolationism ended in World War II, Americans have not fully adjusted to the costs of their new world role, nor have they altered either that role or the international order to the extent that an army has become unnecessary. Divided as it is over the proper kinds of foreign and strategic policies, and even less united over military formats, the country has stumbled along on makeshift formats. In compensation, it has sometimes tried, with varying success, to substitute other armies for its own. It has augmented American forces with those of its European or Asian allies and, overtly or covertly, it has supported indigenous Third World forces as proxies for American military power. Either way, when divergent interests became apparent, so did the limits of this form of military power.[25]

Once again the contrast with Europe highlights the difference in America. Unlike the United States, the continental powers have not abandoned conscription, even though they too have reduced reliance upon the mass army. They have kept the draft partly to maintain their forces, but also to sustain the connection between military obligation and the nation-State.[26] This politico-military type of national integration, so important in continental Europe, has remained alien to the United States. Without universal military training, only a minority of Americans served routinely in uniform; the army was never the nationalizing force that it was in Europe.

The evolution of American nationalism has been a social and economic as much as a political experience. It required the continued recognition of individual, local, and pluralistic interests and loyalties. Uniquely, America has evolved from a society to a nation and only lastly to a State. In Europe, centralized States predated the emergence of nationally conscious "nations." Unlike the political-military nationalism of France and Germany, American nationalism was based upon a socio-economic ideal—the individual's right to liberty and opportunity, and the "pursuit of happiness," in Jefferson's felicitous phrase—rather than on a polity and *raison d'état*. In America, therefore, it has not been self-contradictory for an ardent nationalist, like President Reagan, also to be an opponent of peace-time conscription. The military obligation of American citizenship remains ill defined. The draft remains an episodic and largely unintegrated part of the nation's history.

The American experience with military formats over the past four hundred years demonstrates that they are determined by social conditions and political attitudes as well as military criteria. Whatever the future of the current All-Volunteer Armed Force, its successor will surely be a socio-political and military mechanism rooted in the circumstances of its own time, as well as part of the inherited evolution of the nature of peacetime and wartime armies—an evolution shaped as much by trends in society as by the nature of war itself.

Endnotes

Abbreviations Used in the Endnotes

AVF	All-Volunteer Armed Force	MTCA	Military Training Camps Association
AEF	American Expeditionary Force	NA	National Archives
AF&S	*Armed Forces and Society*	NDB	Newton D. Baker
AHR	*American Historical Review*	NSL	National Security League
AUAM	American Union Against Militarism	NYPL	New York Public Library
		PMG	Provost Marshal General
AWC	Army War College	SCPC	Swarthmore College Peace Collection
BG	Brigadier General		
COHC	Columbia University Oral History Collection	SSS	Selective Service System
		SMAC	Senate Military Affairs Committee
CofS	Chief of Staff		
DAB	Dictionary of American Biography	TR	Theodore Roosevelt
		UMT&S	Universal Military Training and Service
EHC	Enoch H. Crowder		
GS	General Staff	UMTL	Universal Military Training League
JAH	*Journal of American History*		
HLS	Henry L. Stimson	WCD	War College Division, General Staff
HMAC	House Military Affairs Committee		
		WD	War Department
LC	Library of Congress	*WMQ*	*William and Mary Quarterly*
MA	*Military Affairs*		
MG	Major General	WW	Woodrow Wilson

Short Form for the Published Papers of Woodrow Wilson

Link, *PWW*

Arthur S. Link, et al., eds., *The Papers of Woodrow Wilson*, 56 vols. to date (Princeton, N.J., 1966–). I have also cited this immensely valuable compilation even when I used the original manuscript document in the Wilson MSS. In the latter case, I cite the documents also by series, but not box number, since the entire collection was rearranged after it was micro-filmed.

Short Forms for Government Reports

HMAC, *Hrgs: Army Reorganization*
    U.S. Congress, House Military Affairs Committee, *Hearings on Army Reorganization*. 65th Congress, 3rd Sess., Washington, D.C., 1919.

HMAC, *Increase of Military: Hrgs.*
    U.S. Congress, House Military Affairs Committee, *Increase of the Military Establishment of the U.S.: Hearings*. 65th Congress, 1st Sess., Washington, D.C., 1917.

HMAC, *To Increase Efficiency: Hrgs.*
    U.S. Congress, House Military Affairs Committee, *To Increase the Efficiency of the Military Establishment of the U.S.: Hearings*. 64th Congress, 1st Sess., Washington, D.C., 1916.

HMAC and SMAC, *UMT: Gen. Wood.*
    U.S. Congress, House and Senate Committees on Military Affairs, *Universal Military Training: Statements Made by Maj. Gen. Leonard Wood before the Committees*. Washington, D.C., 1917.

House, Special Committee to Investigate the NSL, *National Security League: Hrgs.*
    U.S. Congress, House, Special Committee to Investigate the National Security League. *National Security League: Hearings. . .* 65th Congress, 3rd Sess., 31 parts, Washington, D.C., 1919.

PMG, *First Report.*
    U.S. Provost Marshal General, *Report of the First Draft under the Selective Service Act, 1917.* (Washington, D.C., 1918).

PMG, *Second Report.*
    U.S. Provost Marshal General, *Second Report to the Secretary of War on the Operations of the Selective Service System.* (Washington, D.C., 1919).

PMG, *Final Report.*
    U.S. Provost Marshal General, *Final Report to the Secretary of War on the Operations of the Selective Service System to July 15, 1919.* (Washington, D.C., 1920).

SMAC, *Hrgs: Army Reorganization*
    U.S. Congress, Senate Military Affairs Committee, *Hearings on Army Reorganization*. 66th Congress, 1st and 2nd Sess., Washington, D.C., 1919.

SMAC, *Preparation for National Defense: Hrgs.*
    U.S. Congress, Senate Military Affairs Committee, *Preparation for National Defense: Hearings*. 64th Congress, 1st Sess., Washington, D.C., 1916.

SMAC, *Temporary Increase of Military: Hrgs.*
    U.S. Congress, Senate Military Affairs Committee, *Temporary Increase of the Military Establishment: Hearings*. 65th Congress, 1st Sess., Washington, D.C., 1917.

SMAC, *UMT: Hrgs.*
    U.S. Congress, Senate Military Affairs Committee, *Universal Military Training: Hearings*. 64th Congress, 2nd Sess., Washington, D.C., 1917.

Preface

1. McGeorge Bundy, George F. Kennan, Robert S. McNamara, and Gerard Smith, "Nuclear Weapons and the Atlantic Alliance," *Foreign Affairs*, 60 (Spring 1982), pp. 753–68; Gen. Bernard Rogers, chief, NATO ground forces, *Washington Post*, March 2, 1985; Robert B. Killebrew, *Conventional Defense and Total Deterrence: Assessing NATO's Strategic Options* (Wilmington, Del., 1986); Robert S. McNamara, *Blundering into Disaster: Surviving the First Century of the Nuclear Age* (New York, 1986). After the 1986 summit meeting at Reykjavik, Iceland, the possibility that Ronald Reagan and Mikhail S. Gorbachev might conclude an agreement for major reduction of nuclear weapons led to some warnings that such action would require an increase in NATO's conventional forces to offset the numerical superiority of the Warsaw Pact armies. See "NATO Nervously Contemplates a Conventional Forces Gap," *New York Times*, Oct. 16, 1986; and "The Deeper Challenges of Striking a Missile Deal in Europe," ibid, March 8, June 5, 1987.

2. *Washington Post*, July 9, 1981. For similar views, see Thomas H. Etzold, *Defense or Delusion? America's Military in the 1980s* (New York, 1982), pp. 31–94.

3. Among these were Senator Sam Nunn of Georgia, chair of the Senate Armed Services Committee; former Senator Gary Hart of Colorado; Sen. Ernest F. Hollings of South Carolina; and former Gov. Charles S. Robb of Virginia, chair of the newly formed Democratic Leadership Council. See James W. Davis, "Bring Back the Draft," *New York Times*, Feb. 5, 1987, and ibid., Feb. 15, 1987, March 25, 1987.

Introduction

1. On the *Leviathan*, see *American Yearbook*, 1919, p. 320. The 72 percent figure is extrapolated from Table 80 in U.S. PMG, *Second Report to the Secretary of War on the Operations of the Selective Source System to Dec. 20, 1918* (Washington, D.C., 1919), p. 227. The term "doughboy" for AEF infantrymen apparently derived from Civil War infantry uniform buttons which resembled dumplings made of dough.

2. "Ready or Not? The Real State of the U.S. Military," *U.S. News & World Report*, 97 (Aug. 6, 1984), p. 34; "Armed Farces," *New Republic*, 191 (Aug. 27, 1984), pp. 7–8; Robert K. Fullinwider, ed., *Conscripts and Volunteers: Military Requirements, Social Justice, and the All-Volunteer Force* (Totowa, N.J., 1983).

3. This concept is a modification of Samuel E. Finer "State- and Nation-Building in Europe: The Role of the Military," in Charles Tilly, ed., *The Formation of National States in Western Europe* (Princeton, N.J., 1975), pp. 84–163, esp. 84–102.

4. Compare U.S. documents with the French Republic's Declaration of the Rights of Man and Citizen, and Decree of Aug. 13, 1793 establishing the *levée en masse*. John H. Stewart, ed., *A Documentary Survey of the French Revolution* (New York, 1951), pp. 115, 472–73, 574.

5. The statement is more often made than investigated. See for example,

Caroline F. Ware, K.M. Panikkar, and M. Romein, *The Twentieth Century* (New York, 1966), p. 828, but also the provocative challenge in Richard H. Kohn, "The Social History of the American Soldier: A Review and Prospectus for Research," *AHR*, 86 (June 1981), p. 563. Of course military institutions do not reflect civilian society exactly, but what is correctly implied in the traditional aphorism is that military institutions reflect dominant beliefs and attitudes and are shaped in large part by institutions in civilian society.

6. See Theodore Ropp, *War in the Modern World*, rev. ed. (New York, 1962), p. 161; Edward L. Katzenbach, Jr., "The Mechanization of War, 1880–1919," in Melvin Kranzberg and Carroll W. Pursell, Jr., eds., *Technology in Western Civilization*, 2 vols. (New York, 1967), pp. 551ff.; Bernard and Fawn M. Brodie, *From Crossbow to H-Bomb*, rev. ed. (Bloomington, Ind., 1973), passim.

 New weapons and theories of warfare can certainly result in changes in the nature of armies and war, but considered in a vacuum they leave largely unresolved the question of why some are adopted and used and others are not. Weapons technology has been rejected. See Noel Perrin, *Giving up the Gun: Japan's Reversion to the Sword, 1543–1879* (Boston, 1979), especially pp. 25–26, 81, 92. Constraints on the use of poison gas after World War I and even more on nuclear weapons after World War II have been less the result of technological determination or military strategy than politico-military decisions made by national elites. John Ellis van Courtland Moon, "Chemical Weapons and Deterrence: The World War II Experience," *International Security*, 8 (Spring 1984), pp. 3–35; Lawrence Freedman, *The Evolution of Nuclear Strategy* (New York, 1981).

7. This is certainly the theme and rationale for such books as Peter Paret, ed., *Makers of Modern Strategy: From Machiavelli to the Nuclear Age* (Princeton, N.J., 1986). A number of military historians have specifically asserted the primacy of doctrine and command over evolving weapons technology. For example, see Col. Trevor N. Dupuy, *The Evolution of Weapons and Warfare* (London, 1982), esp. pp. 337–43.

8. See Peter Karsten, "The 'New' American Military History: A Map of the Territory, Explored and Unexplored," *American Quarterly*, 36 (Bibliog. Issue, 1984), pp. 389–418. In American military history more studies are needed like Fred Anderson, *A People's Army: Massachusetts Soldiers and Society in the Seven Years' War* (Chapel Hill, N.C., 1984).

9. Samuel P. Huntington, *The Soldier and the State: The Theory and Politics of Civil-Military Relations* (Cambridge, Mass., 1957); and Morris Janowitz's pioneering work, *The Professional Soldier: A Social and Political Portrait* (Glencoe, Ill., 1960), esp. pp. 215–416.

10. Martin Berger, *Engels, Armies, and Revolution* (Hamden, Conn., 1977); Bernard Semmel, *Marxism and the Science of War* (Oxford, 1981); and Sigmund Neumann and Mark von Hagen, "Engels and Marx on Revolution, War, and the Army in Society," in Paret, ed., *Makers of Modern Strategy* (Princeton, N.J., 1986), pp. 262–80. An influential non-Marxist analysis is Stanislav Andrzejewski (now Andreski), *Military Organization and Society*, 2nd ed. (London, 1968; orig. 1954), esp. pp. 20–75.

11. William H. McNeill, *The Pursuit of Power: Technology, Armed Force and Society since A.D. 1000* (Chicago, 1982) tries ambitiously but not always successfully to link demography, commerce, technology, and the power of the State to the transformation of military institutions.

12. See Peter Karsten, "Armed Progressives: The Military Reorganizes for the American Century," in Jerry Israel, ed., *Building the Organizational Society* (New York, 1972), pp. 197–233; and John W. Chambers II, "Conscripting for Colossus: The Progressive Era and the Origin of the Modern Military Draft in the United States in World War I," in Peter Karsten, ed., *The Military in America* (New York, 1980), pp. 275–96.

13. I have modified and applied to America the concept of military format options developed in Finer's "State- and Nation-Building in Europe," Tilly, ed., *Formation of National States*, pp. 84–163.

14. As used in this work, when capitalized the term "State" denotes a centralized organization, employing specialized personnel, controlling a consolidated territory, and achieving recognition as autonomous and integral. Otherwise, "state" refers to the politico-geographic subdivisions comprising the United States.

15. Traditionally American military historians examined their subject's legal and political standing without significant reference to popular legitimacy and public consent; for example, Lt. Col. Marvin A. Kreidberg and Lt. Merton G. Henry, *History of Military Mobilization in the U.S. Army, 1775–1945* (Washington, D.C., 1955), which for all its detail remains primarily a compilation of data, rather than a work of analysis.

16. The rediscovery of the State and *raison d'état* in much recent historiography has reflected ideological differences—from Perry Anderson, *Lineages of the Absolutist State* (London, 1974) and Peter B. Evans, Dietrich Rueschemeyer, and Theda Skocpol, eds., *Bringing the State Back In* (Cambridge, 1985) on the left, to Reinhard Bendix, *Kings or People, Power and the Mandate to Rule* (Berkeley, Calif., 1978); and Gianfranco Poggi, *The Development of the Modern State: A Sociological Introduction* (Stanford, Calif., 1978), in the Weberian center. See also the extended treatments in "The State," *Daedalus*, 108 (Fall 1979), pp. 1–165; and "State Making," *Comparative Studies in Society and History*, 24 (July 1982); Charles Bright and Susan Harding, eds., *Statemaking and Social Movements: Essays in History and Theory* (Ann Arbor, Mich., 1984); and William E. Leuchtenburg, "The Pertinence of Political History: Reflections on the Significance of the State in America," *JAH*, 73 (Dec. 1986), pp. 585–600.

17. See Charles Tilly, "Reflections on the History of European State-Making," in Tilly, ed., *Formation of National States*, pp. 33–83.

18. Leonard Tivey, ed., *The Nation-State: The Formation of Modern Politics* (Oxford, 1981); Michael Palumbo and William O. Shanahan, eds., *Nationalism: Essays in Honor of Louis L. Snyder* (Westport, Conn., 1981).

19. John Gooch, *Armies in Europe* (London, 1980), pp. 1–144; and V.G. Kiernan, "Conscription and Society in Europe before the War of 1914–1918," in M.R.D. Foot, ed., *War and Society: Historical Essays in Honour and Memory of J.R. Western, 1928–1971* (London, 1973), pp. 141–58.

20. Michael Howard, "War and the Nation-state," *Daedalus*, 108 (Fall 1979), p. 102.

21. See Morton Keller, *Affairs of State: Public Life in Late Nineteenth Century America* (Cambridge, Mass., 1977); Stephen Skowronek, *Building a New American State: The Expansion of National Administrative Capacities, 1877–1920* (New York, 1982); Rhodri Jeffreys-Jones and Bruce Collins, eds., *The Growth of Federal Power in American History* (DeKalb, Ill., 1983).

22. The World War I draft has failed to receive adequate study. The account by John Dickinson, a Harvard-trained lawyer with a Princeton Ph.D. in political science, who served with the General Staff during the war, *The Building of an Army: A Detailed Account of Legislation, Administration, and Opinion in the United States, 1915–1920* (New York, 1922), relied solely on the public record and was prescriptive, not analytical. The most widely cited account, David A. Lockmiller, *Enoch H. Crowder: Soldier, Lawyer, and Statesman* (Columbia, Mo., 1955), is an uncritical, often erroneous, biography of the head of Selective Service.

23. Pro-volunteer policy-driven works include Richard Gillam, "The Peacetime Draft: Voluntarism to Coercion," *Yale Review* 57 (June 1968), pp. 495–517; President's Commission on an All-Volunteer Armed Force [Gates' Commission], *Report* (Washington. D.C., 1970), pp. 6, 159–67; Arthur A. Ekirch, Jr., "The Reform Mentality, War, Peace, and the National State," *Journal of Libertarian Studies*, 3 (1979), pp. 55–72; and Martin Anderson with Barbara Honegger, ed., *The Military Draft: Selected Readings on Conscription* (Stanford, Calif., 1982).

    Conversely, the draft is the American tradition for advocates such as U.S., Selective Service System, *Backgrounds of Selective Service: A Historical Review of the Principle of Citizen Compulsion in the Raising of Armies*, Special Monograph, No. 1 (Washington, D.C., 1947), pp. 1–77; Henry J. Sage, "The Drift Toward the Draft," *U.S. Naval Institute Proceedings*, (June 1979), pp. 38–45.

1 / "Soldiers When They Chose to Be," 1607–1861

1. Francis P. Prucha, *The Sword of the Republic: The United States Army on the Frontier, 1783–1846* (Bloomington, Ind., 1977), pp. 6–7; but see also Russell F. Weigley, *History of the United States Army*, rev. ed. (New York, 1984), p. 81.

2. Michael Duffy, ed., "The Military Revolution and the State, 1500–1800," *Exeter Studies in History*, 1 (Exeter, U.K., 1980), esp. pp. 1–9; Michael Howard, *War in European History* (Oxford, 1976), pp. 20–74.

3. Quote from Daniel J. Boorstin, *The Americans: The Colonial Experience* (New York, 1958), p. 349. A guide to the literature is in John Shy, "Armed Force in Colonial North America: New Spain, New France, and Anglo-America," in Kenneth J. Hagan and William R. Roberts, eds., *Against All Enemies: Interpretations of American Military History from Colonial Times to the Present* (New York, 1986), pp. 3–20.

4. To distinguish these special active-duty units from the *general militia*,

some scholars have referred to them as "volunteer militia" or "organized militia," but these labels are misleading. Recent research is sum-
marized in Allan R. Millett and Peter Maslowski, *For the Common
Defense: A Military History of the United States of America* (New York,
1984), pp. 1–20.

5. See William Pencak, *War, Politics and Revolution in Provincial Massachusetts* (Boston, 1981).

6. Fred Anderson, *A People's Army: Massachusetts Soldiers and Society in
the Seven Years' War* (Chapel Hill, N.C., 1984) demonstrates that, unlike
the underclass of the European regular armies, the 2,500 Massachusetts troops in 1756 included large numbers of young men, aged 14–29,
who were sons of yeomen farmers and thus may have been only temporarily, not permanently, propertyless and "poor." It is not clear if this
example was typical.

7. Ibid., pp. 167–195.

8. Bernard C. Nalty, *Strength for the Fight: A History of Black Americans
in the Military* (New York, 1986), pp. 3–9; Jack D. Foner, *Blacks and the
Military in American History* (New York, 1974), pp. 3–5, 264. Timothy H.
Breen, "English Origins and the New World Development: The Case of
the Covenanted Militia in Seventeenth-century Massachusetts," *Past &
Present*, 57 (Nov. 1972), pp. 74–96.

9. James R. W. Titus, "Soldiers When They Chose to Be So: Virginians at
War, 1754–1763," (Ph.D. dissertation, Rutgers University, 1983), pp.
154–65.

10. See Rhys Isaac, *The Transformation of Virginia Society, 1740–1790*
(Chapel Hill, N.C., 1982), pp. 104–10; following based on Titus, "Soldiers
When They Chose to Be So," pp. 154–65.

11. Joseph Doddridge, *Notes on the Settlement and Indian Wars of the
Western Parts of Virginia and Pennsylvania. . . .* 3rd ed. (Pittsburgh, Pa.,
1912), p. 142; the original 1824 version, p. 184, reads "were soldiers
when they choose to be so. . . ."

12. Titus, "Soldiers When They Chose to Be So", p. 228.

13. Lawrence D. Cress, *Citizens in Arms: The Army and the Militia in Amer-
ican Society to the War of 1812* (Chapel Hill, N.C., 1982), ch. 2, but also
Lois G. Schwoerer, *"No Standing Armies!" The Anti-Army Ideology in
Seventeenth-Century England* (Baltimore, 1974).

14. Russell F. Weigley, *The American Way of War: A History of United States
Military Strategy and Policy* (New York, 1973); John Shy, *A People
Numerous and Armed* (New York, 1976), chs. 9, 10; Charles Royster, *A
Revolutionary People at War* (Chapel Hill, N.C., 1979).

15. See "The American Militia: A Traditional Institution with Revolutionary
Responsibilities," in Don Higginbotham, ed., *Reconsiderations of the
Revolutionary War: Selected Essays* (Westport, Conn., 1978), pp. 83–103.

16. T. Jefferson to J. Adams, May 16, 1777, in Lester J. Cappon, ed., *The
Adams-Jefferson Letters*, 2 vols. (Chapel Hill, N.C., 1959), I, pp. 4–5.

17. Allan Kulikoff, "The Political Economy of Military Service in Revolu-

tionary Virginia," paper presented at the Davis Center Seminar, Princeton University, Feb. 17, 1984.

18. J. Adams to T. Jefferson, May 26, 1777, in Cappon, ed., *Adams-Jefferson Letters*, p. 5.

19. Congress sought a regional balance in appointing general officers; see Jonathan G. Rossie, *The Politics of Command in the American Revolution* (Syracuse, N.Y., 1975), pp. 137–39.

20. Charles Lee and Horatio Gates, two former British officers who settled in America and became radical Whigs, supported citizen-soldiers over regulars. Paul David Nelson, "Citizen Soldiers or Regulars: The Views of American General Officers on the Military Establishment, 1775–1781," *MA*, 43 (Oct. 1979), pp. 126–132; and John Shy, "Charles Lee: The Soldier as Radical," in George A. Billias, ed., *George Washington's Generals* (New York, 1964), pp. 25–37.

21. Mark E. Lender, "The Social Structure of the New Jersey Brigade," in Peter Karsten, ed., *The Military in America* (New York, 1980), pp. 27–44, and his references to similar studies.

22. Linda Grant De Pauw, "Women in Combat: The Revolutionary War Experience," *AF&S*, 7 (Winter 1981), pp. 209–226; John Todd White, "The Truth about Molly Pitcher," in James K. Martin & K.R. Stubaus, eds., *The American Revolution: Whose Revolution?* Rev. ed. (New York, 1981), pp. 99–105. Walter H. Blumenthal, *Women Camp Followers of the American Revolution* (New York, 1952).

23. Eventually, the North recruited companies of free blacks and the South labor units of slaves. Perhaps 5,000 or 2 percent of Americans who served in the war were black. Nalty, *Strength for the Fight*, pp. 10–18; Benjamin Quarles, *The Negro in the American Revolution* (Chapel Hill, N.C., 1961).

24. James K. Martin and Mark E. Lender, *A Respectable Army* (Arlington Hts., Ill., 1982), p. 94. In 1778, 40 percent of the New Jersey Brigade were substitutes for draftees.

25. Howard H. Peckham, ed., *The Toll of Independence: Engagements and Battle Casualties of the American Revolution* (Chicago, 1974), says 200,000; C.H. Lesser, ed., *The Sinews of Independence: Monthly Strength Reports of the Continental Army* (Chicago, 1976), pp. 2–56, calculates 175,000.

26. Robert H. Wiebe, *The Opening of American Society: From the Adoption of the Constitution to the Eve of Disunion* (New York, 1984), p. 354, sees only a "wisp of a nation" in the early 19th century. Yehoshua Arieli, *Individualism and Nationalism in American Ideology* (Cambridge, Mass., 1964); and Paul C. Nagel, *One Nation Indivisible: The Union in American Thought, 1776–1861* (New York, 1971). On localism, Ronald Hoffman and Peter Albert, eds., *Sovereign States in an Age of Uncertainty* (Charlottesville, Va., 1981).

27. Cress, *Citizens in Arms*, focuses on political ideology, but see Richard H. Kohn, *Eagle and Sword: The Federalists and the Creation of the Military Establishment in America, 1783–1802* (New York, 1975).

28. John M. Murrin, "The Great Inversion, or Court versus Country: A

Comparison of the Revolution Settlements in England (1688–1721) and America (1776–1816)," in J.G.A. Pocock, ed., *Three British Revolutions: 1641, 1688, 1776* (Princeton, N.J., 1980), pp. 368–453.

29. Don Higginbotham, "The Debate over National Military Institutions: An Issue Slowly Resolved, 1775–1815," William M. Fowler, Jr. and Wallace Coyle, eds., *The American Revolution* (Boston, 1979), pp. 153–168.

30. Cress, *Citizens in Arms*, pp. 76–78 on militia support from David Ramsey and Mercy Otis Warren. The Newburgh "conspiracy" among officers and mutinies by unpaid soldiers exacerbated distrust of standing armies.

31. John K. Mahon, *History of the Militia and the National Guard* (New York, 1983), p. 47.

32. George Washington's "Sentiments on a Peace Establishment," sent to Congress in 1783, has been much studied. Russell F. Weigley, *Towards an American Army: Military Thought from Washington to Marshall* (New York, 1962), pp. 10–14, 237, 274, definitively corrected the misreading by Gen. John McAuley Palmer who "discovered" the 1783 document in the 1920s and misconstrued it as an endorsement for national UMT, an overemphasis of Washington's commitment to citizen-soldiers as opposed to regulars.

33. Cress, *Citizens in Arms*, pp. 90–92, 116–20.

34. Washington's "Sentiments on a Peace Establishment," in John C. Fitzpatrick, ed., *The Writings of George Washington*, 39 vols. (Washington, D.C., 1932) Vol. 26, pp. 374–98; his former generals' 1783 reports are in George Washington MSS, LC. See Cress, *Citizens in Arms*, pp. 78–79.

35. Kohn, *Eagle and Sword*, p. 79.

36. Speech of Edmund Randolph of Virginia, May 29, 1787, in Charles C. Tansill, ed., *Documents Illustrative of the Formation of the Union of American States* (Washington, D.C., 1927), pp. 924–25.

37. For example, the successful anti-impressment riot in Boston in 1747; John Lax and William Pencack, "The Knowles Riot and the Crisis of the 1740s in Massachusetts," *Perspectives in American History*, 10 (1976), pp. 161–214.

38. Hamilton, *Federalist, No. 31*, Mod. Lib. ed. (New York, 1937), p. 190. Analysis of Founders' attitudes towards the draft has usually been part of contemporary debate on the 20th-century draft. Contrast antidraft assessment of Leon Friedman, "Conscription and the Constitution: The Original Understanding," *Michigan Law Review*, 67 (1969), pp. 1493–1552, with the prodraft rejoinder by Michael J. Malbin, "Conscription, the Constitution, and the Farmers: An Historical Analysis," *Fordham Law Review*, 40 (1972), pp. 805–26. For a dispassionate, insightful historical analysis, see Charles A. Lofgren, "Compulsory Military Service Under the Constitution: The Original Understanding," *WMQ*, 3d series, 38 (Jan. 1976), pp. 61–88.

39. Constitution of U.S., Art. I, Sect. 8, which also reserved to the states the appointment of officers and authority over militia training.

40. Mahon, *History of the Militia*, p. 48.

41. For a discussion of this pluralistic conception of the broad socio-political nature of American citizenship, see Yehoshua Arieli, "Nationalism," in Jack P. Greene, ed., *Encyclopedia of American Political History*, 3 vols. (New York, 1984), II, pp. 841–62. John P. Diggins, *The Lost Soul of American Politics: Virtue, Self-Interest, and the Foundations of Liberalism* (New York, 1984), pp. 65–66, claimed that Hamilton also recognized what Tocqueville would later call the privatization of the American character, the affection for family and neighborhood, and the emphasis upon private concerns to the exclusion of the demands of citizenship, public virtue, and the *res publica*. On Madison, see Charles F. Hobson, "The Negative on State Laws: James Madison, the Constitution, and the Crisis of Republican Government," *WMQ*, 3d series, 36 (1979), pp. 233–35.

42. James H. Kettner, *Development of American Citizenship, 1608–1870* (Chapel Hill, N.C., 1978), pp. 3–10, 208, 334–51; Melvin Yazawa, "Citizenship," in Greene, ed., *Encyclopedia of American Political History*, I, pp. 199–209; Peter H. Shuck and Rogers M. Smith, *Citizenship without Consent: Illegal Aliens in the American Polity* (New Haven, 1985), pp. 1–71.

43. See Alexander M. Bickel, "Citizenship in the American Constitution," *Arizona Law Review*, 15 (1973), pp. 369–87, for a provocative assertion that citizenship was not defined in the Constitution because it was "not important."

44. Rowland Berthoff, "Independence and Attachment, Virtue and Interest: From Republican Citizen to Free Enterpriser, 1787–1837," in Richard L. Bushman et al., *Uprooted Americans: Essays to Honor Oscar Handlin* (Boston, 1979), pp. 97–124.

45. Under southern pressure, this first national militia act excluded blacks, although it was not binding. The bloody overthrow of French rule in Haiti by blacks led most American states to exclude blacks from the militia. Nalty, *Strength for the Fight*, pp. 19–20.

46. The Uniform Militia Act of 1792, U.S., *Statutes at Large*, I, 271. A few days earlier, "An Act to Provide for Calling Forth the Militia" reaffirmed that not over three months of federal service could be required. John K. Mahon, *The American Militia* (Gainesville, Fla., 1960), pp. 14–24

47. Historians have largely neglected to study this important military institution. It originated rather haphazardly. In 1791, to suppress the Indians in the Ohio River Valley, Congress authorized some units of short-term federal volunteers, in addition to several hundred regulars and a number of western militiamen, as part of a 2,700-man expedition under MG Arthur St. Clair, authorizing the president to "employ" up to 2,000 such troops "under the denomination of levies." Although the term "levy" in modern times connotes conscription, in this period it meant simply to "raise." See for example Samuel Johnson, *Dictionary of the English Language*, 2d ed. (London, 1755), II, n.p.; James A.H. Murry, ed., *A New English Dictionary on Historical Principles* (Oxford,

1903), VI, pp. 230–31; Alexander Hamilton, *Federalist, No. 22*, p. 133. These "levies"—"presidential militia" Jefferson later called them— were the embryo of the U.S. Volunteers. See Kohn, *Eagle and Sword*, pp. 109–10; Emory Upton, *The Military Policy of the United States* (New York, 1968, orig. 1904), pp. 78–79. When St. Clair's force was ambushed and decimated, Congress in 1792 authorized a new "punitive" expedition against the Indians, tripling the size of the regular army to 5,000 men and again providing for assistance by western militia and units of six-month federal volunteers; this force, under MG Anthony Wayne, decisively beat the Indians at Fallen Timbers in 1794.

48. The most serious disadvantage of the U.S. Volunteers was the difficulty of maintaining veteran units with replacements, as new officers raised new units.

49. Compiled from data in *Statistical History of the U.S.* rev. ed. (Stamford, Conn., 1965), p. 719. On Jeffersonian fears, see Lance Banning, *The Jeffersonian Persuasion* (Ithaca, N.Y., 1978), pp. 92–270.

50. Thomas P. Slaughter, *The Whiskey Rebellion: Frontier Epilogue to the American Revolution* (New York, 1986).

51. Kohn, *Eagle and Sword*, pp. 193–255.

52. Kohn neglects these brutalities; ibid., p. 251.

53. Not until the federal income tax and American entry into World War I did the U.S. government reach the level of the British State in the 1790s, in raising more revenue through direct taxes than through customs duties. Murrin, "Great Inversion," p. 429, citing Mitchell and Deane, *British Historical Statistics*, pp. 386–88; *Statistical History of the U.S.* II, p. 1106.

54. James H. Hutson, "Intellectual Foundations of Early American Diplomacy," in *Diplomatic History*, 1 (Winter 1977), pp. 1–19; Theodore J. Crackel, "Mr. Jefferson's Army, Political Reform of the Military Establishment, 1801–1809," (Ph.D. dissertation, Rutgers University, 1985).

55. Theodore J. Crackel, "Jefferson, Politics, and the Army: An Examination of the Military Peace Establishment Act of 1802," *Journal of the Early Republic*, 2 (Spring 1982), pp. 21–38; and "The Founding of West Point: Jefferson and the Politics of Security," *AF&S* 7 (Summer 1981), pp. 529–43.

56. Thomas Jefferson to William Duane, March 18, 1811, in Albert E. Bergh, ed., *Writings of Thomas Jefferson*, 20 vols. (Washington, D.C., 1907), VIII, p. 30; quoted in Crackel, "Mr. Jefferson's Army," p. 270.

57. Ibid.

58. Technically, the $200,000 annual appropriation (in the 1808 federal budget of $10 million) was the first federal grant-in-aid, but the precedent was not expanded significantly until the 20th century. See Mahon, *History of the Militia*, p. 66.

59. J.C.A. Stagg, *Mr. Madison's War: Politics, Diplomacy, and Warfare in the Early Republic, 1783–1830* (Princeton, N.J., 1983), pp. 3–119.

60. Ibid., pp. 148–54.

61. In Martin *v.* Mott, 12 Wheat. 19 (1827), the Supreme Court of the United States made the definitive decision that the existence of the triggering conditions for calling the militia into federal service is made by the president, not the governors, thus overturning 8 Mass. 548 (1812). On War Dept. ineffectiveness, Stagg, *Mr. Madison's War*, pp. 162–76, 270–80, 456–57, and Irving Brant, *James Madison: Commander in Chief* (Indianapolis, Ind., 1961), pp. 47–50.

62. Daniel Webster to Ezekiel Webster, Dec. 22, 1814, quoted in Stagg, *Mr. Madison's War*, p. 464n; italics in the original.

63. Thomas Jefferson to James Monroe, Oct. 16, 1814, in Paul L. Ford, ed., *Writings of Jefferson*, 10 vols. (New York 1892–99), IX, p. 492.

64. Since 40,000 were to be a short-term defense force, the term "regular" was a misnomer. In reality, the administration was now using it to mean national as opposed to state troops. The Additional Army had become U.S. Volunteers.

65. Monroe submitted several options to Congress in October 1814, but made it clear that the administration wanted the legislators to authorize national conscription so that if the citizen-soldiers could not be obtained voluntarily, the national government could institute a selective draft directly through local county lieutenants.

66. James Monroe to William Giles, Oct. 17, 1814, *American State Papers: Military Affairs* (Washington, D.C., 1832), I, pp. 514–16. Monroe's plan is in U.S. Congress, *Debates & Proceedings*, 13:3rd (Oct. 27, 1814), pp. 483–88.

67. Daniel Webster, speech of Dec. 9, 1814, reprinted in C.H. van Tyne, ed., *Letters of Daniel Webster* (New York 1902), pp. 56–68. Webster later had ambivalent feelings about his role in blocking a national draft. As a growing champion of nationalism, he prevented the anticonscriptionist speech from being published. Publication came long after his death in 1850.

68. So complex was legislative maneuvering and so inadequate contemporary reporting, that leading historical accounts differ dramatically, even as to which bill was adopted. Compare Jack F. Leach, *Conscription in the United States: Historical Background* (Rutland, Vt., 1952), pp. 69–70, 96–97, 115–18; Stagg, *Mr. Madison's War*, pp. 459–66; Kreidberg and Henry, *History of Military Mobilization*, pp. 53–56.

69. Some 86 percent of approximately 528,000 enlistments among Americans in the War of 1812 were in units *not* under direct control of the War Department. See estimate of the Adjutant General of U.S. Army in 1836, cited in Stagg, *Mr. Madison's War*, p. 162. The total figure represented 47 percent of the white male population of the United States, age 16 to 45, but may have included re-enlistments. Mahon, *History of the Militia*, p. 77, estimates 458,000 enlistments.

70. *Historical Statistics of the U.S.* (1965), pp. 7, 737.

71. Kenneth J. Hagan, ed., *In Peace and War: Interpretations of American Naval History, 1775–1984*, 2nd ed. (New York, 1984), pp. 3–106; Robert S. Browning III, *Two If By Sea: The Development of American Coastal Defense Policy* (Westport, Conn., 1983), covering 1816 to 1905.

72. Reports of Calhoun, 1818, and Poinsett, 1837, in Mahon, *History of the Militia*, pp. 80–83; see also Marcus Cunliffe, *Soldiers & Civilians: The Martial Spirit in America, 1775–1865* (New York, 1973), pp. 101–11.

73. War Dept. General Order, Feb. 18, 1820, in Nalty, *Strength for the Fight*, pp. 25–26. In the 1840s, some 47 percent of recruits were immigrants; Weigley, *History of the U.S. Army*, p. 168. In the American Revolution, foreign soldiers had served. Afterwards, except during wartime, aliens were excluded in law, but not always in practice, from the regular army. James B. Jacobs and Leslie Ann Hayes, "Aliens in the U.S. Armed Forces: A Historico-Legal Analysis," *AF&S*, 7 (Winter 1981), p. 188.

74. Mahon, *History of the Militia*, pp. 80–81.

75. U.S. House of Representatives, 26:1st, *House Rept. No. 584* quoted in "Militia of the United States," *New York Review*, VII (Oct. 1840), pp. 277–305.

76. K. Jack Bauer, *The Mexican War, 1846–1848* (New York, 1974), pp. 71, 397, and Mahon, *History of the Militia*, p. 91; American combat forces were 58 percent U.S. Volunteers, 30 percent regulars, and 12 percent militia. Kreidberg and Henry, *History of Military Mobilization*, p. 78.

77. Mahon, *History of the Militia*, p. 92.

78. Alexis de Tocqueville, *Democracy in America*, P. Bradley ed. (New York, 1945), I, p. 228; Daniel Wells, *An Examination of the Messages of . . . the Governor* (Cambridge, Mass., 1833); Lena London, "The Militia Fine, 1830–1860," *MA*, 15 (Fall 1951), pp. 133–44; Paul T. Smith, "Militia of the U.S., from 1846 to 1860," *Indiana Magazine of History*, 15 (March 1919), pp. 20–47.

79. For example, London, "The Militia Fine," 133–44; exceptions are John Hope Franklin, *The Militant South, 1800–1861* (Boston, 1964), pp. 172–86, and Mahon, *History of the Militia*, p. 83. In its initial constitution of 1817, Mississippi made militia membership a prerequisite for the franchise.

80. Foner, *Blacks and the Military*, p. 21.

81. See Cunliffe, *Martial Spirit*, pp. 215–54.

82. Robert F. McGraw, "Minutemen of '61, the Pre–Civil War Massachusetts Militia," *Civil War History*, 15 (1969), pp. 108–12; Stewart L. Gates, "Disorder and Social Organization: The Militia in Connecticut Public Life, 1660–1860" (Ph. D. dissertation, University of Connecticut, 1975).

83. Gooch, *Armies in Europe*, pp. 50–80. After the French revolution, European monarchs wanted reliable armies, loyal to the regime and the social order, as effective instruments against political and economic unrest. Cost-consciousness also contributed to the use of smaller, elite, professional forces rather than mass conscript armies.

84. Skowronek, *Building a New American State*; Bruce Collins, "Federal Power and Economic Policy: Henry Carey and the 1850s," in Jeffreys-Jones and Collins, ed., *Growth of Federal Power*, pp. 36–48. Compared to the aggregate efforts of state and local governments in socio-economic policies and total spending, the federal government was dwarfed

as it continued to be in peacetime until after World War II. See *Historical Statistics of U.S.* (1960), pp. 718–9, 726.

2 / The Civil War Draft and After, 1861–1914

1. John M. Forbes to Gov. John Andrew of Massachusetts, June 1, 1863, in Sarah Forbes Hughes, ed., *The Letters of John Murray Forbes*, suppl. ed., 3 vols. (Boston, 1905), II, pp. 122–23.
2. The rush to enlistment is recounted in Fred A. Shannon's dated work, *The Organization and Administration of the Union Army, 1861–1865,* 2 vols. (Cleveland, 1928), I, pp. 27–50; and more recently, James M. McPherson, *Ordeal by Fire: The Civil War and Reconstruction* (New York, 1982), pp. 149–51, 163–73, 180–83. Figure from U.S. Dept. of War, *The War of the Rebellion: A Compilation of the Official Records of the Union and Confederate Armies,* 148 vols. (Washington, D.C., 1880–1901), Series 3, I, p. 699; hereafter *Official Records.*
3. If based on total enlistments and re-enlistments—approximately 2,700,000—then 94 percent were volunteers. Many women served as nurses and doctors; at least 400 women joined combat units, disguised as men. Agatha Young, *The Women and the Crisis: Women of the North in the Civil War* (New York, 1959), p. 43; see also Ann Douglas Wood, "The War within a War: Women Nurses in the Union Army," *Civil War History* 18 (Sept. 1972), pp. 197–212. An unknown number of wives and children accompanied the armies in their encampments.
4. McPherson, *Ordeal by Fire,* pp. 171–3; Mahon, *History of the Militia,* pp. 10, 30.
5. Isaiah Price, *History of the Ninety-Seventh Regiment, Pennsylvania Volunteer Infantry during the War of the Rebellion, 1861–65* (Philadelphia, 1875), pp. 11–70.
6. Quoted by Mahon, *History of the Militia,* p. 106. The assertion that the Union Army was roughly representative of the population of the North (more particularly among young males, aged 16 to 30) made by McPherson in *Ordeal by Fire,* pp. 181, 359, is challenged by W.J. Rorabaugh, "Who Fought for the North in the Civil War? Concord, Massachusetts, Enlistments," *JAH,* 73 (Dec., 1986), pp. 695–701. Rorabaugh found that the contingent from that town came disproportionately from the propertyless and from clerks, skilled workers, and farm laborers. Another study fails to confirm high enlistment rates among clerks and skilled workers, but confirms the preponderance of propertyless youths. Mark A. Snell, "A Northern Community Goes to War: Recruiting, the Draft, and Social Response in York County, Pennsylvania, 1861–65," (M.A. thesis, Rutgers University, 1987). York County supported its volunteers and their families during and after the war. See also Gerald F. Linderman, *Embattled Courage: The Experience of Battle in the American Civil War* (New York, 1987).
7. Herman Hattaway and Archer Jones, *How the North Won: A Military History of the Civil War* (Urbana, Ill., 1983), p. 114; McPherson, *Ordeal by Fire,* pp. 181–83, 357–59; Albert B. Moore, *Conscription and Conflict in the Confederacy* (New York, 1924).

8. Preliminary analysis suggests the Confederate Army was *not* composed disproportionately of lower-income groups. McPherson, *Ordeal by Fire*, pp. 357–59. However, such an analysis does not indicate whether conscription was *implemented* equitably.

9. That is 11 percent as draftees and 10 percent as substitutes; Moore, *Conscription*, pp. 356–61. The Confederacy enlisted 87 percent of its white males of military age. Hattaway and Jones, *How the North Won*, p. 721.

10. John Morgan Dederer, "The Origins of Robert E. Lee's Bold Generalship: A Reinterpretation," *MA*, 46 (July 1985), pp. 117–23.

11. Scholars are divided on whether Jefferson Davis—and also the centrally administered national draft (instead of nationally coordinated state drafts suggested by Gen. Pierre G.T. Beauregard)—helped or hurt the southern war effort. Many agree Davis and the draft undermined morale in the long run. See the various interpretations in David Donald, "Died of Democracy," in David Donald, ed., *Why the North Won the Civil War* (New York, 1962) p. 81; E. Merton Coulter, *The Confederate States of America, 1861–1865* (Baton Rouge, La., 1950), pp. 313–28, 566–67; Emory M. Thomas, *The Confederate Nation, 1861–1865* (New York, 1979), pp. 147, 212, 224; Richard E. Berringer et al., *Why the South Lost the Civil War* (Athens, Ga., 1986), pp. 3, 30–34, 288, 421–42; Moore, *Conscription*, pp. 13–17; Wilfred B. Yearns, *The Confederate Congress* (Athens, Ga., 1960), pp. 60–66; and Lowell H. Harrison, "Conscription in the Confederacy," *Civil War Times—Illustrated*, 9 (July 1970), pp. 10–18. William T. Auman, "Neighbor against Neighbor: The Inner Civil War in the Randolph County Area of Confederate North Carolina," *North Carolina Historical Review*, 61 (Jan. 1984), pp. 59–92, lists the literature on the extensive draft evasion and resistance, particularly in the mountainous regions of the South.

12. W. T. Sherman to J. Sherman, Feb. 18, 1863 in Rachel Sherman Thorndike, ed., *The Sherman Letters: Correspondence between General and Senator Sherman from 1837 to 1891* (New York, 1894), pp. 191.

13. Gov. C. S. Olden, quoted in Allan Nevins, *The War for the Union* (New York 1959), II, p. 164.

14. W.H. Seward to T. Weed, July 8, 1862 quoted in Frederick W. Seward, *William Henry Seward*, 3 vols. (New York, 1891), III, p. 115.

15. Figures from Kreidberg and Henry, *History of Military Mobilization*, pp. 94, 103. The 520,000 enlistments did not include militia.

16. Jack F. Leach, *Conscription in the United States: Historical Background* (Rutland, Vt., 1952), despite much valuable research lacks a general analytic framework. See also Shannon, *Union Army*, I, pp. 295–300; Nevins, *War for Union*, II, p. 398; and Eugene Murdock, *One Million Men: The Civil War Draft in the North* (Madison, Wis., 1971), pp. 5–6. Even an extensive legislative history fails to examine adequately the pressures for the draft; see James W. Geary, "A Lesson in Trial and Error: The United States Congress and the Civil War Draft, 1862–1865" (Ph.D. dissertation, Kent State University, 1976), pp. 92–96, and "The Enrollment Act and the 37th Congress," *Historian*, 46 (Aug. 1984), pp. 562–82.

17. Henry C. Lea, "Volunteering and Conscription," *U.S. Service Magazine* 1 (March 1864), p. 240. Lea argued that the itinerant poor—who could best be spared and who composed the bulk of European armies—could easily flee from such service in America, but could be enticed to stay on through liberal bounties.

18. Joe H. Mays, *Black Americans and Their Contributions Toward Union Victory in the American Civil War* (Lanham, Md., 1984); Ira Berlin, et al., eds., *Freedom: A Documentary History of Emancipation, 1861–1867. The Black Military Experience*, Series II (Cambridge, Mass., 1982); Robert L. Peterson and John A. Hudson, "Foreign Recruitment for Union Forces," *Civil War History*, 7 (1961), pp. 176–89.

19. W.T. Sherman to U.S. Grant, June 2, 1863, in U.S. Grant, *The Papers of Ulysses S. Grant*, ed. by John Y. Simon, 14 vols. (Carbondale, Ill., 1967–85), VIII, pp. 395–97; Rachel Sherman Thorndike, ed., *The Sherman Letters: Correspondence Between General and Senator Sherman from 1837 to 1891*, (New York, 1894), pp. 111–13, 196–97; Grant to Lincoln, June 19, 1863. *Official Records*, Series 3, III, pp. 386–88. David Donald, ed., *Inside Lincoln's Cabinet: The Civil War Diaries of Salmon P. Chase* (New York, 1954), pp. 109, 162.

20. Even a number of Unionist Democrats repudiated the party's attachment to states' rights and endorsed national conscription. See August Belmont to Thurlow Weed, July 20, 1862, in Thurlow Weed Barnes, ed., *Memoir of Thurlow Weed*, 2 vols. (Boston, 1884), II, pp. 420–21.

21. In the prosperous farm community of Troy, Mich., the 42 percent casualties suffered by local volunteers in 1861–63 stunned the town and—along with a "war weariness" over lack of victory—led Troy to insulate itself from the trauma. In 1863–64, it turned to non-local recruits, hired through bounties, to fill a large proportion of its quotas of soldiers. Not until 1865 with victory in sight did local volunteers again compose the majority of Troy's recruits. Dale Prentiss, "Troy, Michigan, and the Civil War Draft" (Honors Thesis in History, University of Michigan, 1981), pp. 47–57, copy in the Bentley Library, Ann Arbor, Mich. On the disproportionate share of troops and casualties from the Midwest, see governors' complaints and plea for a national draft in *Official Records*, Series 3, II, pp. 212–13, 223; III, p. 893; IV, pp. 1264–65; V, pp. 730–32. As an example of the Army's sense of mission and its hostility to dissenters, the commander of a volunteer Michigan regiment wrote to his brother after the passage of the draft act: "I hope the people of Mich. will none of them be so foolish as to attempt to resist the Draft. The soldiers of this Regt. would in such a case shoot them, if ordered to, with as little hesitation, as if they [were] so many dogs. Such is the feeling throughout the army. It would be hardly possible for the Govt. itself to stop the war now if it desired. We can whip the Rebels & we mean to do it if it takes fifty years." Col. Charles B. Haydon, 2nd Michigan Volunteers, to his brother, May 1, 1863, Charles B. Haydon, "Diary," Bentley Library, Ann Arbor, Mich. For similar, see Maj. Harrision Soule, 6th Michigan Volunteers, entry of Nov. 14, 1863, Soule Diary, Bentley Library; and Gen. William Sherman to Sen. John Sherman, Jan. 25, 1863 in Thorndike, ed., *Sherman Letters*, p. 184.

22. Lorraine A. Williams, "The Civil War and Intellectuals of the North" (Ph.D. dissertation, American University, 1955), pp. 178–90; Frank Freidel, *Francis Lieber: Nineteenth-Century Liberal* (Baton Rouge, La., 1947), p. 348; Stephen E. Ambrose, *Halleck: Lincoln's Chief of Staff* (Baton Rouge, La., 1962), pp. 103–4. For conservatives' support for conscription to restore social order, see *Harper's Weekly*, (March 1861), p. 554; (Aug. 1861), p. 482; (Jan. 1862), pp. 259–64; (Jan. 1863), pp. 273–77; George Frederickson, *The Inner Civil War: Northern Intellectuals and the Crisis of the Union* (New York, 1968), esp. pp. 23–35, 98–112, 130–50; "Conscription and Volunteering as Methods of Recruiting National Armies," *Brownson's Quarterly Review* (Jan. 1863), pp. 55–77; the last item courtesy of Prof. William J. Gillette.

23. Eric Foner, *Politics and Ideology in the Age of the Civil War* (New York, 1980).

24. Lorraine A. Williams, "Northern Intellectual Reaction to Military Rule during the Civil War," *Historian*, 27 (1964–65), pp. 334–49; William H. Seward to Thurlow Weed, July 8, 1862, quoted in Seward, *Seward*, III, p. 115; Weed to Bigelow, July 27, 1862, in John Bigelow, *Retrospections of an Active Life* 5 vols. (New York, 1909), I, p. 521; *New York Times*, Feb. 20, 1863; Weed's Albany (N.Y.) *Evening Standard*, July 7, 1862; and Horace Greeley's New York *Tribune*, July 9, Aug. 5, 9, 1862.

25. Samuel J. Tilden, *Letters and Literary Memorials of Samuel J. Tilden*, 2 vols. (New York, 1908), I, pp. 175–76, 179–84.

26. Richard H. Abbott, "Massachusetts and the Recruitment of Southern Negroes, 1863–1865," *Civil War History*, 14 (1968), pp. 197–210 and Abbott, *Cobbler in Congress: The Life of Henry Wilson, 1812–1875* (Lexington, Ky., 1972), pp. 131–41.

27. Charles Francis Adams, Jr., to his father, July 16, 1862, in W.C. Ford, ed., *A Cycle of Adams Letters, 1861–1865*, 2 vols. (Boston, 1920), I, p. 165.

28. Diary entry of Aug. 11, 1863, Howard K. Beale, ed., *Diary of Gideon Welles*, 3 vols. (New York, 1960), I, p. 397; Abbott, *Cobbler in Congress*, pp. 131–41; *Congressional Globe* (hereafter *Cong. Globe*), 37:3rd, pp. 978, 1213–14, 3095–98; Freidel, *Francis Lieber*, p. 348. Among the generals consulted were William S. Rosecrans and Samuel R. Curtis.

29. Sen. Henry Wilson, *Cong. Globe*, 37:3rd, pp. 995–97.

30. U.S. *Statutes at Large*, XII, p. 731.

31. Wilson in *Cong. Globe*, 37:3rd, p. 737, 978; and Sen. John Sherman of Ohio, in ibid., pp. 734–35; John M. Forbes to H. Wilson, Feb. 11, 1863, and to Gov. John Andrew, June 1, 1863, both in Hughes, ed., *Letters of John Murray Forbes*, pp. 67–68, 122–23. Horace S. Merrill, *Bourbon Leader: Grover Cleveland and the Democratic Party* (Boston, 1957), p. 12. The law did not exempt Quakers and other pacifists; see Edward N. Wright, *Conscientious Objectors in the Civil War* (Philadelphia, 1931).

32. Benjamin P. Thomas and Harold M. Hyman, *Stanton: The Life and Times of Lincoln's Secretary of War* (New York, 1962), p. 280.

33. *Cong. Globe*, 37:3rd, pp. 1001–02.

34. *Cong. Globe*, 37:3rd, pp. 1225, 1261–62, 1291–93; appendix, p. 163.

35. John Sherman to W. T. Sherman, March 20, 1863, in Thorndike, *Sherman Letters*, p. 195.

36. H. Wilson in *Cong. Globe*, 38:1st (January 8, 1864), p. 143.

37. On the NYC draft riots, see Adrian Cook, *The Armies of the Streets: The New York Draft Riots of 1863* (Lexington, Ky., 1974) p. 194, who estimates 119 known deaths. Iver Charles Bernstein, "The New York City Draft Riots of 1863 and Class Relations on the Eve of Industrial Capitalism" (Ph.D. dissertation, Yale University, 1985) was unavailable when the present manuscript was completed.

38. Stanton offered federal troops to governors if they were needed to carry out the draft, stating: "The Government will be able to stand the test even if there should be a riot and mob in every ward of every city." Quoted in Thomas and Hyman, *Stanton*, p. 282.

39. Boston *Daily Advertiser*, July 14, 1863; also William Dusinberre, *Civil War Issues in Philadelphia* (Philadelphia, 1965), pp. 165–78.

40. W. T. Sherman to E. M. Stanton, Sept. 13, 1864, *Official Records*, Series 3, IV, p. 713.

41. Traditional accounts of draft resisters include, U.S. PMG, *Final Report to the Secretary of War*, hereafter PMG, *Final Report* 1866, pp. 4, 30, 75; Journal of the House of Reps., 39:1st (1866), *House Executive Document No. 1*, IV (serial set nos. 1241–52); also in *Official Records*, Series 3, V, pp. 599–932; Murdock, *One Million Men*, pp. 29, 41, 52, 307, 314. For less hostile treatment, see Richard O. Curry, "The Union as It Was: A Critique of Recent Interpretations of the 'Copperheads,'" *Civil War History*, 13 (March 1967), pp. 25–39.

42. Peter Levine, "Draft Evasion in the North during the Civil War, 1863–1865," *JAH*, 67 (March 1981), pp. 816–34.

43. Ibid.; see also Arnold Shankman, *The Anti-War Movement in Pennsylvania, 1861–65* (Rutherford, N.J., 1980); Frank L. Klement, *Dark Lanterns: Secret Political Societies, Conspiracies, and Treason Trials in the Civil War* (Baton Rouge, La., 1984); and, as part of a much larger focus, Jean H. Baker, *Affairs of Party: The Political Culture of Northern Democrats in the Mid-Nineteenth Century* (Ithaca, N.Y., 1983), pp. 113, 138, 146, 319, 338–39.

44. In an uncirculated memorandum, Taney argued that federal and state governments were sovereign and distinct and possessed some powers that were mutually exclusive rather than concurrent. Taney asserted that "the citizen owes allegiance to the general government to the extent of the power conferred on it, and no further. . . ." That power, he claimed, did not include compulsory military service. Roger B. Taney, "Thoughts on the Conscription Law of the United States," MS copy, NYPL. Taney's memorandum was never used. See Carl B. Swisher, *Robert B. Taney* (New York, 1936), pp. 570–71. The national draft was also criticized by some leading constitutional lawyers including Democrats Samuel J. Tilden and George Ticknor Curtis, see Tilden *Letters and Memorials*, I, pp. 175–84.

45. Kneedler *v.* Lane, 45 *Pa. State Reports* 238 (1863).

46. A. Lincoln, "Opinion on the Draft," Sept. 14, 1863, in Roy P. Basler, ed.,

The Collected Works of Abraham Lincoln, 8 vols. (New Brunswick, N.J. 1953), VI, pp. 445–46.

47. Carl Sandburg, *Abraham Lincoln*, 4 vols. (New York, 1939) IV, pp. 370–77, suggested Lincoln kept silent because of the inequity of commutation.

48. One of the three Democratic judges ran for governor, lost, and was replaced on the court by a Republican.

49. Kneedler *v.* Lane, 45 *Pa. State Reports* 275 (1864). Another Republican quoted Vattel's *The Law of Nations* (1760), that "since then a nation is obligated to preserve itself, it has a right to *everything* necessary for its preservation." Ibid., p. 311. Italics in original.

50. PMG, *Final Report* (1866), I, p. 175, 626; figures are rounded off.

51. MacPherson, *Ordeal by Fire*, pp. 409–10.

52. *DAB*, IV, pp. 47–48; also Geary, "A Lesson in Trial and Error," pp. 186–88, 375–79.

53. James G. Blaine in *Cong. Globe*, 38:1st (Feb. 2, 1864), p. 434; similar, ibid., pp. 140, 158, 528; ibid., 37:3rd., p. 1388.

54. Commutation repealed July 1864; Geary, "A Lesson in Trial and Error," pp. 333–40.

55. Thomas Hillhouse, *The Conscription Act Vindicated* (New York, 1863), pp. 14–16, 22–24; yet Hillhouse also supported the commutation clause. For a similar view, see Alexander Hamilton's son James to Edwin M. Stanton, July 16, 1863, in James A. Hamilton, *Reminiscences* (New York, 1869), pp. 563–64. In the N.Y. *Journal of Commerce*, Nov. 18–24, 1863, George B. Butler made the bold assertion—long denied by champions of states' rights—that the Constitution acted directly upon the citizens instead of through the states. "It follows that in every case in which there exists a right and power in the Constitution [such as the authority of Congress to raise and support armies], there is a correlative duty on the part of the citizen." Reprinted as George B. Butler, *The Conscription Act* in *Pamphlets of the Loyal Publication Society* (New York, 1864).

56. W.T. Sherman to Gen. H.W. Halleck, Sept. 17, 1863 in William T. Sherman, *Memoirs of General William T. Sherman*, 2 vols. (New York, 1875), I, p. 340. After re-election, Senator Wilson agreed; *Cong. Globe*, 38:2nd, (July 24, 1864), p. 604.

57. Garrett Davis, *Cong. Globe*, 37:3rd (February 16, 1863), p. 995.

58. On exclusion of different minority groups from the political community, see Schuck and Smith, *Citizenship without Consent*, pp. 62–71

59. U.S., *Statutes at Large*, XIII, p. 9, sec. 18. Compelling declarant aliens, who were still foreign nationals, to serve in the American army was unprecedented and of questionable legality. American courts had held on numerous occasions that "mere declaration of intention" did not confer U.S. citizenship, yet Congress in 1863 made it the basis for imposing the heaviest obligation of citizenship—military service in war. See John Houck, "Comments [on Aliens and Military Service]," *Michigan Law Review*, 52 (Dec. 1955), pp. 265–76; and Michael Walzer, *Obligations: Essays on Disobedience, War, and Citizenship* (Cambridge, Mass., 1970), pp. 99–119.

60. See note No. 18 *supra*. When Massachusetts enlisted southern blacks to reduce its draft quotas, Congress eventually declared that such soldiers would serve in solely national units.

61. See illustrations in Baker, *Affairs of Party*; Berlin, ed., *Freedom*.

62. "Once let the black man get upon his person the brass letters U.S.; let him get an eagle on his button and a musket on his shoulder, and bullets in his pocket, and there is no power on earth or under earth which can deny that he has earned the right to citizenship in the United States." Frederick Douglass, July 6, 1863, quoted in Charles H. Wesley and Patricia W. Romero, *Negro Americans in the Civil War*, in the *International Library of Negro Life and History* (Washington, D.C., 1967), p. 73. See also Mary F. Berry, *Military Necessity and Civil Rights Policy: Black Citizenship and the Constitution, 1861–1868* (New York, 1977); and William J. Gillette, *The Right to Vote: Politics and the Passage of the Fifteenth Amendment* (Baltimore, 1965), pp. 40, 59, 85.

63. *New York Times*, June 22, 1864; see also *Cong. Globe*, 38:1st, p. 257. PMG figures in *Official Records*, Series 3, IV, p. 421. Traditional interpretations that the commutation fee did not protect the poor or working class (Shannon, *Union Army*, I, pp. 298–99, 308; II, pp. 11–14, 21–34) have been modified by Eugene C. Murdock, "Was it a 'Poor Man's Fight'?" *Civil War History*, 10 (1964), pp. 241–45; and Hugh G. Earnhart, "Commutation: Democratic or Undemocratic?" ibid., 12 (1966), pp. 132–42.

64. *Cong. Globe*, 38:1st, p. 3322; Geary, "A Lesson in Trial and Error," pp. 333–40.

65. Geary, "A Lesson in Trial and Error," pp. 355–67, corrects miscalculations in Earnhart, "Commutation: Democratic or Undemocratic?" On the class composition of the Union Army, see W.J. Rorabaugh, "Who Fought for the North in the Civil War? Concord, Massachusetts, Enlistments," *JAH* 73 (Dec. 1986), pp. 695–701; and McPherson, *Ordeal by Fire*, pp. 357–59. On public financial aid for local draftees, see N.Y. *Tribune*, Jan. 2, 1865; Leach, *Conscription in the U.S.*, pp. 311–13; and Eugene C. Murdock, *Patriotism Limited, 1862–1865: The Civil War Draft and the Bounty System* (Kent, Ohio, 1967), pp. 21–24.

66. PMG, *Final Report* (1866), I, p. 95; also Kreidberg and Henry, *History of Military Mobilization*, pp. 109–11.

67. Most Confederate decisions about the army and the draft were made in the first year, before it became a war of attrition.

68. Yancey quoted in David Donald's essay in Bernard Bailyn, et al., *The Great Republic: A History of the American People*, 2 vols. (Boston, 1977), I, p. 714. See also Paul D. Escott, *After Secession: Jefferson Davis and the Failure of Confederate Nationalism* (Baton Rouge, La., 1978); David M. Potter, "Jefferson Davis and the Political Factors in Confederate Defeat," in Donald, ed., *Why the North Won*, pp. 91–112; and Eric L. McKitrick, "Party Politics and the Union and Confederate War Efforts," in W.N. Chambers and W.D. Burnham, eds., *The American Party Systems* (New York, 1968), pp. 152–81.

69. William A. Ganoe, *History of the U.S. Army* (New York, 1924), p. 286; also

Nevins, *War for the Union*, I, p. 465; Murdock, *One Million Men*, pp. 335–36, 344–49.

70. Brevet (temporary) BG James Oakes, head of the draft in Illinois, recommended that to make conscription politically acceptable and militarily efficient in the future, a series of steps be taken including: quotas by states rather than by congressional districts, service for the duration of the war rather than for terms of one to three years, and elimination of bounties, commutation, and substitution. Oakes' report included in PMG, *Final Report* (1866), II, pp. 1–50. In World War I, General Enoch H. Crowder, one of the principal authors of the Draft Act of 1917 and head of Selective Service, 1917–19, adopted these recommendations, and subsequent draft officials proclaimed General Oakes "the father of modern selective service." U.S. SSS, *Selective Service: Historical Background* (Washington, D.C., 1966). This was misleading, for although several of Oakes' suggestions were adopted, the creation of the Selective Service System was the work of General Crowder and a number of other officers and civilians in 1917.

71. Kettner, *Development of American Citizenship*, pp. 334–49, for references to the Civil Rights Act of 1866 and the 14th Amendment, ratified 1868. See also, Robert J. Kaczorowski, "To Begin the Nation Anew: Congress, Citizenship and Civil Rights after the Civil War," *AHR* 92 (Feb., 1987), pp. 45–68.

72. Patrick W. Riddleberger, *1866: The Critical Year Revisited* (Carbondale, Ill., 1979), pp. 151–55, 168; Gillette, *Right to Vote*, pp. 40, 59, 85.

73. Mary R. Dearing, *Veterans in Politics: The Story of the G.A.R.* (Baton Rouge, La., 1952); Weigley, *History of the U.S. Army*, pp. 265–92.

74. The traditional emphasis on army isolation, portrayed by Huntington, *Soldier and the State*, pp. 222–69, is challenged by John M. Gates, "The Alleged Isolation of the U.S. Army Officers in the Late 19th Century," *Parameters* 10 (Sept. 1980), pp. 32–45; Peter Karsten, "Militarization in the U.S., 1870–1914," in John R. Gillis, ed., *The Militarization of the World* (New Brunswick, N.J., forthcoming, 1987). Enlisted men of the regular army were often held in contempt. See "Drink and Disease in the Army," *Literary Digest*, 43 (July 8, 1911), p. 48.

75. See Joseph J. Holmes, "The National Guard of Pennsylvania: Policemen of Industry, 1865–1905," (Ph.D. dissertation, University of Connecticut, 1971); Kenneth R. Bailey, "A Search for Identity: The West Virginia National Guard, 1877–1921," (Ph.D. dissertation, Ohio State University, 1976); and Lowell D. Black, "The Negro Volunteer: Militia Units of the Ohio National Guard, 1870–1954: The Struggle for Military Recognition and Equality in the State of Ohio" (Ph.D. dissertation, Ohio State University, 1976).

76. David Trask, *The War with Spain in 1898* (New York, 1981); Gerald F. Linderman, *The Mirror of War: American Society and the Spanish-American War* (Ann Arbor, Mich., 1974); and the different perspectives in John M. Gates, *Schoolbooks and Krags: The U.S. Army in the Philippines, 1898–1902* (Westport, Conn., 1973), and the more critical, Stuart C.

298   TO RAISE AN ARMY

Miller, *"Benevolent Assimilation": The American Conquest of the Philippines, 1899–1903* (New Haven, Conn., 1982).
77. See the references in Kenneth J. Hagan, ed., *In Peace and War: Interpretations of American Naval History, 1775–1984*, 2nd ed. (Westport, Conn., 1984), pp. 145–204.
78. On the development of the mass conscript army on the continent in the late 19th century, see Michael Howard, "The Armed Forces," in F.H. Hinsley, ed., *The New Cambridge History*, XI, *Material Progress and World-Wide Problems* (Cambridge, 1967). Traditional accounts such as Hoffman Nickerson, *The Armed Horde, 1793–1939* (New York, 1940) and Alfred Vagts, *A History of Militarism*, 2nd ed. (New York, 1959) and the more objective and wide-ranging, Theodore Ropp, *War in the Modern World*, rev. ed. (New York, 1962), pp. 195–206, have been superseded on Germany by Gordon A. Craig, *The Politics of the Prussian Army, 1640–1945* (New York, 1955); supplemented by Martin Kitchen, *A Military History of Germany* (Bloomington, Ind., 1975), and from a different perspective Dennis E. Showalter, "Army and Society in Imperial Germany: The Pains of Modernization," *Journal of Contemporary History*, 18 (Oct. 1983), pp. 583–618. On France, see Richard D. Challener, *The French Theory of the Nation in Arms, 1866–1939*, 2nd ed. (New York, 1965), supplemented by Allan Mitchell, "'A Situation of Inferiority:' French Military Reorganization after the Defeat of 1870," *AHR*, 86 (Feb. 1981), pp. 49–62, and Sanford Kanter, "Sacrificing National Defense to Class Interest: The French Military Service Law of 1872," *MA*, 49 (Jan. 1985), pp. 5–8. The British still relied on voluntarism; see Hugh Cunningham, *The Volunteer Force: A Social and Political History, 1859–1908* (London, 1975), Gwyn Harries-Jenkins, *The Army in Victorian Society* (London, 1977).
79. Gooch, *Armies in Europe*, pp. 109–44; Brian Bond, *War and Society in Europe, 1870–1970* (New York, 1980), pp. 13–99; Eugen Weber, *Peasants into Frenchmen: The Modernization of Rural France, 1870–1914* (Stanford, Calif, 1976), pp. 98–114, 292–302, 475–77.
80. Bvt. MG Emory Upton, who in the 1880s emphasized regulars over amateurs and advocated copying the extended training and the mass conscript-reservist army system of Europe, wound up demoralized and a suicide. Stephen E. Ambrose, *Upton and the Army* (Baton Rouge, La., 1964) and Weigley's fine essay in *Towards an American Army*, pp. 100–126. James L. Abrahamson, *America Arms for a New Century: The Making of a Great Military Power* (New York, 1981). An alternative to Uptonian professionalism in the form of even greater emphasis upon a volunteer citizen-army was proposed by former Union Army general Sen. John A. Logan (Rep.–Ill.) in *The Volunteer Soldier of America* (Chicago, 1887).
81. James E. Hewes, Jr., *From Root to McNamara: Army Organization and Administration, 1900–1963* (Washington, D.C., 1975), pp. 3–21. A good comparative study is James A. Mowbry, "Militiamen: A Comparative Study of the Evolution of Organization in the Canadian and British Voluntary Citizen Military Forces, 1896–1939," (Ph.D. dissertation, Duke University, 1975).

82. U.S., *Statutes at Large*, XXXII, pp. 775–80. See Martha Derthick, *The National Guard in Politics* (Cambridge, Mass., 1965), pp. 22–29. "The Militia Act of 1903," *North American Review*, 177 (Aug. 1903), pp. 278–87.

83. Attorney General George W. Wickersham to Secretary of War Henry L. Stimson, Feb. 17, 1912, in U.S. War Dept., *Annual Reports, 1912*, pp. 147–50, an opinion prepared in large part by Judge Advocate General Enoch H. Crowder.

84. The Volunteer Act of April 25, 1914; U.S., *Statutes at Large*, XXXII, p. 347, adopted in the wake of revolution and civil war in Mexico, especially U.S. military seizure of Vera Cruz in April 1914 which almost led to war. Dickinson, *Building of an Army* pp. 6–8, 22–26; Kreidberg and Henry, *History of Military Mobilization*, pp. 188–89; "The Volunteer Army Bill," *Nation*, 97 (Dec. 25, 1913), pp. 610–11; ibid., 98 (April 30, 1914), p. 400.

3 / The Conscription Crusade, 1914–1917

1. EHC, typescript of speech, n.d. (summer 1917), Enoch H. Crowder MSS, Box 46, University of Missouri, Columbia, Mo. For similar, see *New York World*, April 30, 1917. Voluntary enlistment in the U.S. Army by draft age men was prohibited Dec. 15, 1917. On Aug. 8, 1918, Voluntary enlistment in any service was prohibited and the Selective Service System supplied men for all branches. PMG, *Second Report to the Secretary of War on the Operations of the Selective Service System to Dec. 20, 1918* (Washington D.C., 1919), pp. 4, 6, 227 (hereafter, PMG, *Second Report*).

2. Louisville (Ky.) *Courier-Journal*, April 25, 1917; *Congressional Record* (hereafter *Cong. Rec.*) 65:1st, p. 1123.

3. Louisville (Ky.) *Evening Post*, April 16, 1917, quoted in the New York *American*, April 20, 1917.

4. John P. Finnegan, *Against the Specter of a Dragon: The Campaign for Military Preparedness, 1914–1917* (Westport, Conn., 1974), p. 188; Weigley, *Towards an American Army*, pp. 219–20; contrast with Arthur A. Ekirch, Jr., *The Civilian and the Military* (New York, 1956), p. 180.

5. Kreidberg and Henry, *History of Military Mobilization*, pp. 242, 254, credit MG Hugh L. Scott, chief of staff, and relegate Enoch H. Crowder simply to writer of the statute. General Wood got primary credit from Scott, *Some Memories of a Soldier* (New York, 1928) and Herman Hagedorn, *Leonard Wood: A Biography*, 2 vols. (New York, 1931), II, p. 205; but Lockmiller, *Enoch H. Crowder*, hailed Crowder as responsible.

6. Michael Pearlman, *To Make Democracy Safe for America: Patricians and Preparedness in the Progressive Era* (Urbana, Ill., 1984), focuses on extremists' attempts to revive the nation's "moral character" through UMT. Finnegan, *Specter of a Dragon* provides a broader canvas but ends in 1917. John Garry Clifford, *The Citizen Soldiers: The Plattsburg Training Camp Movement, 1913–1920* (Lexington, Ky., 1972) offers a compelling narrative of the Military Training Camps Association. William H.

Harbaugh, "Wilson, Roosevelt, and American Intervention, 1914–1917," (Ph.D. dissertation, Northwestern University, 1953) is still insightful.

7. Richard A. Preston and Sydney F. Wise, *Men in Arms: A History of Warfare and Its Interrelationships with Western Society*, 4th ed. (New York, 1979), p. 265.

8. "Our Inadequate Army," *Literary Digest*, 49 (July 25, 1914), p. 146; *Historical Statistics of the U.S.*, p. 718.

9. The preparedness movement remains the subject of significant debate. Those who focus on foreign affairs differ over whether its leaders were perceptive "realists" or dangerous "militarists." For the "realist" assessment, see Huntington, *Soldier and the State*, pp. 263–73; Robert E. Osgood, *Ideals and Self-Interest in America's Foreign Relations* (Chicago, 1953), pp. 125–38, 208–11. In a provocative twist, John Milton Cooper, Jr., *The Warrior and the Priest: Woodrow Wilson and Theodore Roosevelt* (Cambridge, Mass., 1983), pp. 297–302, 307–9, concludes that Wilson was the greater "realist." Some who abandon the realist-idealist dichotomy, portray preparedness leaders as perceptive internationalists; Clifford, *Citizen Soldiers*, pp. 35–38. Conversely, Robert H. Ferrell, *Woodrow Wilson and World War I, 1917–1921* (New York 1985), pp. 103, 201, incorrectly dismisses the preparedness movement as mostly partisan politics. Those who label them "militarists" include Walter Millis, *Road to War: America, 1914–17* (Boston, 1935), pp. 92–97, 148–51, 235–59, 426; Merle Curti, *Peace or War: The American Struggle, 1636–1936* (New York, 1936), pp. 234–35; Ekirch, *Civilian and Military*, pp. 156–75. The predominant liberal interpretation has condemned Roosevelt and Wood in 1915–17 as extremists, if not outright "militarists," who glorified force and sought an over-extensive military establishment. See Arthur S. Link, *Wilson*, 5 vols. (Princeton, N.J., 1947–65), III, pp. 592–93; IV, pp. 15–54; David M. Kennedy, *Over Here: The First World War and American Society* (New York, 1980), pp. 17–18, 31–32. Although most scholars see preparedness leaders as active interventionists, one revisionist has recast them somewhat as isolationists, preparing primarily for postwar defense; Finnegan, *Specter of a Dragon*, pp. 3–4, 38–39, 194–95.

Another issue is whether the preparedness movement was "progressive" or "conservative." For the former stance, see Finnegan, *Specter of a Dragon*, pp. 9–10, 24–25, 109–12; Clifford, *Citizen Soldiers*, pp. 195–203; Abrahamson, *America Arms*, pp. 79–83, 103–27, 148–49, 190–92; Pearlman, *To Make Democracy Safe*, pp. 5–6, 12. William E. Leuchtenburg, "Progressivism and Imperialism: The Progressive Movement and American Foreign Policy, 1898–1916," *Mississippi Valley Historical Review* 34 (Dec. 1952), esp. pp. 497–98, claimed militarism and navalism were rooted in the progressive belief in strong government, a linking of militarism and progressivism which has been widely challenged. See the literature listed in Gerald Markowitz, "Progressivism and Imperialism: A Return to First Principles," *Historian*, 37 (Feb. 1975), pp. 274ff. More recently, some have avoided the dichotomy and portrayed preparedness leaders as "cosmopolitans" and "modernizers;" see Karsten, "Armed Progressives," in Israel, ed., *Building the Organizational So-*

ciety, pp. 221–23; Lane, *Armed Progressive*, pp. xiv, 145–55, 237–39; Abrahamson, *America Arms*, pp. xi–xv, 34–36, 188–194. The majority of historians probably agree with Wilson's pre-eminent biographer that most of the preparedness leaders were political and economic conservatives who sought to constrain American democracy; see Arthur S. Link, *Woodrow Wilson and the Progressive Era, 1910–1917* (New York, 1954), pp. 180–81; Robert D. Ward, "The Origins and Activities of the National Security League, 1914–1919," *Mississippi Valley Historical Review*, 47 (June 1960), p. 61; and Kennedy, *Over Here*, pp. 17–18, 30–36.

10. Many historians do not make an explicit connection between the preparedness movement and the selective draft of 1917–18, or simply imply a causal relationship. "The movement for compulsory military training *veered* into the channel of conscription . . .," concluded Chase C. Mooney and Martha E. Lyman, "Some Phases of the Compulsory Military Training Movement, 1914–1920," Mississippi Valley Historical Review, 38 (March 1952), pp. 633–56. The most common explanation is that the draft was an inevitable part of modern mass warfare. See n. 4, *supra*. Conversely, some have adopted a narrow interpretation, attributing Woodrow Wilson's decision for the draft largely to petty partisanship. See Daniel R. Beaver, *Newton D. Baker and the American War Effort, 1917–1919* (Lincoln, Neb., 1966), pp. 27–30. However, political partisanship is too narrow to be useful, and inevitability too sweeping. Much more was involved.

11. Cooper, *Warrior and Priest*, pp. 288–302.

12. See Jack S. Lane, *Armed Progressive: General Leonard Wood* (San Rafael, Calif., 1978), pp. xiv, 145–55, 237–39, although I disagree that Wood was a true "progressive." See EHC to HLS, March 29, 1917, Henry L. Stimson MSS, Yale University, hereafter HLS MSS; "The Truth about Leonard Wood," *Nation*, 110 (May 29, 1920).

13. Colmar von der Goltz, *The Nation in Arms* (Berlin, 1883; London, 1903), pp. 128–32, 380–81; Hagedorn, *Wood*, I, p. 398; II, pp. 87, 94. On Upton, see ch. 2, n. 80, *supra*.

14. Hagedorn, *Wood*, I, p. 398; Lane, *Armed Progressive*, pp. 116–17. Wood and Roberts were observers of German Army maneuvers in 1902.

15. R.J.Q. Adams, "The National Service League and Mandatory Service in Edwardian Britain," *AF&S*, 12 (Fall 1985), pp. 53–74; but see also the provocative critique by Theodore Ropp, "Conscription in Great Britain, 1900–1914: A Failure in Civil-Military Communications?" *MA*, 20 (Summer 1956), pp. 71–76. On the creation of a new volunteer reserve system (the "Territorials"), see Edward M. Spiers, *Haldane: An Army Reformer* (Edinburgh, 1980).

16. Lane, *Armed Progressive*, pp. 156–96; Clifford, *Citizen Soldiers*, pp. 1–92; see also "Report of the Organization of the Land Forces of the United States," prepared at Wood's direction by the War College Division (hereafter WCD) of the General Staff (hereafter GS), Aug. 10, 1912; in U.S., WD, *Annual Reports, 1912* (Washington, D.C., 1912), pp. 65–182.

17. This profile of the conscriptionist leadership is based upon a list of 42 leaders who held offices or positions on the executive boards in the

organizations devoted to universal military training or who were otherwise recognized as leading champions of UMT within the military or civilian society. Biographical data obtained from *DAB, National Cyclopedia of American Biography, Who's Who in America*, and obituaries in *New York Times* and *Chicago Tribune*. For the list and a fuller analysis, see John |Whiteclay Chambers II, "Conscripting for Colossus: The Adoption of the Draft in the United States in World War I" (Ph.D. dissertation, Columbia University, 1973), pp. 61–63, 395. An adaptation and modification of this compilation is in Pearlman, *To Make Democracy Safe*, pp. 5, 9n. 12, 271–75.

18. The list of leading conscriptionists and a full socio-economic and political profile is also available in John Whiteclay Chambers II, *To Raise an Army: The Draft Comes to Modern America*, enlarged version, (New Brunswick, N.J., bound photocopy, 1987), ch. 3, and Appendix, available through interlibrary loan from Alexander Library, Rutgers Univ., New Brunswick, N.J. 08903. In regard to the exclusion of women, the psychological and cultural-political dimensions of this action have not yet received the attention they deserve, but many of the interpretations of Cynthia Enloe, *Does Khaki Become You?* (Boston, 1983), pp. 10–17, 21–23 and passim are relevant. Barbara J. Steinson, *American Women's Activism in World War I* (New York, 1982), esp. pp. 163–218, includes a study of women's auxiliary groups linked to the major preparedness organizations or patriotic societies such as the Daughters of the American Revolution. Female preparedness advocates often were wives or daughters of male preparedness leaders, and generally held conservative political, social, and economic views. Many were anti-suffragists as well as anti-pacifists and opposed the claim of radical feminists and pacifists like Jane Addams and other leaders of the Woman's Peace Party to speak for American women. Accepting child-rearing and homemaking as women's primary roles, they argued that wives and mothers should also support the military defense of their homes and homeland. See Frances Kellor, *Straight America—A Call to National Service* (New York, 1916), pp. 179–89.

19. Finnegan, *Specter of a Dragon*, pp. 25-27, gives excessive credit to A.P. Gardner; John C. Edwards, *Patriots in Pinstripes: Men of the National Security League* (Washington, D.C., 1982) pp. 1–17, to S.S. Menken. In addition to Root, HLS, and Bacon, the real leadership included Wall Street lawyers Herbert Barry, Frederic R. Coudert, and Charles Lydecker. Root described Menken as simply "a good-natured chucklehead." Elihu Root to George Wharton Pepper, Aug. 8, 1918, Elihu Root MSS, LC, Box 136.

20. National Security League (hereafter NSL), *Officers, Committee, and Branches* (New York, 1915); see also Military Training Camps Association (hereafter MTCA) *List of Members of Camp of Instruction, Regular Troops, Plattsburg, N.Y., Aug. 10–Sept. 6, 1915*, undated pamphlet in the John Purroy Mitchel MSS, LC, Box 49. Huntington, *Soldier and the State*, and Finnegan, *Specter of a Dragon*, greatly underestimate the importance of the new corporate and professional elites in the preparedness movement.

21. On the wealthy donors and their contributions, see congressional audit of the NSL in U.S. Congress, House Special Committee to Investigate the NSL, *National Security League: Hearings*, 65:3rd, 2 vols. (Washington, D.C., 1919), pp. 2044–45, 2060–65; MTCA, *Report of the Treasurer, Nov. 10, 1916*, pamphlet in A. Lawrence Lowell MSS, File #1273, Harvard University Archives; LTG S.B.M. Young to TR, Oct. 26, 1916, TR MSS, Reel 215 (on the Association for National Service); George W. Perkins to TR, July 22, 1916, TR MSS, Reel 212; Guy Emerson to TR, Aug. 15, 1916, and enclosure, UMTL, *Universal Military Training League* (undated pamphlet, c. 1916) in ibid., Reel 213; Guy Emerson, "Memoir," Columbia Oral History Collection, pp. 94–96; Emerson to HLS, Nov. 27, 1916, and HLS to John Crosby, Jan. 31, 1917, both in HLS MSS. See full listing in Chambers, "Conscripting for Colossus" (1973), pp. 52–60.

22. Clifford, *Citizen Soldiers*, p. 62, for ideal of public service. Pearlman, *To Make Democracy Safe*, pp. 35–114, probes psychological drives and domestic concerns, but ignores foreign policy.

23. Quote from Grenville Clark to DeLancey Jay, May 29, 1915, Grenville Clark MSS, Dartmouth College, Hanover, N.H. See also Samuel Gompers to Leonard Wood, Sept. 15, Oct. 6, 1915, Leonard Wood MSS, LC, and John Garry Clifford, "Leonard Wood, Samuel Gompers, and the Plattsburg Training Camps," *New York History* (April 1971), pp. 169–89.

24. Grenville Clark to Thomas W. Miller, March 11, 1916, Clark MSS.

25. Charles W. Eliot, "Shall We Adopt Universal Military Service?" *World's Work*, 33 (Nov. 1916), pp. 16–17.

26. Theodore Roosevelt, *An Autobiography* (New York, 1913), p. 580; Philip C. Jessup, *Elihu Root*, 2 vols. (New York, 1938), II, pp. 274–76.

27. NSL, *Proceedings of the National Security Congress* (Washington, D.C., 1916), pp. 90–91. See also Sidney Ballou, *Compulsory Military Training and Service*, Navy League pamphlet, No. 125 (Washington, D.C., 1916), p. 5.

28. My conclusion is drawn from a reading of published and unpublished views on foreign policy, 1910–1920, by leading conscriptionists of 1915–17. A sampling includes: Joseph H. Choate, "The Right and Duty of Self-Defense," *North American Review*, 201 (March 1915), pp. 363–65; Herbert Barry, "Christianity—International Relations—The Duties of the Nation and the Citizen," address before the American Church Congress, May 5, 1916, reported in SMAC, *UMT: Hrgs.*, 64:2nd (Washington, D.C., 1917), pp. 469–73; Sen. George E. Chamberlain in NSL, *Proceedings of the National Security Congress*, pp. 209–19. Frederic R. Coudert, Philadelphia *Public Ledger*, Dec. 23, 1916, and typescript n.d., pp. 35–36, in Frederic R. Coudert MSS, Vol. 9, Columbia University; Charles W. Eliot to Joseph Choate, April 17, 30, 1917, Joseph H. Choate MSS, Box 13, LC; Leonard Wood to L.S. Rowe, Sept. 30, 1915, Wood MSS, Box 85.

29. Among the most ardent interventionist-conscriptionists were Lyman Abbott, editor of *Outlook*, James Beck, Bacon, Choate, Coudert, George Harvey (conservative editor of the *North American Review*), John G. Hibben, president of Princeton University, Henry Cabot Lodge, Ralph Barton Perry (Harvard philosopher), Stimson, Roosevelt, Root, and

Wood. Given the anti-interventionist mood in America, they could not express publicly what many of them said privately. See Elting E. Morison and John M. Blum, eds., *The Letters of Theodore Roosevelt*, 8 vols. (Cambridge, Mass., 1951–53), VIII, pp. 829–30 (hereafter Morison, ed., *Letters of T. Roosevelt*). Their interventionism also explains why they wanted large numbers of reserve officers as quickly as possible.

30. One exception was scholar-diplomat David Lewis Einstein, who published anonymously before the war, *American Foreign Policy by a Diplomatist* (Boston, 1909), esp. pp. 14, 58, 119; in *A Prophecy of the War, 1913–1914* (New York, 1918), pp. 66–67, Einstein favored conscription.

31. Testimony, Jan. 31, 1917, U.S. Cong., House and Senate Committees on Military Affairs, *UMT: Statements Made by Maj. Gen. Leonard Wood before the Committees* (Washington, D.C., 1917), p. 1101. On evaluation by the General Staff, see BG M.M. Macomb, chief, WCD, Memorandum for CofS, Feb. 29, 1916, subj: Possible Rupture with Germany, WCD, 9433–1, GS Records (RG 165), WCD, Genl. Corres., 1903–1919, Box 444, National Archives (hereafter NA), Washington, D.C.

32. Hudson Maxim, *Defenseless America* (New York, 1915), pp. 76–80; Eric Fisher Wood, *The Writing on the Wall* (New York 1916). "Battle Cry of Peace," *Outlook*, 3 (Sept. 22, 1915), pp. 165–66.

33. Frederick L. Huidekoper, *The Military Unpreparedness of the United States: A History of the American Land Forces from Colonial Times Until June 1, 1915* (New York, 1915).

34. Frederic Coudert, "Proposed Reorganization of the National Guard," *Journal of the Military Service Institution*, 24 (March 1899), pp. 239–45; "Memorandum re Constabulary Bill for Mr. Smith of Evening Post," Jan. 22, 1914 in Coudert MSS, Reel 2; HLS to Samuel Gompers, Feb. 6, 1917, and N.L. Hosford to HLS, Feb. 17, 1917, HLS MSS; Charles W. Eliot and TR, *New York Times*, Jan. 6, 1916 and March 11, 1917.

35. HLS to Walter L. Fisher, Jan. 23, 1917, HLS MSS.

36. Testimony, Jan. 31, 1917, in House and Senate Military Affairs Committees, *UMT: Gen. Wood*, p. 998.

37. Ralph Barton Perry, *The Free Man and the Soldier: Essays on the Reconciliation of Liberty and Discipline (New York, 1916), p. 161.*

38. John Whiteclay Chambers II, *The Tyranny of Change: America in the Progressive Era, 1900–1917* (New York, 1980), pp. 40–42, 107–9.

39. Gunther E. Rothenberg, "Moltke, Schlieffen, and the Doctrine of Strategic Envelopment," and Michael Howard, "Men against Fire: The Doctrine of the Offensive in 1914," in Paret, *Makers of Modern Strategy*, pp. 296–325 and 510–26.

40. TR to H.H. Sheets, Nov. 27, 1915, TR MSS, Reel 359.

41. Peter Paret, "Conscription and the End of the Old Regime in France and Prussia," paper delivered at Davis Center, Princeton Univ., Nov. 19, 1982. See also ch. 2, n. 78, 79, *supra*.

42. Henry S. Hooker, Wall Street lawyer and partner of Langdon P. Marvin and Franklin D. Roosevelt, to WW, Dec. 1, 1916, Woodrow Wilson MSS (hereafter WW MSS), Series VI, LC.

43. TR quoted in "The Movement for Universal Military Training," *Current Opinion*, 61 (Aug. 1916), p. 78.

44. Henry Cabot Lodge to TR, July 2, 1908, April 19, 1910; and Lodge to John T. Morse, Jr., Dec. 14, 1912, in William C. Widenor, *Henry Cabot Lodge and the Search for an American Foreign Policy* (Berkeley, Calif., 1980), pp. 154, 169.

45. Walter Lippmann, *Drift and Mastery: An Attempt to Diagnose the Current Unrest* (New York, 1914); Ronald Steel, *Walter Lippmann and the American Century* (Boston, 1980), pp. 65–67, 77–81; Kenneth McNaught, "American Progressives and the Great Society," *JAH*, 53 (1966), p. 512; Terence H. Qualter, *Graham Wallas and the Great Society* (New York, 1979), pp. 170–71; Jean B. Quandt, *From Small Town to the Great Community: The Social Thought of Progressive Intellectuals* (New Brunswick, N.J., 1970), esp. pp. 17–66, 102–159; Thomas Bender, *Community and Social Change in America* (New Brunswick, N.J., 1978), pp. 8–39, 136–39.

46. Barry D. Karl, *The Uneasy State: The U.S. from 1915 to 1945* (Chicago, 1983), pp. 9–49, 225–39; Ellis W. Hawley, *The Great War and the Search for a Modern Order* (New York, 1979); Skowronek, *Building a New American State*, pp. 3–46, 163–292; Chambers, *Tyranny of Change*, pp. 105–39.

47. Charles Nagel, *Speeches and Writings, 1900–1928*, ed. by Otto Heller, 2 vols. (N.Y., 1931), I, p. 35; Arthur T. Hadley, *Undercurrents in American Politics* (New Haven, Conn., 1915), pp. 125–26; Norman M. Wilensky, *Conservatives in the Progressive Era: The Taft Republicans of 1912* (Gainesville, Fla., 1965), pp. 32–50; Widenor, *Lodge*, pp. 9, 22–30, 53–64, 309–26, 350.

48. Elihu Root, "The Citizen's Part in Government," May 21, 1907, in Root, *Addresses on Government and Citizenship*, ed. by Robert Bacon and James B. Scott (Cambridge, Mass., 1916), pp. 70, 9–10.

49. Elihu Root, "Public Service by the Bar," Aug. 30, 1916, in ibid., p. 539. Italics added.

50. Root, "Citizen's Part in Government," in ibid., pp. 6, 12.

51. Frank A. Vanderlip, *The Need for a United Nation* (n.p., 1916), pp. 14–15, 9–11; italics added. Daniel Guggenheim, "Some Thoughts on Industrial Unrest," *Annals of the American Academy of Political and Social Science*, 59 (May 1915), pp. 209–11; *Magazine of Wall Street*, 19 (Oct. 14, 1916), p. 75.

52. Root, *Addresses*, pp. 74–76; *New York Times*, Oct. 17, 1915; Edward G. Hartmann, *The Movement to Americanize the Immigrant* (New York, 1948), pp. 112–39.

53. Henry Breckinridge, "Solving the Hyphen," *Forum*, 55 (Nov. 1916), pp. 583–88. TR to Capt. George V.H. Moseley, Jr., Nov. 17, 1915, G.V.H. Moseley MSS, LC.

54. The pattern was repeated in the Cold War era of the 1950s and the Vietnam War era in the sixties. In 1971, the 26th Amendment awarded the vote at age 18.

55. Frederic R. Coudert, "Our New Peoples: Citizens, Subjects, Nationals, or Aliens?" 3 *Columbia Law Review* 13 (1903).

56. J. Morgan Kousser, *The Shaping of Southern Politics: Suffrage Restriction and the Establishment of the One-Party South, 1880–1910* (New Haven, Conn., 1974); Milton R. Konvitz, *The Alien and the Asiatic in American Law* (Ithaca, N.Y., 1946), pp. 79–97, 148–70; Arnold J. Lien, "The Acquisition of Citizenship by the Native American Indians," *Washington University Studies*, 13 (1925); Virginia Shapiro, "Women, Citizenship, and Nationality: Immigration and Naturalization Policies in the United States," *Politics & Society*, 13 (1984), pp. 1–26.

57. L. Wood to TR, March 5, 1915, TR MSS, Reel 199; ibid, Dec. 13, 1905, Reel 61; Wood, *Military Obligation of Citizenship*, p. 63; and *Universal Military Training* (New York, 1917), pp. 67–68.

58. Lucien Howe, *Universal Military Education and Service*, 2nd ed. (New York, 1917), pp. 61–62.

59. More was published about U.S. citizenship than at any other time. A sampling: Nathaniel S. Shaler, *The Citizen: A Study of the Individual and the Government* (New York, 1904); Josiah Royce, *The Philosophy of Loyalty* (New York, 1908); Henry Van Dyke, *The Spirit of America* (New York, 1910); Samuel W. McCall, *The Liberty of Citizenship* (New Haven, Conn., 1915).

60. While the South destroyed second-class citizenship by eliminating blacks from the polity entirely, the North strengthened an apprentice citizenship, urging immigrants from southern and eastern Europe to follow the leadership of Anglo-Saxon citizens; see David W. Noble, *The Progressive Mind, 1890–1917*, rev. ed., (Minneapolis, 1981), pp. 72–74, 102–103. Many conscriptionists were active leaders in the Immigration Restriction League and National Americanization Committee.

61. WW, "The Meaning of Citizenship," May 10, 1915, in Woodrow Wilson, *The Papers of Woodrow Wilson*, Arthur S. Link, et al., eds., 56 vols. to date (Princeton, N.J., 1966–), (hereafter, Link, *PWW*), 33, pp. 147–50.

62. Ibid.

63. Arieli, "Nationalism," in Greene, ed., *Encyclopedia American Political History*, pp. 841–62.

64. David P. Thelen, *The New Citizenship: Origins of Progressivism in Wisconsin, 1885–1900* (Columbia, Mo., 1972) and Thelen, *Robert M. La Follette and the Insurgent Spirit* (Boston, 1976).

65. For radical attempts to keep the ideal of a democracy of producers among farmers and workers (as worker-owners), see Lawrence Goodwyn, *Democratic Promise: The Populist Movement in America* (New York, 1976), and Leon Fink, *Workingman's Democracy: The Knights of Labor and American Politics* (Champaign, Ill., 1982).

66. Thomas K. McCraw, *Prophets of Regulation* (Cambridge, Mass., 1984); Charles Forcey, *The Crossroads of Liberalism: Croly, Weyl, Lippmann and the Progressive Era, 1900–1925* (New York, 1961).

67. Joseph H. Choate, later honorary president of the NSL, had successfully argued the case against the federal income tax in 1895.

68. MTCA, *Constitution, By-Laws, Committees* (New York 1916), p. 1, Clark MSS, Series II, Box 36, emphasizing UMT for "promoting internal order, cohesion, and good citizenship."

69. Wood, *Universal Military Training*, p. 94.

70. Conscriptionists played an active role in the efficiency movement. Samuel Haber, *Efficiency and Uplift: Scientific Management in the Progressive Era, 1890–1920* (Chicago, 1964), pp. ix, 68, 71–75, 106–10.

71. Henry C. Emery, Yale economist, former chair of the U.S. Tariff Board, "The Economic Value of Universal Service," *Proceedings of the National Security Congress*, pp. 108–9.

72. W.D. Earnest, testimony, Jan. 11, 1917, U.S. Cong., SMAC, *UMT: Hrgs.*, 64:2nd, 1917, p. 448; Wood, *UMT*, pp. 95–96. Some advocated UMT as part of a larger program of "industrial preparedness." Guy Emerson, a banker and a founder of the Universal Military Training League, confided that "[U]nless there is cooperation between government and business of the most frank and intelligent sort, the leaders of Business in this country believe we will be forced into a subordinate position in the world's affairs." Emerson to TR, May 11, 1916, in Emerson, "Memoir" COHC, p. 124. See also George W. Perkins, "All-Around Preparedness," press release, Feb. 2, 1916, Perkins MSS Box 27; Frank A. Vanderlip, to Edward R. Wood, Jan. 10, 1916, Vanderlip MSS; *Magazine of Wall Street*, 19 (Nov. 25, 1916), p. 236; *Manufacturers Record*, 70 (Dec. 14, 1916), pp. 39–40.

73. Malcolm Jennings to Warren G. Harding, April 5, 1916, Warren G. Harding MSS, Ohio Historical Society, Columbus, O., Reel 261.

74. William T. Hornaday, Brooklyn *Daily Eagle*, Dec. 6, 1915, p. 5, clipping, TR MSS, Reel 202. Several conscriptionists helped build up the Boy Scouts. On Boy Scouts: David I. Macleod, *Building Character in the American Boy: The Boy Scouts, YMCA, and Their Forerunners, 1870–1920* (Madison, Wis., 1983).

75. Perry, *Free Man and the Soldier*, p. 16.

76. TR in NSL, *Proceedings of the National Security Congress*, p. 88.

77. Grenville Clark, "Remarks at the Organizational Meeting of the Business and Professional Men's First Training Regiment," Sept. 1, 1915, typescript Clark MSS, series II, Box 6.

78. HLS to BG John F. Morrison, Nov. 22, 1916 and to George Harvey Putnam, Nov. 15, 1916, both in HLS MSS.

79. HLS to Putnam, Nov. 15, 1916, HLS MSS; also Joseph Choate to Thompkins McIlvaine, Jan. 20, 1916, Clark MSS, Series II, Box 1.

80. HLS to G.A. Slater, March 20, 1916, HLS MSS. "The urgent need for a system of National Military Training for America is not military at all, but economic. In my use of the term National Military Training, I do not

mean simply the drill—a proficiency in the drill can be acquired in a very short time by the American youth—but the forming of habits of personal hygiene, discipline and respect for authority and, through service to the State, a love of and devotion to the fundamental ideals of Democracy." LTG S.B.M. Young (U.S.A., Retired), pres., Assn. for Natl. Service, to Capt. George V.H. Moseley, Gen. Staff, June 16, 1916, copy in Moseley MSS. For similar, Wood, testimony, Jan. 31, 1917, HMAC & SMAC, *UMT: Gen. Wood*, p. 1078; Grenville Clark to Lyman Abbott, April 8, 1916, Clark MSS, Series, II, Box 1.

81. Possibly as Clifford, *Citizen Soldiers*, pp. 37–38, suggests, if the United States already had a large, pretrained force, Germany might not have sunk American ships. However, Germany might have been desperate and reckless enough in early 1917 to hope to sink transports too.

82. On the nature of "militarism," see Volker R. Berghahn, *Militarism: The History of an International Debate, 1861–1979* (Leamington Spa, U.K., 1981). It is possible to consider Theodore Roosevelt, particularly in his unrestrained periods, as being to some extent an anti-materialistic "militarist," but this overlooks the consciously forward-looking purposes of Roosevelt and most other preparedness leaders. It is also true that a pyschological interpretation based on the concept of "negative identity" may help to understand the aggressive pursuit of masculine roles and intense denigration of weakness and "feminine" sentimentality, particularly by Roosevelt, Wood, and Guy Emerson. See the data in Harbaugh, *Roosevelt*; Hagedon, *Wood*, I, pp. 5–11, 18–19, 23, 28–29; Emerson, "Memoir," COHC, p. 2. In my view, the preparedness leaders aimed primarily at specific policies directly related toward America's national unity, potential military strength, and international position.

83. Grenville Clark's life and values stood squarely against "militarism" and he directly repudiated such a charge. "Remarks of Grenville Clark . . . September 1, 1915" typescript, p. 4, Clark MSS, Series II, Box 6. Few conscriptionist organizations were directly connected with munitions companies and the NSL apparently rejected contributions from them for fear of adverse publicity. "[We are] keeping our shirts entirely free from any tainted money. . . ." HLS to George W. Pepper, Jan. 5, 1917, HLS MSS.

84. For a fuller development of this typology, see John W. Chambers, ed., *The Eagle and the Dove: The Peace Movement and U.S. Foreign Policy. 1900–1922* (New York, 1976), pp. 1–80.

85. Elihu Root typified the Taft Republicans and Cleveland Democrats who dominated the UMT movement; so did Sen. James W. Wadsworth (Rep.-N.Y.), see his "The Duty of a True Democracy," in NSL, *Universal Obligatory Military Training and Service* (New York, 1916), p. 14. The few UMT leaders who considered themselves progressives represented the eastern business wing of the progressive movement and advocated UMT&S not simply for reasons of foreign policy and domestic order, but, as a self-styled progressive on the Federal Trade Commission con-

fided in 1916: "If military service and cooperation for the struggle of war and the competition of peace will stimulate in this country a collective spirit, we will lay a foundation for further steps in social reform. . . . The people are not yet prepared. They still cling to mistaken ideas about individual rights and perhaps there is no better way for them to be rid of these than by a period of wars and rumors of wars." Will Culbertson to TR, April 20, 1916, TR MSS, Reel 208. For the positions of specific progressives on UMT, see Chambers, "Conscripting for Colossus," (1973), pp. 396–7; and Chambers, *To Raise an Army*, enlarged edition, Appendix, cited in Note 18 *supra*.

86. Other conservative reform movements included those for immigration restriction and social purity. Many conservatives, as well as progressives, were leaders in movements for prohibition, eugenics (sterilization for population and social control), and compulsory Americanization.

87. This study lends support to the importance of a cosmopolitan "new middle class" described by Robert H. Wiebe, *The Search for Order, 1877–1920* (New York, 1967), pp. 111–32. It also demonstrates the considerable influence of the new corporate and professional elites, although it differs from Gabriel Kolko, *The Triumph of Conservatism, 1900–1918* (Boston, 1968) on the amount of cooperation between big business and the national government and the degree of success achieved by the corporate leaders.

88. Although they had given lip service to the citizen-soldier ideal, Federalists like Washington and Hamilton had not sought UMTS but rather a professional army with a selected reserve.

89. The "Associative State" is a phrase used by Ellis W. Hawley, "The Corporative Component of the American Quest for National Efficiency, 1900–1917," paper presented at the annual conference of the Organization of American Historians, NYC, April 11, 1986.

90. John L. Thomas, *Alternative America: Henry George, Edward Bellamy, Henry Damarest Lloyd and the Adversary Tradition* (Cambridge, Mass., 1983), pp. 243–73.

91. Karsten, "Militarization in the U.S.," in Gillis, ed., *Militarization of the World*; see also Wallace E. Davies, *Patriotism on Parade: The Story of Veterans' and Hereditary Organizations in America, 1783–1900* (Cambridge, Mass., 1955), pp. 215–48, 310–58 and passim.

4 / Resistance and Reform, 1914–1917

1. "Preparedness and Politics," *Literary Digest*, 51 (Nov. 20, 1915), pp. 1143–45.

2. U.S. WD, *Annual Reports, 1915*, pp. 25–27; Rep. T. W. Miller to Grenville Clark, Dec. 20, 1915, Clark MSS, Series II, Box 4.

3. On the controversy, see William E. Dodd to William J. Bryan, May 17, 1916, Bryan MSS, Box 31; Joseph H. Choate to Lord Mount Stephen, July 11, 1916, Choate MSS, Box 15; Link, *Wilson*, III, pp. 592–93; Cooper,

Warrior and Priest, pp. 274, 297–300; Ferrell, *Wilson and World War I*, p. 103.

4. WW to Lindley M. Garrison, Aug. 19, 1915, Link, *PWW*, 34, p. 248; on Democrats' warnings, see Ray S. Baker, *Woodrow Wilson: Life and Letters*, 8 vols. (Garden City, N.Y., 1927), VI, pp. 13, 19.

5. *New Republic*, 4 (Aug. 28, 1915), pp. 82–83.

6. Scholars now emphasize that Wilson had long supported U.S. politico-economic activism in world affairs, but that he grew to recognize the limited effectiveness of military intervention. Arthur S. Link, *Woodrow Wilson: Revolution, War, and Peace* (Arlington Hts., Ill., 1979), pp. 3–13; Lloyd C. Gardner, *Safe for Democracy: The Anglo-American Response to Revolution, 1913–1923* (New York, 1984), pp. 35–44; Cooper, *Warrior and Priest*, pp. 267–71; and Frederick S. Calhoun, *Power and Principle: Armed Intervention in Wilsonian Foreign Policy* (Kent, O., 1986), pp. 250–67.

7. Baker, *Wilson*, VI, p. 8; also WW to John B. Walker, May 5, 1915.

8. MG H.L. Scott to Maj. J.A. Ryan, May 25, 1915, Scott MSS, Box 18; Secretary of War to GS, memorandum July 28, 1915, p. 2, ibid., Box 72.

9. L.M. Garrison, testimony Jan. 6, 1916, HMAC, *To Increase the Efficiency of the Military Establishment of the U.S.: Hearings*, 64th Cong., 1st Sess. (Washington, D.C., 1916), pp. 10–13, 69. Anne W. Lane and Louise H. Wall, eds., *The Letters of Franklin K. Lane* (Boston, 1922), pp. 177–78; Charles Seymour, ed., *The Intimate Papers of Colonel House*, 4 vols. (Boston, 1926), I, pp. 296–302; II, pp. 18–20; Frank Freidel, *Franklin D. Roosevelt: The Apprenticeship* (Boston, 1952), p. 242.

10. CofS to chief, WCD, March 11, 17, 1915; Secretary of War to president, Army War College, April 17, 1915; memorandum for Secretary of War, July 31, 1915, subj: Statement of Military Policy, all in Scott MSS, Box 72.

11. Henry C. Breckinridge, unpublished "Memoir," pp. 193–94, 402, typescript in the Henry C. Breckinridge MSS, LC; see also notes of meeting of WCD, June 29, 1915, WCD 9053–46, GS Records (RG 165).

12. "A Statement of a Proper Military Policy," WCD 9053–90, Sept. 11, 1915, in WD, *Annual Reports, 1915*, pp. 109–35.

13. *New York Times*, Dec. 27, 1915; SMAC, *Preparedness for National Defense: Hearings*, 64th Cong., 1st Sess. (Washington, D.C., 1916), p. 259; HMAC, *To Increase Efficiency: Hrgs.*, pp. 406, 728–38, 859, 936.

14. Scott, *Some Memories*, pp. 469–71; testimony, HMAC, *To Increase Efficiency: Hrgs.*, pp. 83–99, 1150–51.

15. "The Plattsburg Idea," *New Republic*, 4 (Oct. 9, 1915), pp. 148–50; "Preparedness—A Trojan Horse," ibid., 5 (Nov. 6, 1915), pp. 6–7; Norman Hapgood, "The Swiss Army Lesson," *Harper's Weekly*, 61 (July 17, 1915), p. 55–56

16. See the literature cited in Walter Dean Burnham, "The System of 1896: An Analysis," in Paul Kleppner, et al., *The Evolution of American Electoral Systems* (Westport, Conn., 1981), pp. 147–202; and Lewis L. Gould,

Reform and Regulation: American Politics from Roosevelt to Wilson, 2nd ed. (New York, 1986), pp. 3–30.

17. On the archtype, see K. Austin Kerr, *Organized for Prohibition: A New History of the Anti-Saloon League* (New Haven, Conn., 1985).

18. William Jennings Bryan, "The Munitions-Militarist Conspiracy," *The Commoner*, 16 (May 1916), p. 3; Robert M. La Follette, "Impudent Graft: Congress Stampeded into an Astounding Military Program!" *La Follette's Magazine*, 8 (Sept. 1916), p. 2; hundreds of letters from rural constituents such as E.D. Godfrey to Claude Kitchin, Feb. 6, 1916, Claude Kitchin MSS, University of North Carolina, Reel 7; and report from Midwest in Oswald G. Villard to David Lawrence, April 18, 1916, O.G. Villard MSS, Harvard University; also John Milton Cooper, Jr., *The Vanity of Power: American Isolationism and World War I, 1914–1917* (Westport, Conn., 1969).

19. Testimony, HMAC, *To Increase Efficiency: Hrgs.*, pp. 1235–39, 1240, 1246–48; also George B. Tindall, *The Emergence of the New South, 1913–1945 (Baton Rouge, La., 1967), pp. 41, 47*

20. Black support in SMAC, *UMT: Hrgs.*, pp. 336–352; southern white fears of black soldiers, Rep. James Hay, chair, HMAC, to WW, Feb. 8, 1916, Wilson MSS, Series II; "Preparedness and the South," *Current Opinion*, 60 (March 1916), pp. 208–10.

21. On labor support, Matthew Woll, "Trades-Unionism and Military Training," *Proceedings of the Academy of Political Science*, 6 (July 1916), pp. 558–69; A.F. of L., *Proceedings of Convention* (Washington, D.C., 1915), pp. 87, 381–88; Samuel Gompers, "Justice and Democracy: Handmaids of Preparedness," *American Federationist*, 23 (March 1916), pp. 173–80. On labor opposition, HMAC, *To Increase Efficiency: Hrgs.*, pp. 1317–24; John P. White, "Organized Labor and Military Service," *Proceedings of the Academy of Political Science*, 6 (July 1916), pp. 625–29; Alexander Trachenberg, ed., *American Socialists and the War* (New York, 1917), p. 27; Industrial Workers of the World, *Official Proceedings of 1916 Convention*, p. 138.

22. Jane Addams, testimony, HMAC, *To Increase Efficiency: Hrgs.*, p. 210; F.J. Varne, *The Immigrant Invasion* (New York, 1913), pp. 43–44. Joseph Rappaport, "Jewish Immigrants and World War I: A Study of American Jewish Press Reactions," (Ph.D. dissertation, Columbia University, 1951), p. 170; Frederick C. Luebke, *Bonds of Loyalty: German-Americans and World War I* (De Kalb, Ill., 1974), pp. 158–69.

23. Charles Chatfield, *For Peace and Justice: Pacifism in America, 1914–1941* (Knoxville, Tenn., 1971), pp. 15–50; Charles De Benedetti, *The Peace Reform in American History* (Bloomington, Ind., 1980), pp. 79–107.

24. "Committee to Fight 'Huge War Budget,'" *Survey*, 35 (Jan. 1, 1916), p. 370.

25. Sen. William E. Borah (Rep.-Idaho) quoted by Charles T. Hallinan to Executive Committee, April 17, 1918, AUAM MSS, Swarthmore College Peace Collection (hereafter SCPC), Reel 1. Charles T. Hallinan, "American Union against Militarism," typescript history, in ibid.

26. On women in the peace and anti-preparedness movements, see C. Roland Marchand, *The American Peace Movement and Social Reform, 1898–1918* (Princeton, N.J., 1972), pp. 182–222; and Steinson, *American Women's Activism*, pp. 1–162.

27. Biographical data from *Biographical Directory of the American Congress*; Solon de Leon, ed., *American Labor Who's Who* (New York, 1925); *Who's Who in America, 1914–1920*; Blanche Wiesen Cook, "Woodrow Wilson and the Antimilitarists, 1914–1917," (Ph.D. dissertation, The Johns Hopkins University, 1970), pp. 3–6;

28. O.G. Villard, *Preparedness* (New York, 1915); "Sentimental Aspect of Preparedness," *Intercollegiate Socialist*, 5 (Dec.–Jan., 1916–17), pp. 4–8.

29. O.G. Villard, *Universal Military Training Our Latest Cure-All* (Washington, D.C., 1918, orig. 1916), p. 6; see also Rep. George Huddleston (Dem.-Ala.), *Conscription is Undemocratic* (Washington, D.C., 1917). Dudley A. Sargent, *The Effects of Military Drill on Boys* (Chicago, 1916).

30. George W. Nasmyth, *Universal Military Service and Democracy* (Washington, D.C., 1917, orig. 1916), p. 7.

31. Max Eastman, testimony, SMAC, *UMT: Hrgs.*, pp. 544–49.

32. Testimony, HMAC, *To Increase Efficiency: Hrgs.*, pp. 1255–56.

33. Dr. Frank Bohn, quoted in "Does UMT Educate," *Intercollegiate Socialist*, 5 (Dec.–Jan., 1916–17), p. 15.

34. Carlton J.H. Hayes, Jan. 15, 1917, "Four Facts Against Compulsory Universal Training," Columbia College *Spectator*, clipping, n.d., Collegiate Antimilitarism League MSS; SCPC; also Nasmyth, *UMS*, p. 11.

35. See numerous constituent letters in papers of members of Congress such as Warren W. Bailey, Henry A. Cooper, John J. Esch, Simeon D. Fess, Paul O. Husting, Claude Kitchin, Robert M. La Follette, Kenneth D. McKellar, Knute Nelson, Thomas Schall, as well as studies of rural members of Congress such as T.L. Miller, "Oscar Calloway and Preparedness," *West Texas Historical Association Yearbook*, 43 (1967), pp. 80–93; Monroe Billington, *Thomas P. Gore: The Blind Senator from Oklahoma* (Lawrence, Kan., 1967), pp. 56–60. On the value and limitation of congressional mail as an index of public opinion, see David B. Truman, *The Governmental Process* (New York, 1951), pp. 390–91; Leila A. Sussman, "Voices of the People: A Study of Political Mass Mail," (Ph.D. dissertation Columbia University, 1957), pp. 216–217; V.O. Key, *Public Opinion and American Democracy* (New York, 1961), p. 492.

36. Huddleston, *Conscription is Undemocratic*, pp. 6–7; Amos Pinchot, wealthy radical, labor lawyer, brother of the former chief forester, wrote that "The Wall Street interests that are behind the campaign for compulsory service . . . want something that cannot be obtained in any way except by forced service—and that is a meek and disciplined labor group that will make no trouble at home and will fight obediently to defend the American dollar abroad." Amos Pinchot to Samuel Gompers, March 10, 1917, Amos Pinchot MSS, Box 192. It was widely published: *New York Times*, March 13, 1917; *Brotherhood of Locomotive Firemen*

and Engineers' Magazine, 62 (March 15, 1917), pp. 7–9; *Coast Seamen's Journal*, 30 (March 28, 1917), p. 1; and *Railway Carmen's Journal*, 22 (April 1917), pp. 224–27. See also Edward A. Wieck, "Militarism and the Worker," *United Mine Workers Journal* (Feb. 1917), p. 7.

37. O.G. Villard to WW, Oct. 20 (actually 30th), 1915, Villard MSS. The point is developed in Chambers, *Tyranny of Change*, pp. 119–25.

38. Link, *Wilson*, IV, pp. 18–30, 167–94; Alex Arnett, *Claude Kitchin and the Wilson War Policies* (Boston, 1937), chs. 1–2.

39. James Hay, "Woodrow Wilson and Preparedness," typescript, n.d. (probably early 1920s), in James Hay MSS, LC; George C. Herring, Jr., "James Hay and the Preparedness Controversy, 1915–1916," *Journal of Southern History*, 30 (Nov. 1964), pp. 383–404; Mabel Deutrich, *Struggle for Supremacy: The Career of Fred C. Ainsworth* (Washington, D.C., 1962).

40. Herring, "James Hay and Preparedness," p. 394; Finnegan, *Specter of a Dragon*, pp. 80–86.

41. James Hay to WW, Feb. 5, 8, 1916, WW MSS, Series II; also in Link, *PWW*, 36, pp. 134–35, 141–43.

42. Martha Derthick, *The National Guard in Politics* (Cambridge, Mass., 1965), pp. 36–40. Also, by using militia, the South could exclude blacks.

43. On its political effectiveness, see Derthick, *National Guard*, and William H. Riker, *Soldiers of the States* (Washington, D.C., 1957).

44. For example, Henry Stimson believed that the militia was "a hopeless anachronism and a shackle on our future progress both in the states and in the Nation." HLS to Walter L. Fisher, Jan. 23, 1917, HLS MSS.

45. "Beware! National Guardsmen, of Sinister Influences," *National Guard Magazine*, 13 (May 1916), p. 100.

46. Ibid., pp. 104–5; also "The Military Situation in 1916," ibid., 12 (Nov. 1915), p. 197; "The Army and the National Guard," ibid., 13 (Feb. 1916), p. 38.

47. BG Gardner W. Pearson, Mass. N.G., testimony, HMAC, *To Increase Efficiency: Hrgs.*, pp. 1094–95; "Will Pay or Universal Service Solve Our Problems?" *National Guard Magazine*, 12 (Nov. 1915), pp. 197–98.

48. Link, *PWW*, 36, pp. 7–16, 26–48, 52–122. Years later, Garrison condemned Wilson as "a man of high ideals but no principles." L.M. Garrison to W.W. Brooks, Feb. 24, 1929, quoted in Link, *Woodrow Wilson and the Progressive Era*, p. 186n.

49. Chamberlain, a native of Mississippi, became reform governor of Oregon, 1902–9, then U.S. Senator, *DAB*, III, pp. 595–96; on his UMT bill, *Army & Navy Journal*, 53 (Dec. 18, 1915), p. 505. Adoption of Hay bill, *New York Times*, March 18–24, 1916; roll-call votes, *The Searchlight on Congress*, 1 (Oct. 1916), pp. 7–16. Senate vote, *New York Times*, April 7, 19, 1916; *Searchlight on Congress*, 1 (Sept. 1916), pp. 2–8.

50. Charles T. Hallinan, "Putting Pins in Preparedness," *Survey*, 35 (Feb. 26, 1916), pp. 632–33; "Swinging around the Circle against Militarism," ibid., 36 (April 22, 1916), pp. 95–96.

51. WW "A Colloquy with a Group of Antipreparedness Leaders," May 8, 1916, in, Link, *PWW*, 36, p. 645–46, and 634–48. This revealing document, based on shorthand notes of Wilson's personal stenographer, is superior to the somewhat different recollections of antipreparedness leaders in "Transcript of Interview with the President by the American Union against Militarism, May 8, 1916," printed copy in the Lillian Wald MSS, NYPL; abbreviated published versions of the exchange, in *New York Times*, May 9, 1916; *Survey*, 36 (May 20, 1916), pp. 198–99; and an official account released by the White House in 1918, with excerpts in *New York Times*, Aug. 4, 1918.

52. WW, "Colloquy," May 8, 1916, in Link, *PWW*, 36, p. 648.

53. WW to L.M. Garrison, Feb. 10, 1916, Link, *PWW*, 36, p. 163; Breckinridge, "Memoir," p. 421, citing Aug. 24, 1915 diary entry, reported WW told him the administration plan must not include compulsion.

54. WW, "Colloquy," May 8, 1916, in Link, *PWW*, 36, p. 647.

55. WW, statement, May 30, 1916, in Link, PWW, 37, pp. 127–28.

56. *New York Times*, May 14, 21, 1916; National Defense Act of June 3, 1916, U.S. *Statutes, at Large*, XXXIX, p. 166. Congress feared the administration might blame it for obstructing defense if war did break out with Mexico. Charles T. Hallinan, in AUAM, "Bulletin," May 18, 1916, AUAM MSS, Reel 2.

57. ROTC was advocated by General Wood and many college presidents and supported by Congress over the General Staff proposal that candidates first serve a year in the ranks of the regular army. Gene M. Lyons and John W. Masland, "The Origins of ROTC," *MA*, 23 (1959), pp. 7–11.

58. As General Scott put it: "If it [the National Guard] is further paid, its votes will have a tendency to choke the Regular Army and all other branches." H.L. Scott to Gen. W.W. Robinson, Jr., April 7, 1916, misfiled with 1917 correspondence, Scott MSS, Box 28.

59. U.S., *Statutes at Large*, XXXIX, p. 197. The 1916 act reasserted without implementing the principle of universal military *obligation* among able-bodied men 18–45, the so-called unorganized Militia, which had been abandoned in the Militia Act of 1903.

60. Praise came from "Mobilization in Spite of the War Department," *National Guard Magazine*, 13 (Aug. 1916), pp. 153, 159; Gen. Frederick Funston to Gen. H.L. Scott, Nov. 29, 1916, Scott MSS, Box 25; and Craig A. Newton, "Vermonters in Texas: A Reassessment of National Guard Duty on the Mexican Border in 1916," *Vermont History*, 37 (Winter, 1969), pp. 30–38.

61. TR to H.H. Sheets, Nov. 27, 1915, TR MSS, Reel 359. Condemnation of the volunteer system based on 1916 mobilization, see "Case against the Militia System," *Outlook*, 114 (Oct. 25, 1916), pp. 405–6; Sigmund Henschen, "Collapse of Our Militia," *Forum*, 56 (1916), pp. 290–96.

62. John Rae, *Conscience and Politics: The British Government and the*

Conscientious Objector to Military Service, 1916–1919 (New York 1970), pp. 1–67; Cameron Hazlehurst, *Politicians at War: July 1914 to May 1915: A Prologue to the Triumph of Lloyd George* (New York 1971), pp. 265–68, 301–3; and the critical David R. Woodward, *Lloyd George and the Generals* (Newark, Del., 1983), pp. 56–60, 64–65, 88, 173–75.

63. S.K. Ratcliffe, "The British Army and Compulsion," *New Republic*, 1 (Jan. 2, 1915), pp. 13–15; "England Forced to Conscription," *Literary Digest*, 52 (June 17, 1916), pp. 1770–71.

64. Quoted in *Nation's Business*, 4 (March 1916), p. 21; see also Mayor's Committee on National Defense New York City, "Employers Give Views on Preparedness," Jan. 20 [1917], GS Records, WCD (RG 165), AWC-9317, Box 390, NA.

65. Howard Coffin at the National Defense Conference, May 2–3, 1917, "Transcript of Proceedings," Grosvenor Clarkson MSS, Box 1, Columbia University

66. Current Opinion, 61 (Aug. 1916), p. 78.

67. U.S. Chamber of Commerce, *How Business Men Stand on Natl. Defense* (n.p., 1916), p. 1; National Association of Manufacturers, *Proceedings of Annual Convention, 1916* (New York, 1916), p. 119; American Institute of Banking, *Bulletin*, 9 (Oct. 1916), pp. 374–76.

68. On physicians, SMAC, *UMT: Hrgs.*, pp. 247–85; on N.E.A., *New York Times*, May 19, 21, July 8, 1916; on clergy, ibid., June 19, Oct. 8, 31, 1916; John Purroy Mitchel, *Address at National Defense Conference of Mayors* (New York, 1916), p. 12.

69. James Cardinal Gibbons to H.H. Sheets, *New York Times*, Oct. 8, 1916. Other quotations: U.S. Chamber of Commerce, *How Business Men Stand*, p. 15; Henry C. Emery, "The Economic Value of Military Training," *Nation's Business*, 4 (June 1916), pp. 20–21.

70. BG John J. Pershing, "General Pershing Wants Every Man a Soldier," *New York Times Magazine*, Jan. 30, 1916, pp. 3–4.

71. Henry Harrison Sheets, secretary-treasurer of Assn. for National Service, and H.H. Gross, director of UMTl., had previously promoted and publicized the first international tour by an American professional baseball team, a campaign for increased consumption of specific American agricultural products, and the successful lobbying campaign for a Federal Tariff Commission. On Taft, see *New York Times*, June 8, 9, 1916; for many others, NSL, *Proceedings of the National Security Congress*, passim; on press, "Growing Momentum of the Movement for UMT," *Current Opinion*, 61 (Aug. 1916), pp. 77–78; *New York Times* printed whatever Henry Stimson sent, HLS to F.R. McCoy, Feb. 28, 1916, HLS MSS.

72. "Memorial to the President," April 1916, and AUAM, "Bulletin," April 1916, both in AUAM MSS, Reel 1; western report of A.T. Hadley to Charles Evans Hughes, July 26, 1916, Arthur T. Hadley MSS, Yale University.

73. H.C. Lodge to TR, June 14, 1916, TR MSS, Reel 211; on Hughes, see TR to Lodge, July 3, 1916, in Morison, ed., *Letters of T. Roosevelt*, VIII, p. 1086.
74. Kirk H. Porter and Donald B. Johnson, compilers, *National Party Platforms, 1840–1956* (Urbana, Ill., 1956), pp. 201, 208.
75. For conflicting interpretations of the "joker," Sec. 79 of National Defense Act of June 3, 1916, introduced by Rep. Carl Hayden (Dem.-Ariz.), see James W. Pohl, "The General Staff and American Defense Policy: The Formative Period, 1898–1917," (Ph.D. dissertation, University of Texas, 1967), pp. 383–87; Cook, "Woodrow Wilson and the Antimilitarists, 1914–1917," pp. 72–84; and Finnegan, *Specter of a Dragon*, pp. 144–45. Research in newly available sources indicates that the "joker" was not the result of a conspiracy, but neither was it inconsequential, due to the principle of wartime conscription involved. Highlights of debate include C.T. Hallinan to Executive Committee, Aug. 2, 1916, "New Light on the Conscription Situation," [Aug. 11, 1916], mimeo., AUAM MSS, Reel 1; Amos Pinchot to WW, Aug. 9, 18, 1916, Wilson MSS; and WW to Pinchot, Aug. 11, 19, 1916, Pinchot MSS; the latter also in Link, *PWW*, 38, p. 52; WW to James Hay, Aug. 11, 1916, Hay MSS, Box 1; Hay to WW, Aug. 14, 1916, WW MSS, Series IV; "A Federal Conscription Act?" *Survey*, 36 (Sept. 16, 1916), pp. 596–97. See also Link, *PWW*, 38, pp. 190, 445; Link, *Wilson*, V, pp. 160–64. On Sept. 1, Rep. George Huddleston introduced H.R. 1771 for repeal.
76. Secretary of War to Chairman, HMAC, Jan. 3, 1917. The General Staff, while praising conscription, dismissed the "Hayden joker" as "of no great importance," because it lacked provisions for implementation and enforcement. Col. C.W. Kennedy, acting chief, WCD, memorandum for CofS, Jan. 3, 1917, re H.R. 1771, WCD-9317, GS Recds., WCD, Box 390.
77. James Hay quoted in AUAM "Bulletin," No. 59 (Aug. 30, 1916). See also AUAM Executive Comittee, Minutes, Sept. 7, 1916, both in AUAM MSS, Reel 1; C.T. Hallinan to Lillian Wald, Sept. 12, 1916, Wald MSS, Columbia University, Box 88. After re-election, Wilson declined to seek repeal. WW to L. Wald, Dec. 5, 1916, Wald MSS, NYPL; also in Link, *PWW*, 40, pp. 121, 163. Hay's speech, *Cong. Rec.*, 64:1st (March 17, 22, 1916), pp. 4309, 4648.
78. A national militia offered an alternative to a professional standing army or the national mass conscript-reservist forces of continental Europe and, in the late 19th and early 20th centuries, appealed to some socialists and members of the labor movement as a means of limiting the military power of capitalist and aristocratic-monarchical States. This was most fully developed by Jean Jaurès in *L'Armée nouvelle* (1910; paraphrased in English, by C.C. Coulton, ed., *Democracy and Military Service* [London, 1916]). See also Jaurès speech in the Chamber of Deputies reprinted in *Journal Officiel de la République française Déb.* (1912, sess. ext.), pp. 3039–73. Citizens would be trained for six months and then discharged into territorial militia reserve units. The professional army, viewed as an instrument of capitalist aggression and exploitation, would be abolished. The officer corps would be trained in

universities, not military academies, and only one-third would be full-time professionals and they would be more like civil servants than aristocratic soldiers. See David B. Ralston, *The Army of the Republic: The Place of the Military in the Political Evolution of France, 1871–1914* (Cambridge, Mass., 1967), pp. 131–32, 314, 348–55; Harold Weinstein, *Jean Jaurès: A Study of Patriotism in the French Socialist Movement* (New York, 1936); and Richard D. Challener, *The French Theory of the Nation in Arms, 1866–1939* (New York, 1965), pp. 68–74, 87, 109, 162–64. In Germany, some Social Democrats also suggested a *Volkswehr* or "Peoples' Army." See August Bebel, *Nicht stehendes Heer sondern Volkswehr!* (Stuttgart, 1898); Geoff Eley, "Army, State and Civil Society: Some Thoughts on German Militarism, c. 1860–1918," paper presented at the Davis Center, Princeton Univ., Feb. 11, 1983. The same was true in Russia, see George J. Neimanis, "Militia vs. the Standing Army in the History of Economic Thought from Adam Smith to Friedrich Engels," *MA*, 44 (Feb. 1980), p. 31.

79. Walter L. Fisher, a Chicagoan and Secretary of the Interior, 1911–13, wanted an expanded volunteer citizen reserve which would be thoroughly defensive in orientation. Testimony of Feb. 9, 1916, in HMAC, *To Increase Efficiency: Hrgs.*, p. 1280; Fisher, "Fundamental Considerations Affecting the Military Policy of the United States," *Proceedings of the American Academy of Political Science* 6 (July 1916), pp. 455–56. William Jennings Bryan suggested a federally financed program of national roads which enhance the ability of a highly mobile army to defend the coasts while the militia and Volunteers "spring to arms overnight." Conversely, conscriptionists argued for pretrained national reserves, and the use of such a "democratic army" in support of expanded internationalism: Perry, *Free Man and the Soldier*, pp. 24–43; W. L. Stoddard, "For a Citizen Army," *New Republic*, 5 (Sept. 4, 1915), p. 125. Samuel Gompers urged opening the citizen-officer corps to members of the working class. Gompers, "Democratize the Army," *American Federationist*, 24 (June 1917), pp. 543–44. On "Khaki University" idea, see N.D. Baker, "From Bayonets to Books," *Independent*, 99 (Aug. 16, 1919), pp. 218–19. On using the army for peacetime public service, see Sen. John D. Works, testimony, Feb. 4, 1916, and his bill, S. 2684, in SMAC, *Preparation for National Defense: Hrgs.*, 64:1st, (Washington, D.C., 1916), pp. 937–39; and Charles J. Post, "The Army as a Social Service," *Survey*, 36 (May 20, 1916), pp. 201–2. On labor opposition, see White, "Organized Labor and Military Service," p. 629; "A Million Men Out of Work," *Literary Digest*, 49 (Dec. 26, 1914), p. 1264.

On position of European socialists who supported military training for workers, see Neumann and von Hagen, "Engels and Marx on Revolution, War, and the Army in Society," in Paret, ed., *Makers of Modern Strategy*, pp. 262–80. On American socialists' antimilitary position, see "American Socialists and the War," *The New Review*, 3 (Oct., 1914), p. 615; *Appeal to Reason* (Dec. 11, 1915); and *American Socialist* (Dec. 9, 1915; Jan. 29, 1916). A few American liberals and socialists advocated adoption of a form of universal *non*-military public service as an alternative to war, a development of the idea propounded by William James, *The Moral Equivalent of War* (New York, 1910). Most prominent was Randolph Bourne, "Moral Equivalent for Universal Military Service," *New Republic*, 7 (July 1, 1916), pp. 217–19. A few socialists argued for "Socialist Plattsburgs" which would teach community service instead of military service. "The Sentimental Aspect of Preparedness," *Intercollegiate Socialist*, 5 (Dec.–Jan., 1916–1917), pp. 4–8. See also "Democratic Defense" put forward by W.J. Ghent, and seven other nationalistic socialists in *New Republic*, 10 (March 31, 1917), pp. 262–63.

80. On the liberal attitude towards war and the military in America, see John Shy, "The American Military Experience: History and Learning," *Journal of Interdisciplinary History*, 1 (Feb. 1971), pp. 205–28; Ekirch, *Civilian and Military*; and critique in Huntington, *Soldier and the State*, pp. 143–62; and Michael Howard, *War and the Liberal Conscience* (New Brunswick, N.J., 1978), pp. 28–29, 80–82, 115–17, 129–35.

5 / Decision to Draft the Doughboys, February–March 1917

1. On the draft, debate focuses on when and why Wilson made his decision. The traditional date, Feb. 4, 1917, was first put forward by Gen. Enoch H. Crowder, the draft administrator, in a speech, March 15, 1928, typescript EHC MSS, Box 46. David A. Lockmiller, *Enoch H. Crowder, Soldier, Lawyer, and Statesman* (Columbia, Mo., 1955), pp. 152–54, incorporated it, and it remains widely accepted. See John K. Ohl, "Hugh S. Johnson and the Draft, 1917–18," *Prologue*, 8 (Summer 1976), p. 86; Ferrell, *Woodrow Wilson and World War I* (1985), p. 16; Calhoun, *Power and Principle* (1986), p. 163. Others emphasize late March 1917; see Daniel R. Beaver, *Newton D. Baker and the American War Effort, 1917–1919* (Lincoln, Neb., 1966), pp. 27–29. However, Link, *Wilson*, V, pp. 309–409, judiciously declined to pinpoint a date. Regarding Wilson's reasons for the draft, traditional interpretations emphasize the influence of the British experience and the arguments of Generals Scott and Wood; see Kreidberg and Henry, *History of Military Mobilization*, p. 243; Coffman, *War to End All Wars*, p. 24. Recently, more partisan motives have also been emphasized, see Beaver, *Baker*, p. 28; Clifford, *Citizen Soldiers*, p. 226; Kennedy, *Over Here*, p. 148.

2. Woodrow Wilson, *A History of the American People*, 5 vols. (New York, 1901), IV, pp. 214, 236–37.

3. In 1916, he wrote: "What I hope is, that the [army] measure can be so framed as to give us an ample skeleton and unmistakable authority to fill it out at any time that the public safety may be deemed to require it." "W.W.", Memorandum attached to James Hay to WW, April 19, 1916, James Hay MSS, Box 1, LC; See also Hay, "Woodrow Wilson and Preparedness," p. 25.

4. Gould, *Reform and Regulation*, pp. 176–211.

5. WW to Mrs. George Bass, May 4, 1917, WW MSS, Series IV, italics added; also in Link, *PWW*, 42, p. 214.

6. NDB to brother, Frank H, Baker, Jan, 2, 1916, N.D. Baker MSS, Box 2,

Western Reserve Historical Society, Cleveland, O.; NDB to A.R. Horr, June 26, 1916 and to David C. Westenhaver, Dec. 15, 1916, N.D. Baker MSS, LC.

7. WW to Lindley M. Garrison, Aug. 8, 1914, in Link, *PWW*, 30, pp. 360–61; Calhoun, *Power and Principle*, examines the issue.

8. J.A.S. Grenville and G.B. Young, *Politics, Strategy, and American Diplomacy: Studies in Foreign Policy, 1873–1917* (New Haven, 1966), pp. 321–22, 327.

9. Link, *Wilson: War, Revolution and Peace*; compare John A. Thompson, "Woodrow Wilson and World War I: A Reappraisal," (British) *Journal of American Studies*, 19 (1985), pp. 3, 325–48.

10. "A 'State of War' with Germany," *Literary Digest*, 54 (March 31, 1917), p. 882; "Mobilizing Public Sentiment," *Independent*, 90 (April 2, 1917), p. 14.

11. See Chambers, "Conscripting for Colossus" (1973), pp. 255–59. Julius Rosenwald was head of Sears and a founder of the UMTL.

12. *New York Times*, March 23, 25, 30, 1917. Herbert Satterlee.

13. Ibid., Feb. 5, 7, 17, 1917; correspondence, Feb.–March, 1917, WW MSS, Series IV.

14. W. Lippmann to WW, Feb. 6, 1917, WW MSS, Series II, also in Link, *PWW*, 41, pp. 134–35; and to NDB, Feb. 6, 1917, Lippmann MSS, Yale.

15. New York *World*, March 24, 30, 1917; *Independent*, (April 1, 1917), p. 14; AUAM Executive Committee, Minutes, Feb. 14, 27, 1917; C. T. Hallinan to Executive Committee, March 2, 8, 23, 1917, all in AUAM MSS, Reel 1.

16. Meeting of March 14, 1917, in Franklin H. Martin, *Digest of Proceedings of Council of National Defense* (Washington, D.C., 1934), p. 112; see also Samuel Gompers to Frank Morrison, Secretary, A.F. of L., March 27, 1917, A.F. of L. MSS, Series XI, Files of Office of the President (hereafter Gompers MSS), Box 24, State Historical Society of Wisconsin; Samuel Gompers, *Seventy Years of Life and Labor*, 2 vols. (New York, 1925), II, pp. 369–70.

17. Gompers to union presidents, March 2, 24, 1917, Gompers MSS, Box 24; Gompers, "American Labor's Position in Peace or in War," *American Federationist*, 24 (April 1917), pp. 269–84.

18. BG Joseph E. Kuhn, chief, WCD, to CofS, Jan. 27, 1917, subj: Plan for a National Army, WCD-9876–9, GS Records, WCD (RG 165), Box 442, NA; reprinted in U.S. Cong., 65:1st, (April 1917), *Sen. Doc. No. 10*.

19. Ibid; chief, WCD, to CofS, Jan. 30, 1917, WCD-9876–11, GS Records (RG 165), Box 442; chief, WCD, to CofS, subj: A Plan for an Expansible Army of 500,000 men based upon Universal Liability to Military Service, Feb. 20, 1917, WCD-9433–7, GS Records, WCD, Genl. Corres., 1903–19, Box 444.

20. MG Tasker H. Bliss to CofS, Jan. 31, 1917, WCD-9876–13, GS Records WCD, (RG 165), Box 442. On Crowder, see Breckinridge, "Memoir," pp. 193–94, 402; EHC to LTC William G. Haan, April 17, 1916, W.G. Haan

MSS, Box 4, State Historical Society of Wisconsin. The army credited
Scott and Wood, not Crowder, with instigating the draft; John J. Pershing, *My Experiences in the World War*, 2 vols. (New York 1931), I, pp.
15, 20–21; Kreidberg and Henry, *History of Military Mobilization*, pp.
242–43.

21. NDB to G.E. Chamberlain, Feb. 23, 1917, U.S. Cong., 65:1st, *Sen. Doc.
No. 10*, p. 8. On press, New York *World*, Feb. 17, *Army and Navy
Journal*, Feb. 24, 1917.

22. Secy. for CofS, to chief, WCD, Feb. 3, 1917, WCD-9433–7, GS Records
(RG 165), WCD, Genl. Corres., Box 444.

23. NBD to W.H. Taft, Feb. 7, 1917, in Link *PWW*, 41, pp. 153–156.

24. NDB to WW, Feb. 7, 1917, in Link, *PWW*, 41, pp. 151–52; directly
counter to WCD recommendation against volunteers; chief, WCD,
memorandum for CofS, Feb. 3, 1917, subj: Preparation for Possible
Hostilities with Germany, WCD 9433–4, GS Records (RG 165), WCD,
Box 444.

25. BG J.E. Kuhn, chief, WCD, memorandum for CofS, Feb. 20, 1917, subj:
A Plan for an Expansible Army of 500,000 men based upon Universal
Liability to Military Service, WCD 9433–7, GS Records (RG 165), WCD,
Box 444.

26. BG J.E. Kuhn, chief, WCD, memorandum for CofS, March 15, 1917,
subj: 500,000 Volunteers in Addition to Regular Army & National
Guard, WCD 9433–11, in ibid.

27. MG H.L. Scott to Louis Wiley, March 7, 1917, Scott MSS.

28. Link, *Wilson, War, Revolution and Peace*, pp. 65–67; Link, *PWW*, 41,
pp. 86–308, 451n.

29. Contemporary collaboration for the Feb. 22 meeting, but not the origin
of the actual draft law, is in [EHC] to LTC W.G. Haan, Feb. 28, 1917,
Haan MSS, Box 3; and HLS to EHC, misdated Feb. 18 [but probably 28,
from internal evidence], 1917; and EHC, memorandum, Feb. 23, 1917,
to "Mr. Keith," both in Crowder MSS, Box 2.

30. [EHC] to W.G. Haan, Feb. 28, 1917, Haan MSS, Box 3. No copy of the
proposed joint resolution has been located; this account is derived
from references in HLS to EHC, Feb. 18 [probably 28], 1917; EHC to
CofS, March 21, 1917, subj: Joint Resolution for Raising a Force of One
Million Men Prepared Last Month for Secretary of War; both in
Crowder MSS, Box 2.

31. BG J.E. Kuhn, chief, WCD, to CofS, March 24, 1917, WCD 7923–10,
subj: Joint Resolution by JAG for Raising 1,000,000 Men; Crowder
MSS, Box 2.

32. Link, *PWW*, 41, p. 286, my italics; *New York Times*, Feb. 27, 1917.

33. Link, *Wilson, War, Revolution and Peace*, pp. 68–71 and *PWW*, 41, pp.
424–507.

34. EHC to HLS, March 22, 1917, HLS MSS.

35. LTC W.S. Graves, secretary to CofS, memorandum to Adjutant Gen-

eral, March 23, 1917, Records of the Adjutant General's Office (RG 64) File No. 2558228, NA.

36. EHC to HLS, March 26, 1917, HLS, MSS; similar im MG H.L. Scott to BG E. St. J. Greble, March 24, 1917, Scott MSS, Box 28.

37. See entry, March 24, 1917, E. David Cronin, ed., *Cabinet Diaries of Josephus Daniels, 1913–1921* (Lincoln, Neb., 1963), p. 120.

38. EHC to HLS, March 26, 1917, HLS MSS.

39. "Summary of the Bill to Increase Temporarily the Military Establishment of the United States," enclosed with NDB to WW, March 29, 1917, WW MSS, Series II.

40. EHC to HLS, March 29, 1917, HLS MSS.

41. Ibid.

42. NDB to WW, March 29, 1917, WW MSS, also in Link, *PWW*, 41, pp. 500–501, already assumed presidential approval of the basic nature of the plan; NDB probably received that approval orally during his meeting with the president the previous evening. To have initiated such a change on his own would have been uncharacteristic of Baker; see House, Diary, March 28, 1917, in Link *PWW*, 41, p. 497.

43. N.D. Baker, "Some Legal Phases of the War," *American Bar Association Journal* 7 (July 1921), p. 323.

44. Ibid.; see also NDB to Frederick Palmer, Aug. 19, Sept. 8, 1930, N.D. Baker MSS, Box 184, LC; Frederick Palmer, *Newton D. Baker: America at War*, 2 vols. (New York, 1931), I, p. 184.

45. Hugh S. Johnson, *The Blue Eagle: From Egg to Earth* (Garden City, N.Y., 1935), p. 73, and interview in *New York Times*, Feb. 2, 1931; David F. Houston, *Eight Years with Wilson's Cabinet, 1913–1920*, 2 vols. (Garden City, N.Y., 1927), I, pp. 245–46.

46. The new evidence includes the records of the War College Division of the General Staff pertaining to planning for the wartime army between February and May 1917: WCD-9433 and WCD-10050, General Staff Records (RG 165), War College Division, General Correspondence, 1903–19, Boxes 444 and 512, National Archives; declassified in 1973 and 1975. Also essential were key letters from General Crowder, not including the Crowder papers at the University of Missouri, but located by the author in the papers of Henry L. Stimson at Yale University and William G. Haan at the State Historical Society of Wisconsin.

47. Roosevelt's compulsive desire to lead men in battle is examined in Pearlman, *To Make Democracy Safe*, pp. 19–20, 146–50.

48. TR to NDB, July 6, 1916, Morison, ed., *Letters of T. Roosevelt*, VIII, pp. 1087–88.

49. TR to NDB, Feb. 2, 7, 1917 and NDB's replies, Feb. 3, 9, 1917, ibid., VIII, pp. 1149–51.

50. With considerable publicity, General Butler had sheltered runaway slaves, purposely increasing pressure on Lincoln for emancipation.

51. Quote from WW to NDB, Jan. 13, 1917, refusing to send Wood to Europe as a military observer; N.D. Baker MSS, LC, Box 4. On Wood's reassignment, see Beaver, *Baker*, pp. 41–42.

52. TR to NDB, March 19, 1917, reply, March 20, 1917, in Morison, ed., *Letters of T. Roosevelt*, VIII, p. 1164.

53. TR, telegram, to NDB, March 23, 1917, ibid., p. 1166.

54. WW to NDB, March 27, 1917, Baker MSS, Box 4, LC; reply to NDB to WW and enclosure, March 26, 1917, also in Link, *PWW*, 41, pp. 469–70, 478.

55. Meeting reported in EHC to HLS, March 29, 1917, HLS MSS; my inference that formal approval was given then orally.

56. On public debate on TR Volunteers, see William H. Harbaugh, *Life and Times of Theodore Roosevelt* (New York, 1963), pp. 470–74; Seward Livermore, *Politics is Adjourned* (Middletown, Conn., 1966), pp. 19–31.

57. Link, *PWW*, 42, pp. 324–26, 346; *New York Times*, May 19, 1917.

58. Link, *PWW*, 42, pp. 29–32.

59. NDB to TR, April 13, May 11, 1917, Link, *PWW*, 42, pp. 56–57.

60. March 18, 1919 entry, Cary T. Grayson Diary, Office of the Papers of Woodrow Wilson, Princeton University, courtesy of Prof. Arthur S. Link. To be included in Link, *PWW*, 56 (forthcoming 1987).

61. Ferrell, *Wilson and World War I*, p. 50; Coffman, *War to End All Wars*, pp. 26–27; Weigley, *History of the U.S. Army*, pp. 373–74; Kreidberg and Henry, *History of Military Mobilization*, p. 252.

62. For example, Georges Clemenceau, Marshal Joseph J.C. Joffre, and Gen. G.T.M. "Tom" Bridges, chief, military section, British Mission to U.S., April–May 1917. See [G.T.M. Bridges] "General Military Report of Mission," "confidential," pp. 3–4, n.d., probably June 21, 1917, in War Office Records, WO 106/468, ERD/2755, Public Records Office, London.

63. Beaver, *Baker*, p. 44.

64. Quoted in Hagedorn, *Wood*, II, pp. 219–22, citing 1930 memorandum from contemporary notes by John M. Parker, prominent Louisianan, of an interview with WW, May 18, 1917.

65. Ray S. Baker, record of interview with NDB, April 6, 1928, Ray S. Baker MSS, LC, Box 20.

66. TR to H.C. Lodge, March 22, 1917, Morison, ed., *Letters of T. Roosevelt*, VIII, p. 1165.

67. May 14, 1917, House Diary; see also entry, April 16/17, 1917. Senator Chamberlain, for example, offered to raise an Oregon regiment. George E. Chamberlain to Gen. H.P. McCain, Feb. 21, 1917, George E. Chamberlain MSS, Oregon Historical Society, Portland, Ore.

68. NDB to W. Lippmann, April 4, 1917, Lippmann MSS. I am indebted to Prof. J. Garry Clifford for bringing this document to my attention.

69. WW to Elizabeth M. Bass, May 4, 1917, WW MSS, Series IV; also in Link, *PWW*, 42, p. 214.

70. WW to Rep. Guy T. Helvering, April 19, 1917, WW MSS, Series VI; also in Link, *PWW*, 42, pp. 97–98.

71. Baker, testimony, April 1917, HMAC, *Increase of Military: Hrgs.*, pp. 6–13, 77, 127, 145–52, 224; also WW, speech, April 15, 1917, Link, *PWW*, 42, pp. 71–75.

72. NDB to Walter Lippmann, April 4, 1917, Lippmann MSS.

73. Baker, testimony, April 9, 1917, HMAC, *Increase of Military: Hrgs.*, pp. 40–41.

74. Baker, testimony, April 17, 1917, ibid., p. 222; NDB to Lippmann, April 4, 1917, Lippmann MSS.

75. Baker, testimony, April 7, 1917, HMAC, *Increase of Military Hrgs.*, p. 63.

76. "'Limited-Liability' War," *Literary Digest*, 54 (March 3, 1917), pp. 538–39; ibid., 54 (April 7, 1917). pp. 965–67; New York *World*, March 21, 1917.

77. See reports in Link, *PWW*, 41, pp. 336, 428; ibid., 42, pp. 69–75.

78. *New Republic*, 10 (April 21, 1917), p. 332; see also entry of April 12, 1917 in W. Alexander Mabry, ed., "Prof. William E. Dodd's Diary, 1916–1920," *John P. Branch Historical Papers*, n.s. 2 (March 1953), p. 40.

79. WW meeting with pacifists, Feb. 28, 1917, Link, *PWW*, 41, pp. 302–5; Jane Addams, *Peace and Bread in Time of War* (New York, 1922), pp. 63–64. See also, WW interview with AUAM delegation, May 8, 1916, Link, *PWW*, 36, p. 645; and with W.E. Dodd, Aug. 24, 1916 entry, "Prof. Dodd's Diary," Mabry, ed., *John P. Branch Historical Papers*, n.s. 2 (March 1953), pp. 10–11.

80. Herbert C. Hoover to E.M. House, Feb. 13, 1917, enclosed with House to WW, Feb. 14, 1917; WW to NDB, Feb. 16, 1917, all in Link, *PWW*, 41, pp. 226–29. Wilson later adopted all but one of Hoover's nine suggestions.

81. NDB to WW, Feb. 7, 1917, in Link, *PWW*, 41, p. 151; EHC to HLS, March 26, 1917, HLS MSS.

82. H.L. Scott to D.C. Ricketts, April 6, 1917, Scott MSS, Box 28.

83. See war plans, WCD 9433, GS Records (RG 165), WCD, Genl. Corres., 1903–19, Box 444; and "Study and Report of G3 Features of the War Dept. War Plans and Preparations for War . . ." Sept. 17, 1928, Army War College, G-3 Course, 1928–29, typescript in File 352-4A, U.S. Milary History Collection, Carlisle Barracks, Pa.

84. Margin notation by Secretary of War on BG J. E. Kuhn, chief, WCD, memorandum to CofS, Feb. 3, 1917, subj: Preparation for Possible Hostilities with Germany, p. 2, WCD 9433-4, GS Records (RG 165), Box 444.

85. BG J. E. Kuhn, chief, WCD, memorandum for General Bliss, April 13, 1917, subj: Plan for Transporting a Force of 500,000 troops to France, reply to Bliss' "personal memorandum," March 27, 1917, WCD 9433–24 in ibid.

86. The Army's initial focus was on protecting U.S. territories and oil

fields in Mexico. CofS to chief, WCD, Feb. 28, 1917, WCD 9433–12; March 21, 1917, WCD 9433–16; chief, WCD, to CofS, March 24, 1917, subj: Garrisons of Canal Zone, Oahu and the Philippine Islands, WCD 9433–16; T. Bliss, memorandum for CofS, WCD 9433–16, in ibid. Also April 22, 1917 entry, House Diary, Yale University

87. On the missions, Kathleen Burk, *Britain, America and the Sinews of War, 1914–1918* (Boston, 1985); André Kaspi, *Le Temps des ámericains: le concours ámericain à la France en 1917–1918* (Paris, 1976).

88. See W.H. Page to Robert Lansing, April 14, 16, 21, 1917; WW MSS, Series II; and April 17, 19, in Link, *PWW*, 42, pp. 82–3, 109.

89. Report on French casualties, Norman Hapgood (London) to E.M. House, April 5, 1917, enclosed with House to WW, April 19, 1917, WW MSS, Series II; reports to Army War College by American Military attachés in France, April 13, 26 1917, WCD 10050–2, 18; and Britain, April 27, May 4, 11, 1917, WCD 10050–9, 12, all in GS Records, (RG 165), WCD, Box 460.

90. LTG G.T.M. Bridges to chief, Imperial General Staff, April 29, 1917, Cabinet Records, CAB 21/53, Public Record Office, London.

91. [LTG G.T.M. Bridges] to General [Scott], "secret," April 30, 1917, p. 1. Only the first two pages of this document are in the WW MSS, Series II; however, a full copy is included as "Appendix 2," in Bridges to chief, Imperial General Staff, London, "secret," May 3, 1917, W0106/468/ERD/2532, Public Record Office, London. For similar, see account of meeting April 30, 1917 between WW and René Viviani, head of French mission, by unidentified French military officer, MS in *État-Major de l'Armée de Terre*, 14 N 25, Archives of the Ministry of Defense, Vincennes, France; also in Link, *PWW*, 42, pp. 173–76.

92. See notes of meeting, WW with Marshal Joffre, May 1, 1917; NBD to WW, May 2, 1917, WW to NDB, May 3, 1917, in Link, *PWW*, 42, pp. 186–94, 201–2; LTG G.T.M. Bridges to War Office, telegram May 3, 1917, W0106/468/ERD/2532 Public Record Office, London, England. On French concerns, see French Ambassador to U.S., to *Président du conseil ministere des affaires Estranges*, May 4, 1917, and French Ambassador to Great Britain to same, "urgent," May 5, 1917, in *Guerre, 1914–1918, États-Unis*, Vol. 507, Ministry of Foreign Affairs Archives, Quai Voltaire, Paris, France.

93. NDB to WW, May 8, 1917, Link *PWW*, 42, p. 250.

94. T. Bliss to H.L. Scott, May 4, 1917, Bliss MSS; BG J.E. Kuhn, chief, WCD, to CofS, May 10, 1917, subj: Plans for Possible Expeditionary to France, WCD 10050–8, GS Records. (RG 165), Box 460.

95. WW to NDB, May 10, 1917, in Link, *PWW*, 42, pp. 263–64.

96. This significant phrase is in minutes of Joffre-Baker meeting, May 14, 1917, submitted to the French Government by Marshal Joffre and printed in U.S. Army, Historical Division, *U.S. Army in the World War, 1917–1919*, 17 vols. (Washington, D.C., 1948), II, p. 5. However, it does

not appear in the documents Joffre gave to Baker. See M. Joffre to Secretary of War, May 14, 1917, "Note relative à la Coopération de l'Armée Americaine sur le Front des Armées Alliées," encl. in CofS to chief, WCD, June 11, 1917, WCD 10050–66, GS Records (RG 165), WCD, Box 512. Joffre's minutes state "The dispatch of this expeditionary force, as well as of all other units, depends on transportation facilities. The secretary [of war] gives me to understand that, from now on, the efforts of the United States will be restricted only by transportation difficulties." (p. 5).

97. *New York Times*, May 19, 1917.

98. Ray S. Baker, record of interview with N. D. Baker, April 6, 1928, in R.S. Baker MSS, LC, Box 20; see also LTG G.T.M. Bridges, Memorandum, June 14, 1917, S.P. 5, CAB 27/7; and Cabinet Paper G.T. 744 of May 17, 1917, CAB 24/13, both in Cabinet Office Files, Public Records Office, London.

99. NDB to WW, May 27, 1917, in Link, *PWW*, 42, pp. 406–7.

100. Ibid.

101. MG Tasker H. Bliss, acting CofS, to NDB, May 25, 1917, enclosed with NDB to WW, May 27, 1917, in Link, *PWW*, 42, pp. 406–10. See also Donald Smythe, *Pershing: General of the Armies* (Bloomington, Ind., 1986), pp. 5–7, for dates of Pershing–Baker meetings.

102. BG J.E. Kuhn, chief, WCD, memorandum for CofS, June 7, 1917, subj: Tactical Reorganization Required to Meet Requirements in European Theater of War and Program for Progressive Dispatch of Troops to France. WCD 10050–30, p. 1, GS Records (RG 165), WCD, Box 460.

103. Army, Historical Division, *U.S. Army in the World War*, I, pp. 55, 91–93.

104. NDB to WW, Nov. 11, 1917, in Link, *PWW*, 45, p. 6; earlier, see ibid., 42, pp. 373–7, 405–7; ibid., 44, pp. 125–30, 200–203, 239, 361.

105. The Allied Missions awoke America to the need for major mobilization for war. See the (London) *Times*, May 16, 1917; "Our 'Triple Understanding,'" *Literary Digest*, 54 (May 26, 1917), pp. 1582–83; Frank A. Vanderlip to Prince A. Poniatowski, May 22, 1917, Vanderlip MSS. Others sought to limit immediate response to Allies' requests. See *New Republic*, 11 (May 5, 1917), pp. 2–3; Sen. Hiram W. Johnson to his sons, May 17, 1917, and to Charles K. McClatchy, May 1, 1917; Hiram W. Johnson MSS, University of California, Berkeley.

6 / Confronting Congress with Conscription, April–May 1917

1. WW, Address, April 2, 1917, in Link, *PWW*, 41, pp. 519–27.

2. Text of the bill, *New York Times*, April 6, 1917.

3. HMAC, *Increase of Military: Hrgs.*, pp. 3, 25, 42–43, 234.

4. H.Q. Alexander to Members of Congress from North Carolina, April 23, 1917, Kitchin MSS, Reel 17.

5. For example, Gov. Emanuel L. Philipp of Wisconsin to Rep. Henry A.

Cooper, April 10, 24, 1917, Cooper MSS, Box 3, asserting that 80 percent of the state opposed the draft; also Monroe Billington, "Thomas P. Gore and Oklahoma Public Opinion, 1917–18," *Journal of Southern History*, 27 (1961), pp. 344–53.

6. Compare Seward W. Livermore, *Woodrow Wilson and the War Congress, 1916–18* (Middletown, Conn., 1966), pp. 17–18, with HMAC, *Increase of Military: Hrgs.* (1917), pp. 12, 14, 26–27, 35, 63, 145–47, 150, 254.

7. HMAC, *Increase of Military: Hrgs.*, p. 231; my italics.

8. Sen. John S. Williams to M.A. Holt, May 2, 1917, John Sharp Williams MSS, Box 25, LC.

9. HMAC, *Increase of Military: Hrgs.*, pp. 105, 136, 227–28, 243–60.

10. Sen. James K. Vardaman, speech reported in *Vicksburg* (Miss.) *Herald*, April 7, 1917, quoted in William Holmes, *The Great White Chief: James Kimble Vardaman* (Baton Rouge, La., 1970), p. 320; also James K. Vardaman to William J. Bryan, April 2, 1917, Bryan MSS, Box 31. See also references in *New York Age*, April 12, 1917, MG Tasker Bliss to Gen. R.K. Evans, April 4, 1917, Letterbook. 240, Bliss MSS; "Volunteers, Conscription, and Democracy", *Literary Digest*, 54 (April 21, 1917), p. 1147.

11. W.E.B. Du Bois, "Close Ranks," *Crisis*, 16 (July 1918), p. 111; and "The Negro's Fatherland," *Survey*, 39 (Nov. 10, 1917), p. 41.

12. James Weldon Johnson, "The Right to Fight," *New York Age*, April 12, 1917; similarly, Monroe Trotter in Florette Henri, *Black Migration: Movement North, 1900–1910* (New York, 1975), pp. 174–76.

13. Rep. S.J. Nicholls of Spartanburg, S.C., quoted in *New York Age*, May 3, 1917; on NAACP, see Roy Nash to Executive Committee, in Charles Flint Kellogg, *N.A.A.C.P.*, 2 vols., (Baltimore, 1967), I, p. 252.

14. NAACP, Executive Board Minutes, May 14, 1917, cited in ibid.

15. Amendment of Rep. Martin Madden, *Cong. Rec*, 65:1st, pp. 2421, 2429.

16. *New York Times*, April 6, 1917; WW to David F. Houston, secretary of agriculture, April 9, 1917, WW MSS, Series II; WW, Address, April 16, and letter to Rep. Guy T. Helvering, April 19, 1917, in Link, *PWW*, 42, pp. 71–75, 96–98. NDB in HMAC, *Increase of Military: Hrgs.*, pp. 244–45.

17. W.J. Bryan, "At War," *Commoner*, 17 (April 17, 1917), p. 3; see also Bryan to WW, April 6, 1917, Bryan MSS, Box 31.

18. HMAC, *Increase of Military: Hrgs.*, pp. 28, 259; Informal memorandum, EHC to Sen. McKellar, April 17, 1917, Crowder MSS, Box 2; Claude Kitchin to D.W. Pegram, Macon, N.C., May 16, 1917, Kitchin MSS, Reel 18.

19. Gerald W. Patton, *War and Race: The Black Officer in the American Military, 1915–1941* (Westport, Conn., 1981), pp. 32–102; also Emmett J. Scott, *The American Negro in the World War* (New York, 1919).

20. Kreidberg and Henry, *History of Military Mobilization*, p. 282.

21. For an analysis of the situation in Wisconsin where the German-born numbered 10 percent of the state's population, see Rep. John J. Esch to William F. Esch, May 2, 1917, John J. Esch MSS, State Historical Society of Wisconsin, Box 42.

22. Cardinal Gibbons, April 5, 1917, in John T. Ellis, *The Life of James Cardinal Gibbons*, 2 vols. (Milwaukee, 1952), pp. 239–40; also *The Pilot* (Boston Archdiocese), April 17, 1917, p. 1; May 19, 1917; "Call to Patriotism," *Catholic World*, 105 (May 1917), pp. 145–52. J. Harding, S.J., "The Justice of Conscription," *America* 17 (June 23, 1917), p. 263. For opposition: *N.Y. Freeman's Journal & Catholic Register*, June 16, 1917; *New World* (Chicago Archdiocese), April 20, 1917.

23. Labor opposition reported in *New York Times*, April 18, 22, 1917; letters from locals and labor councils, April 11 to 24, 1917, in Gompers MSS, Box 24; SMAC, *Temporary Increase of Military: Hrgs.*, pp. 11–12. On Gompers' support for conscription, see ch. 5, *supra*, notes 16–17; others in New York *Journal*, April 4, 1917.

24. Melvyn Dubofsky, *We Shall Be All: A History of the Industrial Workers of the World* (Chicago, 1969), pp. 355–57.

25. Jane Addams, Lillian Wald, and Norman Thomas to NDB, April 12 and reply, April 12, 1917, Wald MSS, Box 88, Columbia University; Addams to NDB, April 27, and reply April 29, 1917, Women's Peace Party Records, Box 3, SCPC; see also Chatfield, *For Peace and Justice*, pp. 70–86.

26. David A. Shannon, *The Socialist Party of America: A History* (New York, 1955), pp. 94–98; Alexander Trachtenberg, ed., *American Socialists and the War* (New York, 1917), p. 38; "Our Anticonscriptionist Enemies," *Literary Digest*, 54 (June 2, 1917), p. 1686; Harlem Union against Conscription, and its successors, broadsides, April 24, May 18, May 19, 1917, in Henry W.L. Dana MSS, Box 2, SCPC. Alice Wexler, *Emma Goldman: An Intimate Life* (New York, 1984), pp. 230–37.

27. See account in Rep. Anthony's former newspaper, Leavenworth *(Kan.) Times*, April 11, 1917, and HMAC, *Increase of Military: Report, House Report No. 17*, Part 1, 65:1st, (April 1917), pp. 3–5.

28. Ibid., pp. 1–3; speech by Rep. S. Hubert Dent, in *Cong. Rec*, 65:1st, (April 23, 1917), p. 959; *Biographical Directory of the American Congress* and obituary in *New York Times*, Oct. 7, 1933.

29. Rep. James H. Davidson (Rep.-Wis.) to Gov. E.L. Philipp, April 19, 1917, Philipp MSS, Box 4; see also New York *American*, April 17, 1917.

30. There was much discussion outside the House chamber about whether draftees could be sent into foreign service; Rep. Marvin Jones (Dem.-Tex.), unpublished "Memoir" (COHC, 1952), pp. 104, 131.

31. "Many Democrats want a volunteer system for foreign service as well as many Republicans." Rep. Frederick C. Hicks (Rep.-N.Y.), to TR, n.d. (April 18, 1917), TR MSS, Reel 229; see also "America's Part in the War," *New Republic*, 10 (Feb. 19, 1917), pp. 33–34; ibid., (March 31, 1917), p. 250; (April 7, 1917), p. 278; also the Hearst press, New York *American*, Aug 12, 1917; Andrew D. White, former president, Cornell University, to WW, April 26, 1917, WW MSS, Series IV; and constitutional lawyer Hannis Taylor, *Loyalty to the Constitution* (Washington, D.C., 1917). Bills for such a policy were unsuccessfully introduced by Rep. Frederick A. Britten, a Chicago Republican from a heavily German-American district, and later by Democratic Senator Thomas W. Hardwick of

Georgia. See *Cong. Rec*, 65:1st, (April 5, 1917), pp. 397–400, 412; (April 27, 1917), pp. 1400–1401; and (April 28, 1917), p. 1522, with the amendment rejected 120 to 26; and on Hardwick bill, C.T. Hallinan to Sen. K.D. McKellar, Aug. 30, 1917, McKellar MSS, Box 30. On such a policy in Australia, see Roy Forward and Bob Reece, eds., *Conscription in Australia* (St. Lucia, Australia, 1968); F.B. Smith, *Conscription Plebiscites in Australia, 1916–17* (2nd ed.; Clifton Hill, Australia., 1966). A somewhat similar policy was practiced unofficially by Britain in Ireland and later by Canada in dissident Quebec province when Ottawa adopted the draft on Aug. 29, 1917. See J.M. Hitsman, *Broken Promises: A History of Conscription in Canada* (Toronto, 1977), pp. 61–104. Because of Irish resistance, the draft was never put into effect in Ireland. See Rae, *Conscience and Politics*, pp. 34, 65, 156–57; and Alan J. Ward, "Lloyd George and the 1918 Irish Conscription Crisis," *Historical Journal*, 17 (1974), pp. 107–29. I am indebted to Scott B. Cook, Rutgers University, for calling my attention to this article.

32. Analysis based upon data obtained on each member of the HMAC from: *Biographical Directory of the American Congress; Congressional Directory, 1917*, Bureau of the Census, *Thirteenth Census . . . 1910*; and vote, HMAC, *Increase of Military: Rept., House Rept. No. 17*, Pt. II, pp. 5–10.

33. *New York Times*, April 20, 1917; obituary, San Francisco *Chronicle*, Dec. 19, 1924.

34. U.S. Cong., *Senate Report No. 22, Universal Liability to Military Service*, 65:1st, (April, 1917); and minority report Pt. II; *New York Times*, April 18–22, 1917.

35. McKellar to S.W. Farnsworth, March 24, 1917, McKellar MSS, Box 30; obituary, *New York Times*, Oct. 26, 1957.

36. Russell Buchanan, "American Editors Examine America's War Aims and Plans in April, 1917," *Pacific Historical Review*, 9 (Sept. 1940), pp. 262–64.

37. New York *American*, April 16, 1917; for similar, *Manufacturers Record*, April 12, 1917; "Conscription," *New Republic*, 10 (April 14, 1917), pp. 311–12.

38. Henry A. Wise Wood, chair, Conference Committee on National Preparedness, to editor, *The Commonwealth*, Scotland Neck, N.C., April 12, 1917, telegram, Kitchin MSS, Reel 17. NSL, *Annual Meeting, 1917*, (New York, 1917), pp. 12–14; House Special Committee, *NSL: Hrgs.*, p. 2–44.

39. For example, see H.K. Likley, luggage manufacturer, Rochester, N.Y., to Rep. Claude Kitchin, April 27, 1917, Kitchin MSS, Reel 17; Levering Moore, president, mortgage company, New Orleans, to Sen. J.S. Williams, April 21, 1917, Williams MSS, Box 25; Isaac N. Seligman, New York investment banker, *National Economic League Quarterly*, III (May 1917), p. 27; Seward Prosser, president, Banker's Trust, New York, in New York *American*, April 17, 1917; "The Selective Draft," *Iron Age*, 99 (April 12, 1917), p. 911; ibid., (April 19, 1917), pp. 954–57; "Militarism and Economics," *Commercial and Financial Chronicle*, 104 (May 19,

1917), pp. 1948–49; and "Business—Enthusiastic Conscript," *Nation's Business*, 5 (June 1917), pp. 9–11.

40. Benjamin Strong to WW, March 30, 1917, Benjamin Strong MSS, Federal Reserve Bank of New York, and Office of the Papers of Woodrow Wilson, Princeton University, courtesy of Prof. Arthur S. Link. For similar, Judge Joseph M. Molyneux, Minneapolis, Minn., to Sen. Knute Nelson, April 11, 1917, Nelson MSS 39–F–3–7B.

41. John Bakerville, executive, American Merchants Syndicate, Chicago, to Rep. Henry A. Cooper, April 24, 1917, Cooper MSS, Box 3; italics added. For similar, see J.J. Phoenix of Bradley Knitting Co., Delavan, Wis., to Cooper, April 23, 1917, ibid.; Sydney L. Dodds., planter, of Hickman, Ky., to Rep. Alben W. Barkley, April 18, 1917; and L.H. Baekeland, past president, American Institute of Chemical Engineers, Yonkers, N.Y., to Sen. John S. Williams, April 18, 1917, Williams MSS, Box 24; Gov. T.W. Bickett of North Carolina to WW, April 18, 1917, WW MSS, Series IV; and New York *World*, April 21, 1917. On drafting loafers and antiwar socialists, see W.D. Lovell, Minneapolis contractor, to Sen. Knute Nelson, May 4, 1917; William S. Dwinnell, state senator from Minneapolis, to Nelson, April 13, 1917, Nelson MSS 39–F–3–7B.

42. C.M., Eau Claire, Wis., to Rep. John J. Esch, telegram, April 27, 1917, Esch MSS.

43. Telephoned message, Rep. Jouett Shouse (Dem.-Kan.), April 16, 1917, WW MSS, Series IV; see also New York *World*, April 21; New York *American*, April 22–28, 1917.

44. *Cong. Rec.*, 65:1st, (April 27, 1917), p. 1375. See also ibid., pp. 909, 970–80, 1351, 1369 70.

45. Rep. Sydney Anderson (Rep.-Minn.) in *New York Times*, April 25, 1917; Rep. William Adamson (Dem.-Ga.) ibid., April 24, 1917.

46. Frelinghuysen quoted in *New York Times*, April 25, 1917; see also Sen. John S. Williams in *Cong. Rec.*, 65:1st, (April 23, 1917), pp. 909, 946, 1441.

47. Sen. Hardwick, ibid. (April 27, 1917), pp. 1319–24; see also ibid., pp. 978, 1327, 1362.

48. Rep. James Beauchamp "Champ" Clark, ibid. (April 25, 1917), p. 1120. The phrase is from Robert H. Wiebe, *The Search for Order, 1877–1920* (New York, 1967), p. xiii.

49. *Cong. Rec.*, 65:1st (April 25, 1917), p. 1120.

50. Jones, "Memoir," COHC p. 132. For press vilification, *Washington Post*, April 27, 1917; New York *World*, April 28, 1917.

51. See New York *World*, *New York Times*, New York *American*, and *Washington Post*, April 29, 1917, and *Searchlight on Congress*, I (May, 1917), p. 3.

52. Ibid. and *Cong. Rec.*, 65:1st, (April 28, 1917), p. 1408.

53. New York *American*, April 29, 1917.

54. Jones, "Memoir," pp. 136–37. For influences, see New York *Post*, April 26, 1917; the (London) *Times*, April 30, 1917; Gov. E.L. Philipp to Rep.

J.A. Frear, April 30, 1917, Philipp MSS, Box 4; Rep. Simeon Fess (Rep.-Ohio) to his family, April 19, 26, 1917, Simeon Fess MSS, Box 10, Ohio Historical Society, Columbus, Ohio; C.J. Weber to Philip Lehner, April 18, 1917, Esch MSS, Box 41; Rep. Claude Kitchin to Judge R.W. Winston, May 15, 1917, Kitchin MSS, Reel 18. Politically, "a member [of Congress] can always say he supported the Government and get away with it." William F. Esch to brother, Rep. John J. Esch of Wis., April 21, 1917, Esch MSS, Box 41.

55. For example, see Rep. John A. Moon (Dem.-Tenn.), Chattanooga *News*, n.d. [mid-April, 1917], clipping in McKellar MSS, Box 9.

56. Livermore, *Politics is Adjourned*, pp. 27–28.

57. *New York Times*, May 8, 11, 1917. James Cannon, Jr., Anti-Saloon League, to Rep. John J. Esch, April 16, 23, May 1, 1917, Esch MSS, Boxes 41, 42; also Cronon, ed., *Diaries of Josephus Daniels*, p. 136.

58. On Roosevelt, see Livermore, *Politics is Adjourned*, pp. 19–31 and Harbaugh, *Life and Times of Theodore Roosevelt*, pp. 470–74.

59. H. C. Lodge to TR, April 23, 1917, Henry Cabot Lodge MSS Massachusetts Historical Society, Boston; Sen. Warren G. Harding introduced the amendment; see also House Diary, entry of April 19, 1917, Yale University.

60. Although the *New York Times*, May 8, 1917, reported that Roosevelt had enrolled 200,000 men and received several offers of fully equipped units, Livermore, *Politics is Adjourned*, p. 252n. claimed not more than 1,500 men actually signed up. The truth is elusive. The Roosevelt Papers indicate that he corresponded mainly with potential officers who were expected to raise their own units upon approval; also many offers went to the corps' headquarters for processing. Roosevelt and friends never doubted such a force could have been raised. See A.E. Wilson to TR, May 3, 1917, and TR to S. Simpson, May 25, 1917, TR MSS, Reels, 231, 391.

61. For press support for the draft and TR Volunteers, see *Washington Post*, April 22, 1917; Boston *Transcript*, April 14, 1917; April 25, 1917; Franklin (Ind.) *Star*, May 3, 1917, clippings, TR MSS, Reel 231; Louisville *Courier-Journal* quoted in *Current Opinion*, 62 (May, 1917), p. 304; Hearst press in *Literary Digest*, 54 (May 12, 1917), pp. 1241, 1395.

62. Rep. Frank L. Greene (Rep.-Vt.) to Frank E. Howe, May 16, 1917, in Frank L. Greene MSS, LC; F. E. Scobey, San Antonio, Tex., to Sen. Warren G. Harding, May 2, 1917, Harding MSS, Reel 263; Lehr Fess to Rep. Simeon Fess, May 11, 1917, Fess MSS, Box 10; Nathan M. Palmer, Warrenton, N.C., to Rep. C. Kitchin, May 30, 1917, Kitchin MSS, Reel 19.

63. Sen. Kenneth D. McKellar, "Draft Law," pp. 19–20, typescript "Memoir," McKellar MSS, Box 7.

64. The Senate approved the Roosevelt Volunteers by 56–31. *New York Times*, April 29, 1917; the House defeated them, 170–106.

65. Quoted in *Literary Digest* (April 28, 1917), p. 1242.

66. For criticism, see Leonard Wood Diary entry, March 4, 1917, Wood MSS; Pierce Anderson to Grenville Clark, May 15, 1917, Clark MSS.

67. Sen. Claude A. Swanson (Dem.-Va.) in H.C. Lodge to TR, May 4, 1917, Lodge MSS.
68. Lodge to TR, May 4, 1917, and reply May 10, 1917, both in Lodge MSS; *New York Times*, May 12, 1917.
69. House vote, 215–178, May 13, 1917; *New York Times*, May 14, 1917.
70. Ibid., May 14, 17, 1917; *Searchlight on Congress*, 2 (May, 1917), p. 4.
71. *New York Times*, May 19, 1917; "An Act to Temporarily Increase the Military Forces of the United States," U.S. *Statutes at Large*, XL, Pt. 2, p. 1666.
72. WW, statement, May 18, 1917, enclosed with NDB to WW, May 1, 1917, in Link, *PWW*, 42, pp. 179–82. Johnson had sought to replicate Wilsonian rhetoric; see Hugh S. Johnson, *The Blue Eagle: From Egg to Earth* (Garden City, N.Y., 1935), pp. 34–35.
73. WW, statement of May 18, 1917, in Link, *PWW*, 42, p. 181.
74. U.S. Army, *Mobilization Regulations, 1936*, Regulation 1–1, quoted in Army War College, G-1 Course, Report of Subcommittee No. 1, "Wartime Procurement of Volunteers," Nov. 10, 1936, p.3, AWC, G-1 Course, File No. 1–137–1, Military History Collection, Carlisle Barracks, Pa. For 1917 suggestions to use the Volunteer Act of 1914, see "How Shall We Raise an Army?" *Nation*, 104 (April 5, 1917), pp. 390–91.
75. "Everyman's War," *Independent*, 90 (April 14, 1917), p. 98; *Munsey's Magazine*, 61 (June 1917), pp. 53–5; William Cary Sanger, assistant secretary of war, 1901–03, to WW, April 17, 1917, WW MSS, Series IV.
76. On the various alternatives, the European use of colonial and other foreign troops is described in Charles J. Balesi, *From Adversaries to Comrades-in-Arms: West Africans and the French Military, 1885–1918* (Waltham, Mass., 1979); James Wellard, *The French Foreign Legion* (London, 1964); Jeffrey Greenhut, "The Imperial Reserve: The Indian Corps on the Western Front, 1914–1915," *Journal of Imperial and Commonwealth History*, 12 (October 1983), pp. 54–73; DeWitt C. Ellinwood and S.D. Pradhan, eds., *India and World War I* (Columbia, Mo., 1978), pp. 19–74, 177–226; Bryon Farwell, *The Gurkhas* (N.Y., 1984), pp. 86–114; Cynthia H. Enloe, *Ethnic Soldiers: State Security in Divided Societies* (Athens, Ga., 1980), esp. pp. 23–49; and Richard A. Preston, "The Multi-cultural and Multi-national Problems of Armed Forces," in Weigley, ed., *New Dimensions in Military History*, pp. 227–41.

On the American experience, see Frank Thackery, superintendent, Indian Reservation, Sacaton, Ariz., to MG Hugh L. Scott, April 25, 1917, Scott MSS, Box 28, and Scott's reply of April 27 that the General Staff and Secretary Baker were greatly opposed to forming an Indian or other ethnic unit: "I do not see any possibility of the Secretary receding from the position that he does not desire any racial troops [units] other than the negro, which we now have by law. We do not want any German, Slav, Italian or Irish regiments. We want a homogeneous army." The unsuccessful recommendation for 10 regiments of "North American Indian Cavalry" came from Dr. Joseph Kossuth Dixon, *North American Cavalry, Argument before the Committee on Military Affairs, House of Representatives 65th Cong. on H.R. 3970, July 25, 1917*, pamphlet, Scott

MSS, Box 70. A regiment of Puerto Rican Infantry, accepted into the U.S. Army in 1908, served in the Panama Canal Zone from May 1917 to March 1919. U.S. Army War College, *Order of Battle of the U.S. Land Forces in the World War (1917–1919)*, pt. 2 (Washington, D.C., 1949), p. 1405. In 1918, the U.S. drafted 10,000 Puerto Ricans, but they were completing training as the war ended. See also James R. Woolard, "The Philippine Scouts: The Development of America's Colonial Army," (Ph.D. dissertation, Ohio State University, 1975).

On ethnic units, Polish-American leaders offered 100,000 officers and men, and Slovak, Bohemian, Italian, and other immigrant groups were interested in forming such units. Gen. G.J. Sosnowski to WW, April 7, 1917, and NDB to WW, April 14, 1917, both in WW MSS, Series II; WW to NDB, May 21, 1917, ibid., Series IV; also Bruce White, "The American Military and the Melting Pot in World War I," in J.L. Granatstein and R.D. Cuff, *War and Society in North America* (Toronto, 1971), pp. 37–51. On blacks, see Nalty, *Strength for the Fight*, pp. 107–24; Arthur Barbeau and Florette Henri, *The Unknown Soldiers: Black American Troops in World War I* (Philadelphia, 1971), pp. 122–32; Gerald W. Patton, *War and Race: The Black Officer in the American Military, 1915–1941* (Westport, Conn., 1981), pp. 32–103. Although the Army Nurse Corps had been created in 1901, the General Staff refused to relax its prohibition against women in the enlisted ranks in World War I, despite the success of the British in creating women's auxiliary corps to perform many noncombatant tasks and the enlistment of 13,000 "Yeomanettes" by the U.S. Navy and Marine Corps in 1917–18. Mattie E. Treadwell, *Women's Army Corps* (Washington, D.C., 1954), pp. 1–12; Martin Binkin and Shirley J. Bach, *Women and the Military* (Washington, D.C., 1977), pp. 5–6.

77. On the importance of the conscriptionist organisations in preparing public opinion for the draft, see William Cary Sanger, to Joseph P. Tumulty, May 16, 1917, WW MSS, Series IV; Rep. Julius Kahn, HMAC, to H.H. Sheets, May 17, 1917, TR MSS, Reel 233; NDB to H.H. Sheets, Sept. 14, 1917, copy in Crowder MSS, Box 3; New York *Tribune*, July 1, 1918; Sen. George B. Chamberlain, to NDB, July 17, 1918, N.D. Baker MSS, LC; Kreidberg & Henry, *History of Military Mobilization*, p. 242; Finnegan, *Specter of a Dragon*, p. 191; Clifford, *Citizen Soldiers*, pp. 112–27.

78. "Cracks the whip" quote, Rep. Frederick C. Hicks to TR, n.d. [April 18, 1917], TR MSS, Reel 229. "What he wants he gets" quote, Clarence J. Weber, administrative assistant for Rep. John J. Esch (Rep.-Wis.) to Philip Lehner, April 18, 1917, Esch MSS, Box 41; similar in AUAM, "Confidential Bulletin," new series, no. 8 (Nov. 13, 1918), AUAM MSS, Reel 2.

79. BG J.E. Kuhn, chief, WCD, memorandum for CofS, Feb. 20, 1917, subj: A Plan for an Expansible army of 500,000; WCD-9433-7, pp. 5–7, in GS Records (RG 165), WCD, Genl. Corres., 1903–19, Box 444.

80. U.S. *Statutes at Large*, XL, pp. 76–83; Selective Draft Act, sec. 4; NDB to H.S. Johnson, Oct. 12, 1932, copy in Frederick P. Keppel MSS, Columbia University. On importance of "supervised decentralization," see

memos of May 26, June 18, 1917, reprinted in U.S., PMG, *Report of the Provost Marshal General to Secretary of War on the First Draft* (Washington, D.C., 1918), p. 12, (hereafter, PMG, *First Report*).

81. Appeal procedure in ibid., p. 61; PMG, *Second Report*, pp. 48–54.

82. Selective Draft Act, sec. 4. For criticism, *New Republic*, 11 (May 5, 1917), pp. 2–3.

83. Selective Draft Act, sec. 4.

84. See John A. Thompson, "American Progressive Publicists and the First World War, 1914–1917," *JAH*, 58 (Sept. 1971), pp. 364–83; Chambers, *Tyranny of Change*, pp. 230–33; and Frederic C. Howe, *Confessions of a Reformer* (Chicago, 1967, orig., 1925), pp. 17, 305–6.

85. Historians, like contemporaries, have differed over whether the Selective Draft Act was a progressive or conservative measure. The one specific study of the issue fails to reach a conclusion other than that progressives divided over the draft. Joe F. Decker, "Progressive Reaction to Selective Service in World War I," (Ph.D. dissertation, University of Georgia, 1969), esp. pp. 164–66.

86. "The Morality of Conscription," *New Republic*, 11 (May 5, 1917), pp. 7–8.

87. Nelson to O.A. Norman, April 24, 1917, Nelson MSS, 39F–3–7B.

88. Italics added. House Diary, March 26, 1917; also in Link, *PWW*, 41, p. 483; and entry of May 21, 1917, House MSS, Yale University. I am indebted to Prof. J. Garry Clifford for this last reference.

89. Joseph P. Tumulty to WW, May 24, 1917, copy in N.D. Baker MSS, Box 4, LC; also Brand Whitlock to NDB, April 27, 1917, ibid.; see also New York *Post*, April 28, 1917.

90. On the role of conservatives and other non-progressives, as well as progressives, in the changes of the "progressive era," see Chambers, *Tyranny of Change*, pp. 105–39, 230–32.

91. This conclusion is drawn in part from my roll-call analysis of the key votes on the draft, based upon data obtained from *Cong. Rec.*, 65:1st, (April 28, 1917), p. 1408; *Searchlight on Congress*, 1 (May, 1917), p. 3; three New York newspapers: the *World, New York Times*, and *American*, April 29, 1917; and the *Statistical History of the U.S.* The Senate, where the ideology of most members has been identified (H.W. Allen, "Geography of Politics: Voting on Reform Issues in the U.S. Senate, 1911–1916," *Journal of Southern History*, 27 [May, 1961], pp. 224–26), divided on ideological as well as urban-rural and sectional lines. Conservatives endorsed the draft 31–2, while reformers split almost evenly.

92. New York *Tribune*, quoted in *Literary Digest*, 54 (May 12, 1917), p. 1398; see similar editorial in New York *World*, April 30, 1917.

7 / Uncle Sam Wants You!, 1917–1918

1. On the experience of other nations and critiques of "decisionism" (the making of decisions based solely on objective considerations), see Gerald D. Feldman, "Political and Social Foundations of Germany's

Economic Mobilization, 1914–1916," *AF&S*, 3 (Fall 1976), pp. 121–46; and N.F. Dreisziger, ed., *Mobilization for Total War: Canadian, American and British Experience, 1914–1918, 1939–1945* (Waterloo, Ont., Canada, 1981), pp. 1–22, 71–86.

2. For other agencies, see Karl, *The Uneasy State*, pp. 34–49; Robert D. Cuff, *The War Industries Board: Business-Government Relations During World War I* (Baltimore, 1973); Ellis W. Hawley, *The Great War and the Search for a Modern Order* (New York, 1979), pp. 1–37, 226–29; and Kennedy, *Over Here*.

3. Lockmiller, *Crowder*, p. 54. Crowder served as judge advocate in the Philippines, worked in effect as minister of justice in the provisional government of Cuba, 1906–9, and was then appointed judge advocate general of the army. Ibid., pp. 13–152, obituary in *New York Times*, May 7, 1932; and *DAB*, XXI, Suppl. 1, pp. 210–12. On Oakes' report see Ch. 2, n. 70, *supra*.

4. The SSS hails Oakes as the "Father" of modern Selective Service, but the present author contends that despite Oakes' prescience, many of his recommendations clashed with localism, pluralism, and limited central government. Crowder, while accepting Oakes' other suggestions, wisely recognized this fact. PMG, *Second Report*, pp. 7–8.

5. Under pressure from Congress, Baker reluctantly agreed to exclude military officers from draft boards; see change in Baker's testimony between April 9, 10, and April 17, 1917, in HMAC, *Increase of Military Establishment: Hrgs.*, pp. 62, 154, 229. On concept of "supervised decentralization," see Crowder's testimony at meeting May 2–3, 1917, Council of National Defense, typescript in Grosvernor Clarkson MSS.

6. Palmer, *Baker*, I, pp. 212–14.

7. Enoch H. Crowder, *The Spirit of Selective Service* (Garden City, N.Y., 1920), p. 120; see also PMG, *First Report*, pp. 7–8. The suggestion of the voting precinct for registration came independently from former Rep. Burnett M. Chiperfield (Rep.-Ill.) and Sen. Porter J. McCumber (Rep.-N.D.). See B.M. Chiperfield to Peyton C. March, March 29, 1932, Peyton C. March MSS, LC; and Sen. P.J. McCumber to WW, May 10, 1917, Records of the Selective Service System, 1917–19 (RG 163), Federal Records Center, Suitland, Md. (Hereafter, SSS Records [RG 163]), Genl. File 112, Box 64.

8. NDB to Edgar J. Criswell, May 29, 1917, Records of Office of Secretary of War (RG 107), Box 1, NA. Also NDB, speech, May 2, 1917, "Proceedings of the National Defense Conference," p. 7.

9. John P. White in Minutes, Council of National Defense, June 12, 1917, Josephus Daniels MSS, LC. The remaining 10 percent included farmers and other occupational groups. My computation is based on figures in PMG, *Second Report*, p. 227.

10. PMG, *Second Report*, pp. 142, 251–69, 335–337.

11. John Henry Wigmore, "The Conduct of the War in Washington: A Critique of Men and Methods," n.d. [1919], typescript in John Henry Wig-

more MSS, Northwestern University Law Library, Chicago, Ill., Box 1, pp. 63–64. Personnel in PMG, *Second Report*, pp. 335–36.

12. Quoted in "Ten Million Answers to Germany," *Literary Digest*, 54 (June 16, 1917), p. 1831.

13. PMG, *First Report*, p. 14; see also H.S. Johnson to P. Archer, June 6, 1917, SSS Records (RG 163), Genl. File 27–3, Box 15.

14. PMG, *First Report*, pp. 15–21.

15. Only 11 percent of the 1.5 million husbands called in the first draft were taken, ibid., pp. 15–27, 51–53. In 1917–18, it was 25 percent. PMG *Second Report*, pp. 1–7, 49, 108–22. Northern laborers could earn $80 in busy months but had to pay for sustenance.

16. TR to EHC, Aug. 19, 1917, Crowder MSS, Box 3. "Chronicles of the Draft," Local Board, Dickson City, Pa., typescript [1919], SSS Records, (RG 163), Box 3.

17. BG J.E. Kuhn, chief, WCD, to CofS, June 7, 1917, subj: Tactical Reorganization, GS Records (RG 165), WCD 1050–30, Box 460; MG Henry Jervey, chief, Operations Division, GS, "Mobilization of the Emergency Army," lecture, GS Coll., Jan. 3, 1920, WD Records, Historical Branch, G-1, 12–6 (RG 165), Box 51.

18. PMG, *Second Report*, pp. 6, 13, 223. Except for Class I registrants whose number brought them within the current quota, registrants could still enlist in the navy or marines.

19. Ibid., pp. 6, 15, 224–25; *Chicago Tribune*, Aug. 11, 1918.

20. Secretary of War to Governors, May 26, 1917; PMG, *First Report*, p. 13.

21. Cuff, *War Industries Board*; Kennedy, *Over Here*, pp. 111–43.

22. Council of National Defense, meeting, Feb. 15, 1917, cited in Clarkson, *Industrial America in the World War*, pp. 24–25.

23. Public Law, No. 12, May 18, 1917; PMG, *Second Report*, pp. 126–28.

24. PMG, *First Report*, p. 33.

25. Herbert Hoover to WW, Aug. 27, 1917, WW MSS, also in Link, *PWW*, 44, pp. 72–73; "The Farmers and the Selective Draft," *Pierce's Farm Weeklies*, Nov. 15, 1917, clipping, SSS Records (RG 163), Box 28.

26. "Casting Bread Across the Waters," *Literary Digest*, 54 (April 21, 1917), pp. 1151–52; Kankakee (Ill.) *Republican*, May 18, 1917; *Wallace's Farmer*, June 28, 1918, clipping, SSS Records (RG 163), Box 28. NDB to WW, May 29, 1917, Records of Adjutant General's Office (RG 94), File 2638801, Inc. 105, Box 9071, NA.

27. PMG, *Second Report*, pp. 51, 135–37, 145. Crowder prevented the administration from granting blanket exemption to farmers; see NDB to WW, Sept. 2, 1917, WW MSS; also in Link, ed., *PWW*, 44, p. 123; PMG to Secretary of War, Feb. 14, 1918, Crowder MSS, Box 3; letters in Link, *PWW*, 46, pp. 178, 428n, 431, 446; and *PWW*, 51, pp. 212, 250–51.

28. My italics. NDB to WW, May 26, 1917, Baker MSS, LC, Box 4.

29. EHC to NDB, Jan. 7, 1918, N.D. Baker MSS, LC, Box 5; EHC to John H. Wigmore, July 14, 1918, Crowder MSS, Box 22; PMG, *Second Report*,

pp. 138–42; "Draft Exemption for Coal-Miners," *Literary Digest*, 58 (July 13, 1918), p. 16; "The Labor Situation," *Coal Age*, 24 (Aug. 8, 1918), pp. 276–78; NDB to WW, Jan. 14, May 22, 1918, WW to NDB, Jan. 15, 1918, N.D. Baker MSS, Box 8, LC.

30. Florence Kelley, "War and Women Workers," *Survey*, 39 (March 9, 1918), pp. 628–31; D.N. Crosthwaite, Jr., "Making up the Labor Short-ages," *Industrial Management*, 55 (May 1918), pp. 412–13; "Our Man-Power Famine," New York *Tribune*, June 23, 1918.

31. "Labor Shortage," *New Republic*, 12 (Oct. 20, 1917), pp. 316–17; "Skilled Men Drafted for War Duty," *Iron Age*, 100 (Nov. 8, 1917), p. 1118; "Draft Crippling Industries," *Literary Digest*, 55 (Dec. 1, 1917), pp. 31, 80.

32. PMG, Press Release, Dec. 3, 1917, SSS Records (RG 163), Genl. File 13740, Box 47. See also PMG to NDB, Sept. 22, 1917, ibid., Genl. File 22-10, Box 12; Unsigned memorandum, for PMG, Oct. 29, 1917, ibid., Genl. File 31–65, Box 17; PMG to acting CofS, memorandum, Nov. 3, 1917, subj: Exemption & Classification of Skilled Men in Industry & Army, in ibid., Genl. File 298, Box 66; PMG to NDB, Dec. 22, 1917, Crowder MSS, Box 3.

33. NDB to WW, April 22, 1918, Baker MSS, Box 8, LC.

34. PMG, *Second Report*, pp. 2–3, 45–48.

35. "Draft Made Really Selective," *Literary Digest*, 55 (Nov. 3, 1917), p. 10.

36. The states, in order of their adoption, were Maryland, West Virginia, Kansas, Nebraska, New Jersey, New York, Massachusetts, Rhode Island, Delaware, Louisiana, Georgia, Kentucky, and South Dakota. See H.G. Moulton, "Pressing Need: Industrial Conscription," *North American Review*, 206 (Dec. 1917), pp. 894–905; and Sen. McCumber's labor draft bill, *New York Times*, Feb. 26, 1918; also "Loafing a Crime," *Literary Digest*, (March 30, 1918), p. 19; "Compulsory Work Laws," U.S. Bureau of Labor Statistics, *Monthly Review*, 7 (Aug. 1918), pp. 429–30.

37. Louis B. Wehle to WW, Nov. 11, 1917, WW MSS, Link, *PWW*, 45, pp. 7–11.

38. New York *Tribune*, Feb. 15, 1918; also WW to William L. Hutcheson, Feb. 17, 1918, in Link, *PWW*, 46, p. 366.

39. WW to Sen. Joseph I. France, Feb. 14, 1918, WW MSS, Series VI, also in Link, *PWW*, 46, pp. 325–26, 343; on bills by Sens. France and McCumber, *Washington Herald*, Jan. 22, 1918; *New York Times*, Feb. 10, 1918.

40. Samuel Gompers to Louis Lochner, May 10, 1917; to WW, May 29, 1917; L.B. Schram to Maj. Charles B. Warren, May 29, 1917; Gompers to W.S. Gifford, June 2, 1917, all in Gompers MSS, Boxes, 24, 25; NDB, memo-randums, May 26, June 18, 1917, in PMG, *First Report*, p. 13.

41. Samuel Gompers, "Don't Conscript—Mobilize Labor," *American Federationist*, 24 (Dec. 1917), p. 1096. J.W. Sullivan, "There is No Short-age of Labor," ibid., 24 (Oct. 1917), pp. 842–45.

42. PMG, *Second Report*, p. 75. See also Benedict Crowell to WW, April 9, 1918, and reply, April 9, 1918, WW MSS.

43. PMG, *Second Report*, pp. 75–85; NDB to EHC, May 26, 1918, Crowder MSS, Box 22. After its adoption, Crowder suggested that by its effective use "the day of a compulsory [labor] conscription will be far postponed." PMG, memorandum for the President, June 15, 1918, Crowder MSS, Box 22; see also Col. Hugh S. Johnson to EHC, March 8, 1918, Records of Joint Army and Navy Selective Service Committee, (RG 147), File #100, Box 1, NA.

44. "Precis for War Council," March 19, 1918, Crowder MSS, Box 22.

45. Minutes and Resolution adopted by War Council, March 20, 1918, in re: confidential memorandum from PMG, Selective Draft & Adjustment of Industrial Manpower," SSS Records (RG 163), Genl. File 642, Box 67. See also A.S. Burleson to WW, April 5, 1918, in Link, *PWW*, 47, pp. 264–65; Benedict Crowell to WW, April 8, 1918, and reply, April 9, 1918, ibid., 296n, 299–300. On Speaker Cannon, see BG Hugh S. Johnson, "Draft Problems," p. 3, Lecture, AWC, Dec. 22, 1924, G-1 Course No. 22, Genl. File 261, Serv., Mil., U.S., 287 A-22, Military History Collection, Carlisle Barracks, Pa. (Hereafter, Johnson, "Draft Problems," AWC lecture, Dec. 22, 1924.)

46. Johnson, "Draft Problems," AWC lecture, Dec. 22, 1924, p. 3.

47. *Washington Post*, April 5, May 17, 26, 1918; *New Republic* (May 11, 1918), clippings, SSS Records (RG 163), Entry 17, Box 44.

48. San Francisco *Chronicle*, April 6, 1918; *Chicago Tribune*, April 19, 1918; clippings in SSS Records (RG 163), Entry 17, Boxes 44, 60; "work or fight" order of May 17, 1918 in U.S. Committee on Public Information, *Official Bulletin*, May 24, 1918.

49. Johnson, "Draft Problems," AWC lecture, Dec. 22, 1924, p. 3, notes occupations, but does not admit to class bias.

50. August Hermann to NDB, Aug. 20, 1918; NDB to EHC, Aug. 23, 1918; reply, Aug. 24; SSS Records (RG 163), Genl. File 74–75, Box 59.

51. Chicago *Daily News*, May 23, 1918; *Detroit Journal*, May 24, 1918; *New York Times*, May 24, 1918; "War-Work or Fight," *Literary Digest*, 56 (June 8, 1918); *Detroit Free Press*, July 14, 1918; *Cincinnati Inquirer*, July 20, 1918; clippings, SSS Records (RG 163), Entry 17, Box 60.

52. Woodward, *Lloyd George and the Generals*, pp. 282–336.

53. Coffman, *War to End All Wars*, pp. 127ff; Beaver, *Baker*, pp. 110–50.

54. PMG to CofS, memo, July 27, 1918, PMG, *Second Report*, pp. 312–17.

55. PMG, *First Report*, p. 60; see also BG Morrison to HLS, HLS MSS.

56. Gompers to WW, Aug. 14, 1918, N.D. Baker MSS, LC, Box 8; also in Link, *PWW*, 49, pp. 255–56; on management, EHC to John H. Wigmore, July 18, 1918, Crowder MSS, Box 3; PMG, Memorandum for President, June 15, 1918, ibid., Box 22; Rep. Edward Pou, not drafting "boys," New York *World*, July 27, 1918.

57. Louisville (Ky.) *Courier-Journal*, June 14, 1918, clipping, SSS Records (RG 163), Box 44.

58. PMG Memorandum for CofS, subj: "Changes in the Draft;" CofS, memorandum for PMG, Aug. 3, 1918, subj: Limits of Draft Age;" both in CofS

Records (RG 165), File #400, Draft, Box 394–401; see also EHC to Gov. Luke E. Wright, W. Va., July 30, 1918, Crowder MSS, Box 3. *New York Times*, July 24–Aug. 4, 1918.

59. WW to NDB, Aug. 20, 1918, and reply, Aug. 22, N.D. Baker MSS, LC, Box 8, also in Link, *PWW*, 49, pp. 294–95, 328–29.

60. LTC John H. Wigmore, memorandum for PMG, May 28, 1918, subj: Plan of Campaign for Supplying Adequate Numbers of Selectives, July 1, 1918, to July 1, 1919, SSS Records (RG 163), Genl. File 994, Box 70; New York *Tribune*, June 17, 1918; PMG, *Second Report*, pp. 24–32.

61. PMG to CofS, July 27, 1918, subj: Changes of Draft Age, in PMG, *Second Report*, pp. 312–317; *New Republic* (July 27, 1918), p. 361; "To Call on Our 'Uttermost Force,'" *Literary Digest*, (Aug. 17, 1918), pp. 12–13; 40 U.S., *Statutes at Large*, p. 955 (Aug. 31, 1918).

62. PMG, *Second Report*, pp. 24–32, 42–43, 223.

63. WW to NDB, Aug. 24, 1918, N.D. Baker MSS, LC, Box 8. For other governmental intervention in the labor market, mainly through coordination rather than coercion, see Kennedy, *Over Here*, pp. 260–68; Louis V. Wehle's reports in *Quarterly Journal of Economics*, (1917–1919).

64. Col. J.S. Easby-Smith to EHC, Aug. 16, 1918, Joint Army and Navy Selective Service Committee Records (RG 147), File #100, Box 1.

65. Anti-labor quote from LTC J.I. Miller to EHC, memorandum, Oct. 8, 1918, subj: "Proposed Solution of Industrial Slacker Problem," see also H.C. Adler, memorandum for EHC, Oct. 14, 1918, subj: "Industrial Slackerism," both in Crowder MSS, Box 22. On origins of "work or fight," see EHC, memorandum for Secretary of War, Jan. 7, 1918, N.D. Baker MSS, LC, Box 5.

66. WW to Members, District Lodge No. 55, and other striking workers, Sept. 13, 1918, in Link, *PWW*, 49, pp. 539–40. Wilson also ordered the plant managers to reinstate all returning strikers, under threat of government seizure of the plant. WW to Remington Arms Co., Sept. 7, 1918, ibid., 51, pp. 24, 49–50. On Bridgeport, Conn., and Staten Island, N.Y., shipyard incidents, see New York *Tribune*, Feb. 15, 1918; Kennedy, *Over Here*, pp. 261–70; Conner, *National War Labor Board*, pp. 130–34.

67. Army War College, Personnel Committee, "Selective Draft: Study of Draft Laws, Civil War & World War," Jan. 21, 1920, p. 5, Genl. File 261, Serv., Mil., U.S., 190-A/1, in Military History Collection, Carlisle Barracks, Pa.

68. Figures from PMG, *Second Report*, pp. 226–29. The 2,810,296 draftees represented 25 percent of registrants, 67 percent of the army on Nov. 11, 1918, and 72 percent of the soldiers obtained since the U.S. entered the war on April 6, 1917.

69. Walter Millis, *Arms and Men* (New York, 1956), p. 209.

70. PMG, *Second Report*, p. 51.

71. Ibid., p. 80.

72. Unsigned letter to EHC, June 12, 1918, Crowder MSS, Box 3; see also Philadelphia *North American*, July 8, 1918; Chicago *Daily News*, July 9,

1918; clippings, SSS Records (RG 163), Box 60. Indirectly, the federal order may have been most effective in assisting local authorities to enforce state anti-loafing and compulsory work laws; see "Work or Fight in the South," *New Republic* (May 13, 1918); Mandel Serner, "New Bern's Work or Fight Labor Ordinance," *American City*, 19 (Oct. 1918), pp. 310–11.

73. Quoted in PMG, *Second Report*, p. 81.

74. One such critic was Mark Sullivan, *Our Times: The United States, 1900–1925*, Vol. V, *Over Here, 1914–1918* (New York, 1933), pp. 489–91.

75. Cuff, *War Industries Board*, pp. 140–49; Kennedy, *Over Here*, pp. 126–40.

76. The political economy of mobilization has been variously characterized. Emphasis on massive progressive voluntarism is in Benedict Crowell and Robert Wilson, *How America Went to War* (New Haven, Conn., 1921); Grosvenor B. Clarkson, *Industrial America in the World War* (Boston, 1923). Wartime partnership, with big business domination through "dollar-a-year" corporation executives leading government agencies, is the focus of James Weinstein, *The Corporate Ideal in the Liberal State* (Boston, 1968), esp. pp. 172–213; Melvin I. Urofsky, *Big Steel and the Wilson Administration* (Columbus, Ohio, 1969), pp. 66–76; and Paul A.C. Koistinen, *The Military-Industrial Complex* (New York, 1980), pp. 23–46. More recently, some historians have emphasized wartime bureaucratization and greater authority for public administrators as a harbinger of the liberal, regulatory, and administrative State which reached fruition in the New Deal; see Kennedy, *Over Here*, pp. 138–43; Robert D. Cuff, "American Mobilization for War, 1917–45: Political Culture vs. Bureaucratic Administration," in Dreisziger, ed., *Mobilization for Total War*, pp. 71–86.

77. This minimally expanded State, one which went significantly beyond laissez-faire but which fell short of Statism, is described in Ellis W. Hawley, *The Great War and the Search for a Modern Order* (New York, 1979) and Robert D. Cuff, *The War Industries Board* (Baltimore, 1973).

78. My treatment of the Selective Service System has been particularly influenced by Ellis W. Hawley's examination of the Food Administration and other wartime mobilization agencies; see especially, Hawley, "The Great War and Organizational Innovation: The American Case," paper presented at Princeton University, Jan. 21, 1984. Hawley drew upon Kenneth Boulding, "Intersects: The Peculiar Organizations," in Conference Board, *Challenge to Leadership* (New York, 1973), pp. 179–201; and the concept of the "developmental state" (of parallel, but interlinked public-private authorities, central elite, and institutional apparatus for fostering community spirit and building social consensus) pioneered in Japan and studied by Chalmers Johnson, *MITI and the Japanese Miracle* (Stanford, Calif., 1982), esp. pp. 17–34, 305–24.

79. "Associative State" is Hawley's apt term. On the study of corporatism and non-Statist coordinative machinery in Europe, see Philippe C. Schmitter and Gerhard Lehmbruch, eds., *Trends Toward Corporatist*

Intermediation (Beverly Hills., Calif., 1979) and Gerhard Lehmbruch and Philippe C. Schmitter, eds., *Patterns of Corporatist Policy-Making* (Beverly Hills, Calif., 1982).

8 / Critics, Dissenters, and Resisters, 1917–1918

1. Despite the powerful drive of the "organizational synthesis," one of its major limits has been its neglect or trivialization of the unorganized and of those who opposed the development of large-scale, national, bureaucratic institutions. Outside of this synthesis, critics and dissenters in World War I have received considerable attention, particularly in critiques of wartime suppression; for example, Horace Peterson and Gilbert Fite, *Opponents of War, 1917–18* (Madison, Wis., 1957); Paul L. Murphy, *World War I and the Origins of Civil Liberties in the U.S.* (New York, 1979), and Steinson, *American Women's Activism.*

2. For evidence of ethnic opposition despite the dearth of outspoken leadership, see (Chicago) *Illinois Staats-Zeitung*, Feb. 8, 1918; March 14, 1918; (Chicago) *Abendpost*, Aug. 15, 26, 1918; (Chicago) *Dziennik Zwiazkony*, June 4, 1917; March 11, 1918; all in U.S. Works Projects Administration, "The Chicago Foreign Language Press Survey," translations of Chicago newspapers of twenty-two ethnic groups, 1860s–1930s; completed in 1942, microfilm, Newspaper Division, Chicago Public Library.

3. Thelan, *La Follette*; Robert L. Morlan, *Political Prairie Fire* (Minneapolis, 1955), pp. 143–164.

4. Jeffersonian Pub. Co. *v.* West, 245 Fed. 585 (S.D. Ga., 1917); see also Military Intelligence Division, "Weekly Intelligence Summaries," July 7, 1917, p. 12; Aug. 11, 1917, pp. 11–12, copies in N.D. Baker MSS, Cleveland.

5. PMG *Second Report*, pp. 207–12; Peterson and Fite, *Opponents*, pp. 24, 28, 39, 99.

6. Du Bois, "The Black Soldier," *Crisis*, 16 (June 1918), p. 60; and "Close Ranks," ibid. (July 1918), pp. 111–12. Henri, *Black Migration*, pp. 274–76.

7. Jane Addams to Helena Dudley, April 19, 1917, Jane Addams MSS, Box 6, SCPC; the Women's Peace Party became the WILPF in 1919.

8. T. Roosevelt, "Conscientious Objectors, Spies and Slackers," Sept. 24, 1918, in *Roosevelt in the Kansas City Star: Wartime Editorials* (Boston, 1921), pp. 221–24.

9. AUAM, Executive Committee Minutes, April 4, 9, 30, May 7, 1917, AUAM MSS; C.T. Hallinan to Villard, Dec. 1, and reply Dec. 3, 1917, Villard MSS.

10. Wilson quoted in Josephus Daniels, Diary, Aug. 31, 1917, in Link, *PWW*, 44, p. 107. John A. Fitch, "Organized Labor in Wartime," *Survey*, (Dec., 1917), pp. 232–33; Samuel Gompers, "America's Labor Convention in War Time," *American Federationist* 25 (Jan. 1918), pp. 32–3; Frank L.

Grubbs, *The Struggle for Labor Loyalty: Gompers, the A. F. of L., and the Pacifists, 1917–1920* (Durham, N.C., 1968), pp. 16–18.

11. William L. O'Neill, *The Last Romantic: A Life of Max Eastman* (New York, 1978), pp. 58–81.

12. Judge Julius M. Mayer in U.S. Supreme Court, Transcript of Record, October Term, 1917, No. 702, Emma Goldman & Alexander Berkman, Plaintiffs in Error *v.* U.S. (Southern District of New York), p. 13.

13. Murphy, *World War I*, pp. 104–5, 173 is highly critical of Wilson, but the president may have considered prosecuting I.W.W. leaders under the Espionage Act to be preferable and milder than the extreme suggestions from western governors and editors for federal indictment of all I.W.W. activists and deportation of those found to be aliens.

14. In mail balloting, Socialist party members upheld the St. Louis resolution 21,000 to 8,000. Milton Cantor, "The Radical Confrontation with Foreign Policy: War and Revolution, 1914–1920," in Alfred F. Young, ed., *Dissent: Explorations in the History of American Radicalism* (DeKalb. Ill. 1968), pp 223–30. Quotation from Trachtenberg, ed., *American Socialists and the War*, p. 42.

15. James Weinstein, *The Decline of Socialism in America, 1912–1925* (New York, 1965), pp. 140–59.

16. Burleson quoted in *Literary Digest*, 55 (Oct. 4, 1917), p. 2.

17. Nick Salvatore, *Eugene V. Debs: Citizen and Socialist* (Urbana, Ill, 1982), pp. 291–300; Weinstein, *Decline of Socialism*, pp. 119–76.

18. For recent reinterpretations, challenging the federal wartime radical-suppression concepts enunciated by Zechariah Chaffee, Jr., *Freedom of Speech* (New York, 1920); Peterson and Fite, *Opponents*; and others, see David M. Rabban, "The First Amendment in Its Forgotten Years [1890–1917]," *Yale Law Journal*, 90 (Jan. 1981), pp. 514–96; and Arthur S. Link, "That Cobb Interview," *JAH*, 72 (June 1985), pp. 7–17. Pressed by ultra-nationalists and focusing upon foreign affairs, Wilson partially lost control to zealous subordinates less resistant to local pressures for suppression. See Link, *PWW*, 46, pp. 458–61; ibid., 47, pp. 135–36. Half of the 2,000 federal prosecutions under the Espionage and Sedition Acts occurred in six western judicial districts. Also, imprisonment of 1,200 of the half million German aliens in U.S. was mild compared with Britain's internment of all its 45,000 German nationals. The suggestion that chauvinism and repression derives more from local authorities and private groups than from the national government receives theoretical support from Grant McConnell, *Private Power and American Democracy* (New York, 1967) and Richard M. Brown, *Strain of Violence: Historical Studies of American Violence and Vigilantism* (New York, 1975); and specific confirmation in World War I from Bruce Fraser, "Yankees at War: Social Mobilization on the Connecticut Home Front, 1917–1918," (Ph.D. dissertation, Columbia University, 1976), pp. 144–233, 286–340; and William J. Breen, *Uncle Sam at Home: Civilian Mobilization, Wartime Federalism, and the*

Council of National Defense, 1917–1919 (Westport, Conn., 1984), pp. 79–89, 94, 106–7.

19. "The Enemy Within Our Cities," *National Service*, 2 (Dec. 1917), p. 307.

20. Joan Jensen, *The Price of Vigilance: The American Protective League* (Chicago, 1968).

21. T. Roosevelt, "Yankee Versus German Blood," Aug. 26, 1918, in *Theodore Roosevelt: His Life, Meaning and Messages*, ed., William Griffith, 3 vols. (New York, 1919), III, p. 958, see also 946–47, 867. On Taft, see *New York Times*, Feb. 22, April 4, 1918.

22. On the Chamberlain bill, the *New York Times*, April 17, 24, 28, 1918. In Britain, the Defense of the Realm Act, Aug. 4, 1914, authorized court martial for civilians communicating with the enemy or interfering with the means of communication, docks, or harbors. The Law of Siege, Aug. 4, Sept. 8, 1914, placed France under jurisdiction of summary courts martial, with trial within 24 hours of arrest. In Germany, the Law of Siege divided the country into military districts under commanding generals, ultimately with virtually dictatorial powers to "maintain public safety." Gooch, *Armies in Europe*, pp. 147–48.

23. Link, "That Cobb Interview," p. 14; Peterson and Fite, *Opponents*, pp. 14–15, 210, 216.

24. John C. Farrell, "John Dewey and World War I: Armageddon Tests a Liberal's Faith," *Perspectives in American History*, 9 (1975), pp. 308–9, 316–17.

25. WW to Max Eastman, Sept. 18, 1917, in Link, ed., *PWW*, 44, pp. 210–11, 169–72. The president frequently overruled the postmaster general's censorship; see WW to A.S. Burleson, Sept. 16, 1918, ibid., 51, p. 12.

26. Murphy, *World War I*, esp. pp. 39–47 and Paul L. Murphy, *The Meaning of Freedom of Speech* (Westport, Conn., 1972), pp. 11–21.

27. See Note 18, *supra*, also Arthur Marwick, *The Deluge: British Society & the First World War* (Boston, 1965), pp. 36–38, 80–85, 139–42; John Williams, *The Other Battleground: The Home Fronts, Britain, France, and Germany, 1914–18* (Chicago, 1972), pp. 6, 20–26, 64–65, and passim.

28. See Johnson, lecture, "Draft Problems", Dec. 22, 1924; also John Henry Wigmore, memorandum for EHC, Jan. 10, 1919, "Some Interesting Facts Developed in the PMG's Report," p. 2; Crowder MSS, Box 4. "Ten Million Answers to Germany," *Literary Digest*, 54 (June 16, 1917), p. 1831.

29. EHC to W.C. Fitts, Nov. 5, 1917, SSS Records (RG 163), Genl. File 229, Box 66.

30. Crowder's estimate that some 150,000 of an estimated 1,000,000 new 21-year-olds had successfully evaded draft registration on June 5, 1918 is in PMG, memorandum for Secretary of War, Aug. 3, 1918, subj: "Contemplated Measures for Securing 100 Per Cent Registration under Proposed Law to Extend Draft Registration Ages," SSS Records, Genl., 74–49, Box 59. On Mexico City antidraft colony, see *Kansas City Star*, July 7, 1918.

31. Dept. of Justice, Circular. No. 742, Oct. 8, 1917, and Statistics Compiled from Responses of U.S. Attorneys, Dept. of Justice Records. (RG 60), Numerical file 186233, Box 2033, NA.

32. T.J. Day to EHC, Jan. 25, 1918; also "In Re: Henry Terrill, Colored. Failure to Register," and other cases in Records of U.S. Attorney, Mobile, Ala., Selective Service Act Enforcement Records, 1917–18, Box 22, National Archives and Records Center, Atlanta, Ga.

33. James R. Green, *Grass-Roots Socialism: Radical Movements in the Southwest, 1895–1943* (Baton Rouge, La., 1978), pp. 354–68; Garin Burbank, "The Social Origins of Agrarian Socialism in Oklahoma, 1910–1920" (Ph.D. dissertation, University of California, Berkeley, 1974); Charles C. Bush, "The Green Corn Rebellion," (M.A. thesis, University of Oklahoma, 1932); PMG, *Second Report*, pp. 207–10; "Uncle Sam's Little War in the Arkansas Ozarks," *Literary Digest*, (March 8, 1919), pp. 107–9; James F. Willis, "The Cleburne County Draft War," *Arkansas Historical Quarterly* 26 (1967), pp. 24–39.

34. PMG, *Final Report of the Provost Marshal General to the Secretary of War on the Operations of the Selective Service System to July 15, 1919* (Washington, D.C., 1920), (hereafter, PMG, *Final Report*), pp. 52–53. Compare with draft delinquency rates of 1/2 of 1 percent in World War II, and over 20 percent early in the Vietnam War; Dept. of Justice, *Report of the Attorney General FY 1946*, p. 15; SSS, *Annual Report of the Director, FY 1965*, pp. 17–22.

35. Bergoll went into hiding when his draft notice arrived, but taunted federal agents and the press by sending postcards as he traveled. Captured after the war during a visit to his mother, Bergdoll escaped again and fled to Germany where he remained until 1939. He returned voluntarily to spend five years in military prison during World War II. His son, Albert, was arrested for draft evasion during the Korean War. Roberta E. Dell, *The U.S. against Bergdoll* (New York, 1977). Figures from PMG, *Second Report*, 192–97, 225–26. On evasion along the Mexican border, see diary entry, Oct. 23, 1917, LTC Samuel D. Pepper MSS, University of Michigan.

36. See T.W. Gregory to WW, Sept. 9, 1918, citing NDB to Gregory, Aug. 5, 1918, in Link, *PWW*, 49, p. 500; also Peterson and Fite, *Opponents*, pp. 57–60, 79, 203.

37. Jensen, *Price of Vigilance*, pp. 188–218, Murphy, *World War I*, pp. 125–26, 221–23; Peterson and Fite, *Opponents*, pp. 230–34.

38. Frank I. Cobb to Joseph P. Tumulty, Sept. 5, 1918, Link, *PWW*, 49, p. 451; editorial, New York *World*, Sept. 6, 1918; see also Peterson and Fite, *Opponents*, pp. 230–32.

39. T.W. Gregory to WW, Sept. 9, 1918, Link, *PWW*, 49, pp. 501–2; Murphy, *World War I*, pp. 126–27, 223–34. On the reorganization of the FBI, see entry, June 4, 1919, Grayson diary, Office of Papers of Woodrow Wilson, Princeton University, courtesy of Prof. Arthur S. Link. To be included in Link, *PWW*, 59 (forthcoming, 1989).

40. NDB to WW, May 11, 1920, and reply, N.D. Baker MSS, LC, Box 13–13a. Figures, PMG, *Final Report*, pp. 52–53.

41. EHC to A.B. Bielaski, chief, FBI, June 15, 1918, SSS Records, North Carolina File, 17–21; Box 225; EHC to Bielaski, Oct. 18, 1917, ibid., Genl. File 17–34, Box 7. Figures, Wigmore to PMG, "Some Interesting Facts in [PMG] Report," Jan. 10, 1919, Crowder MSS, Box 4.

42. See Chatfield, *For Peace and Justice*, pp. 42–70 and Norman Thomas, *The Conscientious Objector in America* (New York, 1920).

43. John Nevin Sayre to WW, April 27, 1917, and reply, May 1, 1917, Link, *PWW*, pp. 159–60, 179.

44. "I had more criticism for befriending conscientious objectors than I have had for any sort of oppressive action towards them." NDB to Myrta L. Jones, Dec. 21, 1921, Frederick Keppel MSS, Columbia University.

45. Secretary of War, *Statement Concerning the Treatment of Conscientious Objectors in the Army* (Washington, D.C., 1919), p. 17.

46. Leonard Wood to Jacob Greenberg, Oct. 21, 1918, ACLU Files, Vol. 96, p. 17, Princeton University. The names of the objectors who died in military prisons, a number from pneumonia or other ailments connected with their harsh treatment and one, Ernest Gellert, from suicide, are listed in "C.O.s Who Died in Military Prisons," typed list, ACLU Files, 1918, Vol. 71, p. 67; clippings, pp. 87–97; news release, n.d., Federated Press Service, Vol. 122, p. 69 (which differ on whether 13 or 15 deaths); and 17 names listed by Stephen M. Kohn, *Jailed for Peace: The History of American Draft Law Violators, 1658–1985* (Westport, Conn., 1986), pp. 29, 42n.

47. Secretary of War, *Statement Concerning . . . C.O.'s*, p. 16.

48. Quoted in James C. Juhnke, *Mennonite Life* (Jan. 1970); see also A. Teichroew, "World War I and the Mennonite Migration to Canada to Avoid the Draft," *Mennonite Quarterly Review*, 45 (1971), pp. 219–49.

49. Mark A. May, "The Psychological Examinations of C.O.'s," *American Journal of Psychology*, 31 (April 1920), pp. 154–61.

50. Addams, *Peace and Bread*, p. 4.

51. Figures from May, "Psychological Examinations of C.O.'s," pp. 160–61, but see also Chatfield, *For Peace and Justice*, chs. 1–2.

52. Secretary of War, *Statement Concerning . . . C.O.'s*, pp. 17–19. Under prodding, the administration on March 21, 1918, specified non-combatant activities within the army for c.o.'s. Only after congressional action did the government begin in June 1918 to furlough some c.o.s to work in civilian agricultural and relief activities. See NDB to WW, Aug. 22, 27, 1917, Link, *PWW*, 44, pp. 29, 74; Benedict Crowell to WW, March 19, 1918, ibid., *PWW*, 47, p. 72–73.

53. Figures, Secretary of War, *Statement Concerning . . . C.O.'s*, p. 25; SSS, *Conscientious Objection*, I, p.60; an account by head of the board is Walter G. Kellogg, *The Conscientious Objector* (New York, 1919).

54. Evan Thomas, "Disciplinary Barracks," *Survey*, 41 (Feb. 1, 1919), pp.

625–29; Ernest L. Meyer, *Hey! Yellowbacks!* (New York, 1930); David D. Lee, *Sergeant York: An American Hero* (Lexington, Ky., 1985), pp. 10–39. I am indebted to Prof. Edward M. Coffman for this last reference.

55. Roger N. Baldwin, *The Individual and the State: The Problem as Presented by the Sentencing of Roger N. Baldwin* (New York, 1918), p. 6.

56. George F. Peabody to WW, Oct. 31, 1918, Link, *PWW*, 51, pp. 534–35; "Mercy for C.O.'s," *Literary Digest*, 60 (Feb. 8, 1919), p. 33; the Wilson administration released the last 33 c.o.'s in November 1920.

57. NDB to WW, July 22, 1918, *Cong. Rec.*, 65:3rd (Feb. 12, 1919), p. 3237; WW to B. Crowell, Sept. 13, 1918, WW MSS. On WW's general desire for a wide amnesty for c.o.'s, see NDB to WW, July 1, 1919, Link, ed., *PWW*, 61 (forthcoming, 1989). The WWII experience is treated in Mulford Q. Sibley and Philip E. Jacobs, *Conscription of Conscience: The American State and the Conscientious Objector, 1940–1947* (Ithaca, NY, 1952).

58. John Henry Wigmore to Alice and Frank [Dains], Mollie [Height], Dec. 9, 1917, Wigmore MSS.

59. Arver et al. *v.* U.S., the *Selective Draft Law Cases*, 245 U.S. 366 (1918). On their socialism, Alfred Jaques, U.S. Attorney to the Attorney General, Aug. 10, 1917, Dept. of Justice Records, (RG 60) File No. 186233–118. The other cases were Goldman et al., *v.* U.S., 245 U.S. 474 (1918); Ruthenberg et al. *v.* U.S., 245 480 (1918). Briefs for Plaintiffs and for the U.S. in Supreme Court briefs, October Term (Washington, D.C., 1954), microfilm copy 216, Reel 15. Plaintiffs were represented by Harry Weinberger and Clarence Darrow; the U.S. by the solicitor general, John W. Davis. See William H. Harbaugh, *Lawyer's Lawyer: The Life of John W. Davis* (New York, 1973), pp. 124–25; Murphy, *World War I*, p. 215.

60. Arver, et al. *v.* U.S., 245 U.S. at 377–78 (1918); on White's commitment to the expansion of national power in emergencies, see Marie C. Klinkamer, *Edward Douglass White* (Washington, D.C., 1943), pp. 61, 221, 238; Paul L. Murphy, *The Construction in Crisis Times, 1918–1969* (New York, 1972), pp. 10–13.

61. Arver, et al., *v.* U.S., 245 U.S., at 390.

62. Goldman *v.* U.S. 245, U.S. 474, 477 (1918); Ruthenberg et al. *v.* U.S. 245, U.S. 480 (1918).

63. Legal debate over the *Arver* opinion has generally accompanied popular controversy over conscription: over the first prewar draft in 1940, the possibility of postwar UMT&S, and the operation of the draft in the Vietnam War. See Ch. 1, note 38, *supra*. On contemporary legal support for the draft, see Charles E. Hughes, "New Phases of National Development," *American Bar Association Journal* 4 (Jan. 1918), pp. 54, 93; Thomas W. Gregory, ibid., pp. 309–16.

64. Oliver W. Holmes quoted in Tennant S. McWilliams, *Hannis Taylor: The New Southerner as an American* (University, Ala., 1978), p. 80. Taylor was arguing on behalf of Robert Cox, a drafted Missouri militiaman, who sued to prevent General Wood and the U.S. government

from sending him to Europe. Taylor argued that the power to compel military service was linked historically and legally to short-term home defense, not overseas expeditionary forces. Cox *v.* Wood, 247 U.S. 3 (1918); motions, briefs, and correspondence in Dept. of Justice Records (RG 60) File 160492–39, declassified, 1969. For a rejection of Taylor's argument, see J.R.C. "Memo. for the Atty. Genl.," enclosed with T.W. Gregory to WW, Sept. 1, 1917, in Thomas W. Gregory MSS, Box 1, LC; letter, not memorandum, also in Link, *PWW*, 44, pp. 60, 119–20.

65. Lofgren, "Compulsory Military Service," pp. 61–88; see also Loren P. Beth, *Development of the American Constitution, 1877–1917* (New York, 1971), p. 164.

66. SSS Records, Okla., File 17–19, Box 240; Richmond (Va.), *Journal*, Aug. 22, 1917, ibid., Box 28; William T. Hutchinson, *Lowden of Illinois*, 2 Vols. (Chicago, 1957), I, p. 368. On partisanship, see William G. McAdoo to NDB, July 3, 10, 1917; W.G. McAdoo MSS, LC, Letterbook No. 50; Josephus Daniels to NDB, July 14, 1917, Daniels MSS, LC; "'Politics' in Draft-Exemptions," *Literary Digest*, 55 (July 14, 1917), pp. 9–10.

67. Arthur Barbeau and Florette Henri, *The Unknown Soldiers: Black American Troops in World War I* (Philadelphia, 1974); William W. Griffin, "Mobilization of Black Militiamen in World War I: Ohio's Ninth Battalion," *Historian*, 40 (Aug. 1978), pp. 686–703; Gerald W. Patton, *War and Race: The Black Officer in the American Military, 1915–1941* (Westport, Conn., 1981), pp. 32–102.

68. Robert V. Haynes, *A Night of Violence: The Houston Riot of 1917* (Baton Rouge, La., 1976).

69. "Where to Encamp the Negro Troops," *Literary Digest*, 55 (Sept. 29, 1917), pp. 14–15; also Richard C. Brown, "Social Attitudes of American Generals 1898–1940," (Ph.D. dissertation University of Wisconsin, 1951), pp. 189–196.

70. Henri, *Black Migration*, pp. 294–95; see also chief, WCD, memorandum for CofS, Nov. 13, 1917 in GS Records (RG 165), WCD 8142–46; BG Henry Jervey, Acting Assistant CofS., Director of Operations, memorandum to Adjutant General, March 21, 1918, subj: "Disposition of the Colored Draft, Called into Service Beginning March 29, 1918," CofS Records (RG 165), file 400, "Draft," Box 393–401.

71. H.G. Learned, Adjutant General's Office, to PMG, Sept. 14, 1917, attached to MG Tasker Bliss, Assistant CofS, memorandum for Secretary of War, Sept. 7, 1917, subj: "Mobilization and utilization of colored drafted men," SSS Records, Genl. 61–30, Box 36.

72. M. Bolton to C. Kitchin, Sept. 18, 1917, Kitchin MSS, Reel 20; see also EHC to HLS, Sept. 15, 1917, HLS, MSS; EHC memorandum for CofS, Sept. 18, 1917, SSS Records, Genl. 28–24, Box 16.

73. EHC to Sen. Thomas Hardwick, n.d., SSS Records, Ga. 27–4, Box 111. Italics in original. See also EHC to Governors of Southern States, Dec. 10, 1917, ibid., Genl. 28–42, Box 16. Blacks were classified separately, such as "Colored Class I."

74. Rep. Claude Kitchin to Sucie Hays, Jan. 7, 1917 (actually 1918), Kitchin

MSS, misfiled in Reel 14; EHC, memorandum for Dr. Keppel, Feb. 27, 1918, SSS Records, Genl. 61–87, Box 36; EHC memorandum for Emmett J. Scott, March 23, 1918, ibid., Genl. 68–127, Box 48, and May 3, 1918, ibid., Genl. 28–63, Box 16; and PMG to CofS, May 11, 1918, subj: "Deferment of call for colored troops," and reply by BG Henry Jervey, Director of Operations, May 21, 1918, both in ibid., Genl. 61–112, Box 37.

75. EHC, memorandum for Third Assistant Secretary of War (Keppel), Sept. 30, 1918, SSS Records, Genl. 1449, Box 73.

76. Third Assistant Secretary of War Frederick Keppel, former dean of Columbia College who twenty years later as president of the Carnegie Foundation would commission Gunnar Myrdal's historic investigation of the circumstances of American blacks, found 48 percent of black registrants were held eligible for military service (Class I) compared to 26 percent of the whites. F.P. Keppel to PMG, Sept. 27, 1918, SSS Records, Genl. 1449, Box 73. By the end of the war, the PMG reported the figures as 52 percent of blacks compared to 33 percent of whites in Class I. Although blacks were 10 percent of the population and 9 percent of the registrants, they made up 13 percent of draftees. PMG *Second Report*, pp. 191–92; J.H. Wigmore, "Some Interesting Facts Developed in the [PMG] Report," Jan. 10, 1919, Crowder MSS, Box 4.

77. EHC, memorandums for Third Assistant Secretary of War, Sept. 27, 30, 1918, SSS Records, Genl. 1449, Box 73. For criticism, see John F. Baker, Flint, Mich. to NDB, Dec. 3, 1918, in ibid., Mich. 68–72, Box 168.

78. Crowder erred in stating that practically all 650,000 white enlistments among those between the ages of 21 and 30 could be considered in Class I reservoir for comparative purposes; many of these volunteers could have obtained occupational or other deferments. John H. Wigmore claimed the higher Class I ratio among blacks was due to a higher ratio of delinquencies than among whites and to a lower level of dependency deferments among blacks; however, these could have been due to racial discrimination.

79. PMG, *Second Report*, p. 193.

80. Quoted in Foner, *Blacks and the Military*, p. 112. EHC to L. Wood, July 20, 1918, Crowder MSS, Box 3.

81. NDB to John F. Baker, Dec. 12, 1918, SSS Records, Mich. 68–72, Box 168; EHC to Keppel, Sept. 30, 1918, ibid., Genl. 1449, Box 73.

82. Paul T. Murray, "Blacks and the Draft: A History of Institutional Racism," *Journal of Black Studies*, 2 (Sept., 1971), pp. 57–76. Since many blacks had low incomes, the soldier's pay of $30 a month plus family allotments of $15 to $50 a month through War Risk Insurance frequently meant a family would receive more money with the man in the army, a computation often used by southern boards. Roscoe Conklin to EHC, Nov. 5, 1917, Joint Army and Navy Selective Service Committee Records (RG 147), #100, Box 1.

83. Northern Republican critics charged the method chosen by the Census Bureau aided the Democratic South since registration was conducted

more efficiently in urban than rural areas. Determination of population by multiplying draft registrants by ten (the proportion of the entire population who were males, age 21–30), therefore produced large, fictitious populations—and inflated initial draft quotas—in the industrial North. New York *Sun*, July 18, 1917; New York *Tribune*, Sept. 17, 1917. Census Director Samuel L. Rogers denied any conscious regional benefit. New York *Sun*, July 18, 1917. The distortion was confirmed by the 1920 Census and publicized by the GOP before the election; Republican Publicity Association press release, Oct. 1920, "The Cards Were Stacked," in Rep. Frank L. Greene MSS, Box 24, LC; also New York *Tribune*, Oct. 12, 25, 1920; clippings in Crowder MSS, Box 29.

84. PMG, *Second Report*, pp. 89–90.

85. New York *Tribune*, Sept. 17, 1917; "To Draft Aliens," *Literary Digest*, 55 (Sept. 29, 1917), p. 13.

86. Frederic F. Purdy, et al., to WW, Aug. 16, 1917, WW MSS; Kennedy, *Over Here*, p. 157.

87. Quoted in *Literary Digest* (Sept. 29, 1917), p. 13.

88. "To Get the Alien Slacker," *Literary Digest*, 55 (Aug. 4, 1917), p. 22.

89. Wilfred A. White, "British Recruiting in the U.S.," *National Service* 4 (Sept., 1918), pp. 81–83. On Lansing's negotiations and congressional frustration, see New York *Tribune*, Nov. 29, 1917; New York *World*, Jan. 31, Feb. 28, 1918, clippings, SSS Records, Boxes 32, 44. The treaties with half a dozen nations were ratified between July and November 1918.

90. PMG, *Second Report*, pp. 86–108.

91. Ibid., pp. 94–95. Figures extrapolated from Table 26A, p. 400.

92. PMG, *First Report*, p. 96. Figure of 9 percent extrapolated from Jacobs and Hayes, "Aliens in U.S. Armed Forces," *AF&S*, p. 193.

93. PMG, *Second Report*, pp. 102, 104–7.

94. BG Lytle Brown, director, War Plans Division, to CofS, July 6, 1918, CofS Records (RG 165), file 10762; also WPD, memorandum for CofS, May 22, 1918, ibid.

95. Memorandum for CofS, Jan. 10, 1918, file 10073; March 3, 1918 and BG Henry Jervey, Adjutant General, to Isaac Kushner, March 13, 1918, CofS Records, (RG 165) file 10050.132; on alien officers, National Defense Act of 1916, ch. 134, Par. 24; Jacobs & Hayes, "Aliens in the U.S. Armed Forces," p. 190.

96. Memorandum for CofS, May 17, 1918, ibid., file 10050; also White, "American Military and the Melting Pot," p. 43.

97. PMG, *First Report*, pp. 44–47; *Second Report*, pp 150–68. However, John Henry Wigmore warned that the figures on illiteracy were mere guesswork. Selective Service never compiled such figures on a national scale. Wigmore to Crowder, Jan. 10, 1919, "Some Interesting Facts Developed in the [PMG] Report," p. 6; Crowder MSS, Box 4. On the IQ tests, see Daniel J. Kevles, "Testing the Army's Intelligence:

Psychologists in World War I," *JAH*, 55 (Dec. 1968), pp. 565–81; and James Reed, "Robert Yerkes and the Mental Testing Movement," in M. Sokal, ed., *Psychological Testing and American Society* (New Brunswick, N.J., 1987).

98. PMG, *First Report*, pp. 44–47; *Second Report*, pp. 150–68. "Fitting the Unfit: Physical Rejections," *Everybody's Magazine* (Dec. 1917), p. 128; C.B. Davenport and Albert G. Love, "Defects Found in Drafted Men," *Scientific Monthly*, 10 (Jan.–Feb. 1920), pp. 5–25, 125–41.

99. Dr. John H. Quayle, "Reclamation Camps for the Physically Unfit," *Forum*, 58 (Nov. 1917), pp. 579–84; "Reclaiming our Man-Power for War," *Literary Digest*, 57 (April 6, 1918), pp. 32–33. Adjutant General's Office to PMG, Aug. 28, 1918, subj: Induction of Limited Servicemen for Clerical Work, SSS Records, Genl. 57–38, Box 34.

100. "Teaching New Selectives," *Americanization Bulletin* (Sept. 15, 1918), SSS Records, Box 28; War Plans Division to CofS, June 3, 1918, subj: Plan for Preliminary Military Instruction of Class I Registrants, GS Records, WCD (RG 165) AWC 9317–103, Box 390; PMG, *Second Report*, pp. 298–303.

101. Jacobs and Hayes, "Aliens in the U.S. Armed Forces," p. 194.

102. Act of May 9, 1918, 40 *Statutes at Large*, XL, p. 542; P. Hazard, "Administrative Naturalization Abroad of Members of Armed Forces of U.S.," *American Journal of International Law* 46 (1952), pp. 295 ff.; figure, PMG, *Second Report*, p. 102.

103. PMG, *Second Report*, pp. 197–99; Kettner, *Development of American Citizenship*, pp. 292–93, 300n; Yazawa, "Citizenship," Greene, ed., *Encyclopedia of American Political History*, pp. 206–8.

104. Army War College, Historical Division, *Order of Battle*, pt. 2, pp. 661–62; PMG, *Second Report*, pp. 33, 219, 321–22.

105. Jose A. Cabranes, *Citizenship and the American Empire: Notes on the Legislative History of the U.S. Citizenship of Puerto Ricans* (New Haven, Conn., 1979), pp. 13–17. For traditional views, see Manuel Maldonado-Denis, *Puerto Rico* (New York, 1972), p. 108; L. Crips, *Puerto Rico* (Cambridge, Mass., 1974), pp. 23–24.

106. U.S., Bureau of Supplies, *Report of the Adjutant General to the Governor of Puerto Rico on the Operation of . . . Selective Draft in Puerto Rico* (Washington, D.C., 1924), p. 93; see also Cabranes, *Citizenship*, pp. 14–17, 37, 95–101.

107. Kankakee (Ill.) *Daily Republican*, April 18, 19, 1917.

108. Chicago *Tribune*, Nov. 1, 1917; *New York Times*, Feb. 6, 26, March 28, 1918; Washington *Herald*, May 9, 1918; Allan Nevins and Frank E. Hill, *Ford: Expansion and Challenge, 1915–1933* (New York, 1937), pp. 77–78; PMG, Memorandum for Secretary of War, Dec. 1, 1917, subj: Appeals to the President: Case of Robert Scripps, Baker MSS, LC, Box 14; PMG, *Second Report*, pp. 52–54. Most of 24,000 appeals to SSS HQ were rejected. PMG, *Second Report*, pp. 52–54. Wilson refused personal

requests for exemptions, even from friends. See WW to Kate D.M. Simons, Aug. 21, 1918, in Link, *PWW*, 48, pp. 305–6.

109. Between September and November 1918, draft-eligible college students were organized into units of a Students Army Training Corps, attending classes in uniform on their campuses. See Carol S. Gruber, *Mars and Minerva: World War I and the Uses of Higher Learning in America* (Baton Rouge, La., 1975), pp. 213–52.

110. "Memoir of the Draft," p. 4, District Board, Helena, Mont., in "Chronicles of the Draft" (1919), SSS Records, Entry 38, Box 3.

111. EHC, memorandum for Secretary of War, May 22, 1917, SSS Records, Genl. 114, Box 64; EHC to HLS, Oct. 10, 1917, HLS MSS.

112. On officer selection and training in World War I, see Beaver, *Baker*, pp. 37–39; Coffman, *War to End Wars*, pp. 54–58.

113. C.P. Crosby to Gov. J.A.A. Burnquist, Jan. 22, 1917, Burnquist Adm. MSS, 56–A–9–5B; Sen. Knute Nelson to Mrs. L.R. Noegle, April 24, 1917, Nelson MSS, 39–F–3–7B.

114. On the degree to which this was a progressive army, see Coffman, *War to End All Wars*, pp. 54–85, and Kennedy, *Over Here*, pp. 185–90. On the draftees' experience, see (Irving Crump) Conscript 2989, *Experiences of a Drafted Man*, (New York, 1918); Fred David Baldwin, "The American Enlisted Man in W.W. I," (Ph.D. dissertation, Princeton University, 1964).

115. Report of Dr. Thomas W. Salmon, enclosed with NDB to WW, July 18, 1919, in Link, ed., *PWW*, 61 (forthcoming, 1989). I am indebted to Prof. Arthur S. Link for bringing this document to my attention. See also *Report of the Chairman of Training Camp Activities to the Secretary of War, 1918* (Washington, D.C. 1918); N.D. Baker, "The Responsibility of an Officer of the Army of the United States," in Baker, *Frontiers of Freedom* (New York, 1918), pp. 63–66; Herbert F. Margulies, "The Articles of War, 1920: The History of a Forgotten Reform," *MA.*, 43 (April 1979), pp. 85–89.

116. "How Old Are You," *World's Work* (Aug. 1917); *Chicago Tribune*, June 25, 1917.

117. Cincinnati *Inquirer*, Feb. 9, 1918; "Identification of Dead Soldiers," *National Service*, 5 (April, 1919), p. 248, which lists European methods.

118. Gordon Snow, "Reflections of a Draft-Board Man," *Atlantic*, 122 (Aug. 1918), pp. 196–205; G. Taylor, "Draft: A Great Human Experience," *Survey*, 38 (Aug. 4, 1917), p. 404; E.H. Crowder, *The Selective Service System, Its Aims and Accomplishments, and Its Future* (Washington, D.C., 1917). Figures from PMG, *Second Report*, pp. 251–53.

119. John Kennan, chair, Local Board No. 47, Philadelphia, Pa., "Report," "Chronicles of the Draft" (1919) SSS Records, Entry No. 38, Box 3.

120. A.B. Stoughton and Harry A. Fricke, L.B. No. 45, Northeast Philadelphia, Pa., "Report" in ibid. On IRS, see John H. Judge, chair, legal advisory board, to Local Board No. 129, New York City, in New York *Sun*, Dec. 4, 1918, Crowder MSS, Box 26.

121. Local Board No. 39, in south Philadelphia, Pa., *Our Board* (Philadelphia, 1918) and *History of Draft Board 40 of Philadelphia*. (Philadelphia, 1919) pamphlets; Philadelphia *Record*, Oct. 28, 1918, clipping, SSS Records, Entry 38, Box 3.

122. U.S., WD, Acting Chief, Militia Bureau, *Annual Report, 1918* (Washington, D.C., 1918), pp. 8–11; Mahon, *History of the Militia*, pp. 156–61.

123. American draftees did not engage in combat in massive numbers until the last two months of the war; most of the 50,000 American battle deaths were reported in the press after the Armistice. A study of two subsequent wars showed popular support declined in direct proportion to sharp increases in casualty rates, without evidence of ultimate victory. John E. Mueller, "Trends in Popular Support for the Wars in Korea and Vietnam," *American Political Science Review*, 65 (June 1971), pp. 365–67.

9 / The Legacy of the Draft, 1919–1987

1. John H. Wigmore, memorandum for PMG, Nov. 8, 1918, Wigmore MSS, Box 1; PMG memorandum for CofS, Nov. 11, 1918, subj: Demobilization, Crowder MSS, Box 3. So linked was the draft to the war, that when news of the armistice arrived, trains carrying draftees to training camps were ordered to turn around and return the young conscripts to their home towns, *New York Times*, Nov. 12, 1918.

2. NDB to Peyton C. March Nov. 23, 1918, CofS Records (RG 165), File 400, Box 393–401. J.H. Wigmore to Louis D. Brandeis and Felix Frankfurter, Nov. 11, 1918, Crowder MSS, Box 3. "The President Relapses," *New Republic* (Dec. 14, 1918). But see Peyton C. March, "Demobilization," *National Service*, 5 (April 1919), pp. 201–206; Edward M. Coffman, *The Hilt of the Sword: The Career of Peyton C. March* (Madison, Wis., 1966), pp. 154–60.

3. *New York Times*, Jan. 12, 1919; James R. Mock and Evangeline Thurber, *Report on Demobilization* (Norman, Okla., 1944), p. 210.

4. John Henry Wigmore to Frank Dains, Jan. 1, 1919, Wigmore MSS.

5. *American Yearbook, 1919*, p. 200; obituary, *New York Times*, May 7, 1932; *DAB*, XXI, Suppl. 1, pp. 210–12; Lockmiller, *Crowder*, pp. 230–56.

6. NSL, *National Security League: Before the War, During the War, After the War* (New York, Nov. 1918), pp. 12–13; pamphlet, NYPL. Attempt by Sen. Harry S. New to draft boys aged 19–21 into UMT, *New York Times*, March 25–30, 1918; defeated 36 to 26. Wilson rejected UMT, WW to NDB, July 30, 1918, WW MSS, Series VI.

7. BG Joseph E. Kuhn, "When Two Strong Men Stand Face to Face," *Military Surgeon* (Oct. 1917), p. 411; "Democracy and Military Service," *Infantry Journal* (Oct. 1918), p. 325.

8. Coffman, *Hilt of the Sword*, pp. 174–181; Gen. Frank McIntyre to Gen. Lytle Brown, memorandum, Dec. 2, 1918, File No. 50, CofS Records (RG

165); NDB to EHC, Dec. 30, 1918, SSS Records (RG 163), Genl. No. 1685, Box 75; N.D. Baker, "From Bayonets to Books," *Independent*, 99 (Aug. 16, 1919), pp. 218–19.

9. SMAC, *Hearings on Army Reorganization*, 66:1st and 2nd (Washington, D.C., 1919), pp. 27–28, 39, 43–44, 1178–1182.

10. NDB to G.F. Peabody, May 23, 1919, N.D. Baker MSS, LC, Box 10; see also HMAC, *Hearings on Army Reorganization*, 65:3rd (Washington, D.C., 1919), pp. 3–12, 40–44, 64–65.

11. NDB to Beecher Stowe, Sept. 20, 1929 [misdated, actually 1919], copy in Peyton C. March MSS, LC, Box 22. On Wilson's foreign policy aims in 1919, Link, *Woodrow Wilson: Revolution, War, and Peace*, pp. 72–128; Gardner, *Safe for Democracy*, pp. 231–80.

12. Tompkins McIlvaine, "Universal Training and Army Reorganization," *National Service*, 5 (Jan. 1919), pp. 23–25; Clifford, *Citizen Soldiers*, pp. 264–65; Charles Lydecker to Elihu Root, Dec. 5, 1918, Root MSS, Box 136. The effectiveness of the NSL was crippled when it sought to unseat some members of Congress in 1918 and was subsequently investigated by a House Committee which exposed its reliance on contributions from big business. See U.S. Cong., House, Special Committee to Investigate the NSL, *National Security League: Hearings*, 31 parts (Washington, D.C., 1919).

13. McIlvaine to NDB, Sept. 5, 1919, G. Clark MSS, Series II, Box 3.

14. John McAuley Palmer to G. Clark, April 17, 1919, Clark MSS, Ser. II, Box 4; see his memoir-biography, Irving B. Holley, Jr., *Gen. John M. Palmer, Citizen Soldier, and the Army of a Democracy* (Westport, Conn., 1982), pp. 413–79; but also Weigley, *Towards an American Army*, pp. 223–41. On the Uptonian emphasis on regulars and long-term training over briefly trained civilian "amateur" soldiers, see Ch. 2, note 80, *supra*.

15. T. McIlvaine, "A People's Army—Plan of the MTCA in Congress," *National Service*, 6 (Sept. 1919), pp. 150–65; G. Clark to T. McIlvaine, May 7, 1919, Clark MSS, Ser. II, Box 3.

16. T. McIlvaine, "American Legion," *National Service*, 5 (June 1919), pp. 348–49; HLS, Diary, Dec. 10, 1919; "What Civilians Say about UMT," press release, Oct. 22, 1919, MTCA Records, Box 12, Chicago Historical Society.

17. Martin L. Fausold, *James W. Wadsworth, Jr.: The Gentleman from New York* (Syracuse, N.Y., 1975), pp. 112–22.

18. MTCA, Secretary's Report, Jan. 15, 1920, Clark MSS, Ser. II, Box 6.

19. Editorial, *National Service*, 5 (April 1919), p. 235.

20. Howard H. Gross, president, UMTL, SMAC, *Hrgs.: Army Reorganization*, p. 1064; George Sutherland, "Military Preparedness: The Best Guarantee of Peace," Edwin Wildman, ed., *Reconstructing America* (New York 1919), p. 384.

21. Most senior officers opposed the League and supported a nationalist view; Brown, "Social Attitudes of American Generals," pp. 280–83. Charles Eliot and Grenville Clark supported the treaty and League, but

Lodge, Root, and Stimson favored a limited, defensive alliance. Jessup, *Root*, II, pp. 372–417; Widenor, *Lodge*, p. 306n. On Taft and A. Lawrence Lowell, see Roland N. Stromberg, "Uncertainties and Obscurities about the League of Nations," *Journal of the History of Ideas*, 33 (Jan.–March, 1972), pp. 139–54; "Peace and the League," *National Service*, 5 (May 1919), p. 262.

22. "Red flag" quote from UMTL, *The Real Melting Pot* (n.p., UMTL, 1919), booklet, U.S. Military History Collection, Carlisle Barracks, Pa.; "democracy safe" quote from Gen. Charles W. Martin, speech, unidentified newspaper clipping, Dallas, Tex., Oct. 11, 1919, enclosed with Charles W. Martin to William G. Haan, Oct. 22, 1919, Haan MSS, Box 5.

23. "Outline of Plan for UMT," memorandum, n.d., enclosed with A.F. Cosby to G. Clark, May 5, 1919, Clark, MSS, Ser. II, Box 1; also H.H. Gross, "Universal Military Training," *National Service*, 3 (April 1918), p. 135; and George W. Perkins in Elisha M. Friedman, ed., *American Problems of Reconstruction* (New York, 1918), p. 52.

24. Ekirch, *Civilian and Military*, pp. 195–206; Chatfield, *For Peace and Justice*, pp. 91–151; Chambers, *Eagle and the Dove*, pp. 68–73.

25. AUAM, Executive Committee, Minutes, Nov. 27, 1918; Feb. 14, Sept. 24, Oct. 23, 1919; AUAM MSS, Reel 1; Nov. 5, 1920, Reel 2; Steinson, *American Women's Activism*, pp. 350–80; National Farmers Union, *Minutes of the Annual Meeting, 1919* (Texarkana, [1920]), p. 50; *Farmer's Yearbook* (New York, 1919), p. 149; A.F. of L., *Report of Proceedings, 39th Annual Convention* (Washington, D.C., 1919), p. 78; Ekirch, *Civilian and Military*, p. 200; "Militarism is Waning," *Nation*, 108 (June 21, 1919), p. 973. On fears of southern whites, see AUAM Executive Committee, Minutes, Sept. 24, 1919, AUAM MSS, Reel 1; and AUAM, "Bulletin," new series No. 19 (Oct. 6, 1919); ibid., Reel 2; George F. James, MTCA education secretary, "Some Lessons of the Great War," typescript speech, n.d., (1919–20), MTCA Records, Box 12; Arthur F. Cosby, MTCA Secretary's Report, Jan. 15, 1921, in G. Clark MSS, Ser. II, Box 6.

26. Frank Mondell, *Cong. Rec.*, 66:2nd, p. 2119; and subsequently in New York *Post*, Jan. 28, 1920. On Chamber of Commerce and N.A.M. support for budget-cutting and reduction of the military, see Henry Mussey, successor to C.T. Hallinan as AUAM lobbyist, AUAM "Bulletin," new series, No. 30 (Dec. 16, 1920), AUAM MSS, Reel 2.

27. George F. Peabody to NDB, June 24, 1919, N.D. Baker MSS, LC, Box 10; Peabody to NDB, May 17, 1919, ibid.; Gerald Robinson, "Military Paternalism and Industrial Unrest," *Dial*, 67 (Aug. 23, 1919), pp. 137–39. However, some isolationists saw a drafted citizen-army as a check on overseas adventurism. Chicago *Daily News*, April 26, 1919.

28. "Universal Training vs. Preparedness," *New Republic*, 22 (March 17, 1920), pp. 70–72.

29. Bennett Champ Clark quoted in National Guard Association, *The First One Hundred Years: National Guard of the U.S.* (Washington, D.C., 1978), p. 15; an eastern minority, which supported increased cooperation with the War Department, was led by MG John F. O'Ryan, N.Y. N.G.; Army-

Guard rivalry is best described in Karsten, "Armed Progressives," pp. 223–31.

30. S. 3424 and H.R. 10583 are discussed in HMAC, *Hrgs: Army Reorganization*, pp. 1904–20. On results of 1920, see Mahon, *History of the Militia*, pp. 170–71; the four states were Maine, Vermont, New York, and Maryland. See AUAM Executive Committee, Minutes, April 29, 1919; AUAM "Bulletin," new series, No. 20 (Dec. 9, 1919), AUAM MSS, Reels 1,2.

31. WW, speech at St. Louis, Mo., Sept. 5, 1919, in Baker and Dodd, eds., *Public Papers of Wilson*, V, p. 638; For similar, consult ibid., VI, pp. 50–51, 392, 412–13. See also Coffman, *Hilt of the Sword*, p. 198; and Calhoun, *Power and Principle*, pp. 250–67.

32. Bernard L. Boylan, "Army Reorganization 1920: The Legislative Story," *Mid-America*, 49 (April 1967), pp. 115–28. But Coffman, *Hilt of the Sword*, pp. 173–211, and Clifford, *Citizen Soldiers*, pp. 262–95, offer more sophisticated accounts. The present account also draws upon the reports of AUAM and MTCA lobbyists, revealing much partisan maneuvering.

33. *New York Times*, Jan 4, Feb 10, 1920. Pershing's testimony, Oct. 31 to Nov. 5, 1919, SMAC, *Hrgs: Army Reorganization*, pp. 1517–1794. When Sen. Boies Penrose of Pennsylvania, chair of Finance Committee, repudiated UMT, Republican commitment rapidly eroded. C.T. Hallinan in AUAM "Bulletin", new series, No. 19 (Oct. 6, 1919). By Dec. 1919, the Baker-March bill was also dead. It was too expensive, and administration's endorsement allowed Republicans to take a "lofty" position against a large standing army and "militarism." C.T. Hallinan in AUAM "Bulletin," new series, No. 2, AUAM MSS, Reel 2.

34. C.T. Hallinan in AUAM "Bulletin", new series No. 22 (Feb. 14, 1920); approval of Wadsworth-Kahn UMT bill was 8–5 in SMAC, 11–9 in HMAC; ibid. new series, No. 23 (March 17, 1920); both in AUAM MSS, Reel 2 *New York Times*, Jan. 28, Feb. 4, 10, 1920.

35. WW to NDB, Feb. 7, 1920, N.D. Baker MSS, LC, Box 11; C.T. Hallinan, "Bulletin", new series No. 22 (Feb. 14, 1920), AUAM MSS, Reel 2. *New York Times*, Jan. 28, Feb. 4, 10, 1920.

36. J. W. Wadsworth to HLS, April 1, 1920, copy in Crowder MSS, Box 6; on House Republicans, C.T. Hallinan in AUAM "Bulletin," new series, No. 23 (March 17, 1920), AUAM MSS, Reel 2. *Cong. Rec.*, 66:2nd (March 18, 1970), p. 4560.

37. Memorandum of telephone conversation with Senator Wadsworth, April 12 [1920] by Arthur F. Cosby, MTCA executive secretary, enclosed with Cosby to Grenville Clark, misdated April 9, and to Archibald Thacher, April 12, 1920, all in G. Clark MSS, Ser. II, Box 1.

38. Memorandum, ibid.; see also AUAM "Bulletin," new series No. 24 (April 15, 1920), AUAM MSS, Reel 2; *Cong. Rec.*, 66:2nd, Sen. Vol. 59, (April 8, 1920), p. 5402; *New Republic*, 22 (April 21, 1920), p. 234. *New York Times*, April 10, 1970.

39. House adoption was 236–106, *Cong. Rec.* 66:2nd, (May 28, 1920), p. 7844; the Senate quickly followed. Ibid. (May 29, 1970), p. 7916.

40. C.T. Hallinan, AUAM "Bulletins," Oct. 6, 1919; Feb. 2, 14, and April 27, 1920; AUAM MSS, Reel 2. The Senate-House Conference Committee dropped the draft provision. Hallinan, "Bulletin," new series, No. 27 (June 8, 1920), AUAM MSS, Reel 2.

41. Hallinan, "Bulletin," new series No. 22 (Feb. 14, 1920) AUAM MSS, Reel 2.

42. Ibid., No. 26 (April 27, 1920); AUAM "Bulletin," No. 27 (June 8, 1920), AUAM MSS, Reel 2. Congress relied instead upon the more circuitous statement, Sec. 57 of the National Defense Act of 1916, that citizens not in the U.S. Army or National Guard were part of the "Unorganized Militia," an indirect, assertion that they were liable to some kind of military service in wartime.

43. Proposed veto message prepared by N.D. Baker, enclosed with NDB to WW, June 4, 1920; in response to Wilson's request, June 3, 1920, in N.D. Baker MSS, LC, Boxes 12, 13.

44. NDB to WW, June 3, 1920, ibid., Box 13. The National Defense or Army Reorganization Act of June 4, 1920 is U.S., Statutes at Large, XLI, pp. 759–812.

45. The 1920 act provided the basic legislation governing the organization and regulations of the U.S. Army until 1950. U.S. Army, American Military History, 1607–1953 (Washington, D.C., 1956), p. 363. Consistent with the prevailing anti-immigrant sentiment, Congress in 1920 re-imposed the 1894 prohibition against enlisting non-declarant aliens and the War Department made U.S. citizenship an absolute requirement for officers. These prohibitions were not relaxed until World War II. See Jacobs and Hayes, "Aliens in the U.S. Armed Forces," pp. 189–190. Blacks were limited to the four traditional regiments and all recruitment of blacks, except veterans, was suspended in July 1919. Memorandum for CofS, July 19, 1919, File No. 8591–116, CofS Records (RG 165).

46. Bernard M. Baruch, "The War Industries Board," "confidential" lecture, Army War College, Feb. 12, 1924, copy in Grosvenor Clarkson MSS, Box 1; Hugh S. Johnson, "Fallacies of 'The Universal Draft,'" Army Ordnance, 10 (Nov.–Dec., 1929), pp. 155–57; "Conscription of Men and Money in Time of War," Nation, 130 (April 16, 1930), p. 439; Paul A.C. Koistinen, "The Industrial-Military Complex in Historical Perspective: The Interwar Years," JAH, 56 (March 1970), pp. 828–30.

47. Army War College, Personnel Committee, "Selective Draft: Study of Draft Laws Civil War and World War," Jan. 21, 1920, p. 1, Carlisle Barracks, Pa.; Hugh S. Johnson, "Industrial and Manpower Mobilization," (Dec. 11, 1922), p. 9; in ibid., Genl. File 261; 250–10; Joint Army and Navy Selective Service Committee (JANSSC), "Selective Service: Plans of Organization and Administration," mimeographed report, revised 1933, JANSSC Records (RG 147) No. 100.01, Box 2, NA.

48. J. Garry Clifford and Samuel P. Spencer, Jr., The First Peacetime Draft (Lawrence, Kans., 1986), pp. 41–47; see also Forrest C. Pogue, George C. Marshall: Ordeal and Hope, 1939–1942 (New York, 1966), pp. 56–63, for a more favorable view of Marshall's role.

49. Hugh S. Johnson, "Selective Service" Oct. 23, 1939, Lecture No. 5 (1939–40), G-1 MSS, Military History Collection, Carlisle Barracks, Pa. Italics added.

50. The Army's actions were not technically illegal, but neither were they *specifically* authorized by Congress. Without informing the national legislature, the Army had proceeded on a broad interpretation of Section 5 of the Army Reorganization Act of 1920 which gave the General Staff responsibility for *planning* "the mobilization of the manhood of the nation." See Maj. Lewis B. Hershey, Secretary, Joint Army and Navy Selective Service Committee (JANSSC), to Rep. Bruce Barton, Sept. 27, 1939, JANSSC Records (RG 147), No. 100.07, Box 2.

51. George Q. Flynn, *Lewis B. Hershey, Mr. Selective Service* (Chapel Hill, N.C., 1985), p. 63.

52. JANSSC, "Selective Service: Plans of Organization and Administration," memorandum report, 1933, p. 5, JANSSC Records (RG 147), No. 100.01, Box 2.

53. Murphy, *Constitution in Crisis Times*, pp. 80, 126–27; Ronald Schaffer, "The War Department's Defense of ROTC, 1920–1940," *Wisconsin Magazine of History*, 53 (Winter, 1969–70), pp. 108–20.

54. Commonwealth of Massachusetts, *Proceedings of the Constitutional Convention, 1917–18*, 4 vols. (Boston, 1920), III, pp. 20–79. Arthur Capper, "Let Us Tax the Vote Slacker," *New York Times Magazine* (Dec. 19, 1926); Henry J. Abraham, *Compulsory Voting* (Washington, D.C., 1955), pp. 3–33.

55. "The draft shattered the illusion of the melting pot and the little red school house," U.S. Commissioner of Education, *Annual Report 1919*, pp. 42–46, and 11–12, 50, 123; "A Nation-wide Drive for Social Reconstruction," *Survey*, 41 (March 1, 1919), p. 785; Horace M. Towner, "Federal Aid to Education," *University of Illinois Bulletin*, 19, no. 17 (Dec. 26, 1921), pp. 82–95; Howard J. Beard, "Physical Rejection for Military Service: Some Problems in Reconstruction," *Scientific Monthly*, 9 (July 1919), pp. 5–14; U.S. Cong., House, Committee on Immigration and Naturalization, *Prohibition of Immigration: Hearings*, 65:3rd (Washington, D.C., 1919), pp. 220, 284–85, 295–96.

56. Hugh S. Johnson to Albert Shaw, June 30, 1917, Crowder MSS, Box 3.

57. Quotation, EHC to Walter W. Davis, Nov. 26, 1919, Crowder MSS, Box 6. See also EHC to Julius H. Cohen, March 19, 1920, ibid.; E.H. Crowder, *The Spririt of Selective Service* (New York, 1920), pp. 224–54, 309–47, 398.

58. Praise in *Daily Metal Reporter* (Sept. 12, 1918); Martin Egan to EHC, Dec. 18, 1919; and other letters, Crowder MSS, Box 6. But for criticism, especially for assuming re-creation of wartime unity and restrictions on individual liberty, see J. Reuben Clark, Jr. to EHC, Jan. 7, 1919, ibid., Box 4, and a dozen book reviews in ibid., Box 29.

59. The Transportation Act of 1920 allowed the ICC to use state organizations by holding joint hearings of federal and state regulatory commissions. Following widespread evasion of Prohibition, the Coolidge ad-

ministration decided that federal enforcement could not be effective without state cooperation; state officials were appointed federal prohibition enforcement officers under supervision of U.S. Treasury Department.

60. William E. Leuchtenburg, "The New Deal and the Analogue of War," in John Braeman, et al., *Change and Continuity in Twentieth Century America* (Columbus, Ohio, 1964), p. 83; Gen. John J. Pershing, "We Are at War," *American Magazine*, 113 (June 1932), p. 74.

61. Charles W. Johnson, "The Civilian Conservation Corps: The Role of the Army," (Ph. D. dissertation, University of Michigan, 1968); Calvin W. Gower, "'Camp William James,': A New Deal Blunder?" *New England Quarterly*, 38 (December 1965), pp. 475–93; John A. Salmond, *The Civilian Conservation Corps, 1933–1942: A New Deal Case Study* (Durham, N.C., 1967). On the NRA, Hugh Johnson, and comparisons with the old SSS, see Russell Owen, "General Johnson Wages a Peace-Time War," *New York Times Magazine*, July 30, 1933, p. 3. Samuel Grafton, "The New Deal Woos the Army," *American Mercury*, 33 (Dec. 1934), pp. 436–37; Ruth McKenney, *Industrial Valley* (New York, 1939), p. 107; and [John F. Carter] "Unofficial Observer," *American Messiahs* (New York, 1935), p. 223.

62. The legislation empowered the ICC, Federal Power Commission, and SEC to use comparable state commissions.

63. Jane P. Clark, *The Rise of a New Federalism, Federal-State Cooperation in the United States* (New York, 1938), pp. 90–93, 296; and Jesse I. Miller, "General Crowder and the Wagner Act," typescript, n.d. [1938], Crowder MSS, Box 23.

64. Felix Frankfurter to EHC, n.d. (prob. July, 1918), Crowder MSS, Box 1; Ernest H. Gruening to EHC, July 6, 1918, ibid., Box 3; Gen. Peyton C. March quoted in *New York Times*, Dec. 6, 1918; Preston Slosson, *The Great Crusade and After, 1914–1928* (New York, 1940), pp. 37–38; Coffman, *War to End All Wars*, p. 29; Weigley, *History of the U.S. Army*, p. 358; Kreidberg and Henry, *History of Military Mobilization*, p. 279; Ferrell, *Woodrow Wilson and World War I*, pp. 15–16.

65. Hugh S. Johnson, "Industrial & Manpower Mobilization.," p. 1, lecture, Dec. 11, 1922, G-1, Course No. 7, Army War College, Washington, D.C., copy at U.S. Military History Collection, Genl. File 261, U.S., 250–10, Carlisle Barracks, Pa.

66. On the period, see John Braeman, "Power and Diplomacy: The 1920s Reappraised," *Review of Politics*, 44 (July 1982), pp. 342–69; Robert K. Griffith, Jr., *Men Wanted for the U.S. Army: America's Experience with the All-Volunteer Army Between the World Wars* (Westport, Conn., 1982).

67. Clifford and Spencer, *First Peacetime Draft.*

68. John O'Sullivan, *From Voluntarism to Conscription: Congress and Selective Service, 1940–1945* (New York, 1982); Flynn, *Lewis B. Hershey*, pp. 84–142; Albert A. Blum, *Drafted or Deferred: Practices Past and Present* (Ann Arbor, Mich., 1967); George Q. Flynn, *The Mess in Washington:*

Manpower Mobilization in World War II (Westport, Conn., 1979).

69. Melvyn P. Leffler, "The American Conception of National Security and the Beginnings of the Cold War, 1945–48," *AHR*, 89 (April 1984), pp. 346–81, and critiques, pp. 382–400, as well as from differing perspectives, John Lewis Gaddis, *Strategies of Containment: A Critical Appraisal of Postwar American National Security Policy* (New York, 1982); and Stephen E. Ambrose, *Rise to Globalism*, 3rd rev. ed. (New York, 1983).

70. The draft was re-enacted June 19, 1948 as a temporary solution to manpower shortages during a period of increasing tensions with the Soviet Union. Although the bill passed a month before the Berlin Blockade began in full on July 14, 1948, Russian harassment along the access routes had begun in April 1948 and undoubtedly contributed to public support for draft resumption. See Flynn, *Lewis B. Hershey*, pp. 170, 337n. On UMT, Frank D. Cunningham, "The Army and Universal Military Training, 1942–1948," (Ph.D. dissertation, University of Texas, Austin, 1976); Michael S. Sherry, *Preparing for the Next War: American Plans for Postwar Defense, 1941–1945* (New Haven, Conn., 1977).

71. James M. Gerhardt, *The Draft and Public Policy: Issues in Military Manpower Procurement, 1945–1970* (Columbus, O., 1971) provides a legislative history.

72. Burton I. Kaufman, *The Korean War: Challenges in Crisis, Credibility, and Command* (New York, 1986).

73. From an average of 500,000 a year from 1950–53, draft calls dropped from 251,000 in FY 1954 to 136,000 in FY 1956 and 90,000 in FY 1960; Flynn, *Hershey*, pp. 192–93, 341n. On Eisenhower era, see Stephen E. Ambrose, *Eisenhower: The President and Elder Statesman, 1952–1969* (New York, 1984); Douglas Kinnard, *President Eisenhower and Strategy Management: A Study in Defense Politics* (Lexington, Ky., 1977).

74. George C. Herring, *America's Longest War: The United States and Vietnam, 1950–1975*, 2nd ed. (New York, 1986); see also Andrew F. Krepinevich, Jr., *The Army and Vietnam* (Baltimore, 1986); Nancy Zaroulis and Gerald Sullivan, *Who Spoke Up? American Protest Against the War in Vietnam, 1963–1975* (New York, 1984); John E. Mueller, "Trends in Popular Support for the Wars in Korea and Vietnam," *American Political Science Review*, 65 (June 1971), pp. 358–75; Michael Useem, *Conscription, Protest and Social Conflict* (New York, 1973); Lawrence M. Baskir and William A. Strauss, *Chance & Circumstance: The Draft, the War, and the Vietnam Generation* (New York, 1978). Stephen M. Kohn, *Jailed for Peace: The History of American Draft Law Violators, 1658–1985* (Westport, Conn., 1986).

75. Gary L. Wamsley, *Selective Service and a Changing America: A Study of Organizational-Environmental Relationships* (Columbus, O., 1969); and the forthcoming study by George Q. Flynn, *The Draft and American Society, 1940–1973*.

76. See the contrasting assessments of Hershey in Flynn, *Lewis B. Hershey*, pp. 216–68; and Wamsley, *Selective Service*, pp. 181–242.

77. For a defense of Army leaders as supportive of a return to an all-

volunteer army, see Robert K. Griffith, Jr., "About Face? The U.S. Army and the Draft," *AF&S*, 12 (Fall, 1985), pp. 108–33; and "The Transition of the U.S. Army from the Draft to the All-Volunteer Force, 1968–1974," preliminary version, 1986, of book for U.S. Army, Center of Military History, Washington, D.C. The political basis of the decision to end the draft is emphasized in Gus C. Lee and Geoffrey T. Park, *Ending the Draft: The Story of the All-Volunteer Force* (Alexandria, Va., 1977). On Nixon's replacement of General Hershey, and elimination of local boards and inductions by 1973, see contrasting accounts by Flynn, *Lewis B. Hershey*, pp. 268–309; and by Hershey's successor, Curtis W. Tarr, *By the Numbers: The Reform of the Selective Service System, 1970–1972* (Washington, D.C., 1981).

78. For various views, see, Congressional Quarterly, *U.S. Draft Policy and Its Impact* (Washington, D.C., 1968), pp. 7–9, 25–32; Sol Tax, ed., *The Draft: A Handbook of Facts and Alternatives* (Chicago, Ill., 1968).

79. Richard M. Pious, *The American Presidency* (New York, 1979), pp. 400–15; Martin Binkin, *U.S. Reserve Forces* (Washington, D.C., 1974).

80. Draft registration was suspended in April 1975 by President Ford and later terminated; President Carter resumed it in July 1980. James B. Jacobs and Dennis McNamara, "Selective Service Without a Draft," *AF&S*, 10 (Spring 1984), pp. 361–79. On the resurgent attitudes towards increased military strength, see Philip Odeen, "Domestic Factors in U.S. Defence Policy," in Christopher Bertram, ed., *America's Security in the 1980s* (New York, 1983), pp. 22–31; and William Schneider, "Conservatism, Not Interventionism: Trends in Foreign Policy Opinion, 1974–1982," in Kenneth A. Oye, et al., eds., *Eagle Defiant: U.S. Foreign Policy in the 1980s* (Boston, 1983), pp. 33–64.

81. On the Reagan administration, see Jacobs and McNamara, "Selective Service Without a Draft," pp. 365–76. For opposition, see Gillam Kerley, "Do You Feel a Draft?" *The Progressive* (March 1985), pp. 20–23.

82. Caspar Weinberger quoted in the *New York Times*, June 21, 1981. President Ronald Reagan, in his second State of the Union Address, declared: "Defense is not just another budget expense. Keeping America strong, free, and at peace is solely the responsibility of the Federal Government; it is Government's prime responsibility." *New York Times*, Feb. 5, 1986.

83. On the student-aid requirement, introduced by Rep. Gerald B.H. Solomon, an upstate N.Y. Republican, see Edward B. Fiske, "Colleges Perplexed by New Draft Law," *New York Times*, July 19, 1983.

84. For the debate, see Robert K. Fullinwider, ed., *Conscripts and Volunteers: Military Requirements, Social Justice, and the All-Volunteer Force* (Totowa, N.J., 1983); Martin Anderson, ed., *Registration and the Draft* (Stanford, Calif., 1982); Brent Scowcroft, ed., *Military Service in the United States* (Englewood Cliffs, N.J., 1982).

85. For a perceptive recognition of this relationship, see Irving Louis Horowitz, "Human Resources and Military Manpower Requirements," *AF&S*, 12 (Winter 1986), pp. 173–92; and Morris Janowitz and Charles C.

Moskos, Jr., "Five Years of the All-Volunteer Force: 1973–1978," ibid., 5 (Winter 1979), pp. 171–218.

86. Gary Hart and Robert G. Torricelli, "Create a System of Universal National Service," *New York Times*, April 14, 1985; Peter McCloskey, "Argument for National Service," in Anderson, ed., *Registration and the Draft*, pp. 173–78; Morris Janowitz, Margaret Mead in Tax, ed., *The Draft*, pp. 73–90, 99–109.

10 / Conscription and America

1. Ole R. Holsti and James N. Rosenau, *American Leadership in World Affairs: Vietnam and the Breakdown of Consensus* (Winchester, 1984); William H. Chafe, *The Unfinished Journey: America since World War II* (New York, 1986), esp. pp. 457–68 on liberal goals and challenges to them.

2. Lawrence J. Korb and Linda P. Brady, "Rearming America: The Reagan Administration Defense Program," *International Security*, 9 (Winter 1984/85), pp. 3–18.

3. Peter H. Shuck and Rogers M. Smith, *Citizenship without Consent: Illegal Aliens in the American Polity* (New Haven, Conn., 1985), pp. 107, 159n. Civic republicanism emphasizes the importance of compulsory military or national service as an essential ingredient of a meaningful concept of citizenship or *civitas* (the spontaneous willingness to make sacrifices for the public good, and a political philosophy that justifies normative rules of priorities and allocations in the society), as well as a means of providing troops for the armed forces. See Morris Janowitz, *The Reconstruction of Patriotism: Education for Civic Consciousness* (Chicago, 1983); Benjamin R. Barber, *Strong Democracy: Participatory Politics for a New Age* (Berkeley, Calif., 1984), pp. 298–305.

4. Shuck and Smith, *Citizenship without Consent*, pp. 103–8, argue that the key status is no longer U.S. citizenship, for Graham *v.* Richardson 403 U.S. 365 (1971) and succeeding decisions have defined membership in the welfare state far more broadly than political membership. Increasingly welfare state membership, not citizenship, is the most valuable category. See also Charles Reich, "The New Property," *Yale Law Journal* 73 (1964) p. 733; Hull, "Resident Aliens and the Equal Protection Clause: The Burger Court's Retreat from Graham *v.* Richardson," 47 *Brooklyn Law Review* 1 (1980).

5. Section 1113 of the FY 1983 DOD Authorization Act (Public Law 97–252, Sept. 9, 1982) denied federal educational grants, loans, or work assistance to persons required to register for the draft who could not prove compliance; Rutgers University *Daily Targum*, Feb. 24, 1983. On "workfare," see Lawrence M. Mead, *Beyond Entitlement: The Social Obligations of Citizenship* (New York, 1985), and the approach of Gov. Thomas H. Kean of N.J. who envisioned welfare as part of "the social contract between the citizen and the state." *New York Times*, Jan. 15, 1987.

6. On the opening of armed forces to women and racial minorities as a

result of institutional needs and public pressures, see Warren L. Young, *Minorities and the Military* (Westport, Conn., 1982), pp. 191–243; Martin Binkin, et al, *Blacks and the Military* (Washington, D.C., 1982); Edwin Dorn, ed., *Who Defends America? Essays on Blacks in the Armed Forces* (Washington, D.C., 1985); Charles C. Moskos, "Success Story: Blacks in the Army," *Atlantic Monthly*, 257 (May, 1986), pp. 64–72; Nancy Loring Goldman, ed., *Female Soldiers—Combatants or Noncombatants?* (Westport, Conn., 1982), esp. pp. 217–36; David R. Segal, Nora Scott Kinzer, and John C. Woelfel, "The Concept of Citizenship and Attitudes Towards Women in Combat," *Sex Roles*, 3 (1977), pp. 469–77; Jeanne Holmes, *Women in the Military: An Unfinished Revolution* (Navato, Calif., 1982). But see contrasting view of Cynthia Enloe, *Ethnic Soldiers: State Security in Divided Societies* (Athens, Ga., 1980); and *Does Khaki Become You: The Militarization of Women's Lives* (Boston, 1983). Jean Bethke Elshtain, *Women and War* (New York, 1987) stresses the complexity and ambiguity of the issue.

7. For a recent complaint that upper status young men continue to avoid military service, see Arthur T. Hadley, *The Straw Giant: Triumph and Failure: America's Armed Forces* (New York, 1986).

8. Ralph B. Perry, *The Free Man and the Soldier* (New York, 1916), p. 16.

9. Ibid., p. 13. Reflecting values of personal autonomy and communal self-definition, some liberal philosophers have linked military obligation solely to clearly defensive wars. Michael Walzer, *Obligations: Essays on Disobedience, War, and Citizenship* (New York 1970); *Just and Unjust Wars: A Moral Argument with Historical Illustrations.* (New York, 1977).

10. Russell F. Weigley, *The American Way of War: A History of U.S. Military Strategy and Policy* (Bloomington, Ind., 1977), pp. 167–91, 223–41.

11. Melvin Small and J. David Singer, *Resort to Arms: International and Civil Wars, 1816–1980* (Beverly Hills, Calif., 1982), pp. 92–99, 229–32, identify 44 civil wars, 30 interstate, and 12 "extra-systemic" wars between 1945 and 1980.

12. Eliot A. Cohen, "Distant Battles: Modern War in the Third World," *International Security*, 10 (Spring 1986), pp. 143–71. On the Reagan administration's foreign and defense policies, see, from differing perspectives, Barry R. Posen and Stephen Van Evera, "Defense Policy and the Reagan Administration: Departure from Containment," *International Security*, 8 (Summer 1983), pp. 3–45; Edward N. Luttwak, "Delusions of Soviet Weakness," *Commentary*, 79 (Jan. 1985), pp. 32–38. On the administration's controversial 5-year plan, "Defense Guidance," see *New York Times*, May 30, 1982; *Defense Week* 4 (March 14, 1983), pp. 1–2.

13. Specific criticism of the AVF includes, "Military Sees Signs of Enlisting Problems," *Wall Street Journal*, Aug. 24, 1984; Charles Doe, "Analyst Warns U.S. Forces Are Over-Committed," *Army Times* (Oct. 8, 1984), pp. 23, 65; Richard Halloran, "Enlistment Decline Brings Call for New Draft," *New York Times*, April 9, 1985. AVF is supported by Military Manpower Task Force, *Report to the President on Status and Prospects*

of the All-Volunteer Force (Washington, D.C., 1982); Martin Binkin, *America's Volunteer Military: Progress and Prospect* (Washington, D.C., 1984); Lawrence Korb and Gen. John A. Wickham, Jr., *New York Times*, April 23, 1985. A critique of America's search for a durable military format since 1945 is provided in Eliot A. Cohen, *Citizens and Soldiers: The Dilemmas of Military Service* (Ithaca, N.Y., 1985), esp. pp. 152–82, which is better at policy analysis than at reconstructing past events.

14. Eliot A. Cohen, "Why We Need a Draft," *Commentary*, 73 (April 1982), pp. 34–40; and "When Policy Outstrips Power—American Stategy and Statecraft," *The Public Interest* (Spring 1984), pp. 3–19; and Sam C. Sarkesian, "Low-Intensity Conflict," *Air University Review*, 46 (Jan–Feb. 1985), pp. 4–23.

15. Earl C. Ravenal, *Never Again: Learning from America's Foreign Policy Failures* (Philadelphia, 1978); David Landau, "Civil Liberties, National Security, and the Draft," in Anderson, ed., *Registration and the Draft*, pp. 61–80, 331–42.

16. Cohen, *Citizens and Soldiers*, pp. 87–116, 183–90.

17. Since the AVF is official policy, few military officers are willing publicly to advocate a return to the draft. However, conversations by the present author with officers in each of the armed services indicate that such a view is widely held. See also James Fallows, *National Defense* (New York, 1981), pp. 129–33. William C. Westmoreland, "U.S. Military Readiness Requires the Draft," *Wall Street Journal*, May 26, 1981; Maxwell D. Taylor, "Volunteer Army: Long Enough," *Washington Post*, June 16, 1981; Am. Enterprise Institute, *A Conversation with Gen. E. C. Meyer: The Army of the Future* (Washington, D.C., 1981), pp. 11–16. Gen. Bernard Rogers, NATO commander, *New York Times*, March 2, 1985; James L. Lacy, "The Case for Conscription," in Scowcroft, ed., *Military Service*, pp. 195–219; James Coates and Michael Kilian, *Heavy Losses: The Dangerous Decline of American Defense* (New York, 1985), pp. 196–98.

18. Reps. Robert G. Torricelli and Leon E. Panetta, "National Service Can Become a Source of Pride," *New York Times*, Jan. 20, 1987; Charles C. Moskos, "Making the All-Volunteer Force Work: A National Service Approach," *Foreign Affairs*, 60 (Fall 1981), pp. 17–25; U.S. Congress, Budget Office, *National Service Programs and Their Effects on Military Manpower and Civilian Youth Problems* (Washington, D.C., 1978); Timothy Noah, "We Need You: National Service, an Idea Whose Time Has Come," *Washington Monthly*, 18 (Nov. 1986), pp. 34–41; "Enlisting the Young in Public Service," *New York Times*, April 13, 1987.

19. Gene Sharp, *Making Europe Unconquerable: The Potential of Civilian-based Deterrence and Defense* (Cambridge, Mass., 1985); Dietrich Fischer, "Invulnerability Without Threat: The Swiss Concept of General Defense," *Journal of Peace Research (Oslo)*, 19 (1982), pp. 205–25; see also American Friends Service Committee, *In Place of War: An Inquiry into Nonviolent National Defense* (New York, 1967).

20. Support for AVF, Secretary of Defense Caspar Weinberger, *Annual Re-*

port to Congress, FY 1986, pp. 107–23; Richard V. L. Cooper, "Military Manpower and Procurement Policy in the 1980s," in Scowcroft, ed., Military Service, pp. 151–94. In 1987, 49 percent of the Army's combat strength was in reserve units. For skepticism that these could be deployed within 15 days as planned and for criticism that they were inadequately trained and equipped, see Barbara A. Hensler, et al., eds., Reserve Component Manpower Readiness and Mobilization Policy (Washington, D.C., 1984) and New York Times, March 3, 1987. See also Andrew Hamilton, "Redressing the Conventional Balance: NATO's Reserve Military Manpower," International Security, 10 (Summer 1985), pp. 111–36.

21. For alternative service provisions in the conscription laws of various countries, see Asbjorn Eide and Mubanga-Chipoya, "Question of Conscientious Objection to Military Service," Annex I, pp. 26–30, mimeographed report, June 27, 1983, prepared for the UNESCO Commission on Human Rights, Subcommission on Prevention of Discrimination and Protection of Minorities. See also the earlier summaries in Devi Prasad and Tony Smythe, ed., Conscription: A World Survey (London, 1968).

22. William James, "The Moral Equivalent of War," (1910), in Bruce Wilshire, ed., William James: The Essential Writings (New York, 1971), pp. 349–61.

23. On Americans' traditional sense of natural security, see C. Vann Woodward, "The Age of Reinterpretation," AHR, 66 (1960), pp. 1–19. Shy, "The American Military Experience: History and Learning," Journal of Interdisciplinary History 1 (1971), pp. 205–28; Colin S. Gray, "National Style in Strategy: The American Example," International Security, 6 (Fall 1981), pp. 21–47. On temporary aspect of formal U.S. colonialism, see Robin Winks, "American Imperialism and Colonialism," in C. Vann Woodward, ed., Comparative Approaches to American History (New York, 1968), pp. 253–70.

24. The "decline of the mass army," the reduced emphasis on the "nation-in-arms," has been evident throughout the industrialized world since the 1960s, especially in Britain and the U.S. since they ended the draft in 1960 and 1973 respectively. See Morris Janowitz, "Volunteer Armed Forces and Military Purpose," Foreign Affairs, 50 (April 1972), pp. 427–43; and Jacques van Doorn, "The Decline of the Mass Army in the West," AF&S, 1 (Feb. 1975), pp. 147–57.

25. For the context, see John Lewis Gaddis, Strategies of Containment: A Critical Appraised of Postwar American National Security Policy (New York, 1982). The use of "regional influentials" to sustain U.S. interests through their military forces was formalized in the Nixon Doctrine.

26. See Morris Janowitz's insightful essay "Military Institutions and Citizenship in Western Societies," in Gwyn Harries-Jenkins and Jacques van Doorn, eds., The Military and the Problem of Legitimacy (Beverly Hills, Calif., 1976), pp. 77–92; also Michel L. Martin, "Conscription and the Decline of the Mass Army in France, 1960–1975," AF&S, 3 (May

1977), pp. 365–80, 394–96; Catherine McArdle Kelleher, "Mass Armies in the 1970s: The Debate in Western Europe," ibid., 5 (Nov. 1978), pp. 3–30, esp. 8–12, 21; Michel L. Martin, *Warriors to Managers: The French Military Establishment since 1945* (Chapel Hill, N.C., 1981). Conscripts comprise two-thirds of the French army, a percentage similar to that in Germany and much less than the 80 percent in Italy.

Note on Sources and Guide to Further Reading

In addition to the endnotes in the present volume, references to specific documents, books, articles, periodicals, newspapers, government publications and unpublished works used in this study may be found in the 325 single-spaced typed pages of endnotes as well as in the 59 pages of bibliography contained in John Whiteclay Chambers II, *To Raise an Army: The Draft Comes to Modern America*, enlarged version, (New Brunswick, N.J., bound photocopy, 1987), available through interlibrary loan from Alexander Library, Rutgers University, New Brunswick, N.J. 08903.

The best guides to American military history are Robin Higham and Donald J. Mrozek, *A Guide to the Sources of United States Military History* (Hamden, Conn., 1975), *Supplements, I* (1981), *II* (1986), and the bibliographical essays in Kenneth J. Hagan and William R. Roberts, eds., *Against All Enemies: Interpretations of American Military History from Colonial Times to the Present* (New York 1986); Allan R. Millett and Peter Maslowski, *For the Common Defense: A Military History of the United States of America* (New York 1984); and Russell F. Weigley, *History of the United States Army* (rev. ed.; New York 1984); as well as in Peter Karsten, "The 'New' American Military History: A Map of the Territory, Explored and Unexplored," *American Quarterly*, 36 (Bibliographic Issue, 1984), pp. 389–418; and Edward M. Coffman, *The Old Army: A Portrait of the American Army in Peacetime, 1784–1898* (New York, 1986), which appeared too late for inclusion in the present study. Thomas G. Paterson, J. Garry Clifford, and Kenneth Hagan, *American Foreign Policy: A History* (3rd ed.; Lexington, 1987) provides an excellent guide to the literature on foreign policy.

Recent works on the growth of the State in America are placed in historical perspective in William E. Leuchtenburg, "The Pertinence of Political History: Reflections on the Significance of the State in American History," *Journal of American History*, 73 (December 1986), pp. 585–600. See also Peter B. Evans, Dietrich Rueschemeyer, and Theda Skocpol, eds., *Bringing the State Back In* (Cambridge, 1985); Charles Bright and Susan Harding, eds., *Statemaking and Social Movements: Essays in History and Theory* (Ann Arbor, 1984); Barry Karl, *The Uneasy State: The United States from 1915 to 1945* (Chicago, 1983); Stephen Skowronek, *Building a New American State:*

The Expansion of National Administrative Capacities, 1877–1920 (New York 1982); and Morton Keller, *Affairs of State: Public Life in Late Nineteenth Century America* (Cambridge, Mass., 1977). For a seminal essay on the European military experience, consult Samuel E. Finer, "State- and Nation-Building in Europe: The Role of the Military," in Charles Tilly, ed., *The Formation of National States in Western Europe* (Princeton, N.J., 1975), pp. 84–163. On citizenship, see James H. Kettner, *The Development of American Citizenship, 1608–1870* (Chapel Hill, N.C., 1978) and Peter H. Shuck and Rogers M. Smith, *Citizenship without Consent: Illegal Aliens in the American Polity* (New Haven, 1985); and Morris Janowitz, *The Reconstruction of Patriotism: Education for Civic Consciousness* (Chicago, 1983). An excellent guide to historical studies about the progressive era is Arthur S. Link and Richard L. McCormick, *Progressivism* (Arlington Heights, Ill., 1983). See also the bibliographies in Neil A. Wynn, *From Progressivism to Prosperity: World War I and American Society* (New York 1986); John A. Thompson, *Reformers and War: American Progressive Publicists and the First World War* (New York, forthcoming, 1987); and John D. Buenker, ed., *Historical Dictionary of the Progressive Era* (Westport, Conn., forthcoming, 1988). James T. Kloppenberg, *Uncertain Victory: Social Democracy and Progressivism in European and American Thought, 1870–1920* (New York, 1986) appeared too late for inclusion in the present work.

The study of the American mobilization in World War I, the nation's first experience with the "total warfare" of the 20th century, has become a major subfield in itself. For example, see Robert H. Ferrell, *Woodrow Wilson and World War I, 1917–1921* (New York 1985); Robert D. Cuff, *The Home Front and War in the Twentieth Century: The American Experience in Comparative Perspective* (Washington, D.C., 1984); N.F. Dreisziger, ed., *Mobilization for Total War: Canadian, American, and British Experience, 1914–1918, 1939–1945* (Waterloo, Ont., Canada, 1981); David M. Kennedy, *Over Here: The First World War and American Society* (New York, 1980); Ellis W. Hawley, *The Great War and the Search for a Modern Order* (New York 1979). Particular aspects of that experience are examined in William J. Breen, *Uncle Sam at Home: Civilian Mobilization, Wartime Federalism, and the Council of National Defense, 1917–1919* (Westport, Conn., 1984); Valerie Jean Conner, *The National War Labor Board* (Chapel Hill, N.C., 1983); Barbara J. Steinson, *American Women's Activism in World War I* (New York 1982); Stephen Vaughn, *Holding Fast the Inner Lines: Democracy, Nationalism, and the Committee on Public Information* (Chapel Hill, N.C., 1980); Maurine W. Greenwald, *Women, War, and Work: The Impact of World War I on Women Workers in the United States* (Westport, Conn., 1980); Paul A. C. Koistinen, *The Military-Industrial Complex: A Historical Perspective* (New York 1980), pp. 23–46; Paul L. Murphy, *World War I and the Origins of Civil Liberties in the U.S.* (New York 1979); Frederick C. Luebke, *Bonds of Loyalty; German Americans and World War I* (DeKalb, Ill., 1974); Robert D. Cuff, *The War Industries Board* (Baltimore, 1973); Arthur Barbeau and Florette Henri, *The Unknown Soldiers: Black American Troops in World War I* (Philadelphia, 1974); Joan Jensen, *The Price of Vigilance: The American Protective League* (Chicago, 1968); Daniel R. Beaver, *Newton D. Baker and the American War*

Effort. 1917–1919 (Lincoln, Neb., 1966); Edward M. Coffman, *The War to End All Wars: The American Experience in World War I* (New York 1966); Horace Peterson and Gilbert Fite, *Opponents of War, 1917–1918* (Madison, Wis., 1957). A useful guide is David R. Woodward and Robert Franklin Maddox, *America and World War I: A Selected Annotated Bibliography of English-Language Sources* (New York, 1985).

Previously, no adequate study existed of the selective draft of 1917–1918. John Dickinson's contemporary narrative, *The Building of an Army: A Detailed Account of Legislation, Administration, and Opinion in the United States, 1915–1920* (New York 1922), relies solely upon the public record and is prescriptive rather than analytical. The most widely cited account, David A. Lockmiller, *Enoch H. Crowder: Soldier, Lawyer, and Statesman* (Columbia, Mo., 1955), is an uncritical, often erroneous, biography of the head of the Selective Service System. For all its detail, the standard work on raising America's armies, Lt. Col. Marvin A. Kreidberg and Lt. Merton G. Henry, *History of Military Mobilization in the United States Army, 1775–1945* (Washington D.C., 1955), remains primarily a compilation of data, rather than a work of historical analysis.

The present study of the World War I draft draws upon a number of recently opened, or otherwise largely unexamined, manuscript collections. It is the first to use the voluminous administrative records of the Selective Service System, 1917–19 (RG 163) at the Federal Records Center of the National Archives in Suitland, Md. It is also the first to identify vitally important letters from General Enoch H. Crowder in the papers of William G. Haan at the State Historical Society of Wisconsin, and of Henry L. Stimson at Yale University, documents not included in the Crowder papers at the University of Missouri. It is among the first to use the records of the interwar Joint Army and Navy Selective Service Committee (RG 147) at the National Archives. It drew upon recently declassified documents from the War College Division of the General Staff (RG 165) on mobilization planning for war with Germany between February and May 1917. In addition, newly available "personal and confidential" letters between Theodore Roosevelt and Henry Cabot Lodge in the Lodge Papers at the Massachusetts Historical Society provided new insights, as did relatively recently opened records in Paris and London, including reports between April and May 1917 of the British and French Military Missions to the United States.

Manuscript Collections Consulted

Manuscript Collections in Europe

ENGLAND
    Cabinet Records, Public Records Office, London
    War Office Records, Public Records Office, London

FRANCE
    Ministry of Foreign Affairs Archives, Paris
    Ministry of War Archives, Vincennes

Manuscript Collections in the United States

ANN ARBOR, MI., BENTLEY LIBRARY, UNIVERSITY OF MICHIGAN
Americanization Committee of Detroit Records
Roy D. Chapin Papers
Lewis C. Crampton Papers
Arthur Dunham Papers
Harold Grey Papers
William G. Haan Diary
William H. Hobbs Papers
Samuel D. Pepper Papers

ATLANTA, GA., NATIONAL ARCHIVES AND RECORDS CENTER
U.S. Selective Service Act Enforcement Records, 1917–1919

BERKELEY, CA., BANCROFT LIBRARY, UNIVERSITY OF CALIFORNIA
Hiram W. Johnson Papers

BOSTON, MA., MASSACHUSETTS HISTORICAL SOCIETY
Henry Cabot Lodge Papers

CAMBRIDGE, MA., HOUGHTON AND PUSEY LIBRARIES, HARVARD UNIVERSITY
Oswald Garrison Villard Papers
David F. Houston Papers
A. Lawrence Lowell Papers

CARLISLE BARRACKS, PA., ARMY WAR COLLEGE
U.S. Army Military History Collection
U.S. Army War College Records

CHAPEL HILL, N.C., UNIVERSITY OF NORTH CAROLINA LIBRARY
Claude Kitchin Papers

CHICAGO, IL., CHICAGO HISTORICAL SOCIETY
Military Training Camps Association Records

CHICAGO, IL., NORTHWESTERN UNIVERSITY LAW SCHOOL LIBRARY
John Henry Wigmore Papers

CHICAGO, IL., UNIVERSITY OF CHICAGO LIBRARY
Harry Pratt Judson Papers
Frank Lowden Papers

CLEVELAND, OH., THE WESTERN RESERVE HISTORICAL SOCIETY
Newton D. Baker Papers

COLUMBIA, MO., UNIVERSITY OF MISSOURI LIBRARY
Western Historical Manuscripts Collection
Enoch H. Crowder Papers
George N. Peek Papers

COLUMBUS, OH., OHIO HISTORICAL SOCIETY
Simeon D. Fess Papers
Warren G. Harding Papers

HANOVER, N.H., DARTMOUTH COLLEGE LIBRARY
Grenville Clark Papers

LOS ANGELES, CA., UNIVERSITY OF CALIFORNIA
Charles Daniel Frey Papers

MADISON, WI., STATE HISTORICAL SOCIETY OF WISCONSIN
  Henry A. Cooper Papers
  John J. Esch Papers
  Samuel Gompers Papers, Records of the Office of the President of the
      American Federation of Labor
  William G. Haan Papers
  Morris Hillquit Papers
  Paul O. Husting Papers
  Louis P. Lochner Papers
  Emanuel L. Philipp Papers
MEMPHIS, TENN., SHELBY COUNTY ARCHIVES
  Kenneth D. McKellar Papers
MINNEAPOLIS, MN., MINNESOTA HISTORICAL SOCIETY
  Governor J.A.A. Burnquist Administration Papers
  Knute Nelson Papers
  Thomas Schall Papers
MUNCIE, IN., BALL STATE UNIVERSITY LIBRARY
  Norman Angell Papers
NEW HAVEN, CT., YALE UNIVERSITY LIBRARY
  Arthur T. Hadley Papers
  Edward M. House Diary
  Walter Lippmann Papers
  Henry L. Stimson Papers
NEW YORK, N.Y., COLUMBIA UNIVERSITY LIBRARY
  Grosvenor Clarkson Papers
  Frederic R. Coudert Papers
  Frederick P. Keppel Papers
  George W. Perkins Papers
  Frank A. Vanderlip Papers
  Lillian D. Wald Papers
  Columbia Oral History Collection
  Guy Emerson Papers and Memoir
  Marvin Jones Memoir
  Langdon P. Marvin Papers and Memoir
  James W. Wadsworth Memoir
NEW YORK, N.Y., NEW YORK PUBLIC LIBRARY
  William C. Church Papers
  Emma Goldman Papers
  Norman M. Thomas Papers
  Lillian D. Wald Papers
PHILADELPHIA, PA., HISTORICAL SOCIETY OF PENNSYLVANIA
  Charles G. Darrach Papers
PORTLAND, OR., OREGON HISTORICAL SOCIETY
  George E. Chamberlain Papers
PRINCETON, N.J., PRINCETON UNIVERSITY LIBRARY
  American Civil Liberties Union Records
  Bernard M. Baruch Papers

Warren W. Bailey Papers
Lindley Garrison Papers
STANFORD, CA., STANFORD UNIVERSITY
David Starr Jordan Papers
SUITLAND, MD., WASHINGTON NATIONAL RECORDS CENTER
U.S. Selective Service System, 1917–1919, Records (RG 163)
SWARTHMORE, PA., SWARTHMORE COLLEGE PEACE COLLECTION
Jane Addams Papers
American Union Against Militarism Records
Collegiate Anti-Militarism League Records
Henry Wadsworth Longfellow Dana Papers
Fellowship of Reconciliation Records
Jessie Hugham Papers
Women's Peace Party Records
WASHINGTON, D.C., LIBRARY OF CONGRESS
Fred C. Ainsworth Papers
Newton D. Baker Papers
Ray Stannard Baker Papers
Tasker H. Bliss Papers
Henry C. Breckinridge Papers
William Jennings Bryan Papers
Joseph H. Choate Papers
William E. Dodd Papers
Frank L. Greene Papers
Thomas W. Gregory Papers
James G. Harbord Papers
James Hay Papers
Robert M. La Follette Papers
Breckenridge Long Diary
William G. McAdoo Papers
Frank R. McCoy Papers
Robert McElroy Papers
Peyton C. March Papers
John Purroy Mitchel Papers
George Van Horn Moseley Papers
Amos Pinchot Papers
Theodore Roosevelt Papers
Elihu Root Papers
Hugh L. Scott Papers
James W. Wadsworth, Jr., Papers
John Sharp Williams Papers
Woodrow Wilson Papers
Leonard Wood Papers
WASHINGTON, D.C., NATIONAL ARCHIVES
U.S. Army, Adjutant General's Office Records (RG 94)
U.S. Army, General Staff Records (RG 165)
U.S. Army, Office of the Secretary of War (RG 107)
U.S. Army War College Records (RG 165)

U.S. Department of Justice Records, (RG 60)
U.S. Joint Army and Navy Selective Service Committee Records (RG 147)

Newspapers

The following newspapers were consulted: Boston *Transcript*, Boston *Pilot*; Chicago *New World, Chicago Tribune*, Kankakee (Ill.) *Daily Republican*; Leavenworth (Kan.) *Times*; London *Times*; Manchester (England) *Guardian*; New Orleans *Times-Picayune; New York Age*, New York *American*, New York *Call*, New York *Evening Post*, New York *Evening Journal*, New York *Freeman's Journal and Catholic Register*, New York Journal of Commerce, *New York Times, New York Tribune*, New York *World*; Redding, (Calif.) Shasta Courier; *Washington* (D.C.) *Post*

Contemporary Periodicals

Among the contemporary periodicals read were *Advocate of Peace, America, American Federationist, Annals of the American Academy of Political and Social Science, Army and Navy Journal Atlantic Monthly, The Blast, Bulletin of the American Institute of Banking, Catholic World, Cavalry Journal, Collier's, Commercial and Financial Chronicle, The Commoner, The Crisis, Current Opinion, The Dial, Efficiency Society Journal, Everybody's Magazine, Forum, Harper's Weekly, The Independent, Infantry Journal, Intercollegiate Socialist, Iron Age, Journal of the Military Service Institution, La Follette's Magazine, Literary Digest, Living Age, McClure's Magazine, Magazine of Wall Street, Manufacturers Record, The Masses, Mother Earth, Munsey's Magazine, Nation, National City Bank Circular, National Economic League Quarterly, National Guard Magazine, National Service, Nation's Business, New Republic, North American Review, Outlook, Pierce's Farm Weeklies, The Public, Review of Reviews, Saturday Evening Post, Searchlight on Congress, Scientific American, Scientific Monthly, Scribner's Magazine, Survey, System: The Magazine of Business, United States Service Magazine, Viereck's Weekly, Wallace's Farmer, World's Work.*

Works on the Draft and the All-Volunteer Army

Guides to the historical literature on the issue of compulsory military service in the American past are included in several anthologies of documents, among them Martin Anderson, ed., *Conscription: A Select and Annotated Bibliography* (Stanford, Calif., 1976); John Whiteclay Chambers II, *Draftees or Volunteers: A Documentary History of the Debate over Military Conscription in the United States, 1787–1973* (New York 1975); and John O'Sullivan and Alan M. Meckler, eds., *The Draft and Its Enemies: A Documentary History* (Urbana, Ill., 1974). See also some of the recent historical works on aspects of the draft, including John Garry Clifford and Samuel R. Spencer, Jr., *The First Peacetime Draft [1940]* (Lawrence, Kan., 1986); John O'Sullivan, *From Voluntarism to Conscription: Congress and Selective Service, 1940–1945* (New York 1982); Lawrence M. Baskir and William A.

Strauss, *Chance and Circumstance: The Draft, the War, and the Vietnam Generation* (New York, 1978); Michael Useem, *Conscription, Protest, and Social Conflict* (New York, 1973); Stephen M. Kohn, *Jailed for Peace: The History of American Draft Law Violators, 1658–1985* (Westport, Conn., 1986); George Q. Flynn, *Lewis B. Hershey: Mr. Selective Service* (Chapel Hill, N.C., 1985); and Flynn's forthcoming book, *The Draft and American Society, 1940–1973*; as well as Robert K. Griffith, Jr.'s forthcoming work, *The Transition of the U.S. Army from the Draft to the All-Volunteer Force, 1968–1974.*

Debate over the proper military format for the United States in the 1980s and 1990s has already produced an extensive literature. Among the most valuable guides are Martin Anderson, ed., *Registration and the Draft* (Stanford, Calif., 1982), a collection edited by one of the leading libertarian exponents of an all-volunteer armed force; Brent Scowcroft, ed., *Military Service in the United States* (Englewood Cliffs, N.J., 1982), a debate among former policy makers and advisers; and Robert K. Fullinwider, ed., *Conscripts and Volunteers: Military Requirements, Social Justice, and the All-Volunteer Force* (Totowa, N.J., 1983), a compilation of essays primarily in favor of some form of compulsory service. See also Martin Binkin, *America's Volunteer Military: Progress and Prospect* (Washington, D.C., 1984); Eliot A. Cohen, *Citizens and Soldiers: The Dilemmas of Military Service* (Ithaca, N.Y., 1985); Irving Louis Horowitz, "Human Resources and Military Manpower Requirements," *Armed Forces and Society*, 12 (Winter 1986), pp. 173–92; and James B. Jacobs, *Socio-Legal Foundations of Civil-Military Relations* (New Brunswick, N.J., 1986).

Index

UB 343 .C483 1987
Chambers, John Whiteclay.
To raise an army